PSYCHOLOGY OF MOTOR LEARNING

Proceedings of

C.I.C. Symposium

on

Psychology of

Motor Learning

University of Iowa, 1969

October 10-12, 1969

Edited by

LEON E. SMITH

University of Iowa

Library of Congress
Catalog Card Number 79-123217

$7.50 PER COPY

The Athletic Institute   SBN 87670-851-3   Chicago

PREFACE

At the 1964 meeting of the Physical Education Directors of the Western (Big Ten) Conference, the "Big Ten Body-of-Knowledge Project" was born —the brain-child of Dr. King J. McCristal, Dean, College of Physical Education, University of Illinois, and the late Arthur S. Daniels, then Dean, School of Physical Education, Indiana University. The fundamental aim of the project was to identify and revitalize the fundamental body of knowledge in physical education for seven specified areas. In 1965, a "seed" grant was obtained from the Committee on Institutional Cooperation (CIC), a voluntary association of Big Ten universities and the University of Chicago, which aided materially in the continued planning and development of the Project.

The Project has evolved into a series of CIC Symposiums, each focused on the presentation and discussion of research relative to a specialized area in physical education. These symposiums are supported financially by the Departments of Physical Education in Big Ten Universities, The Athletic Institute, and appropriate professional organizations.

The first CIC Symposium was held at the University of Wisconsin in November, 1968, on the topic, "Aspects of Contemporary Sport Sociology." Present plans call for two such symposiums each year, which arrangement will insure that the research in each specialized area will be reviewed and published at about four-year intervals.

The principal emphasis of the Second CIC Symposium, which was held at the University of Iowa, was directed toward the presentation and discussion of theoretically-oriented research in motor learning and sport psychology. It is anticipated that the interaction between the lecturers, the professors, and the graduate students who attended the Symposium, together with the published Proceedings, will contribute to the understanding of creative research in motor learning as an area of fundamental knowledge in physical education.

Because there were times when the lecturers and the members of the audience did not speak clearly or directly into the microphone, sections of the tape recordings were inaudible. However, the Editor is solely responsible for any errors which inadvertently have been included in the Proceedings.

I am greatly indebted to the participants in the Symposium who provided an outstanding program and significantly contributed to the body of fundamental knowledge in Motor Learning. Also, I would like to specially thank my secretary, Mrs. Betty Tipton, who was a great source of assistance during the Symposium and the typing of the Proceedings. Appreciation is also afforded for the assistance given me by the following people: Dr. Louis Alley, Head, Department of Physical Education, University of Iowa; Dr. King McCristal, Chairman, C.I.C. Conference Group; Dr. Frank Jones, President of The Athletic Institute; and Mr. C. J. Yttri, Director of Publications, The Athletic Institute.

Leon E. Smith
Iowa City

ACKNOWLEDGEMENT

The Steering Committee is indebted to the Committee on Institutional Cooperation, and in particular to its Director, Dr. Stanley F. Salwak, and to the Deans, Directors, and Chairmen of Departments or Colleges of CIC Institutions, for their generous financial support.

iv

THE CIC

The Committee on Institutional Cooperation is made up of one member from each of the Big Ten Universities and the University of Chicago. Its objective is to foster cooperation among the member institutions through the sharing of human and material resources for educational and research purposes.

THE CIC CONFERENCE GROUP
ON PHYSICAL EDUCATION

KING J. MCCRISTAL, *University of Illinois, Chairman*

JOHN ALEXANDER, *University of Minnesota*

LOUIS E. ALLEY, *University of Iowa*

GERALD S. KENYON, *University of Wisconsin*

LEON E. SMITH, *University of Iowa, Symposium Chairman*

EARL F. ZIEGLER, *University of Illinois*

FOREWORD

This report is the second of the symposia staged by the Big 10 Directors of Physical Education in their pioneering project on determining the body of knowledge for physical education. Motor Learning is a recent area of study. Many of the papers presented here are reports of research from psychology and physical education. The application of these data to physical education must be attempted by the educator working with boys and girls, men and women. The findings will require more than casual study on the part of the student, professor or research worker.

Leon Smith, Iowa, and his steering committee deserve much praise for their judicious selection of speakers. The men and women who made the presentations, reacted to other papers and discussed their data with the symposium participants were outstanding. Basmajian, K. U. Smith, Henry, the Ammons, Bilodeau, Kroll, Layman and all the other speakers were at their best during the two days of the meeting.

The Athletic Institute is very pleased to have had a role in this project. It is my privilege to extend a hearty "Good Show" to Leon Smith, Lou Alley and the other faculty members at the University of Iowa. And to the overall Steering Committee for the project it is a pleasure to again thank them for asking the Institute to share with them this vital undertaking.

FRANK B. JONES

President, The Athletic Institute

vi

WELCOMING REMARKS
MOTOR LEARNING SYMPOSIUM

LOUIS E. ALLEY

Professor and Head Physical Education for Men

University of Iowa

On behalf of the University of Iowa, in general, and the Department of Physical Education for Men, in particular, I want to welcome you to this Symposium on Motor Learning. To those of you from out of town, a warm welcome to our campus. We are proud to serve as host for this Symposium and pledge our best efforts in making your stay here both professionally profitable and personally enjoyable.

Dr. Leon E. Smith, of our staff, has had the sole responsibility for arranging all aspects of the Symposium, including the arranging of the program. I am certain you will agree that he has done an excellent job and that the program is truly outstanding. We are looking forward eagerly to participating in it with you.

To those of you from out of town, I cordially invite you to inspect our facilities while you are here. I am particularly hopeful that you will visit Dr. Smith's Motor Performance Research Laboratory and Dr. Charles Tipton's Exercise Physiology Laboratory. I think you might enjoying seeing them.

If during your stay here you have any questions or problems, Dr. Smith or I—or any member of our staff—will do our best to help in any way we can. Feel free to ask—your wish is our command.

Again, welcome to the Symposium and to the University of Iowa. We are glad you are here!

THE SYMPOSIUM SERIES - AN HISTORICAL PERSPECTIVE

By KING McCRISTAL

*University of Illinois**

Ladies and Gentlemen:

We welcome you to this, the second in a series of C.I.C. Physical Education Body of Knowledge Symposiums. The first of the series was held last November in Madison, Wisconsin in the area of Sports Sociology. The Madison Symposium was directed by Dr. Gerald Kenyon of the University of Wisconsin.

The Symposium Series is a project of the Western Conference Physical Education Directors' Organization which has been meeting as an informal group every year since 1930. The Symposium project is the outgrowth of a plan which started more than seven years ago following a discussion I had with the late Arthur Daniels, Dean of the School of Health Physical Education and Recreation at Indiana University. For several years we had discussed the need for identifying and building the Body of Knowledge in Physical Education. As the result of our preliminary deliberations we met again during the summer of 1964 to lay the plans which would incorporate this idea in the Big Ten Directors' Annual Meeting, which was to be held the following December at the University of Illinois.

The Big Ten Body of Knowledge Steering Committee (appointed at the Illinois meeting) met the following summer with Dr. Stanley Salwak, Director of the Committee on Institutional Co-operation (University of Chicago and Big Ten Universities) to inquire about planning money to assist with the development of this project. As the result of Dr. Salwak's interest in our proposal the C.I.C. provided a seeding grant of $1500 to help work out some of our initial problems.

Subsequent meetings of the Steering Committee established the format associated with disciplines closely related to the field of Physical Education. It was decided that the following six areas were those on which the Body of Knowledge project should concentrate:

(1) Exercise Physiology,
(2) Biomechanics,
(3) Motor Learning and Sports Psychology,
(4) Sociology of Sport Education,
(5) History and Philosophy of Sport, and
(6) Administrative Theory.

---

* These introductory remarks were made by Dean King J. McCristal of the University of Illinois at the Symposium on Motor Learning and Sport Psychology held at the University of Iowa, Thursday, October 10, 1969.

These topics have comprised the areas of concentration for the Agenda of the Annual Meetings of the Big Ten Physical Education Directors for the past several years.

Physical Education like other disciplines has great need to join in the process by which new knowledge is created. Obviously this entails a planned procedure. If such a pattern is to follow, an opportunity must be provided for specialists in the various areas of Physical Education to probe at increasingly deeper levels in their special areas of interest. If Physical Education is to equal the pace set in other academic disciplines we must go beyond our efforts by extending research opportunities to more people and provide contributions from a broader base.

As a case in point there is great need today for a Physical Education researcher in Sports Psychology and Motor Learning to have an opportunity to exchange ideas with nationally prominent psychologists, not a psychologist from one department in a University but leading psychologists interested in sport and physical education from the best universities in the country. Only in this kind of setting can we hope to apply the techniques and findings of this related discipline to the problems of Physical Education. Hopefully in this process new knowledge will be born, which may then become the substance of the Body of Knowledge in our field.

It is redundant to say that it takes money to run a Symposium, to run several, simply compounds the problem. In our search for funds we have had contacts with the U. S. Office of Education, the National Science Foundation and with Illinois based foundations to no avail. Two years ago at our Annual Meetings in Madison, Wisconsin we finally hit upon the idea of requesting financial aid from the universities which constitute the Big Ten Organization. This was done at our first Symposium last November in Madison, Wisconsin and is also being carried out at these meetings. I am happy to report this year that we have added the support of Women's Physical Education departments and have almost one hundred per cent participation from Big Ten Universities.

We are particularly grateful to The Athletic Institute of Chicago whose Board of Directors and President, Frank B. Jones, have agreed to underwrite the publication of this Symposium's proceedings as they did a year ago. I am sure you have seen copies of the last Symposium proceedings on display, the cost of which is five dollars. The publication of these proceedings permits the information generated at our meetings to become a part of the literature of the field. Some of it also becomes a part of our Body of Knowledge to be shared by everyone in the profession.

We owe a vote of thanks to Dr. Leon Smith, a member of the Body of Knowledge Steering Committee, for the planning and managment of this Symposium. He has worked diligently during the past year in laying out the specific details for these meetings. From the exchange of letters and telephone calls we have had during the past several months I know it has not been an easy task. There were times when we were sincerely worried about whether or not we could make expenses. Hopefully now that worry is behind us and we will concern ourselves with other problems incident to the operation of this Symposium.

At this time I should like to introduce the members of the Body of Knowledge Steering Committee, who are in attendance at the meetings today.

Dr. Jack F. Alexander, University of Minnesota - Exercise Physiology.

Dr. Louis E. Alley, University of Iowa - Biomechanics.

Dr. Leon E. Smith, University of Iowa - Motor Learning and Sports Psychology.

In addition to acting as Chairman of this Committee I represent the area of Administrative Theory.

Obviously we have high hopes for these meetings, the second in our series of Symposiums. The third Symposium will be held at Indiana University, October 19th and 20th, 1970. Dr. John Cooper, President of the American Association for Health Physical Education and Recreation, will direct that Symposium which will focus on the area of Bio-mechanics. The fourth Symposium will be held at Ohio State University March 1-3, 1971. The area of interest will be "History of Physical Education and Sport", and will be directed by Dr. Bruce Bennett.

In closing let me say that we are greatly indebted to the Big Ten Universities that have underwritten the major portion of this Conference's expense. We express appreciation to Dr. Louis E. Alley of the University of Iowa for hosting these meetings and to Dr. Leon E. Smith our Symposium Chairman. I know that the meetings are going to be all we had hoped for. Thank you.

CONTENTS

xi

Information Feedback In
Positioning Problems
and Progress[1]

Ina McD Bilodeau
Tulane University

Marshall B. Jones
Pennsylvania State University

Doubtless there remain more feedback problems in human motor learning than there have been problems solved in the last year or two. Many of the problems are long standing. Some are open to experimental attack—for example, how R (response)-measures other than accuracy behave; how Ss (subjects) handle different simultaneous IF (information feedback) transformations; what transfer there is between different transformations. Some are matters of theoretical inclination and will be slow to fade and quick to recover. Some come from diversity of vocabulary and organization and are as much signs of health as of trouble. Smith's (1962) distinction of reactive, instrumental, and operational feedback is basic and necessary to the central concern of feedback, displacement or transformation; Holding (1965) has organized the various kinds of manipulations of feedback that have been used.

Overviews of the recent status of problems and progress in feedback being abundantly available for motor behavior in general (Adams, 1969; I. McD. Bilodeau, 1966; Smith, 1966; (Smith & Sussman, 1969) and for positioning (I. McD. Bilodeau, 1969), this paper will be restricted to research in progress under the IF portion of a current project on individual differences. Our recent work on information feedback overlaps studies of motor forgetting, and it is difficult to distinguish them. They have a common origin in the analysis of within-trial events and the temporal variables in a trial, and a common present emphasis on individual differences. Our recent progress falls into two parts, both concerned with individual differences.

One part, being pursued by Jones (1966, 1969a, 1969b) is a molar correlational reanalysis of acquisition data under an assortment of IF manipula-

[1]The work reported in this paper was supported by the Air Force Office of Scientific Research, Office of Aerospace Research, United States Air Force, under AFOSR Contract No. F 44620-68-C-0072.

tions. These are data for which mean and variance trends were reported over the last 5-15 years. The second major concern has been forgetting, with IF's close neighbor, instructions, and time as major variables.

Retention

The mixture of IF and forgetting began in studies of temporal variables in simple positioning tasks and the question of what, other than the R he just made, that S could lose in time. The rational answers were that he could begin forgetting R as soon as he finished it and continue to forget it after, as well as before IF. He could forget his IF, his planned next response or R-correction, an earlier correct R, and alternative Rs that he had made or planned to make (E. A. Bilodeau & Bilodeau, 1958b, 1961). If he forgot only one of the events of the immediately preceding trial, his next R would reflect it. For example: S could remember R_n, but not IF_n; his IF_n but not R_n; or his intention to make a longer R, but neither R_n nor IF_n. In the learning studies in which this concern developed, S had also made other Rs and had other IFs, alternative events themselves subject to forgetting. A series of studies followed in which one or more possibilities for forgetting were explored, with a good bit of evidence that a number of events were subject to forgetting, that alternative Rs were sources of interference, and that recall of one within-trial event could be controlled to some extent through reminders of the other events. This work on motor memory has been recently reviewed (E. A. Bilodeau, 1969a) and details of experimental outcomes are introduced below only where particularly relevant. We should note, however, that variance and correlation measures, consistency indices, were favored over central tendency measures of forgetting, partly because Es were looking for relationships between forgetting trends in a number of events (R and IF, for example), partly because decreasing accuracy need not be accompanied by any change in mean.

The most recent studies in motor forgetting, following an experiment by E. A. Bilodeau, Jones, and Levy (1964), have used within-S design, repeated retrievals by the same S. The molar correlational approach that has been used for analyzing acquisition of a positioning habit (again recently reviewed in detail elsewhere—Jones, 1969a) is, thus, appropriate to treating the forgetting studies as well.

E. A. Bilodeau, Jones, and Levy (1964), after guiding S to a response of large amplitude and another of small amplitude on a lever, asked S to choose one of the two responses and try to repeat it. E recorded R amplitude and gave S IF. Whichever R S chose was called wrong—a pull closer to the longer R was called too long, one closer to the shorter R was called too short. The magnitude of reported error was preprogrammed at random from the series 27, 54, 81, . . ., 324. Retention of the arbitrarily incorrect response, R_o, was nonetheless tested 3 min., 20 min., 2 days, and 6 weeks later (four tries at repeating for every S). The outcome of the experiment was interesting in several ways—first, the forgetting trends in means and variances were very like those previously found for the same retention intervals, but with different groups at each interval (E. A. Bilodeau & Levy, 1964). The authors considered within- and between-groups trends similar enough to conclude that their results did not depend on repeated recalling.[2] The most significant finding, however, was the pattern of correlations between successive attempts to retrieve a response. Repeated attempts to reproduce both R_0 and the other R, the alternative S did not choose (R^a), led to a monotonic hierarchy in the correlation pattern of successive recoveries, rather than the near-universal superdiagonal pattern for learning trials—an ill-defined pattern in levering (Jones, 1969a). The feedback recalls, on the other hand, did yield a superdiagonal pattern—ragged, but at least not at all a monotonic hierarchy. The authors stressed the point that motor forgetting was neither the same thing as motor learning nor its exact opposite. A single common factor could account for the intercorrelation pattern over retrieving trials, and this is not possible for the intercorrelation pattern over acquisition trials.

Of two alternative interference positions, systematic and random, the authors favored random interference as more in keeping with their results. Persistent, systematic interference processes act to produce constant errors; adjacent Rs would share directional determinants and be similar, and Rs would be more alike the closer the two responses were in time. This is not consistent with the obtained monotonic hierarchy. Random interference processes, either transient or not acting to produce constant errors, are tenable with the obtained correlation pattern.

The follow-ups use instructions as a way to steer S toward persistence or unsystematic change over a series of related responses. E. A. Bilodeau, Jones, and Levy (1964) inferred a likely process from an interresponse matrix and the studies described below work from the opposite direction, attempting to set S toward constant or variable error where interresponse pattern is the dependent variable.

The first manipulation of instructions (an unpublished experiment by E. A. Bilodeau in 1967) used the same apparatus (lever) as E. A. Bilodeau, Jones, and Levy, but under much simpler conditions as to what S could forget and what events could interfere over time. Ss were asked to make a first move, R_0, a free R; IF, as an important directing variable, and thus, a complication, was omitted; E did not introduce proacting alternative Rs nor give any hint that one amplitude of R was preferable to another. After R_0, S was read one of three sets of instructions aimed, respectively, toward

[2]R. A. Dick and P. W. Fox in a paper presented at the 1968 annual meeting of the Psychonomic Society have shown that the lever R S repeatedly recalls does affect amount, if not general trend, of forgetting. Two groups of Ss made a free R_0 before goal training (R_+) and were tested after 4 weeks for retention of both their last try at R_+ and R_0. In the first week after training one group tried three retrievals of R_+ the other group tried each time to retrieve R_0 as well. The group repeatedly tested for both R_+ and R_0 held up better in R_0 at the end of 4 weeks and less well in R_+.

constant error ("Repeat"), variable error ("Move to some other place"), and ambiguity ("Move").

The apparatus was Lever D (Sulzer, 1963) with a range of R from 44° above the horizontal to 100° beyond, left to right movement required without visual guidance. Amplitude of R was recorded to the nearest 0.2 deg. of arc. The Ss were airmen in basic training, 78 in Group Repeat, 98 in Group Other, and 63 in Group Move. They were checked out on the apparatus (how to hold the lever, when to move, etc.) in small groups, and trained and tested individually. There were two copies of the lever and two Es (in different rooms). In training all Ss had the instructions: " . . . move the lever to the first place you think of . . . ." The test was three Rs at 30 sec. intervals in which Group Repeat was instructed: "The next time repeat your last move . . ."; Group Other was told: "The next time move to some other place . . ."; and Group Move: "Get ready to move the lever . . ." S stayed in position at the lever between trials in order to avoid the complications of disengaging (Boswell & Bilodeau, 1964). E gave no IF and there was no goal R. S's own R_0, a free response, was his reference. Both Es ran all three treatments and the data were pooled after a comparison showed no difference between Es or apparatuses.

Table 1 gives group means and SDs by trials. Groups and Groups x Trials effects are well beyond the .01 level (F=11.67, df=2, 708 and F=5.90, df=6, 236, respectively) and Trials is not significant (F<1). Group Repeat is the most stable; its mean increases slightly over trials but neither mean nor SD changes greatly. Group Other, with a very large R_0 and SD_0, shows a progressive decrease in R amplitude. Group Move has a large increase from R_0 to R_1, and, though later moves have no systematic trend, between-trial differences are bigger than Group Repeat's.

Table 1

Summary of Lever Performance for Groups Repeat, Other, and Move

in Degrees

	Responses							
	0		1		2		3	
Group	M	SD	M	SD	M	SD	M	SD
Repeat	62.4	18.6	64.2	18.8	66.2	19.6	67.0	19.4
Other	76.2	25.8	60.4	19.8	57.2	22.2	58.4	25.2
Move	59.6	21.6	74.8	22.2	74.4	22.8	71.4	21.8

Table 2

Mean Square Components of Total Within-Group Variances in Four

Lever Responses for Each of Three Instruction Groups

Group	Trials[a]	Subjects[b]	T X S[c]
Repeat	320	1,400	20
Other	7,680	480	560
Move	3,280	120	240

[a] 3 <u>df</u>

[b] 77, 97, 62 <u>df</u>, respectively

[c] 231, 291, 186 <u>df</u>, respectively

Table 2 breaks down within-groups variability into Ss, Trials, and S x Trials mean squares. Group Repeat is noteworthy for its small Trials term and large individual differences. Groups Other and Move rank the three sources in the same order, though Group Other has larger mean squares. Table 3 gives a slightly different look at the same effects of instructions— encouraging within-S consistently in Repeat Ss vs. change and alternation in Other Ss. Performance was rescored, O if S fell below his group's median on a given trial, 1 if he fell above; S has a repetition pattern if he remained in the same half of his distribution throughout, alternation if he shifted back and forth on alternate trials. Perfect alternation patterns are few, but most common for Group Other (24%). Repeat Ss follow their instructions, with 82% staying in the same half of the distribution on all trials, and none alternating. Half the Move Ss have the repetition profile, 6% alternate.

Table 4 presents intertrial correlations by groups. Group Repeat shows a tidy superdiagonal pattern and a mean intertrial correlation of about .94 —quite like the effect of omitting IF in learning studies where S is under general instructions to do his best on every trial. Both means and intercor- relations support the hypothesis that little or nothing happens, and, inci- dentally, that S can repeat an original R with little wandering. The short (30 sec.) intervals between trials adds, of course, to the level of intertrial correlation, but does not change the pattern.

Table 3

Proportion of S̲s Fitting Repetition and Alternation Patterns

of Lever Response for Three Instruction Groups

	Group		
	Repeat	Other	Move
Repetition			
1111	.40	.05	.25
0000	.42	.05	.25
Alternation			
1010	0	.12	.03
0101	0	.12	.03

The picture is very different for Group Other; the intercorrelation level is near zero, and only one coefficient ($r_{23} = -.23$) reaches the .05 level. Adjacent Rs have insignificant negative coefficients, alternate Rs have insignificant positive correlations. "Move to some other place" might, over a sufficiently long test series, produce trial-to-trial consistency and predictability, but not within 3 test Rs.

The "Move" instructions, deliberately ambiguous, produce moderate positive correlations and no clear pattern; the Ss do not all give the same interpretation to the instructions (see Table 3). Ss given a free R and then told to move again do not show the individual consistencies that "Repeat" produces, nor the absence of between-trial communality when S is told to change his R. Again, there is a hint of pattern (monotonic recession from the end of the series), but too few trials for concluding that Rs are becoming more predictable.

The three sets of instructions have considerably different effects: "Repeat" produces highly reliable constant errors—nothing significant for the differential composition of the task happens. "Move to some other place" leaves very little common variance between trials; Ss are affected very differently, and though alternating large and small Rs is common, it is not everyone's interpretation of the instruction. Ss also produce another new R on every trial, rather than a different R from the last one.

In summary, this first attempt to change pattern and level of intertrial correlation is encouraging. Individual consistency fell as the instructions departed from a demand for repetition to non-directive to a demand not to repeat. But though pattern was affected and neither "Move" nor "Move to some other place" resulted in a superdiagonal, clear-cut patterns did not emerge in Groups Move and Other. Group Repeat's correlations indicate improvement, increasing consistency in reproducing the last R of the series. E. A. Bilodeau, Jones, and Levy (1964) found that Ss modeled successive retrievals on R_1 (not R_o); the present procedures resulted in S's using R_{n-1}

Table 4

Intercorrelation Matrices of Lever Responses for Three

Instruction Groups

		Responses			
		0	1	2	3
Repeat					
	0	–	.92	.92	.90
	1		–	.97	.97
	2			–	.98
			(n = 78)		
Other	0	–	-.07	.10	-.05
	1		–	-00	.06
	2			–	-.23
			(n = 98)		
Move	0	–	.39	.52	.57
	1		–	.47	.48
	2			–	.57
			(n = 63)		

as a model for R_n. Perhaps all three groups are stabilizing, closing on an end point, rather than receding from a fixed beginning. If this is so, then Group Move may be settling, though slowly, toward repeating R_n, and Group Other toward predictable avoiding—or two Rs in alternation. Within the present experiment, the most common strategy for Move Ss was to vary the magnitude of test Rs about R_o. That is, half the Move Ss persisted with their R_o's directional bias, long or short, and shifted unsystematically about in their original half of the distribution. These "random" errors led to a fair-sized S x Trials variability and lowered intertrial correlations. More trials under a Move treatment are needed to answer the important questions of what (if any clear) r pattern emerges, and if S x Trials variability does decline progressively—i.e. support or contradiction of the hint that S may be slowly closing on an endpoint, and if R_o is the endpoint. The Other instructions, with their wider swings, also need more trials to test whether Ss are closing on two Rs on alternate trials—if odd and even trials lead to saw-toothing in a single matrix, but separately to smooth patterns.

The first retention experiment, summarized above, raised questions, and a second experiment was designed to follow up on some of them. (The data have been presented in an unpublished thesis by Preilowski, 1968.)

Telling S to repeat his *last* R led to a superdiagonal pattern of intertrial correlations for repeated responding (Table 4), while intertrial r's fell into a monotonic hierarchy when S was told to repeat his *first* R (E. A. Bilodeau, Jones, & Levy, 1964). Other procedures also differed. In the latter study, R_o was an attempt to reproduce one of two guided Rs and S got IF that R_o was wrong, whereas Ss told to repeat their last R started with a free R_o and had no IF. One purpose of the next study, then, was to compare interresponse matrices of a group instructed to repeat the *first* move and a group told to repeat the *last* move, with other procedures the same. "Move" and "Move to some other place" treatments were repeated to check on the matrices they produced, and with more test Rs to test the hint that S was closing on an endpoint in these treatments. Finally, the first study pointed so strongly to between S variability as an important dependent variable of instructions that an individual difference variable, AFQT score, was also considered.

The Ss were 320 airmen in basic training. The Dial Trainer (DT), a device developed for group testing (E. A. Bilodeau and Rosenquist, 1963), was modified by substituting a sturdy wire paper clip for the original cardboard start. S held the frame in his left hand, closed his eyes, and turned the dial with a pencil in his right hand. The stop limits R amplitude to a maximum of $355°$. After every move, S turned the DT over and read and recorded a two-letter code used to reduce IF. E later transformed the letter code to degrees of movement in steps of $5°$. (Note that this procedure, unlike the lever treatments, does give S some IF; that is, if the letter code S records on one trial differs from the letter code on the next trial, then the two Rs are different; if letter codes for two Rs are the same, then those two

Rs are not different. The letter-code sequence is not related to the difference in R amplitudes, though the letters may be misleading or misinformative IF to an *S* who assumes alphabetical ordering.)

Ss had two sessions. In the first, pretraining, *E* demonstrated the DT and its scoring to about 80 Ss at a time and gave two practice trials to check Ss out. Ss then went to another room for routine paper-and-pencil testing and returned 30-45 min. later in groups of 13-20 for the experiment proper. The same instruction treatment was given to all Ss in one of these small groups and treatment was assigned by a simple counter-balance. Both sessions were run in a large classroom with tablet armchairs. Three proctors helped *E*. In the experimental session, *S* made 6 Rs at 60 sec. intervals. The first, R_o, was free; *S* was asked to move to the first place he thought of. Instructions for the test, Rs 1-5, differed from group to group (n=80) and were repeated before every test trial, "again" being used on test trials 2-5 for groups First and Other. There were two *repeat* groups, First and Last, The instructions for Group First were: " . . . repeat your first move (again);"

Table 5

Mean and Standard Deviation of Amplitude of Dial Trainer

Response in Degrees of Arc by Trials and Instructions

				Responses			
Group		0	1	2	3	4	5
First	M	152	154	158	156	156	153
	SD	63	72	73	68	73	69
Last	M	154	158	157	157	159	156
	SD	70	73	75	77	82	82
Move	M	154	176	168	186	181	180
	SD	72	71	71	77	78	82
Other	M	155	183	161	167	184	178
	SD	64	73	87	84	97	92

(n = 80)

for Group Last they were: " . . . repeat your last move.". For Group Other, the instructions were: " . . . move to some other place (again)"; and for Group Move: " . . . move the wheel again." *E* recorded the amplitude of the 6 Rs and *S*'s AFQT score, and examined means, variances, and inter-correlation matrices of R amplitude for intact groups and for *S*s in the top and bottom quarters of their group's AFQT distribution.

Table 5 summarizes performance by groups, giving mean and SD for every R. Mean amplitude of R_0 and SD_0 are about the same in all groups, and smaller than for test Rs 1-5. The two repeat groups' test means stay close to R_0, and Groups Move and Other have larger shifts in amplitude. Mean absolute change from one trial to the next is $2°$ for Groups First and Last, $11°$ for Group Move, and $16°$ for Group Other. None of the four groups has a regular trend over successive test Rs.

Table 6 presents frequencies of repetition and alternation profiles, but this time for near-perfect patterns, those with no more than one failure. Most of the *S*s in Groups First and Last, asked to repeat, do repeat; *S*s whose R_0s are in the upper half of the distribution score in the upper half on test Rs 1-5, those whose R_0s are below the median stay below the median. More *S*s of Group Move repeat than alternate, but 26% of the Move *S*s have no more than one exception to an alternating pattern. *S*s in Group Other obey their instructions too. Only 5% of the group has near perfect repetition and Group Other has the highest frequency (33%) of alternation; but the profiles of roughly two thirds of the Other *S*s are not accounted for by these two simple classes.

Table 6

Proportion of Subjects with Repetition and Alternation Profiles

over Responses on the Dial Trainer, by Instruction Group

	Group			
Pattern[a]	First	Last	Move	Other
Repetition	.91	.88	.48	.05
Alternation	.03	.03	.26	.33

[a] No more than one break in pattern

Table 7

Interresponse Correlation Matrices for Amplitude of Dial Trainer

Response for the Four Instruction Groups[a]

		Responses				
Group		1	2	3	4	5
First	0	95	91	96	95	97
	1		97	94	96	93
	2			92	94	89
	3				94	98
	4					94
Last	0	94	90	89	83	83
	1		95	96	85	88
	2			96	95	94
	3				94	95
	4					95
Move	0	37	47	19	34	21
	1		36	50	22	47
	2			23	50	40
	3				38	50
	4					31
Other	0	-03	17	11	-15	06
	1		-39	-02	09	-05
	2			-21	-10	16
	3				-11	-27
	4					-17

[a] Decimal point omitted

(n = 80)

Table 7 contains the intertrial correlations of the four groups. The groups that replicate earlier treatments show some high points of agreement with the earlier findings. That is, "Last R" instructions result in large intertrial correlations in a superdiagonal pattern on the DT as on the lever; "Move" again yields moderate, positive r's; and "Move to some other place" mixed positive and negative values, both generally insignificant (only $r_{1.2}$ and $r_{3.5}$,)

Table 8

Means and Standard Deviations of AFQT Score and Amplitude of

Dial Trainer Response in Degrees of Arc for High and

Low AFQT Quarters of Instruction Groups

Group	AFQT Quarter		AFQT Score	Responses					
				R_0	R_1	R_2	R_3	R_4	R_5
First	High	$\overline{X}$	91	155	156	158	161	158	161
		SD	4	65	72	66	65	65	63
	Low	$\overline{X}$	37	140	137	144	149	142	145
		SD	12	59	66	67	67	70	71
Last	High	$\overline{X}$	86	166	166	162	160	164	160
		SD	5	74	78	81	83	88	88
	Low	$\overline{X}$	26	134	145	158	149	141	141
		SD	3	51	54	54	57	60	64
Move	High	$\overline{X}$	83	184	179	179	182	193	218
		SD	9	81	86	77	92	91	87
	Low	$\overline{X}$	30	144	156	168	178	182	166
		SD	4	81	78	82	85	88	89
Other	High	$\overline{X}$	87	168	166	169	179	172	160
		SD	6	53	76	102	94	99	91
	Low	$\overline{X}$	30	134	208	142	167	172	172
		SD	5	71	56	65	82	101	78
Grand Mean	High		87	168	167	167	170	172	175
	Low		31	138	162	153	161	159	156

(n = 20)

both negative, exceed the .05 level). Group Move in Table 7, however, is patterned, see-sawing across rows and down columns. Correlations peak on odd-odd and even-even trials; odd-even r's are smaller, though still positive. With a little strain one can see something of see-sawing in Group Move in the lever experiment (Table 4), erratic and as if Ss lost place at R_3. The perfect alternation of positive and negative r's of Group Other on the lever (Table 4), on the other hand, does not hold up on the DT; all Group Other's adjacent trials in Table 7 have negative correlations, but so do some pairs of odd (even) trials—again as if Ss fell out of step on R_3. Group First, a new instruction in the free-R_0 procedure, has an even higher average level of intercorrelation than Group Last (.94 compared to .91) and no hint of superdiagonal patterning; neither is there much trace of the monotonic patterning E. A. Bilodeau, Jones, and Levy found (1964), nor any indication that the process begins with R_1 and that R_0 is outside the pattern.

The Ss in the top and bottom quarters of their group's distribution in AFQT were selected for leads on the interaction of instructions and ability. Table 8 gives mean and SD of the AFQT score and amplitude of the 6 positioning Rs for these subgroups. There are small sampling differences in AFQT about the general subgroup means of 87 for High Ss and 31 for Low, small differences relative to the High-Low difference. High and Low subgroups have roughly comparable variability. The most obvious relation between AFQT level and DT behavior is in amplitude of R_0—high AFQT Ss make a large R_0 ($\overline{X}=168°$) and low AFQT Ss a small R_0 ($\overline{X}=138°$). High Ss continue to make larger Rs on test trials, and it is only under Other instructions that Ss low in AFQT score make larger Rs than Ss who score high.

Table 9 gives the percentage of Ss with repetition and alternation profiles in R amplitude, by instructions and ability level. *First* instructions lead to 100% repetition profiles for both ability levels. *Last* works nearly as well at getting the High Ss to repeat, but only 75% of the Low Ss have repetition profiles, and 5% fit the alternation pattern; the Low Ss of Group Last, it should be noted, have the lowest AFQT mean and SD of all. *Last* instructions, as on the lever, lead to a preponderance of repetition profiles, and repetition is dominant at both ability extremes, but Ss do shift across the median more often when they follow instructions to repeat their last, rather than their first R. In both Group Move and Group Other the ability subgroups differ in the preferred profile. Ability level, defined by AFQT, affects behavior on the DT (a very simple device) on the very first R, and that a free turn. Table 9 indicates that instructions and ability levels also have later interactions.

The intercorrelation matrices of the AFQT extremes are shown in Table 10, with the warning that $n=20$ and one can easily make too much of the differences. For the *First* subgroups, differences pose no problem—all intertrial r's are in the high 90's. Though the maximum r's are on the superdiagonal, the patterns for High and Low subgroups of First, and the High

Table 9

Proportion of Subjects with Repetition and Alternation Profiles

over Responses on the Dial Trainer by AFQT Level

and Instruction Group

		Group			
Pattern[a]	AFQT	First	Last	Move	Other
Repetition	High	1.00	.95	.40	.05
	Low	1.00	.75	.60	.20
Alternation	High	.00	.00	.40	.35
	Low	.00	.05	.20	.20

[a] No more than one break in pattern

(n = 20)

subgroup of Last instructions, might as well be called unit matrices. In the left half of Table 10, only the intercorrelations of the Low Ss of Group Last (by sampling error or interaction of ability and instructions) are of suitable magnitude to reveal an unambiguous pattern, and it is obviously super-diagonal. Group Move's High Ss have the saw-toothed pattern, but the Low Ss have fairly high intercorrelations over Rs 1-5 and R_o does not belong with the test Rs (except R_1). The extreme quarters of Group Other are both marked by generally insignificant intertrial r's, many negative; and the opposite sign of $r_{o.1}$ in High and Low subgroups is the most suggestive difference.

Summary. The variations between top and bottom quarters of instruction groups are less important than the main effects of instructions. The First and Last groups on the DT are particularly important to the hypotheses

Table 10

Interresponse Correlation Matrices of Dial Trainer Responses

for High and Low AFQT Quarters by Instruction[a]

		Responses					Responses				
AFQT		R_1	R_2	R_3	R_4	R_5	R_1	R_2	R_3	R_4	R_5
		Group First					Group Move				
High	R_0	98	99	97	98	98	23	73	-02	21	11
	R_1		99	98	98	98		25	43	03	69
	R_2			99	99	99			-07	45	29
	R_3				99	99				39	62
	R_4					99					16
Low	R_0	98	96	95	96	95	62	37	48	44	35
	R_1		98	97	99	97		65	74	77	83
	R_2			97	96	96			66	85	60
	R_3				98	97				79	73
	R_4					99					64
		Group Last					Group Other				
High	R_0	99	99	98	97	97	-27	15	07	24	-18
	R_1		100	99	98	98		-30	-30	-09	27
	R_2			99	99	99			-22	-27	10
	R_3				99	99				-01	-19
	R_4					99					-10
Low	R_0	69	65	59	62	44	49	22	-04	-05	01
	R_1		75	82	55	65		04	-31	37	19
	R_2			84	88	88			10	-02	-03
	R_3				86	85				-30	-58
	R_4					86					01

[a] Decimal point omitted

(n = 20)

offered in earlier research. Group Last confirms the lever finding that telling S to repeat the last R does result in the superdiagonal pattern of correlation. "Repeat your last response" was intended to introduce deliberately an accumulating, systematic bias that would act as a hypothetical systematic interference process—to produce persistant directional communalities between Rs close in time. Though the means show little of this, the trends in intertrial r's are as they shoud be.

Instructions to repeat the original DT response do not deliberately introduce directional bias—which might, of course, build up in the normal course of forgetting—and do not produce a superdiagonal pattern of intertrial correlations (over 5 retrievals 60 sec. apart). The two kinds of "Repeat" instructions are different, they lead to different kinds of between-trial error (or interference), and they produce different intercorrelation patterns. Group First does leave us with two problems: the DT matrix did not reproduce the lever's earlier monotonic pattern, either, though there are many reasons why it might not, and to some extent *First* instructions led to such high interresponse consistency that looking for a trend is futile—Ss do not forget much in three minutes.

Group Move is also relevant to the kind of interference processes, or trial-by trial-fluctuation, that might build up between R_o and tests of retention. The instructions are neutral, no deliberate systematic bias is introduced, and, though large within-S variability is induced, there is no superdiagonal ordering. The lever matrix hinted at a monotonic pattern from a terminal reference, but the DT, overall, did not. With this free instruction DT, Ss of Low ability partly confirmed the lever finding—i.e., to the extent that the smallest correlations were between R_o and test Rs—but Ss of High ability had a different pattern, more in keeping with instructions to make some other R, with alternate peaks and troughs across rows and down columns of the intertrial matrix.

ACQUISITION

Jones (1969a) has found that positioning tasks, unlike continuous motor tasks, have at best a very weakly defined superdiagonal pattern of intertrial correlation in acquisition. Low intertrial r's and rough patterns obtained in the three tasks that he analyzed—lever, knob, and line-drawing—all frequently used positioning apparatuses. This departure from the hitherto invariable intercorrelation pattern of motor learning trials is not as surprising on second as on first thought. They are devices chosen originally to show the effects of IF variables relatively uncomplicated by ability to execute the R. E's intent was to use a task in which R amplitude was heavily dependent on the immediately preceding IF. Correlation between adjacent Rs would follow only indirectly, through the contingency of IF on R. Reducing initial individual differences by controlling the amplitude of the first attempt (asking S to make a specified number of turns, guiding S by using an endstop), and eliminating IF's dependence on R might act to reduce the level of intertrial correlation between responses.

The data Jones (1969a) reported, however, were from standard, control-group treatments, with IF=1.0 R + 0; only in one (turning a knob) had E controlled amplitude of the first R. Turning a micrometer knob gave a very weak superdiagonal pattern over the first eight trials, none over the last eight, an outcome quite in line with Jones' working hypothesis that learning is a process of simplification and that knob-turning is indeed so simple that individual differences, other than error variance, can be eliminated with practice. Lever and line-drawing tasks, though confirming that pattern definition is poor in positioning, did not show the break from superdiagonal pattern between early and late trials. To the very slight extent that there was a correlation pattern, it was present in late as well as early trials, perhaps because these tasks require a single movement in a trial, a simpler task than turning a knob several times per trial, or because learning is a process of complication and perfect performance at drawing lines and moving levers does not take much complication, and turning a knob takes a little more (Jones, 1969a).

Jones has been following his earlier leads in three ways, that add up to the most significant recent contribution to understanding IF's role in learning.[3] The acquisition analysis has two related interests; its implications for the differential processes in learning and its bearing on previous conclusions about IF's role in learning. (1) One analysis, closest to the differential interest uses knob-turning Rs from an experiment on linear IF transformations that produced large between-group differences early in practice, but a common asymptote for all degrees of transformation (E. A. Bilodeau, 1953). The purpose is to test for intercorrelation pattern under conditions in which between-S differences develop and decline at different rates across treatments and are eventually reduced to trifling, nearly pure error variance. The more severe the transformation, the longer it should take for the pattern to break. (2) A second analysis uses data from a modified version of the same apparatus in an experiment that repeated the variation in linear transformation but with motor error eliminated from the beginning by letting S watch a pointer and scale (R, not score) as he turned. Jones' first guess at explaining the low terminal intertrial r's in positioning was that the between-S differences late in practice are motor error, unreliability only (Jones, 1969a). What correlation pattern will develop when this source of between-S differences is removed? These two inquiries are at present under way; for the third there is an answer. (3) Jones' third approach to the learning process and to IF's function in it is the very direct one of analyzing the effects of omitting IF 1969b. A group of Ss who made 20 pulls on a lever before getting IF showed no trend in mean over the 20 Rs (E. A. Bilodeau, Bilo-

---

[3]More properly: The present discussion is limited to the three most relevant analyses and there is no intended implication that this paper is a complete overview of Jones' current project on IF and individual differences.

deau, & Schumsky, 1959), and here " . . . the correlations among the 20 trials without KR showed strong superdiagonal form" (Jones, 1969b, p. 331). These findings are the opposite of the clear trend in mean error and the merely vestigial superdiagonal pattern in correlations between lever trials that include IF.

The outcome is even more dramatic in a second lever study in which IF was given on a fixed ratio schedule, after every 10th, 4th, or 3rd R (E. A. Bilodeau & Bilodeau, 1958a). The patterns previously obtained with IF on every trial and without any feedback at all were checked out on two groups in the experiment on periodic IF. A control group received IF on every trial and a correlational analysis of trials 2-11 showed no real trace of a superdiagonal pattern; Table 11 gives these correlations. But a group given feedback after the first R and not again until after the 11th R clearly showed the superdiagonal pattern of intercorreleation over trial 2-11; Table 12 presents the intercorrelations among these 10 successive Rs after a single IF.

In the original report, the analysis of means for intermittent IF, R error

Table 11

Intertrial Correlations for Group 100, IF after Every Response

Trial	2	3	4	5	6	7	8	9	10	11
2	–	.08	.02	-.09	-.16	.05	-.02	-.17	.08	.14
3		–	-.02	.04	.19	.17	.08	.09	.09	.13
4			–	-.10	.11	.25	-.10	-.09	-.01	.24
5				–	.14	.03	.25	.25	.12	.20
6					–	.10	.11	.09	.31	.11
7						–	.24	.04	.23	.12
8							–	.09	.17	.23
9								–	.03	.11
10									–	.15
11										–

(after Jones, 1970)

Table 12

Intercorrelations among Trials 2 through 11, Responses between

IFs, for a Group with IF after Every Tenth Response

Trial	2	3	4	5	6	7	8	9	10	11
2	–	.87	.71	.59	.41	.51	.47	.41	.51	.26
3		–	.85	.71	.60	.64	.64	.60	.70	.48
4			–	.84	.74	.79	.75	.73	.74	.64
5				–	.90	.91	.81	.76	.75	.74
6					–	.93	.83	.80	.76	.77
7						–	.88	.84	.80	.78
8							–	.92	.83	.81
9								–	.89	.88
10									–	.88
11										–

(after Jones, 1970)

was shown to decrease by steps. The R immediately after the occasional IF showed a reduction in error, and until the next IF, R held roughly constant —error declined again only on the trial after S's next IF. For the group with 10% IF, Jones made a comparable analysis of correlation pattern, examining within-block r's in successive blocks of responses between IFs. The analysis supports the conclusions made from the means. Each block of 10 trials (2-11, 12-21, . . ., 92-101) has the superdiagonal pattern, but both regularity of pattern and level of correlation fall off from block to block, i.e., with additional feedbacks. Jones reports (1969b) that the average level of intertrial r's for group 10% is in the high 60's and low 70's in the intertrial matrices of the first three 10-trial blocks, and that within-block correlation level has shrunk to the mid 30's in the last three 10-trial blocks. The pattern also becomes increasingly ragged over successive within-block matrices.

These findings were validated on groups with 25% and 33% IF; successive matrices for intertrial r's fell in level and sharpness of pattern when 3 Rs (2-4, 5-7 . . .) or 4 Rs (2-5, 6-9 . . .) defined a block of Rs between IFs. Jones' conclusion is similar to the conclusion one makes from the central tendency measures. The effect of IF is cumulative and learning depends on IF, not on making Rs. Intrablock level of correlation depends upon the total number of IFs in preceding trials, i.e. the absolute frequency of IF; correlation level is independent of the relative frequency of feedback. Table 13 gives the average level of intertrial correlation in each of 10 successive matrices for the groups with IF on 10, 25, and 33% of their trials.

Table 13

Average Correlations in Blocks of Trials between IFs in Groups

33, 25, and 10

		Group		
Block	33	25	10	Average
1	.677	.678	.726	.694
2	.710	.700	.669	.693
3	.580	.698	.661	.646
4	.447	.592	.408	.482
5	.530	.705	.491	.575
6	.397	.553	.257	.402
7	.530	.277	.369	.392
8	.533	.222	.369	.375
9	.327	.468	.310	.368
10	.203	.128	.388	.240
X̄	.493	.502	.465	.487

(after Jones, 1970)

The three columns look remarkably alike, though one is based on blocks of 3 Rs, and one on blocks of 10. Merely making Rs does not count any more toward changes in consistency than making Rs counts toward changes in R amplitude; it is IF that makes the difference by either approach. In Jones' 2-way χ^2 analysis for dependent correlations, between-block effects were significant beyond the .001 level, and the between-groups effect was unreliable. Finally, when only the first 10 Rs immediately after IF were intercorrelated, the matrices of 10, 25, and 33% groups were very poorly defined, though all (unlike group 100 in Table 11) showed the expected faint patterning.

In summary, Jones concluded that previous correlational and central-tendency analyses were supported. IF weakens or removes the superdiagonal pattern in positioning, and it is IF that is responsible; the pattern is present when IF is withheld. The chief advance is on how IF acts on the superdiagonal pattern, and slowing up the changes over time by using intermittent IF shows that IF acts gradually and by stages, rather than in an all or none fashion. It is an accrual process, and what IF does to the intertrial r's is not a side effect, but central to learning. Whatever eliminates the superdiagonal pattern over successive IFs is a major and fundamental part of learning itself (Jones, 1969b).

Summary. IF and instructions have been noted as related ways of giving S information and getting him to repeat or to modify his behavior. But in practice instructions are usually (not always: Grant, 1964; E. A. Bilodeau, 1969b) something to be written unambiguously to control individual differences or written with inspiration to raise the level of drive. The two retention experiments reported here use both directive and ambiguous instructions. The obvious expectation that instructions and IF have like effects is verified: instructions to repeat lead to the large between-S differences and the within-S stability characteristic of repeating the IF, "correct, no error;" telling S to do something different reduces individual constant error and increases within-S variability over trials as does an increased error treatment in IF. Though obvious expectations sometimes need experimental demonstration, these obvious consequences of instructions are important mostly as incidental verification that Ss follow their instructions and, thus, that comparing intercorrelation patterns is meaningful.

The kind of accelerated forgetting trend induced by asking S to repeat his last response rather than the same response at every try is not the variety found in standard retention tests—supporting earlier suspicion (E. A. Bilodeau, Jones, & Levy, 1964) that the interference processes in motor forgetting are not attributable to *systematic* accumulating variance. The instruction treatment closest to standard retention-test instructions directed S to repeat his original R every time and was associated with high intertrial correlation and no obvious trend for systematic differential change over 5 attempts at retrieving. Instructions to "move again" and "move to some other place" did not show the same trends in r-pattern in two experiments, but again supported the hypothesis that long-term directional interference does not happen in positioning unless E tries to introduce it.

The analysis of IF's role in learning is quite clear on the issue with which it is concerned—that IF is central learning in positioning. The super-diagonal pattern of intertrial correlations of Rs between successive IFs indicates that IF too can exert a systematic bias, when E's instructions do not. If the relative frequency analyses are included—as they deserve to be—with the present and earlier experiments on repeated responding, they point to further inquiry into goal-training and IF in retrieving. Giving S only general instructions to do his best leads to a different intercorrelation pattern over Rs following a single IF than is found when Ss have one IF ("wrong") and are asked to repeat the wrong R. Recall intervals as well as procedures differ and both replication and extension are needed.

REFERENCES

Adams, J. A. Motor behavior. In M. H. Marx (Ed.), *Learning: Processes.* New York: Macmillan, 1969. Pp. 481-494.

Bilodeau, E. A. Speed of acquiring a simple motor response as a function of the systematic transformation of knowledge of results. *American Journal of Psychology,* 1953, 66, 409-420.

Bilodeau, E. A. Retention under free and stimulated conditions. In E. A. Bilodeau (Ed.), *Principles of skill acquisition.* New York: Academic Press, 1969. Pp. 121-203. (a)

Bilodeau, E. A. Supplementary feedback and instructions. In E. A. Bilodeau (Ed.), *Principles of skill acquisition.* New York: Academic Press, 1969. Pp. 235-253. (b)

Bilodeau, E. A., & Bilodeau, I. McD. Variable frequency of knowledge of results and the learning of a simple skill. *Journal of Experimental Psychology,* 1958, 55, 379-383. (a)

Bilodeau, E. A., & Bilodeau, I. McD. Variation of temporal intervals among critical events in five studies of knowledge of results. *Journal of Experimental Psychology,* 1958, 55, 603-612. (b)

Bilodeau, E. A., & Bilodeau, I. McD. Motor-skills learning. *Annual Review of Psychology,* 1961, 12, 243-280.

Bilodeau, E. A., & Levy, C. M. Long-term memory as a function of retention time and other conditions of training and recall. *Psychological Review,* 1964, 71, 27-41.

Bilodeau, E. A., & Rosenquist, H. S. A simple skills device for research on learning and memory. *Perceptual and Motor Skills,* 1963, 16, 521-524.

Bilodeau, E. A., Bilodeau, I. McD., Schumsky, D. A. Some effects of introducing and withdrawing knowledge of results early and late in practice. *Journal of Experimental Psychology,* 1959, 58, 142-144.

Bilodeau, E. A., Jones, M. B., & Levy, C. M. Long-term memory as a function of retention time and repeated recalling. *Journal of Experimental Psychology,* 1964, 67, 303-309.

Bilodeau, I. McD. Information feedback. In E. A. Bilodeau (Ed.), *Acquisition of skill.* New York: Academic Press, 1966. Pp. 255-296.

Bilodeau, I. McD. Information feedback. In E. A. Bilodeau (Ed.), *Principles of skill acquisition.* New York: Academic Press, 1969. Pp. 255-285.

Boswell, J. J., & Bilodeau, E. A. Short-term retention of a simple motor task as a function of interpolated activity. *Perceptual and Motor Skills,* 1964, 18, 227-230.

Grant, D. A. Classical and operant conditioning. In A. W. Melton (Ed.), *Categories of human learning.* New York: Academic Press, 1964. Pp. 1-31.

Holding, D. H. *Principles of training*. Oxford: Pergamon, 1965.

Jones, M. B. Individual differences. In E. A. Bilodeau (Ed.), *Acquisition of skill*. New York: Academic Press, 1966, Pp. 109-146.

Jones, M. B. Differential processes in acquisition. In E. A. Bilodeau (Ed.), *Principles of skill acquisition*. New York: Academic Press, 1969. Pp. 141-170. (a)

Jones, M. B. Knowledge of results and intertrial correlations in a simple motor task. *Journal of Motor Behavior*, 1969, 1, Pp. 329-338. (b)

Preilowski, B. F. Instructed recall of alternative positioning responses. Unpublished master's thesis, Tulane University, 1968.

Smith, K. U. *Delayed sensory feedback and behavior*. Philadelphia: Saunders, 1962.

Smith, K. U. Cybernetic theory and analysis of learning. In E. A. Bilodeau (Ed.), *Acquisition of skill*. New York: Academic Press, 1966. Pp. 425-482.

Smith, K. U., & Sussman, H. Cybernetic theory and analysis of motor learning and memory. In E. A. Bilodeau (Ed.), *Principles of skill acquisition*. New York: Academic Press, 1969. Pp. 103-139.

Sulzer, J. L. Manual Lever D: a basic psychomotor apparatus for the study of feedback. *Perceptual Motor Skills*, 1963, 16, 859-862.

CRITIQUE OF BILODEAU'S AND JONES' PAPER
by J. Richard Simon

I know that I speak for this entire group in thanking Dr. Bilodeau for her very interesting paper. Those of us who have followed the Bilodeaus' exceptionally productive career know that we owe them a tremendous debt of gratitude, not only for their many original contributions to motor skills research but also for bringing together in their recent text much of what we know about the acquisition of skill.

The Bilodeau and Jones' paper leaves little room for criticism, so let me respond instead by pointing to several characteristics of their approach to research which seem to me to illustrate important and general lessons.

One lesson must certainly be the importance of examining ones data in a variety of different ways. We must not limit ourselves by looking at just one measure such as the difference between the means. As Dr. Bilodeau's data indicate, other indices such as intertrial correlations often reveal trends which would not otherwise be apparent. I am a firm advocate of becoming thoroughly familiar with one's raw data. By using a variety of different measures and approaches, we get a better feel for underlying processes, and we can often formulate hypotheses to guide our subsequent research.

In this connection, I wonder whether Dr. Bilodeau has considered other ways of examining the alternation and repetition patterns which she observes in her data. I am thinking, for example, of computing trial-to-trial change scores for each individual or computing the difference between a particular response and the initial free response if this happens to be of interest. Since the measure I am suggesting is independent of the responses made by other *S*s in the particular treatment group, it might be more sensitive to repetition and alternation behavior than the measure employed in the studies just described.

Another general lesson to be drawn from this paper is the necessity for caution in generalizing from our findings. We might all do well to spend more time repeating our experiments. If journal editors insisted on a replication before accepting an article for publication, the motor skills literature would certainly be less confusing, and we would all have an easier time keeping up with our reading. But we should do more than simple replications. We should be concerned, as Bilodeau and Jones were, with determining whether the findings in a specific experimental situation will generalize to other tasks, different ability groups, etc. They point out that while certain findings from the levering task were replicated on the Dial Trainer, certain other findings were not.

Let me go further in discussing this problem of generalizing from our results. I think that we ivory tower experimental psychologists should become more sensitive to real world problems and begin to design our research accordingly. In this connection, let me report a recent experience. Last month, I attended an International Symposium on Man-Machine Systems and presented a paper describing some of the research which I will report to you later this morning. Following my presentation, a member of the audience, presumably an engineer, arose and asked how I would suggest that display designers utilize the results of my research. My initial response was the stock answer that a) I was an experimental psychologist who did basic laboratory research aimed at better understanding information processing, and that b) I was not primarily interested in applications and that c) I hoped that he and the rest of my audience might be able to help point out applications for my findings. In one sense, my response reflected the way I think about what I do, but in another sense, I think that it represented a "cop out." (Actually, I didn't "cop out" entirely because I had anticipated just that kind of question and *was* able to suggest some practical implications of my research.) Some experimental psychologists would view the question put to me as being completely out of order. I think, however, that in that particular setting it was not. I think too that we ivory tower types might benefit from periodically examining the broader relevance of our research.

Certainly we know quite a lot about information feedback, and certainly Bilodeau and Jones know more than most of us. And yet, if I try to look at their paper through the eyes of a physical education teacher or a coach, I find very little there which I would be able to apply in teaching someone a particular athletic skill. I'm reasonably sure Dr. Bilodeau would agree with that last statement, and it is certainly not meant as a criticism of the research she has reported. I am simply suggesting that we psychologists should be pretty humble before a group such as this because we still haven't very much to offer.

I would like to see you people do more systematic research concerned with the role of feedback in teaching "real world" motor skills such as bowling, golf, shot putting, etc. The feedback employed in these studies should be relevant to the response and not be arbitrary or misleading. One might want to manipulate the amount of feedback, the point in learning at which feedback is introduced, and also the type of feedback; e.g., verbal coaching *vs* visual feedback from a videotape. I was intrigued with the suggestion in the Bilodeau and Jones paper that different ability groups might respond differently to different instructions. Feedback studies could easily be designed to be sensitive to possible interactions between feedback conditions and ability level.

Let me close by simply underlining Dr. Bilodeau's opening statement that " . . . there remain more feedback problems in human motor learning than there have been problems solved in the last year or two."

DISCUSSION OF BILODEAU'S AND JONES' PAPER

UNIDENTIFIED SPEAKER: You indicated that one is more accurately able to repeat his first trials than his last trials.

BILODEAU: If I said that I didn't mean it. On the first test response, *first* and *last* instructions are equivalent directions, since the last response was the original response. Thereafter, however, the instructions do imply something different; the attempt to repeat may fail, and the subject may be aware that he did not repeat his original response. Under *first* instructions, the subject is told to try to make the original response; he has a constant standard and the instructions allow him to correct any error in an earlier try. Under *last* instructions, the subject might know his attempt to repeat was wrong, but the "wrong" response is his new standard and on his next test trial he should try to repeat his mistake. Does that answer you or not? What the subject has closest to him in either case is his last response.

UNIDENTIFIED MAN'S VOICE: If the subject has gone through Responses 1 through 10 and now there is a short rest period and you ask him in one case to repeat Trial 1, and in another case to repeat Trial 10, which would you expect to have greater effect in repetition?

BILODEAU: You are asking me an experimental question that hasn't been answered in these studies, if I understand you.

UNIDENTIFIED SPEAKER: It may be that I misinterpreted the comments along the way. I thought that you were refuting the matter of recency of response being an important factor.

BILODEAU: No.

BASMAJIAN: Ladies and Gentlemen, I find that we have quite a bit of time, in fact, so that we can field a few more questions. At least I hope Dr. Bilodeau will field a few more.

RICHARD SCHMIDT, UNIVERSITY OF MARYLAND: I am not familiar with the AFQT test and I wonder if you could reindicate what it is.

BILODEAU: I could do better if I had a copy of it with me. Are you familiar with the Army General Classification Test? It is a paper and pencil test; it includes—perhaps Dr. Bechtoldt can help me on this—general information, spatial relations, arithmetic computations, reasoning, I think, and so on. It is pretty much an aptitude test with achievement impurities, no doubt, fairly liberal in it.

LARRY LOCKE, UNIVERSITY OF NEW MEXICO: In regard to your earlier comments, I wish you would comment regarding the larger initial excursions of the high quartile AFQT.

BILODEAU: Well, this may help the first questioner. A large response is generally a smart thing to do. It is noticeable. Here the brighter people made a big, first response with plenty of feel from it. The low AFQT group, who may be timorous, made a small response and got less arm stimulation, a smaller sensory effect to relate to their score. That is, if you are going to move something, move it enough so you can feel it.

BASMAJIAN: Are there any other questions at the moment? I'd like to ask a question and it is not a frivolous one, though it may sound like it. I have a couple of daughters, teenagers, who are pianists and I have given a great deal of thought to the playing of the piano—feedback systems as a consequence of listening to phrases repeated over and over again. I wondered what the effect of repetition rates are in such a phenomenon as simply getting the right trills in piano playing, and whether this work might in some way help the piano teachers in their teaching of students—and any other comments you have on the skill of piano playing and deliberate attempts to repeat exactly what one has done before or to improve upon it.

BILODEAU: No. My little boy takes piano lessons on the Tulane campus and when I go over there, I feel that the next time I ought to take a notebook and record some interesting ideas and techniques that the piano teachers are using. At least at this stage of the game and the sort of thing I've done, I think for piano playing I could learn more from them than they from me.

BASMAJIAN: This brings me to the admission that in a lot of the work on information theory the engineers, the electronics people, thought that they were going to teach the neurophysiologists something about the way the bodily systems work, but for the last 8 or 10 years they have been more sitting at our feet learning about how to adapt the bodily systems to the technological developments in electronics than vice versa. In fact, to my knowledge, we havn't learned anything from the information theory people on the mechanisms on the neurophysiological control of muscle for example; so, perhaps in this case we could learn from the practitioners, the music teachers.

Stereotypic Reactions In
Information Processing

J. Richard Simon
University of Iowa

I want to describe for you the results of a series of experiments which we have been conducting over the past several years. These experiments have been concerned with increasing our understanding of an extremely potent stereotype which affects the speed of processing information from visual and auditory displays. This stereotype seems to be a strong tendency to react toward the source of stimulation.

Our research on this stereotype began quite by accident (Simon & Rudell, 1967). We were originally interested in the phenomenon of hemispheric dominance for speech and designed an experiment to investigate the possible interaction between ear stimulated and handedness in an auditory reaction time (RT) task. Without going into a detailed rationale, let me simply say that we wanted to demonstrate that right-handed subjects would respond faster to a verbal command in their right ear than in their left and that left-handed subjects would respond faster to a command in their left ear than in their right.

We selected two groups of subjects. One group consisted of 48 strongly right-handed students, and the other consisted of 32 strongly left-handed students. There was an equal number of males and females in each handedness group. Our subjects wore earphones and sat at a table with their right and left index fingers each resting on a telegraph key. The subjects were told to press the right-hand key as quickly as possible after hearing the word "right" and to press the left-hand key as quickly as possible after hearing the word "left." A Hunter klockounter started when a command was presented and stopped when the subject pressed the key.

The stimulus material was recorded on tape and presented at 70 dB by a Sony Stereocorder. Each subject responded to the same series of 132 commands, each command consisting of the word "right" or the word "left." The commands were presented to either the right ear or the left ear in a predetermined random sequence. The subject had no way of knowing prior to the presentation of each command which ear would be stimulated or what the command would be. He was simply told, "When you hear the word 'right,' press the right key, and when you hear the word 'left,' press the left

key." A ready signal was presented 2 sec. prior to each command, and there
was a 6 sec. interval between commands.

We calculated the median RT for each subject for each of the four experimental conditions—i.e., "right" and "left" commands in the right and
the left ear, and then subjected these data to an analysis of variance. To
our disappointment, the analysis revealed that the predicted interaction
between ear stimulated and handedness was not significant. There was,
however, another effect—totally unexpected—and, as it turned out, much
more interesting than the effect which was our original concern.

The left half of Fig. 1 pictures this effect, a significant command x ear
stimulated interaction. RT is plotted on the ordinate as a function of commands heard in the right ear and in the left ear. You will note that RT was
markedly faster when the "right" command was heard in the right ear than
when it was heard in the left ear, and, similarly, RT to the "left" command
was markedly faster when it was heard in the left ear than when it was heard
in the right ear. Obviously, an irrelevant cue, the ear in which the subject
heard the command, was interfering with his processing of the symbolic content of the command.

At this point, we were still interested in trying to detect an interaction

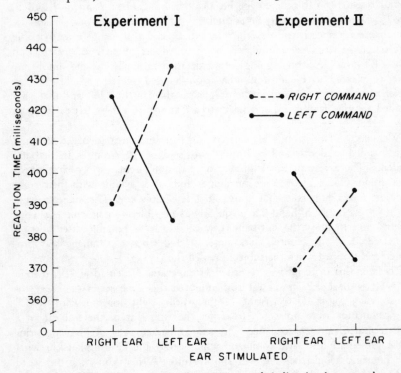

Fig. 1 Effect of ear stimulated on RT to verbal directional commands.

between ear stimulated and handedness. We conjectured that, if we could remove the subject's uncertainty as to the source of the command, then the variance contributed by this irrelevant cue would be eliminated, and we might be able to demonstrate the ear stimulated x handedness interaction. We, therefore, conducted another experiment which was essentially the same as the first except that, this time, trials were presented in blocks rather than in the random-ear order employed previously. Thirty-two right-handed subjects and 32 left-handed subjects performed on two blocks of trials. In one block, the commands were presented to the right ear, and, in the other block, the commands were presented to the left ear. Instructions prior to each block of trials stressed the fact that the commands would be heard in the right ear *only* or in the left ear *only* as the case may be. Each block consisted of 62 test trials in which the commands "right" and "left" appeared an equal number of times in a predetermined random sequence.

Again, we computed the median RT for each subject under the four experimental conditions; i.e., "right" and "left" commands in the right and left ear. Again, our analysis of variance provided no evidence for the predicted ear stimulated x handedness interaction. But again, as in the first study, the major source of variance was the command x ear stimulated interaction pictured in the right half of Fig. 1.

Results of these studies clearly indicated that the speed of processing verbal commands was affected by a cue irrelevant to the task itself; that is, the ear in which the command was heard. RT was significantly faster when the content of the command corresponded to the ear stimulated than when it did not. Our first explanation for these findings was that there must be a strong tendency to associate right-ear stimulation with a right-hand response and left-ear stimulation with a left-hand response. If this were true, we reasoned, then the interaction should *not* occur on a unimanual task. If the interaction *did* occur on a unimanual task, this would indicate that it did not derive from a simple isomorphic association between ear stimulated and ipsilateral hand.

Fig. 2 pictures the one-hand task used in our next experiment (Simon, 1968). The subject moved the control handle to the right or left from a center position in response to the same recorded series of verbal commands used in the first study. A klockounter, which measured RT, started when a command was presented and stopped when the subject had moved the handle away from the center position. Another klockounter, which measured movement time, started when the handle had been moved from the center position and stopped when the 10 in. lateral movement had been completed. The subject was instructed to react and move as fast as he could on each trial.

Sixty-four right-handed university undergraduates, 32 males and 32 females, served as subjects. Half of the males and half of the females performed with their right hand while the other half of each group performed with their left hand.

An analysis of variance of the RT data revealed that males reacted faster

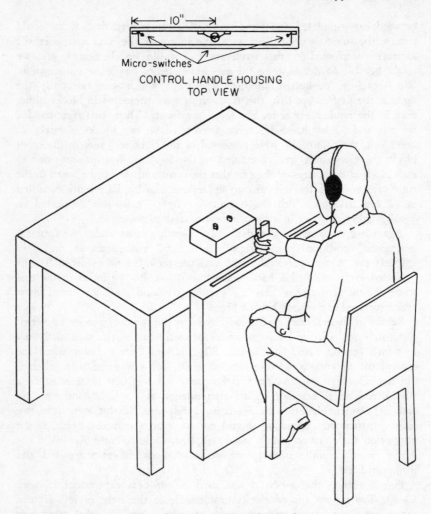

Fig. 2 Unimanual choice of RT task.

than females but that there were no differences as a function of ear stimulated, command, or responding body member. Again, the major finding was a significant command x ear stimulated interaction. This effect is pictured in the left half of Fig. 3. You will note that RT to the "right" command was faster when it was heard in the right ear than when it was heard in the left ear, and, similarly, RT to the "left" command was faster when it was heard in the left ear than when it was heard in the right ear.

The right half of Fig. 3 shows that the same command x ear stimulated interaction also occurs for movement time. That is, movements to the right were faster when the "right" command was heard in the right ear than

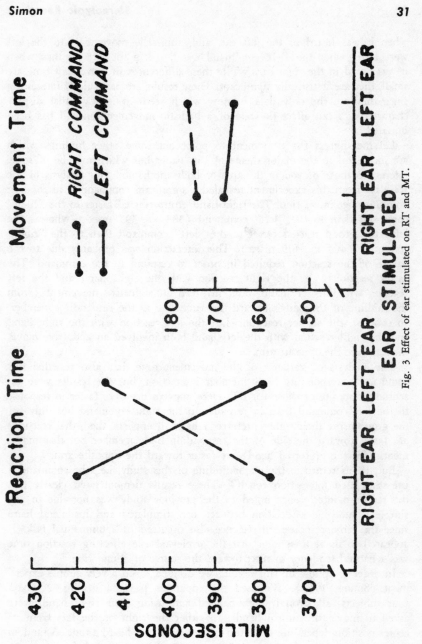

Fig. 3 Effect of ear stimulated on RT and MT.

when it was heard in the left ear, and, similarly, movements to the left were faster when the "left" command was heard in the left ear than when it was heard in the right ear. While these differences in movement time are small, they are statistically significant. These results are particularly interesting since they are the only data I know which seem to indicate that display characteristics can affect the rate of a ballistic movement once it has been initiated.

Let me digress for a moment to point out some other findings which are incidental to the major theme of this paper but which may be of some interest to those of you in the area of body mechanics. Our analysis of the RT data from this experiment revealed a significant command x responding body member interaction. The right-hand group reacted faster to the "right" command than to the "left" command (383 *vs.* 395 msec.) whereas the left-hand group reacted faster to the "left" command than to the "right" command (404 *vs.* 409 msec.). This interaction was probably due to the nature of the reaction required in order to respond to the command. The faster reactions, i.e., the right reaction with the right hand and the left reaction with the left hand, both involved an abductive movement (from the midline of the body) toward the same side as the responding member. In contrast, the slower reactions, i.e., the left reaction with the right hand and the right reaction with the left hand both involved an abductive movement toward the opposite arm.

The analysis of variance of the movement time data also revealed this command x responding body member interaction, but the results were essentially opposite of those for RT. Here, movements were faster in response to the left command than in response to the right command but only for the group using their right (preferred) hand. It appears, then, that reactions are faster toward the side of the responding body member but that movements (for the preferred hand) are faster toward the opposite arm.

But, let us return to the major finding of this study, i.e., the command x ear stimulated interaction for RT. These results demonstrated clearly that the response interference noted in the previous study was not due to any simple isomorphic association between ear stimulated and ipsilateral hand since the same response interference also occurred in a unimanual task. It appeared to us at this point that the irrelevant cue affecting reaction time was a natural tendency to react toward the source of stimulation.

In order to follow up this notion, we decided to do a very simple experiment (Simon, 1969). We used the apparatus pictured in Fig. 2. Sixty-four subjects, all strongly right-handed and using their right hand, were asked to move the control handle to either the right or the left from its center position depending upon the ear in which they heard a tone. A random sequence of 50 stimulus tones (1000 cps, 85 dB) was recorded on tape, 25 in the right channel and 25 in the left. A 2000 cps binaural ready signal was presented 2 sec. prior to each tone. Subjects were told, "This is a test to see how quickly you can react and move in response to a tone that you will hear in either your right ear or in your left ear." In one block of trials, they were instructed to "move the control handle away from the side of the ear stimulated. In other words, when you hear the tone in your left ear, move the control handle to the right as quickly as possible; and when you hear the tone in your right ear, move the control handle to the left as quickly as possible." In a second block of trials, subjects heard the same sequence of stimulus tones, but this time they were instructed to move the control handle *toward* the side of the ear stimulated. Half of the males and half of the females performed the "away" block first and the "toward" block second, while the other half of each group performed in the reverse sequence.

An analysis of variance of these data revealed that subjects reacted significantly faster when instructed to move the control handle toward instead of away from the side of the ear stimulated (292 *vs.* 351 msec.). These results can be explained by postulating a natural tendency to react toward the source of stimulation. The necessity for overriding this stereotype before responding to the tones presented in the "away" block of trials would account for the slower information processing during that block. Incidentally, this study also confirmed the findings from our previous study which employed the same motor response. That is, RT was significantly faster for abductive reactions to the right, but movement time was significantly faster for movements to the left.

Let me now back-track a moment to our studies involving RT to verbal directional commands. Our results there suggested that the auditory display provided two cues, one relevant; i.e., the content of the command, and the other irrelevant; i.e., the ear stimulated, and that the time required to process the former cue was somehow affected by the presence of the latter cue. At this point, we felt that the ear stimulated x command interaction was due to the irrelevant cue *interfering* with information processing on trials where it did not correspond with the symbolic content of the command. It was possible, however, that the interaction was due to the irrelevant cue *facilitating* information processing on trials where it corresponded with the symbolic content of the command. It was also possible that the irrelevant cue operated to *both* facilitate responding on the corresponding trials *and* interfere with responding on the noncorresponding trials.

We decided to design an experiment to determine how the command x ear stimulated interaction was produced (Simon & Small, 1969). This same experiment was designed to determine the generality of the command x ear stimulated interaction. That is, was the phenomenon limited to situations involving verbal commands, or did it also occur when simple stimuli such as pure tones were used to provide the relevant directional information?

Our subjects' task, this time, was to press the correct one of two finger keys as quickly as possible after hearing a tone. Sixty-four subjects heard either a high-pitched tone (1000 cps) or a low-pitched tone (400 cps) presented to one ear or the other. The subjects had no way of knowing prior to the presentation of a tone which ear would be stimulated or what

the tone would be. Half of the subjects were instructed to press the right
key when they heard the high-pitched tone and to press the left key when
they heard the low-pitched tone. The other half of the subjects were given
the opposite tone-key rule. There were 56 monaural test trials in which
the 400 and 1000 cps tones were presented equally often to each ear in a
predetermined random sequence.

In addition to this monaural block of trials, each subject also performed
on a block of trials involving binaural stimulation. Half of the subjects
performed the monaural block first and half the binaural block first. Each
subject performed both blocks using the particular tone-key rule to which
he was originally assigned.

Fig. 4 shows RT to the right and left tonal commands which were presented to the right ear, the left ear, or to both ears simultaneously. It can

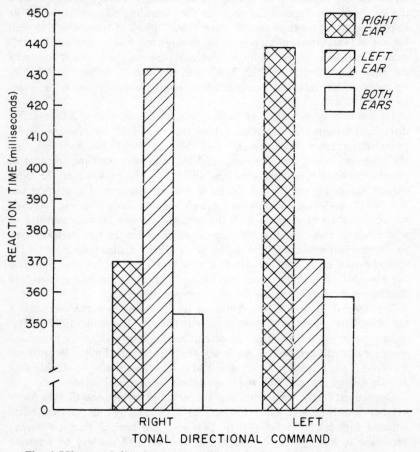

Fig. 4 RT to tonal directional commands as a function of ear(s) stimulated.

be seen that RT was markedly faster when the right command was heard in the right ear than when it was heard in the left ear, and, similarly, RT to the left command was faster when it was heard in the left ear than when it was heard in the right. Clearly then, subjects responded significantly faster on trials where the symbolic content of the command corresponded with the ear stimulated than on trials where it did not. This result demonstrates that the command x ear stimulated interaction, heretofore only observed with verbal directional commands, also occurred when pure tones were used to signal the appropriate response. It appears, then, that the interaction reflects a basic and general phenomenon which exists independently of whether the command is communicated verbally or nonverbally. It also appears that the interaction is unrelated to prior symbolic associations since, in contrast to verbal directional commands, the tones had no implicit directional significance.

The major purpose of this experiment, however, was to determine whether the tonal command x ear stimulated interaction was due to a facilitation of information processing on the corresponding trials or to an interference with information processing on the noncorresponding trials. On the monaural trials, the ear in which the tone was heard provided an irrelevant cue which, of course, was absent on the binaural trials. Therefore, binaural RT provides the appropriate baseline for evaluating the effect of this irrelevant cue. Statistical tests revealed that binaural RT was significantly faster than the average RT on noncorresponding as well as corresponding monaural trials. On the noncorresponding monaural trials, the irrelevant cue apparently conflicted with processing the relevant cue and resulted in slower RT than on the binaural trials. On the corresponding monaural trials, the irrelevant cue coincided with the relevant cue, but this correspondence did not facilitate information processing. Results of this experiment, then, clearly indicated that the tonal command x ear stimulated interaction observed on the monaural trials was a result of interference with information processing on the noncorresponding trials rather than a facilitation of the corresponding trials.

Our next experiment was concerned with determining whether the same phenomena which we had observed with auditory displays would also occur with visual displays (Craft & Simon, 1970). My student, John Craft, modified a stereoscope by removing the lenses and inserting an opaque partition which divided the visual field into two halves (see Fig. 5). In the center of each half of the field, he mounted a small red light and a small green light.

Sixty-four subjects operated finger keys with either their right or left index fingers. Half of the subjects were told, "If you see a red light, push the right-hand key, and if you see a green light, push the left-hand key." The other half of the subjects were given the opposite light-key associations. A warning light was presented two sec. prior to the presentation of the stimulus light. Subjects performed on two blocks of trials, a monocular block and a binocular block. In the monocular block, a red light or a green light was presented to either the right eye or the left eye in a random sequence. In the binocular block, the red light or the green light was presented to both eyes at the same time.

Fig. 6 shows the results of this experiment. RT to the right command was faster when it appeared in the right eye than when it appeared in the left eye, and RT to the left command was faster when it appeared in the left eye than when it appeared in the right eye. This command x eye stimulated interaction is a direct parallel to the command x ear stimulated interaction observed in our previous studies. Note, too, that RT on the binocular trials was faster than on either the corresponding or noncorresponding monocular trials indicating that the interaction observed on the monocular trials was due to interference on the noncorresponding trials rather than facilitation on the corresponding trials.

Craft next addressed himself to the question of whether the command x ear stimulated interaction observed on the monocular trials was due to the eye stimulated per se, or to a directional cue associated with the eye stimu-

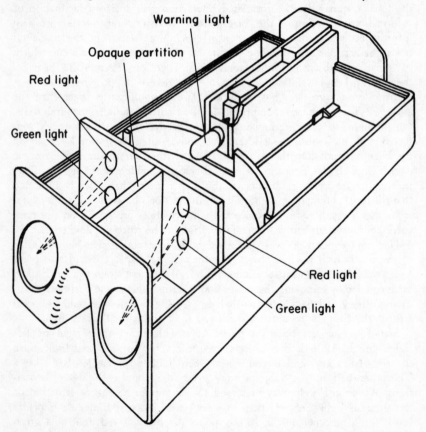

Fig. 5 Modified stereoscope with lenses removed and partition installed.

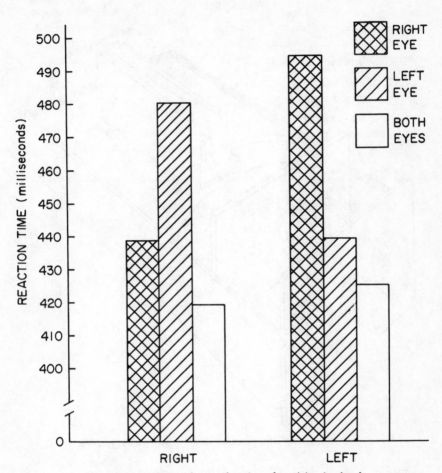

Fig. 6 RT to commands as a function of eye(s) stimulated.

lated. In order to answer this question, Craft reassembled the stereoscope (see Fig. 7). That is, the opaque partition dividing the visual fields was removed and the lenses were reinstalled.

Sixty-four subjects then responded to the same random sequence of monocular trials used previously; i.e., either a red light or a green light was presented to either the right eye or the left eye, and the subject pressed the right-hand key if he saw one color and the left-hand key if he saw the other color. This time, however, with the stereoscope intact, the subject saw the signal light in the center of his visual field, and so could not tell which eye was being stimulated on a given trial. In other words, the directional cue associated with the eye stimulated was effectively removed.

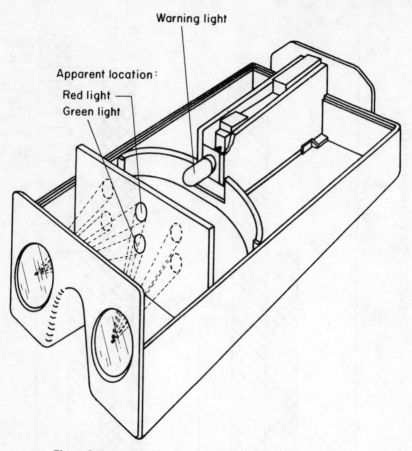

Warning light

Apparent location:
Red light
Green light

Fig. 7 Stereoscope with partition removed and lenses installed.

Fig. 8 shows that, with the directional cue eliminated, the command x eye stimulated interaction disappeared. This experiment, then, demonstrated conclusively that the interaction observed in Craft's first study was due, not to the eye stimulated per se, but to the directional cue associated with the eye stimulated.

Our next experiment was designed to determine whether the command x ear stimulated interaction observed in our previous studies was due to the ear stimulated per se or to a directional cue associated with ear stimulated. Obviously, these two factors were confounded in all of the experiments on auditory displays which I have reported thus far. That is, a signal to the right ear appears to come from the right side, and a signal to the left ear appears to come from the left side. The question was how to unconfound these two factors. We could think of no way of eliminating the directional cue as Craft had done with his visual display. So, instead, we decided to retain the directional cue and eliminate the ear stimulated as a factor.

By employing a phase shifting device, it was possible to stimulate both ears simultaneously and yet make it appear to the subject as if the tone were coming from one side or the other. The experiment consisted of 32 subjects performing on two blocks of trials. The first block was a monaural block identical to that of previous studies. That is, the subject heard either a high- or low-pitched tone in either his right or left ear. He was instructed to press the right key if he heard the "right" command and the left key if he heard the "left" command. In a second block of trials, the subject heard the same random sequence of tonal commands, but this time the tone was

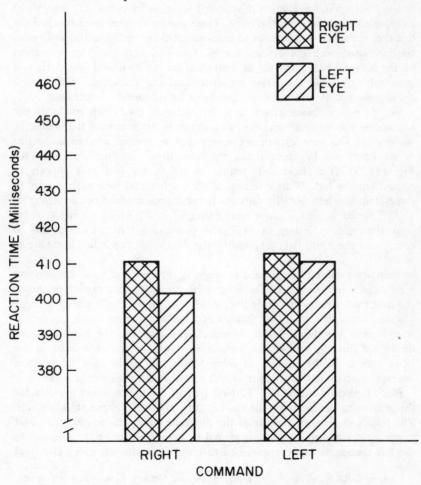

Fig. 8 RT to commands when directional cue is eliminated.

presented through the phase shifter. That is, both ears were stimulated simultaneously, but the tone appeared to come from one side or the other.

Fig. 9 shows the data from this experiment.[1] The left half of the figure pictures the results from the monaural block. The tonal command x ear stimulated interaction is, by now, a familiar one. The right half of the figure shows the results from the binaural block. With a 270° phase shift setting, the tonal command appeared to come from the right. With a 90° phase shift setting, the tone appeared to come from the left. Note that here we got the same significant interaction as on the monaural trials. The subjects responded faster to the "right" command when it appeared to come from the right than when it appeared to come from the left and responded faster to the "left" command when it appeared to come from the left than when it appeared to come from the right. These results demonstrated conclusively that the interaction was not due to ear stimulated per se but to the directional cue associated with the ear stimulated. You will note that the interaction on the binaural block was not as marked as on the monaural block. This is, presumably, because the irrelevant directional cue produced by the phase shifter was not as potent as that produced by monaural stimulation.

We have now demonstrated that the irrelevant cue which produced the interaction was a directional cue, a tendency to react toward the source of stimulation. Our next experiment represented an attempt to change the size of the interaction by manipulating the strength of the directional cue (see Fig. 10). With a phase shift setting of 90°, a binaural tone appears to come from the left. With a setting of 45°, a binaural tone still appears to come from the left, but the directional cue is, presumably, not as strong as at 90°. Similarly, with a phase shift setting of 270°, a tone appears to come from the right. A setting of 315° also produces a tone which appears to come from the right, but, presumably, the directional cue is not as strong as at 270°.

Thirty-two subjects responded to high- or low-pitched tones by pressing a right- or a left-hand key. The tones were presented in a random sequence at phase shift settings of either 90°, 270°, 45°, or 315°, all within a single block of trials. We predicted that a command x apparent source interaction would occur for the 270°-90° condition and also for the 315°-45° condition but that the size of the interaction would not be as marked in the latter case as in the former. In other words, we predicted a triple order interaction of command x apparent source x strength of directional cue.

Fig. 11 pictures the results. The left half of the figure shows the data for the maximum deviation condition; i.e., the 270°-90° phase shift settings. The results duplicated those from the previous study. Subjects reacted faster to the right command when it appeared to come from the right side and to the left command when it appeared to come from the left side. The right

[1] Simon, J. R., Small, A. M. Jr., Ziglar, R. A., and Craft, J. L. Response interference in an information processing task; Sensory versus perceptual factors. *Journal of Experimental Psychology,* 1970, *85,* 311-314.

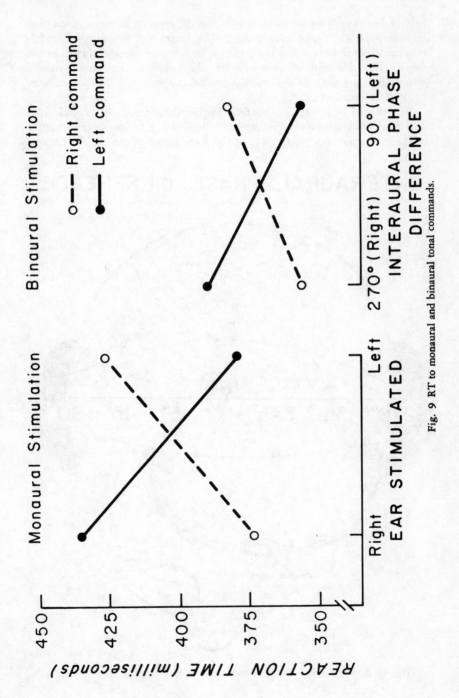

Fig. 9 RT to monaural and binaural tonal commands.

half of Fig. 11 shows comparable data for the reduced deviation condition; i.e., the 315°-45° phase shift settings. This interaction was also statistically significant but did not differ in size from the interaction under the maximum deviation condition. In other words, the phase shift settings which we had selected for the reduced deviation condition did not produce the predicted triple order interaction.

We decided to try again, this time further reducing the interaural phase difference, and therefore, presumably, also further reducing the strength of the irrelevant directional cue. For this experiment, phase shift settings of

INTERAURAL PHASE DIFFERENCE

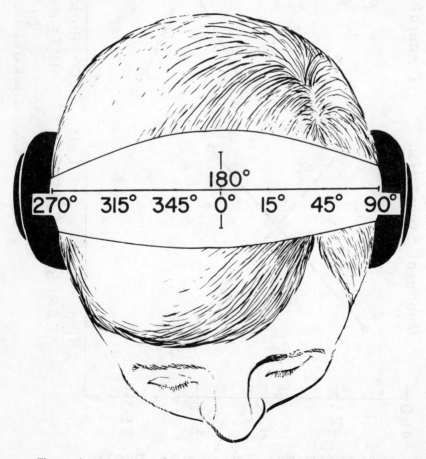

Fig. 10 Apparent source of tonal commands at various phase shift settings.

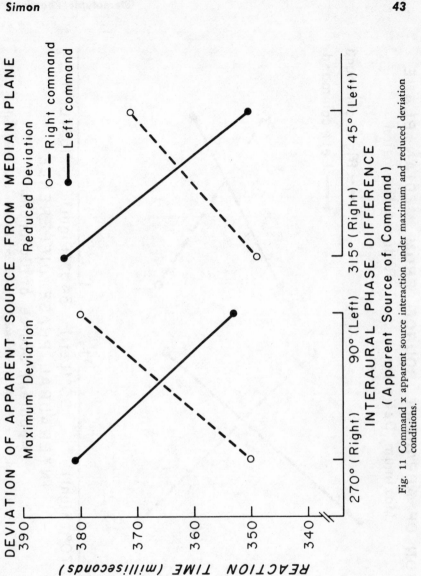

Fig. 11 Command x apparent source interaction under maximum and reduced deviation conditions.

345° and 15° were selected for the reduced deviation condition (see Fig. 10), and these were again contrasted with the 270°-90° maximum deviation condition.

Fig. 12 shows the results. The left half of the figure shows the data from the maximum deviation condition. Note that these data replicate exactly the results of the previous two experiments. The right half of the figure shows the data for the reduced deviation condition. This time, just

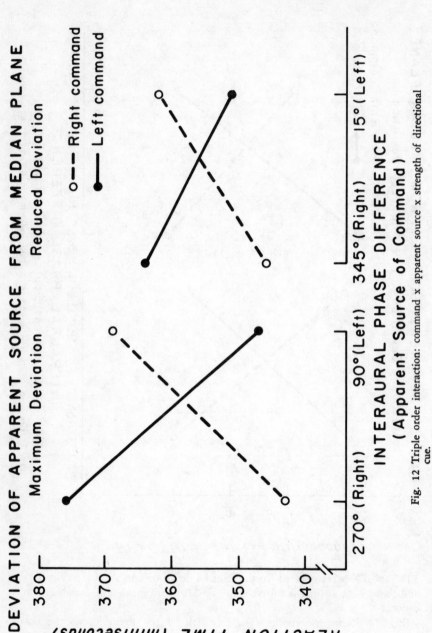

Fig. 12 Triple order interaction: command x apparent source x strength of directional cue.

as we had predicted, the command x apparent source interaction was significant and was also statistically significantly smaller than the same interaction under the maximum deviation condition. We have demonstrated, then, that we can significantly alter the size of the command x apparent source interaction by manipulating the strength of the irrelevant directional cue. These results provide convincing evidence that the irrelevant cue affecting information processing is a stereotypic tendency to react toward the source of stimulation. The stronger the directional cue, the stronger is the tendency to react toward the stimulus source.

The next question we asked was, "Is this stereotype a tendency to react toward the major source of stimulation or is it a specific tendency to react toward the relevant stimulus?" If it is a tendency to react toward the major source of stimulation, it should be possible to eliminate the command x ear stimulated interaction by presenting an irrelevant stimulus to the opposite ear simultaneously with the relevant tonal command. It should also be possible to alter the size of the command x ear stimulated interaction by manipulating the dB level of the irrelevant stimulus to the opposite ear. It might even be possible to reverse the direction of the interaction by increasing the dB level of the irrelevant stimulus to exceed that of the relevant tonal command.

To investigate some of these notions, we conducted a series of experiments similar to those previously reported.[2] In the first experiment in this series, 32 subjects were told to press a right- or a left-hand key in response to high- or low-pitched tonal commands. Half of the trials in a block were exactly the same as those in previous experiments; i.e., a tonal command was presented to one ear or the other, and there was no stimulus provided to the opposite ear. On the other half of the trials, an 89 dB white noise was presented to the opposite ear simultaneously with the introduction of the tonal command.

Fig. 13 shows the results of this experiment. Note that, under the no-noise condition, we obtained the same command x ear stimulated interaction observed so many times before. When the noise was introduced into the opposite ear, however, the command x ear stimulated interaction was eliminated.

Our next experiment was designed to determine whether we could alter the size of the command x ear stimulated interaction by manipulating the strength of the stimulation to the opposite ear. We reasoned that, if an 89 dB noise eliminated the interaction, then a noise of less than 89 dB might reduce but not eliminate the interaction, and a noise of more than 89 dB might even reverse the direction of the interaction.

Thirty-two subjects again pressed a right- or left-hand key in response to a random sequence of high- and low-pitched tones presented equally

2 Simon, J. R., Craft, J. L., and Small, A. M. Jr. Manipulating the strength of a stereotype: Interference effects in an auditory information-processing task. *Journal of Experimental Psychology*, 1970, *86*, 63-68.

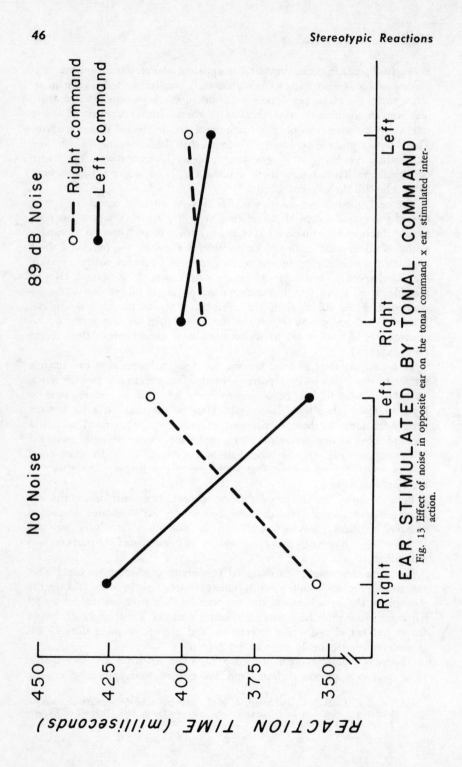

Fig. 13 Effect of noise in opposite ear on the tonal command x ear stimulated interaction.

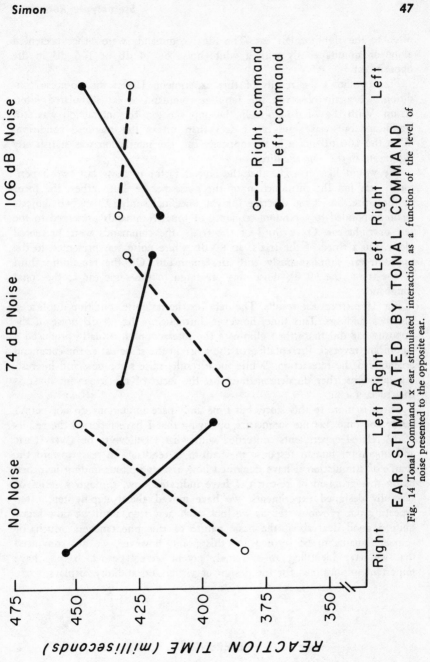

Fig. 14 Tonal Command x ear stimulated interaction as a function of the level of noise presented to the opposite ear.

often to the right or left ear. The tonal commands were either presented alone or simultaneously with a white noise of 74 dB or 106 dB in the opposite ear.

Fig. 14 shows the results of this experiment. Under the no-noise condition, we again observed the familiar command x ear stimulated interaction. With the 74 dB noise in the opposite ear, the interaction was still significant but was significantly less than under the no-noise condition. With the 106 dB noise in the opposite ear, the interaction was statistically significant in the *opposite* direction.

We would like to argue that the crucial factor in these last two experiments was not the introduction of the noise per se, but, rather, the locus of the noise. So let me describe for you one final study. Thirty-two subjects again responded to a random sequence of tonal commands presented to the left or right ear. On a third of the trials, the commands were presented alone. On a third of the trials, an 89 dB white noise was presented to the opposite ear simultaneously with the command. On the remaining third of the trials, the 89 dB noise was presented to the same ear as the tonal command.

Fig. 15 pictures the results. The data for the no-noise condition duplicated previous findings. This time, however, introducing the 89 dB noise in the opposite ear did more than eliminate the interaction. It actually produced a significant reversal. Presentation of the noise in the same ear as the command accentuated the interaction. While these results raise some new and interesting questions, they do demonstrate that the locus of the irrelevant noise is the crucial factor.

There is more to this story, but time and space limitations do not permit me to continue. Let me summarize by saying that I have reported the results of 13 related experiments concerned with what I believe to be a very basic and important human response mechanism, a tendency to react toward the source of stimulation. I have described how a serendipitous finding launched us on this program of research. I have indicated how, through a series of carefully designed experiments, we have moved ahead step-by-step, often repeating our previous step as we took each new step, until we now know quite a good deal about the basic nature of this phenomenon. Much, of course, remains to be learned. At this point, however, we are convinced that we have identified an extremely potent stereotype which may have important implications for the design of visual and auditory displays.

REFERENCES

Craft, J. L., & Simon, J. R. Processing symbolic information from a visual display: Interference from an irrelevant directional cue. *Journal of Experimental Psychology,* 1970, *83,* 415-420.

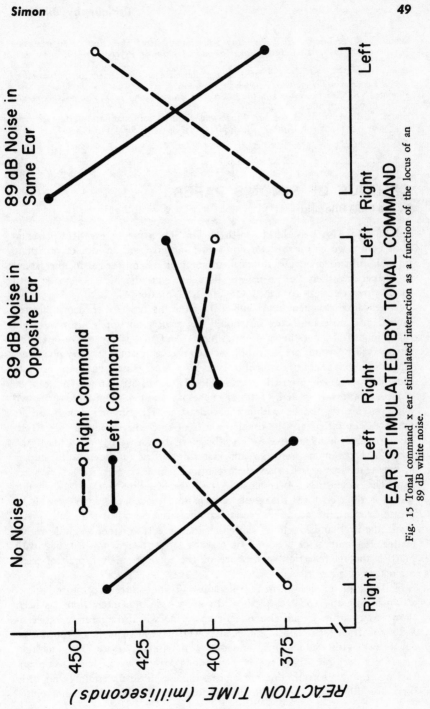

Fig. 15 Tonal command x ear stimulated interaction as a function of the locus of an 89 dB white noise.

Simon, J. R., & Rudell, A. P. Auditory S-R compatibility: The effect of an irrelevant cue on information processing. *Journal of Applied Psychology*, 1967, 51, 300-304.

Simon, J. R. Effect of ear stimulated on reaction time and movement time. *Journal of Experimental Psychology*, 1968, 78, 344-346.

Simon, J. R. Reactions toward the source of stimulation. *Journal of Experimental Psychology*, 1969, 81, 174-176.

Simon, J. R., & Small, A. M., Jr. Processing auditory information: Interference from an irrelevant cue. *Journal of Applied Psychology*, 1969, 53, 433-435.

CRITIQUE OF SIMON'S PAPER
by Ina McD Bilodeau

BASMAJIAN: I would like to thank Dr. Simon for his excellent presentation. Before we go on to discussing it, let me give you an idea of our plan. First, I will call upon Dr. Bilodeau to speak in a semi-formal manner about this paper and then we can have a discussion period which can go on until 12:30 when we break for lunch. Dr. Bilodeau, please.

When an experimenter presents data from 13 new experiments directed toward an important issue, he should not expect anything but praise and eager inquiries about the next installment. And that is my response to Dr. Simon's clear account of a careful attack on the source of a striking phenomenon and the variables that control it. If I have some questions to ask, they stem from an aroused interest, not from dissatisfaction, and can be reduced to less than half a dozen general inquiries. Only the first two questions are legitimate, within the context of Dr. Simon's paper and its purpose. The others are the usual rewards of catching an outsider's interest. Most of the comments that follow thus, can be answered in advance: the program Dr. Simon presented put first things first; a dozen solid studies in two years is more than adequate continued inquiry.

a. The interaction of command (or response direction) and stimulus source is referred to as the result of a natural tendency. It may as well be pre-experimentally acquired; certainly the studies with red and green lights and high and low tones show that the stereotype is not a simple verbal matter. But natural or acquired, it may be strengthened or weakened with practice and its reflection in the size of the interaction over practice trials is a matter of interest.

b. The kind of design used to demonstrate the source x command interaction brings up a related question. In every case, the interaction has been shown as a within-S (subject) phenomenon. Does it also appear in between-S design? If it does, then it is indeed powerful—independent of contrast or any rule that the subject may adopt as a mnemonic device. This question may not be critical, of course. If S responds with only one hand to an unvarying stimulus to only one eye or ear, there is little uncertainty and little room for differences in information processing. On the other hand, eliminating the uncertainty about which ear would be stimulated (the second experiment) did not greatly change the interaction, though it did lower RT. While an independent-groups design might not put the stereotype to a crucial test, its demonstration in a simple RT setup would be striking.

c. The presentation leads the reader through a series of stimulus manipulations in a way that makes one ask for the next question as *E* (experimenter) is about to reveal its answer. This reader's interest was directed increasingly toward the effects of manipulating responses as a way of changing the agreement between command to respond and source. (What happens as the response choices are changed from left-right toward north-south or up-down? If *S* crosses his hands? If the stimulus is aversive?) Only one of the early experiments was concerned with the response side, but the response-centered questions are not likely to have been evoked by accident; presumably some are among the questions already answered in experiments not included in this report. The last experiments also point strongly toward using a different sensory modality for relevant and irrelevant cues and I am curious about what happens there, too.

d. The stereotype is an interference effect, an increase in the time *S* needs to process information. Put this way, then, the interference would not have to be reflected in overt errors. But is it? Could a tendency to orient the body toward the major source of stimulation produce the same effects?

e. The reversal of the direction of the effect when the biggest stimulus is irrelevant and opposite is most striking. The prominant irrelevant stimulus is of real benefit to RT under the unfavorable ear-command combinations as well as detrimental to the favorable combinations. I am not entirely straight on how the speed-up in information processing takes place, though the slow-down seems clear enough. It seems that the experiments with the irrelevant cue and those comparing monocular and binocular (and monaural and binaural) RTs have an important bearing on summation-effect interpretation, as well as implications for equipment design, beyond the competence of an outsider to RT.

SIMON'S REPLY TO
Bilodeau's Critique

SIMON: Well, I could respond to a few of Dr. Bilodeau's comments. First she took me to task for labelling this a "natural" tendency to respond toward the source of stimulation. I think she is right there. I don't have any evidence that it is in fact a "natural" tendency. I think of it as a mechanism built into the human organism, but it might very well be learned; I just don't know. We've looked for analogues of this sort of phenomenon in other areas. Investigators have noted, for example, that infants, after about six months of age, turn toward the source of a loud sound and may even reach toward it. Then there are the taxes or directed orientation reactions in lower organisms where they move toward the source of stimulation. These seem to be built-in sorts of things. I thought for awhile that this phenomenon might be related to the orienting reflex which is very popular now in Russian psychology, but the orienting reflex disappears after a few presentations and our phenomenon does not.

Dr. Bilodeau also asked me about whether the phenomenon was related to intensity of stimulation. That was something that I thought we might investigate in the future. In that last study I reported where we presented noise to the same ear as the relevant stimulus; it looked as if the interaction actually became larger, so maybe this interaction is a function of intensity of stimulation. I have often thought that we might want to increase the decibel level of the tone so that it really blasts the subject. You know, instead of 85 or 100 decibels, have it 110 or 115 so it's almost painful. I wouldn't be surprised under those conditions to find a tendency to react away from the source instead of toward the source. That's something we want to try.

She asked me about possible north-south differences. We are thinking on the same wave length, because I thought of that too and, in fact, that is an experiment we have planned. We are going to put speakers up here and down here and have the subject respond up or down to tones coming from one or the other speaker and see if we get the same phenomenon as we did with the left-right signals.

Concerning the effect of crossing the hands, we just completed that experiment. That was kind of an interesting one. The subjects were presented again with a high- or low-pitched tone, in one ear or the other. One tone signalled a response with the right hand and the other tone signalled a response with the left hand. As long as the right hand operates the key on the right and the left hand operates the key on the left, you get the same interaction we had observed before. But then, on another block of trials, we had the subjects cross their hands. Now the right hand operates the key on the left and the left hand operates the key on the right. Subjects are given the same instructions as before. Under these conditions, the interaction is significant, but in the reverse direction. In other words, it is not the hand that is responsible, it is the location of the keys with respect to the ears. I think I have covered most of the questions you raised, and I am open to any others.

BASMAJIAN: Can we please have questions from the audience?

DISCUSSION OF SIMON'S PAPER

GEORGE VANIS, UNIVERSITY OF MICHIGAN: Did you test your subject as to eye dominance? What I am wondering is, would a person that's right-handed with left-eye dominance follow your pattern?

SIMON: No, we didn't. We tested their hearing in the range that we were working in, to make sure that they had normal hearing in right and left ears, but there were no tests of eye dominance.

BRUCE ANDERSON, UNIVERSITY OF MINNESOTA: I had just a quick, added question on the red and green light. Did you test them for color blindness?

SIMON: No.

ANDERSON: O.K. Then, I want to get to the real question, that is if you used the crossover or not crossover but possibly used the mirror image, would you expect the same kind of results? Where you don't see the hand but the mirror? Would you expect the same kind of results as you got in the cross hands?

SIMON: I have to think about that.

WILLIAM STRAUB, ITHACA COLLEGE: At the chance of being branded a practitioner rather than a theoretician, I would like to try and relate this to a practical situation in physical education. Do your results indicate, for example, that when our right-handed quarterbacks come over to the sidelines, we should give our information in their right ear? My question is really this—I think the physical educator would be interested in knowing about the retention. In other words, in so many situations in physical education we are giving instructions and the subject has to move to another location. Generally when he moves, he is confronted with other stimuli. I was wondering, for example, would your next experiment suggest that after receiving directions, the subject—moved to another location and subjected to other stimuli—perform other tasks faster than the initial directions? Let's take the quarterback as he comes over to his coach to receive some type of information. When he returns to the huddle, if this particular information called for executing a right-handed forward pass, can the subject —after hearing this in his right ear—execute it? Getting off the pass is the prime factor involved. Can he perform this task faster after an interval— such as, going back to the huddle? Would you care to comment about some of the practical aspects of this?

SIMON: I would be very cautious about generalizing about the results of my studies. I think my research probably has very little to do with what most of you are concerned. I warned your Chairman of that when he asked me to give this paper, so I have very little I can say in response to your question. I just hope that this research, which deals with what I think is a basic response mechanism, may be of general interest to you. I can't, myself, see much practical application to physical education.

STRAUB: Would you like to comment on this? In football, if the play were moving to the right and my linemen on the right side were to react from the right, might they not react more quickly, if the signal of the count to the ball—the count when the ball is snapped—were given in the right ear?

SIMON: Yes.

DR. HUBBARD, UNIVERSITY OF ILLINOIS: I will try to get you

out of the hole as an old coach. Weren't they faster when it was binaural?
SIMON: Yes.
HUBBARD: O.K. You don't select the ear.
BASMAJIAN: The answer to that is your other ear is not as fair.
K. U. SMITH: I think the problem here has a practical relationship to the control of fixation. The real problem here is not vision, because the eye has to be directed toward the direction of the stimulus to bring it to focus. Basically, the directional stereotype here in the case of vision is the fixation above the eye.

The real question, however, is in the auditory fixation. What is the auditory fixation process? Is it something connected with the head movement? Head tremor is necessary for auditory localization and direction. Or is it in the ear; is it in the impeding system in the ear? Now, the impeding system—that is, the capacity of each ear to selectively tune in and out conversation—would be quite different from the general head orientation mechanism. I might say, parenthetically, that there is some evidence that the feedback delay is possibly differentiated for right-handed and left-handed individuals. At least in right-handed individuals the speech delay to the right ear has more effect on the perturbance of speech. Now, again, if the impedance mechanism to the two ears were differentiated rather than the middle ear in processing the sound mechanism, you could get the reverse direction effect, rather than the intensity. But I don't see why you would get the reversal effect with the excessive sound unless there were something in the ear itself to signal the differential sound effects.

That's really a question.
SIMON: I don't think this phenomenon can be explained neurophysiologically or anatomically. I don't see any evidence from any of my data that it is related to the ear itself or to hemispheric dominance. There just weren't any of those main effects or interactions in any of the experiments. I think it is a tendency to react towards the source of stimulation not necessarily towards the relevant source but towards the major source.

ELSIE BURTON, OHIO STATE: At the risk of muddying the waters still further, I recently completed a reaction time study in the Behavioral Science Laboratory at Ohio State University, involving the relationship of visual and auditory stimuli to spoken and written responses. I found that written responses were faster to visual than to auditory stimuli, while spoken responses were faster to auditory than to visual stimuli.

Perhaps I could clarify that somewhat. The subjects received visual stimuli from printed digits flashed onto a small panel in front of them. Auditory stimuli were presented through headphones operating from a tape recorder. Auditory stimulation occurred simultaneously in both ears, as there was no attempt to separate ear stimulation in this study.

I found that the subjects responded faster when corresponding sense modalities were involved, that is, visual stimulation resulted in faster written responses, whereas auditory stimulation produced faster spoken responses.

SIMON: I see . . . very interesting.

BURTON: My study involved 10 year old subjects. However, this study was also conducted by Dr. Anthony Greenwald utilizing college students as subjects. Similar results were obtained. Another study utilized five-year old subjects but was limited to the auditory modalities due to the difficulty encountered in obtaining written responses from subjects who could not write.

BASMAJIAN: Are there further questions from the audience?

HOLDING, UNIVERSITY OF LOUISVILLE: I don't know if you remember Jackson's Whistling Kettle experiments. It was in the *Journal of Experimental Psychology* in 1953 or 1954—I don't remember the exact reference. What happened was that he had a row of kettles in his laboratory and he could make noises issue from any of these sites and any one of these kettles would show a cloud of steam. Now, under these circumstances if you show steam issuing from a kettle over here and make a noise over here, then people tend to attribute the source of the noise not merely the visual source. Now, he concluded that the visual localization showed primacy over auditory localization. Since Dr. Simon has already moved from the position of saying one goes faster in the direction of the stimulation— saying one moves faster in the direction of apparent stimulation—this is a further variation of what I might call parency, which I thought might be interesting.

SIMON: Yes. Thank you very much, Dr. Holding.

A PARTICIPANT: I would like to make a comment to point out the importance of attention to stimulation. Novich of Wisconsin did a study of key-tapping and in this study a person would press a key. There would be an auditory signal to each key tap, and corresponding to this, a flash of light from a stroboscope. The intensity of the light flash was subjectively higher than the dB level of the tone; before the experiment he equated the subjectivity of the intensity of the spot to the subjectivity of the loudness of the tone. He didn't know exactly what was loudness, and he found that the intensity of the visual spot was greater than the dB level of the tone. The subject was told to respond just to the sound. He found the intensity was higher; the delayed feedback of the auditory sound did not have that great an effect when the visual signals were greater, for when the visual signal—which was really not supposed to be part of the task—was made less, the delayed auditory sound had a detrimental effect. He showed that the intensity of the stimulation did effect the task even when it wasn't an integral part of it.

SIMON: Yes, it certainly seems to be related. Was that published some-where?

A PARTICIPANT: Yes, in *Perceptual and Motor Skills.*

SIMON: Questions from this side?

BASMAJIAN: I would like to make a few comments, because I think the work that Dr. Simon is doing has intense interest not just to the group in this room but to the general area—that no man's land between neurophysiology and neuropsychophysiology. If you want another no man's land beyond that—psychology. There is very real evidence here, from what he has produced that the phenomena cannot be explained by ordinary neurophysiological methods. I think most of the audience knows enough neuroanatomy, neurophysiology to already have come to that conclusion. Maybe we're wrong in so concluding that, Dr. Simon, but I too cannot even imagine this having what we would call an ordinary feedback loop of the simplest reflex type. This is no simple reflex. Therefore, there is obviously a process going on, and this process is a complex one which probably has been conditioned into the subject. It has an element of naturalness to it that bears a great deal of study. Thus, I would like to see—rather than doing more, shall we say refinements, of what you have been doing—you go in a completely different direction and that is to go to babies, and here —this is odd for me to suggest—the use of animals. Normally, they ask, can that be done in an animal? But I wonder if there is some way in which the development of this laterality can be worked out; I would suggest that babies are the best source of evidence rather than animals to see whether it is natural to the species. Is there a response of the baby towards the side from which the sound comes—or anything comes—to a speaking sound, or not? In other words, what is the genesis of the phenomena? I would certainly like to see you go in that direction as well as in the obvious direction of refinement. Now, you have got to the point of anticipating the arguments of others who try to shake you on your main hypothesis. I think the hypothesis is fully documented; now, I think it is about time to stop worrying about the critics and to put a new type of underpinning under what you're doing. I wish you would go on with babies—studying them.

C. AMMONS, UNIVERSITY OF MONTANA: May I comment on something? I would just like to remark on this business of using babies in research. By the time our seventh infant was coming along, I had learned enough about labor, delivery, and nursing infants and had enough presence of mind to conduct an experiment beginning when this child was three hours old. She was very alert, having been born naturally in a very short time. I used the stimuli developed by Gershon Berkson for his studies with infant chimpanzees. (One appeared in *Perceptual And Motor Skills.*) This child was able, over a period of several trials given at four-hour intervals during her first five days of life, to learn to make a visual-looking response to these stimuli which varied in level of complexity. Responding at first was quite variable and preference (longer looking) was only gradually suggested by the fifth day or after 22-24 trials. This was a rather difficult experimental situation in which to work, but it was great fun. However, I recommend, Dick, that you start training your wife immediately to deliver naturally. Then you teach her to present the simple procedures to the infant when hungry before feeding. Very simple methodology is feasibly handled by the mother-experimenter. It might be, with cooperation of the hospital staff, that one could introduce a foreign experimenter (the father) and more complex procedures, making experimentation with human neonates really entirely feasible.

SIMON: I'll take your comments under advisement. I don't much like babies and college sophomores are much too handy; therefore, I doubt whether I'll go to the direction you suggest, although I see its value. I'll leave that to someone else.

BASMAJIAN: Any further comments or questions?

K. U. SMITH: May I make a comment? There have been several studies in the past four or five years and some quite a bit earlier by ourselves which show that an infant between six and seven months to three years orients very naturally without training of any sort to television images displayed outside of a moving playpen. These television images weren't controlled; they were both visual and auditory. The critical thing is that the infants would not orient just to any stimulus. Their orientation was largely dynamic. They oriented more to movement of Mother, than to the movements of strangers. There was a definite developmental function between six months and three years in this dynamic orientation. I am quite sure crawling children use this orientation. Youngsters who can walk and grab onto the side of the playpen do this and do it with their head while sitting still.

Learning Without Errors

D. H. Holding
Tulane University[1]

Controlling behaviour by administering subsequent feedback, or knowledge of results, or reinforcement, can be extremely effective. These corrective techniques have been relatively well explored, and are backed by a network of theory derived from the learning laboratory. The alternative to the use of trial-and-error methods is to provide sufficient information or constraint to ensure that subjects make only correct responses. The corresponding set of cueing, prompting and guidance techniques, which emphasize error prevention rather than error correction, have received far less experimental and theoretical attention. It is true that during the last few years the issue of "prompting versus confirmation" has begun to attract attention, but we still lack detailed analyses of the guidance side of the dichotomy.

Cueing the correct response in perceptual tasks, prompting correct responses in verbal tasks, and guiding correct responses in motor tasks all represent training methods which rely to varying extents upon constraining the actions available to the learner. In the case of guidance the constraints have been mainly physical, although the term has traditionally included also the visual and verbal methods of guiding motor responses. Morever, particularly in the maze-learning work, physical methods have been as much or more directed toward supplying perceptual information as toward shaping the motor pattern of response.

Cueing and Prompting

In experiments on perceptual learning, techniques relying upon cueing the correct response have generally been found successful in comparison with feedback corrections. Annett (1966), for example, has shown that training for detection of the gap orientation in Landolt rings, can be better assisted by colour cueing, arranging red backgrounds for right-hand gaps and green for left-hand gaps, than by giving "right-wrong" information or summary scores; further, giving supplementary visual cues for sonar detec-

---

[1]Now at the University of Louisville, Kentucky.

tion resulted in better discrimination than lowering the background noise level, while administering knowledge of results led to riskier judgments, with an increase in the number of false positives. Many other instances of cueing effectiveness, particularly in the areas of perceptual identification and signal monitoring, are reviewed by Aiken and Lau (1967).

In the area of programmed learning *prompting* has typically been so heavy as to "give the answer away", as Skinner (1961) himself suggests. The suspicion that the prompting itself is responsible for the high degree of learning achieved, rather than the subsequent confirmatory reinforcement, was given prominence by Cook (1963). Many direct comparisons of the two procedures in verbal paired-association learning, also reviewed by Aiken and Lau (1967), have shown prompting to be as good a training technique, or a better one, than the confirmation method. The model proposed by Cook and Kendler (1956) suggests that these effects should result from the interference introduced into the associative process by the confirmation procedures (a) due to the delay occasioned by the overt anticipating response, and (b) due to the high occurrence of overt errors early in learning, which have later to be extinguished. This second suggestion, concerning an error-dependent mechanism is of particular interest. An analogous mechanism has earlier been prepared for motor learning (Kay, 1951; 1954), and its evaluation is of importance to the present paper.

The object here is to assemble the available evidence on the error-free techniques in motor learning, in an attempt to separate out a number of relevant variables and their effects. Direct comparisons with knowledge of results and feedback techniques will be of subsidiary interest, since the efficiency of either form of training will vary greatly in accordance with the correspondence between the training variables and the task demand characteristics. Guidance is certainly not a panacea, and will be ill-suited to many practical tasks, but it is important to delimit the conditions of its applicability. A first step is to look briefly at the earlier studies of guidance.

Guidance: Brief History

The very earliest guidance investigators all used animal subjects. Thorndike (1898) produced debatable results by forcing cats into puzzle boxes, but Cole (1907) found better learning of a similar task by raccoons, who responded well to guided training in opening problem latches. Koch (1923), who also guided human subjects in a comparative study, showed that placing blocks in the blind alleys of a maze for one trial assisted rats to learn as well as several unaided trials. Blocking the incorrect choice is one form of guidance by restriction, as opposed to the forced-response techniques in which the trainer takes complete charge of the response movement. An intermediate method was used by Alonzo (1926), who obtained indifferent learning by attaching collars to his rats in order to lead them through the maze.

Tsai (1930) tried an early "vanishing" technique, in which guidance was withdrawn gradually, an alley at a time, but with no different effects from abrupt withdrawal of all guidance. Maier and Klee (1945) used guidance in the frustration experiment in order to overcome fixated response choices, and Maier and Ellen (1952) showed that early guidance helped to preserve behavioural flexibility in the rat throughout later frustrating conditions; Haslerud (1953), on the other hand, concluded that the most important function of restrictive guidance lay in establishing new habits. The well known results of Gleitman (1955) and McNamara, Long and Wike (1956), achieved by trolley pulling in a simple elevated T-maze, appear to depend primarily upon visual guidance. More recently a trolley pulling guidance technique has been shown by Pritchatt and Holding (1966) capable of assisting mice in the learning of quite complex mazes.

Maze learning was the task used in all the early human studies. Koch (1923), using restriction in finger mazes patterned on the model used for the rat experiment, found poorer guided learning in human subjects. This might have been due to the small size of the finger maze, presenting considerable manipulative difficulty, and to the fact that glass doors in the rat maze gave "knowledge of alternatives" which was denied to the human learners. Never-the-less, two guided trials at the outset had the effect of seven trials of regular practice. As one might expect from the shape of the learning curve, the effects of a larger number of guided trials, or of guided trials inserted later in the sequence, showed similar savings. The conclusion of Carr's (1930) widely-quoted review, to the effect that guidance is best employed in small amounts early in learning, relies heavily upon these results. However, it has been shown (Holding, 1965) that the Carr index of learning efficiency introduces an artefact, while in any case the Ludgate (1924) work exhibits a different trend. In this experiment manual forced-response, achieved by pulling the subject's stylus through the correct sequence of pathways, improved in efficiency when introduced towards the middle of the learning process. Broadly similar findings are suggested by an incomplete study by Melcher (1934). The Ludgate (1924) study also showed better transfer of training from one maze problem to another following guidance practice.

Further human maze-learning work was carried out by Waters (1930), finding some increase in the value of guidance up to as many as 80 forced-response trials. Waters and Ellis (1931) made the useful precaution of equating the time spent in guided practice against the control practice time, instead of equating the number of trials under both conditions; twice the proportion of unguided subjects failed to learn the maze to criterion. Waters (1931) administered to guided subjects both the correct responses and the errors of paired control subjects, with a resulting decrease in the number of trials needed to learn the maze, but at the expense of a larger number of errors.

Other maze studies have used versions of visual guidance. Carr (1921) anticipated Von Wright (1957) in showing that presenting clearly marked blind alleys is more efficient than restricting the available information by displaying the true path or by not marking the blinds. Carr and Osborn (1922) explored the effect of allowing subject to watch his hand and stylus. Twitmyer (1931) showed a large effect due to the mere observation of control practice. A solitary study on verbal guidance was produced by Wang (1925), who found large amounts of saving produced by talking subjects through the maze.

The maze work raised a number of issues—the comparison of forced-response with restriction, the relative weight of perceptual versus motor components of guidance, parametric problems of amount and point of insertion of guidance, its utility in transfer of training, the comparison of error scores with other criteria of learning and the apparent requirement for knowledge of alternatives. However, these investigations into the serial choice task posed by the maze were followed by relatively few studies of finer adjustive skills.

Lincoln (1956) provided verbal feedback or mechanical guidance in learning to turn a handwheel at a constant rate, finding no differences in performance after the supplementary cues were removed. A restrictive technique was employed by Bilodeau and Bilodeau (1958) in two handed tracting of a cloverleaf pattern. Some positive transfer occurred in both directions between free and guided conditions, the guidance being provided by recessing the correct tracking path. Holding (1959) used small amounts of forced-response guidance, subjects being required to grasp a control knob locked to the course generator of a pursuit tracking task, with results equivalent to normal practice in learning and in transfer to other target courses. These preliminary findings led to the series of experiments described in greater detail below.

Guidance and Skill

The experiments covered a wide range of motor skills, requiring discrete, serial or continuous adjustment. The tasks varied not only in degree of continuity, but in the balance between the demand for response precision or for perceptual complexity. The simplest was a blindfold mechanical "line-drawing" task, high in response demand but with a minimal perceptual component. Next was a serial tracking task, in which a succession of display lights had to be extinguished by movements of a lever. Varying the spatial relationship between lights and lever varied the perceptual demand, leaving response demand constant and fairly low. Finally, the effects of guidance were investigated in a continuous, pursuit tracking task, which was high in both response and perceptual demands.

In the first experiment (Holding and Macrae, 1964) different kinds of guidance were compared with different amounts of knowledge of results on the "line-drawing" task. This was designed as an analogue of the task used in Thorndike's (1927) early demonstration of the "law of effect;" the task actually consisted of pushing a small knob along a metal rod, blind-folded, attempting each time to move an exact distance of four inches. For guidance by restriction a stop was placed on the rod at the four-inch mark; forced response was achieved by attaching to the control knob an ordinary door return spring, modified so as to drag the Ss hand along for an exact four inches. Knowledge of results took the form of calling "right" or "wrong" after each attempt in one condition, or in another of calling the exact amount and direction of error.

All subjects made 20 blind movements to establish initial accuracy, nine sets of 20 movements under the appropriate training conditions, and a further 20 blind movements showing the gains due to training. A control group made the entire series of movements without correction or guidance, and showed negligible change in accuracy. The best results (Table 1) appeared to be those of the restriction group, although these gains were not significantly different from the two sets of knowledge of results data. The forced-response technique gave a significant improvement in accuracy which has some theoretical interest, although for practical purposes the amount of learning was relatively small.

There seem to be two reasons for the superiority of the restriction over the forced-response technique. One is that subjects whose arms are dragged along tend to resist the spring and thus to practice *pulling,* while they are later tested on *pushing.* They are thus practising a movement directly opposed to that finally required, with a resulting tendency toward negative transfer. This possibility was checked in the next experiment (Macrae & Holding, 1965a) by reconstructing the apparatus to replace the pushing

Table 1.   Amount and significance of improvements

Condition	Initial error (inches)	Training gain (inches)	Significance (Wilcoxon, two-tailed)
Control	0.83	-0.03	
Forced response	0.79	0.19	0.05
Restriction	0.91	0.50	0.01
Right-Wrong	0.68	0.35	0.01
Full K.R.	0.84	0.42	0.01

(From Holding & Macrae, 1964)

movement by a releasing one. Testing subjects on the new, if somewhat artificial, version neatly reversed the effectiveness of the two guidance procedures, since the movement made during forcing now clearly resembled the test movement (Table 2).

The other possible reason derives from the repetitive nature of the task. During guided training the forced-response subject has little chance to compare the right distance with the wrong alternatives, and thus cannot improve upon existing discriminations. However, it is not necessary to commit errors in order to broaden experience, since the same effects may be produced by varying guidance. In the same experiment two further groups were tested on the 'push' version of the task, receiving guidance in cycles at 4, 6, 4, 2, 4, 5, 4, 3 and 4 inches before test at 4 inch mark. This also brought about an improvement in the accuracy following forced-response training, bringing it up to the same apparent ceiling reached by the restriction group. The indication is that guidance will be inefficient when it deprives subjects of perceptual information in the form of knowledge of alternatives, just as the previous comparison showed inefficiency when the form of movement provided by guidance was incompatible with the response demands of the task.

Knowledge of alternatives presents no problems in the serial tracking task, since the subject is constantly moving the lever between different posi-

Table 2.   Error scores and significance of improvements

Condition	Initial error (inches)	Final error (inches)	Significance
Push			
Forced	0.77	0.72	Not
Restricted	0.75	0.47	$p < 0.05$
Release			
Forced	0.95	0.55	$p < 0.01$
Restricted	0.87	0.84	Not
Push			
Forced (varied)	0.86	0.54	$p < 0.05$ (one-tailed)
Restricted (varied)	0.77	0.47	$p < 0.05$ (one-tailed)

(From Macrae & Holding, 1965a)

Table 3. Comparison of direct and reversed tasks

	No. of guided runs	Mean total lights extinguished per subject	Improvement over control	Percentage improvement
Direct	0	106.75		
	1	116.95	10.2	9.6
	9	123.35	16.6	15.6
Reversed	0	81.10		
	1	96.20	15.1	18.6
	9	100.40	19.3	23.8

(From Macrae & Holding 1965b)

tions in order to put out the signal lights. There were ten of these lights, programmed to appear in an effectively random order. Forced-response guidance was provided by wiring a motor in with the stepping switches which programmed the signal lights, so that by way of a clutch it could power the control lever. Under guidance conditions the machine tracked itself automatically, and subject had merely to grasp the lever while lights were extinguished at a fixed rate.

In the first experiment with this apparatus (Macrae & Holding, 1965b), an attempt was made to test the hypothesis that the main advantage of guidance lay in preventing errors. If errors which are rehearsed early in learning tend to persist and require later unlearning, guidance which eliminates error practice should prove more effective for a high-error task than for a low-error task. The serial tracking task lends itself to such a comparison, since reversing the display-control relationship between lights and lever increases the error potential by increasing perceptual difficulty, while leaving the response demands unchanged. Guidance on the direct version was therefore compared with guidance on the reversed version, and with two corresponding control groups. To provide further information on the effect of varying amounts of guidance, groups were run with either one or nine guided trials.

All subjects received 10 scored trials. The total number of lights extinguished during three test trials (Table 3) show significant differences between the direct and reversed versions of the task, and between amounts of guidance. Nine trials of guidance provide more learning than does one trial, although not by any means nine times as much. The main issue is the comparative efficiency of guidance between the direct and reversed version of the task. The hypothesis of greater efficiency in the high error case receives considerable support; it can be seen, for instance, that one trial of guidance produces approximately twice the percentage of improvement on the reversed task as on the direct, low-error, version.

Two variations of response compatibility were explored with the serial tracking equipment, the first being a change in rate of guidance. Increasing the speed of the guided movement leads to a higher rate of scoring, and this has two possible consequences: the higher scores achieved during training may raise the subject level of aspiration, with some benefit to his scores on later tests or, alternatively, the higher rate of movement will represent a deviation from the natural movement pattern and will lead to a deterioration in performance. A comparison of the two rates of guidance on the reversed serial task showed the slower rate, equated with the movements of the most efficient control subjects, to be the better. Since in forced-response guidance the trainer takes complete control of subject's response pattern, it is clearly important for the evaluation of guidance that the movements induced take an optimal form.

As part of the same experiment (Holding and Macrae, 1966) the comparison was also made between forced-response and a continuous task analogue of the restriction method, called "hinting". This technique was arranged by controlled slippage of the clutch mediating between the motor and the control lever. At the correct setting, the transmitted power of the motor is exactly balanced by the static friction of the control lever and its associated switching. At this point, the lever is no longer self-actuated. However, it has zero effective friction when moved in the correct direction, whereas when subject attempts to move the lever in the wrong direction, or overshoots a correct position, he encounters considerable resistance.

Like restriction in the discrete adjustment task, hinting appeared more effective than forced-response. The comparison was checked on the most perceptually demanding version of the task, in which the correlation between display light and control lever position was reduced to zero. For light positions 1 through 10, the corresponding lever positions were now 5, 9, 1, 4, 7, 8, 2, 10, 6, 3. Subject received eight control trials of normal practice, or four guided trials of either kind followed by four test trials. At this level of task difficulty, the final scores (Table 4) of both the hinting and the forcing group are significantly superior to the final trials of the control group; in fact, the difference between the final hinting and control scores is larger than the entire improvement during control learning.

The three versions of the serial tracking task form a progression in which the spatial correspondence between display and control elements have varied from direct through reversed to zero correlation, with an increasing demand on perceptual-motor translation processes, while response demands have remained constant. Although there are minor differences in experimental design, a clear trend seems to emerge from the data. From the small effects

Table 4.   Scores on the zero correlation serial tracking task

	Trial 1	Lights Extinguished per Minute			
		5	6	7	8
Control	13.1	16.3	18.5	17.9	19.2
Forcing	(42.0)	15.4	19.4	21.3	23.4
Hinting	(32.9)	23.6	24.7	25.8	27.3

(From Holding & Macrae, 1966)

found with the direct task to the major differences appearing in the zero correspondence task, the outcome of the increase in perceptual load is a substantial increase in the value of guidance as a training procedure. Clearly, for many purposes even the physical forms of guidance will be best regarded as techniques of showing subject what to do, with functions more perceptual than motor. Thus, the differences between forced-response, restriction and the visual and verbal methods may be of minor importance in many tasks. Nevertheless, as in the line-drawing task or the differences in guidance speeds for the serial tracking task, to the extent that the response demands of a task are emphasized, it will be predicted that differences in effectiveness will appear as a result of the differential compatibility of the several forms of guidance with these demands.

The guidance methods have so far been discussed in terms of their capacity to supply information to the learner. In the next experiment, on the most difficult task, a limit to the amount of information which the operator can handle appears to have been reached; in this case, the value of guidance appears instead to lie in obviating surplus information. The task here (Macrae & Holding, 1966) was the continuous pursuit tracking of a target spot shown on an oscilloscope. Three target courses were used, a simple sine wave at 0.7 cps; an intermediate course combining two sine waves at 0.4 and 0.7 cps; and a complex course composed of four sine waves at 0.3, 0.4, 0.7 and 1.0 cps. Forced-response guidance could be provided by feeding the target course motions to the control knob which subject gripped.

Six groups were tested, receiving either guidance or normal practice on the simple, intermediate or complex courses. After five training trials, all groups were transferred to, or continued on, normal practice with the intermediate target course. The effect of guidance on the intermediate course was reasonable, the error scores of the guided subjects finishing on the fifth trial at the same level as those of the control subjects on their tenth. After normal practice, transfer was better from the simple course than from the complex course. From the simple course, transfer after guidance was approximately equivalent to transfer after normal practice.

The most unexpected finding, although reminiscent of Ludgate's (1924) results, was that after transfer from the complex course the final error scores (Table 5) of the guided group was significantly lower than those of the normal practice group. During practice on the complex task the decrease in subjects error scores was relatively small, so that little learning was available for transfer. The advantage of guidance appears to have lain in reducing the amount of information to be processed by the operator, while of course accustoming him to a low error rate. The reduction of load is selective, relieving subject of motor demands while automatic tracking continues to supply the necessary perceptual information. The guided subject is thus able to develop a grasp and anticipation of the course and display-control characteristics, unhampered by the effects of erroneous responses which degrade the information available to the normally practising subject.

More Recent Studies

In exploring the potential of these methods, the experiments described above have in the main shown guidance techniques in a favorable light. It is important, therefore, to consider some less favorable findings. Gordon

Table 5.   Transfer from Single or Complex to Intermediate Courses

	Training	Error Scores (Degrees)		
		Single	Intermediate	Complex
First Score:	Practice		(15.1)	
Final Scores:	Practice	9.9	(10.1)	11.5
	Guidance	9.6	10.0	10.0

(From Macrae & Holding, 1966)

(1968) compared three forms of training for pursuit motor tracking. A control group practised tracking a glass-covered target light rotating at 60 r.p.m. An augmented feedback group received an ambient light signal whenever contact with the target was lost. For a third, mechanical-visual guidance group, a recessed circular guide was provided to restrict radial errors. After 21 training trials under the appropriate conditions on the first day, and 12 on the second, all three groups practised normally during the remaining blocks of trials.

Time-on-target scores, and mean time per target contact, show the transfer scores of the guided group to be inferior to those of the control group although better, of course, than no prior training. The transfer scores after augmented feedback were better than those of the control group, an effect attributed to the superior capacity of augmented feedback over the guidance procedure for facilitating response sets based upon the available intrinsic cues. However, it should be noted that the guidance method employed did not lead to particularly high scores during training, the guided scores during the final 12 trials before transfer being no higher than those of the control group. Further, the restriction of radial errors had no effect upon lead-lag errors which, in the absence of comparative data, must be assumed to possess at least equal importance in the development of pursuit motor skill.

Imperfection in the pattern of guided movements, in contrast to the automatic and near-perfect guidance used in the prior studies, also makes interpretation difficult for the results of Baker (1968). In this study, guidance for two-dimensional pursuit tracking was administered by connecting the joystick controls of "slave" subjects to those of equally unpractised "master" subjects. A third group, of "watchers", received only visual information. Throughout the first two days after training, the performance of the slaves appears consistenly superior to the equivalent scores of the masters, the differences being significant for the first trial of each day. It must be assumed that during training the slave subjects acquire sufficient correct perceptual information temporarily to overcome the erroneous response tendencies which simultaneously develop. However, in a retention test made after an interval of six weeks the relative position of the groups changed to leave the masters superior to both slaves and watchers; the drop in the scores of the slave subjects was significant. These results are in some ways parallel to the findings of Waters (1931) on incorrect guidance. Although the maze results are not simple to interpret, owing to points of design and the multiplicity of differing learning measures, it is important to notice that: partially incorrect guidance, achieved by matching control subjects records, initially saves trials at the expense of a tendency to increase errors; after an interval of one week, the guided group show poorer recall on times and blind alley errors; this contrasts with the effects of correct guidance, in which no errors are practised, in that at first learning this leads to a greater reduction in total and retracing errors, total times and final speed; in retention, the absolute recall scores and most relearning criteria show correct guidance superior to incorrect. It seems legitimate, therefore, to assume that the results of Baker (1968) are at least in part attributable to the uses of "incorrect" form of guidance.

Although it may be expected that early exposure to errors will lead to their later reappearance, there is very little direct evidence of the way in which errors function in learning. What the prompting, cueing, forced-response and restriction methods have in common is the freedom from error which they engender in early learning. However, we lack the elaborated psychology of errors which should underlie the application of the error-free methods of training. It has, for instance, been suggested (Kay, 1954) that it is "a feature of adult learning to repeat mistakes", while Kay (1951) concluded from a serial light-and-keys study that "in so far as subjects learned their repeated errors, final learning involved unlearning". It may be true that subjects learn and therefore repeat the errors which they commit, but the hypothesis requires further confirmation and elaboration. It has been further suggested (Macrae and Holding, 1965b) that it is unlikely that all errors will have the same effect and that those errors to which a subject is strongly committed are more likely to recur than those wrong responses which are tentative, but no direct test has been made. There is, therefore, a need to examine the conditions of occurence and reappearance of errors, an attempt at which is discussed in the final section.

The Problem of Errors

The task used in this study (Holding, 1970) was the discrimination reaction timer. This displays sequences of four red-green light pairs, to be extinguished by the appropriate one of four response keys. Responses were recorded on paper tape to permit the tracing of errors throughout the learning process. Various modifications were made to the apparatus in order to eliminate task-structured bias in the determination of error-responses, a difficulty which complicates interpretation of the Kay (1951) data.

Three groups of subjects were used. A control group, which provided most of the error data, practised until 60 correct matches had been achieved. In addition, an attempt was made to vary error "committal" by running a response-practice group—executing but not selecting errors by depressing the response keys in accordance with sequences read from the records of paired control subjects—and a non-response group, who merely observed the paired control subjects. Following the first block of practice, all three groups practised normally for a further 60 correct trials. The response records of individual subjects were scored separately, the errors being marked for identification. The data were used to investigate (a) whether, during the course of learning, subjects come to repeat individually identifiable errors, (b) whether any repetition could be attributed to the specific learning of subjects' own errors, and (c) whether any learned repetition of errors depended upon the degree of subjects' committal to the early, presumably formative, wrong responses.

In order adequately to answer the first question concerning error persistence, it is clearly not sufficient to show that some errors occur more than once; it must be shown that certain errors, different for different subjects, are made disproportionately often. Analysis showed no significant bias in the usage of these categories over control subjects as a whole, so that analysis by individual subjects was justified. With three erroneous response keys available for the four stimulus pairs, there are 12 error categories. Ascertaining whether these are used disproportionately is not easy since it is not the case, for instance, that chance expectancy would assign one of 12 random errors of each to the 12 categories. In fact, combinatorial analysis suggests that the probability of an even distribution is only 0.000005, while the most likely outcome would be a distribution of 3, 2, 2, 1, 1, 1, 1, 1, 0, 0, 0, and 0 errors.

Fortunately, it is possible to show that usage of the error categories changes as learning proceeds. Table 6 shows that there is marked tendency for control subjects in the later stages of learning to increase their commission of errors repeated three or four times at the expense of those repeated once or twice. A convenient statistical test can be made by counting the number of error categories used. For the early control trials a mean of 8.2 categories were used, which is extremely close to the 7.8 expected on a chance basis. In the later test trials the number falls to a mean 6.6, a Wilcoxon test showing the drop to be significant. It appears true, therefore, that subjects come to develop an increasing persistence with certain errors.

The extent to which later errors may be regarded as the learned consequences of earlier ones depends upon the number of errors which are the same at both stages. This implies the use of a correlation technique. Product-moment correlations, used to avoid the problem of multiple ties, were calculated separately for individual subjects between various early and later

Table 6. Mean Number of Errors Repeated

Number of times repeated	1	2	3	4
Control Group: First 12	5.1	5.4	1.3	0.2
Control Group: Last 12	3.2	4.2	1.8	2.8

error profiles. It appears that the last 12 errors made by the control group were to some extent predicted by the errors made during the first block of trials; the mean correlation of 0.25, while small, is drawn from data on 15 component correlations and is significant at $p < .01$. There is therefore some limited support for the specific error learning hypothesis.

The two less-committed groups, whose overall error scores in the test block were not significantly different from the control group, nevertheless showed reduced predictability in the expected order. The correlation between the control group first block errors and the last 12 made by the response practice group is positive at 0.20 ($p < .05$) With the non-response group, the mean correlation falls to 0.09 and is not significant.

It seems, therefore, that certain errors tend to become ingrained as learning proceeds and that some of the persisting errors may be predicted from knowledge of the errors occurring earlier. The inaccuracy of prediction is largely due to those early errors which do not recur, but which may be presumed to have non-specific effects. Errors which do not become learned responses will nevertheless degrade perceptual information about the task at the time of their occurrence and will contribute either to a general confusion effect, or to the formation of incorrect strategies, or hypotheses.

Any benign influence of errors must be limited to one or two special cases. "Learning by one's errors" may occur in a negative sense when the structure of a task tends strongly to elicit erroneous responses; executing the incorrect responses will then offer an opportunity for their extinction or amendment. Alternatively, learning by errors may occur in circumstances where gaining extra information about the task depends upon executing a wide range of responses. In this case, practising or guiding only the correct response will deprive subjects of "knowledge of alternatives," with the detrimental effects already noted.

Guidance methods which restrict information in this way will be inefficient, as will those which fail to meet response demands for adequate speed, direction or form of movement. On the other hand, as perceptual demands rise, the need for avoiding errors becomes greater and the value of correct guidance seems to increase. Restriction methods are probably better at supplying information, while forced-response methods are obviously suited to dealing with overload. Both methods derive some justification from the avoidance of error practice which their use implies. However, the consequences of error committal are by no means fully analysed, and the part played by error in human learning requires clearer definition.

REFERENCES

Aiken, E. G., & Lau, A. W. Response prompting and response confirmation: a review of recent literature. *Psychological Bulletin,* 1967, 68, 330-341.

Alonzo, A. S. The influence of manual guidance upon maze learning. *Journal of Comparative Psychology,* 1926, 6, 143-158.

Annett, J. Training for perceptual skills, Ergonomics, 1966, 9, 459-468.

Baker, C. H. An evaluation of guidance in learning a motor skill. *Canadian Journal of Psychology*, 1968, 22, 217-227.

Bilodeau, I. McD., & Bilodeau, E. A. Transfer of training and physical restriction of responses. *Perceptual & Motor Skills*, 1958, 8, 71-78.

Carr, H. A. The influence of visual guidance in maze learning. *Journal of Experimental Psychology*, 1921, 4, 399-417.

Carr, H. A. Teaching and learning. *Journal of Genetic Psychology*, 1930, 37, 189-218.

Carr, H. A. & Osbourn, E. B. Influence of vision in acquiring skill. *Journal of Experimental Psychology*, 1922, 5, 301-311.

Cole, L. W. Concerning the intelligence of raccoons. *Journal of Comparative & Neurological Psychology*, 1907, 17, 211-261.

Cook, J. O. "Superstition" in the Skinnerian. *American Psychologist*, 1963, 18, 516-518.

Cook, J. O., & Kendler, T. S. A. A theoretical model to explain some paired-associate learning data. In G. Finch & F. Cameron (Eds.), *Symposium on Air Force human engineering, personnel and training research*. Washington, D.C.: National Research Council, 1956, Pp.90-98.

Gleitman, H. Place learning without prior performance. *Journal of Comparative & Physiological Psychology*, 1955, 48, 77-79.

Gordon, N. B. Guidance versus augmented feedback and motor skill. *Journal of Experimental Psychology*, 1968, 77, 24-30.

Haslerud, G. M. Anticipative transfer of mechanically guided turns. *Journal of Experimental Psychology*, 1953, 45, 431-436.

Holding, D. H. Guidance in pursuit tracking. *Journal of Experimental Psychology*, 1959, 57, 362-366.

Holding, D. H. *Principles of Training*. Oxford: Pergamon Press, 1965.

Holding, D. H. Repeated errors in motor learning. *Ergonomics*, 1970, 13.

Holding, D. H. & Macrae, A. W. Guidance, restriction and knowledge of results. *Ergonomics*, 1964, 7, 289-295.

Holding, D. H. & Macrae, A. W. Rate and force of guidance in perceptual-motor tasks with reversed or random spatial correspondence. *Ergonomics*, 1966, 9, 289-296.

Kay, H. Learning of a serial task by different age groups. *Quarterly Journal of Experimental Psychology*, 1951, 3, 166-183.

Kay, H. The effects of position in a display upon problem solving. *Quarterly Journal of Experimental Psychology*, 1954, 6, 155-169.

Koch, H. L. The influence of mechanical guidance upon maze learning. *Psychological Monographs*, 32, 5, 1923.

Lincoln, R. S. Learning and retaining a movement with the aid of kinesthetic and verbal cues. *Journal of Experimental Psychology*, 1956, 51, 199-204.

Ludgate, K. E. The effect of manual guidance upon maze learning. *Psychological Monographs*, 33, 148, 1924.

Macrae, A. W. & Holding, D. H. Method and task in motor guidance. *Ergonomics*, 1965a, 8, 315-320.

Macrae, A. W. & Holding, D. H. Guided practice in direct and reversed serial tracking. *Ergonomics*, 1965b, 8, 487-492.

Macrae, A. W. & Holding, D. H. Transfer of training after guidance or practice. *Quarterly Journal of Experimental Psychology*, 1966, 18, 327-333.

Maier, N. R. F. & Ellen, P. Studies of abnormal behavior in the rat. XXIII. The prophylactic effects of 'guidance' in reducing rigid behavior. *Journal of Abnormal and Social Psychology*, 1952, 47, 109-116.

Maier, N. R. F. & Klee, J. B. Studies of abnormal behavior in the rat. XVII. Guidance versus trial and error in the alteration of habits and fixations. *Journal of Psychology*, 1945, 19, 133-163.

McNamara, H. J., Long, J. B. & Wike, E. L. Learning without response under two conditions of external cues. *Journal of Comparative & Physiological Psychology*, 1956, 49, 477-480.

Melcher, R. T. Children's motor learning with and without vision. *Child Development*, 1934, 5, 315-350.

Pritchatt, D., & Holding, D. H. Guiding Deutsch's model in reverse. *British Journal of Psychology*, 1966, 57, 17-23.

Skinner, B. F. *Cumulative Record*. (London: Methuen.) 1961.

Thorndike, E. L. Animal intelligence. *Psychological Review Monograph Supplements,* 1898, 2, No. 8.

Thorndike, E. L. The law of effect. *American Journal of Psychology,* 1927, 39, 212-222.

Tsai, L. S. Gradual vs abrupt withdrawal of guidance in maze learning. *Journal of Comparative Psychology,* 1930, 10, 325-331.

Twitmyer, E. M. Visual guidance in motor learning. *American Journal of Psychology,* 1931, 43, 165-187.

Von Wright, J. M. A note on the role of guidance in learning. *British Journal of Psychology,* 1957, 48, 133-137.

Wang, G. H. The influence of tuition in the acquisition of skill. *Psychological Monographs,* 1925, 34, No. 154.

Waters, R. H. The influence of large amounts of manual guidance upon maze learning. *Journal of General Psychology,* 1930, 4, 213-227.

Waters, R. H. The effect of incorrect guidance upon human maze learning. *Journal of Comparative Psychology,* 1931, 12, 293-301.

Waters, R. H. & Ellis, A. L. The relative efficiency of free and guided learning when equated in terms of time. *Journal of Comparative Psychology,* 1931, 12, 263-277.

CRITIQUE OF HOLDING'S PAPER
by Harold Bechtoldt

Over the years a number of us have been impressed by the provocative papers on problems of human skill and performance from the British psychologists at Cambridge. Professor Holding's paper is in this tradition although he worked at Leeds. The paper contains an interesting combination of theoretical concepts and of pragmatic approaches to some problems of motor learning. This combination will provide the framework for most of my brief comments. I intend to note, at first, some points in the approach taken by Professor Holding that might be sources of possible confusion. Finally, I wish to comment on the idea of error as presented in this paper. Professor Holding, at the end of his paper, provided me with a summary statement when he said: "the part played by errors in human learning requires clearer definition."

In line with my continuing concern about the referents of commonly-used terms in Psychology, my first comments will deal with the possibly minor matter of semantic issues which may have arisen from our different backgrounds. Although an investigator is constrained in the use of his terms only by the demands of speed and accuracy of communication, changes in definitions can be a source of confusion. The distinction between the perceptual and motor components of a task, for example, is neither clearly specified nor apparently in line with the tradition of the American experimental laboratory. A related semantic problem develops from the concept of perceptual load and load-shedding. A line-drawing task carried out under blindfold conditions is considered by Professor Holding as requiring more motor skill than perceptual components, while a serial light-tracking task is characterized as having the requirements weighted in the reversed order. In the laboratory, we ordinarily consider a task with reduced or degraded cue systems, but with a simple available response, as more perceptual or even sensory than motor in nature. Perhaps the term "motor" is used by Professor Holding for both the sensory feedback and the efferent action phases found in response systems. However, as another example of the semantic problems one may encounter, the word "hinting" is used by Professor Holding to refer to a treatment condition in which the apparatus has a slipping clutch; perhaps the phrase "slipped disk" would be more accurate than the word "hinting." The use of new names for old things, generally, does not seem desirable, especially when additional or surplus meanings thereby introduced into the discussion are irrelevant or inadequate ones.

The particular combination of theoretical and pragmatic matters found in the paper is the concern of my next few comments. There seems to be an implicit plea for considering prompting and guidance as good things, but this view is more clearly evident in the Annett (1966) and in the Aiken and Lau (1967) papers to which favorable reference is made by Professor Holding. The problem lies in the relevance of the results of these studies for investigations of behavior in other situations. In the paper by Annett, in addition, the statistical procedures employed produced the unfortunate effect of misrepresenting the valuable process of *data mining* as *hypothesis testing*.

The relevance of the Annett studies and of several of the papers reviewed by Aiken and Lau tends to be reduced by the overgeneralization of results as reported in these articles. In both of these papers as well as in those of Professor Holding that I have read, the conclusions imply that the results are reproducible and also are relevant to performances of subjects other than English and American high-school or college students. Only limited note is taken of the extensive literature on perceptual and discrimination learning in nonarticulate subjects—such as human infants, chimpanzees, cats, rats, etc. Another feature reducing the relevance of these several studies to the development of explanations of behavior is the absence of dimensional representations of the treatment conditions. Such representations generally have been used in laboratory investigations. For example, work on the so-called "instructional variable" has included giving the instructions to the subject either *before* or *after* the stimulus presentation. Of course, for some conditions the separate instructions are so different that only a list of noncomparable characteristics rather than levels of a variable is implied. However, the addition of graded amounts of physical cues to a standard stimulus complex is a common way of using the dimensional representation of treatment conditions in the laboratory. Added stimulus components may include both associational and physical cues when transfer designs are used.

A comparison of the effectiveness of reinforcement and of prompting or guidance is a point of emphasis in these studies; the results, however, seem to be only of suggestive value for a theoretical development because of the lack of such controls as those for different initial response tendencies in a two-stage transfer paradigm. Of course, other controls are also needed in an analytic study of the influence of guidance and reinforcement.

The many behavioral differences between populations sampled in these several studies could develop from differences in the prior experiences and work habits acquired by the subjects over a period of fifteen to twenty years of exposure to various educational and cultural situations. The lack of control over current activities and the incomplete information about the prior experiences of human adult subjects are reasons for the emphasis in theoretical work on using infants and animals as subjects. The investigation by Bower (1966) of constancy phenomena with human infants and the study conducted by Gardner and Gardner (1969) of the acquisition of sign language by a chimpanzee both clearly indicate the value of reinforcement in early stages of learning. The influence of early experience on adult performance is another question that to date has been studied extensively only with animal subjects. The time in a training program when, if at all, the reinforcing stimuli become internalized within the subjects to such a degree that external signals are no longer needed is an interesting and possibly testable question. The evidence from elementary-school subjects seems to suggest that the shift may well take place for humans in the early elementary grades as a facet of the child's cultural development. Certainly, the observable motivational orientation of young adults in the Iowa high schools and colleges with whom I am acquainted can be described as competitive, experiment-oriented, and generally cooperative with an experimenter. In such cases, instructions and cues, obvious or subtle, from the experimenter as to the action to be performed by the subject are adequate to maintain performance and improvement over rather long periods of time and without the obvious direct payoff procedures we use with subjects' having less cultural training.

The emphasis in these comments up to this point has been on the possible value of studies of perceptual-motor performance for a theory of behavior. Possibly, the emphasis has been misplaced; Melton (1967), for example, has said: ". . . as everyone knows, we have at this time no general theory of human learning and performance" (p. 242). Investigations of human performance, however, when they are properly designed, may indicate the dimensions along which empirical S-R generalization takes place in given populations of subjects. Such empirical generalization functions may be of value in designing procedures for educational, industrial, or military training programs. Professor Holding suggests, in this connection, that the efficiency of a training procedure will vary with the correspondence between the training conditions and the task-demand characteristics. Apparently, the efficiency is to be evaluated in terms of the number of trials to a criterion or the speed or accuracy of performance on a given block of trials; it is not clear to me whether a transfer paradigm is of central importance. One problem with this suggestion is the difficulty of determining the relevant task-demand characteristics and the degree of correspondence between the task and the training procedure; the problem arises in trying to attribute the performance differences to the differences in methods.

The variations in an error function observed after different treatment conditions appear to be the source of the suggestion by Professor Holding as to the value of prompting and guidance; prompting by preventing errors is said to preclude the learning of the wrong thing. When the task is learned with errors, these errors must be extinguished before success is achieved. The prompting and guidance activities also are supposed to aid in the selection of cues and the reduction of surplus information in tasks with high perceptual loads. This second suggestion, as was the case with the tuning hypothesis of a number of years ago, might be investigated by varying the time of the instruction and the type of instruction used in a series of tasks systematically varied along some dimension. The current approaches to human problem-solving behavior provide other paradigms of interest in connection with this filtering or tuning hypothesis.

Professor Holding suggests that, as yet, there is no elaborated psychology of errors for the application of error-free methods of training. There exist, however, several relevant observations and some interesting suggestions regarding the problem of stimulus control developed by H. S. Terrace from a series of studies on errorless discrimination training in pigeons. Terrace (1966) suggests that a differential reinforcement procedure is necessary for the typical unimodal generalization functions for such animals. He also points out that initial response tendencies, some of which may involve innate factors, will influence the distinctiveness and choices with respect to a particular stimulus dimension. For the development of an errorless discrimination performance, Terrace reported considerable success with a shaping technique; he started with only one positive stimulus and then introduced S— while gradually progressing from large S+ and S— differences along several dimensions to the smaller stimulus differences of interest to him. The evidence reported by Terrace indicates differences for pigeons both in performance measures and in emotional responses after training with errors and without errors. The performances tended to be more stable when learned with errors.

Although the performance of human subjects rather than that of pigeons is of concern at the moment, the relevance of the data from Terrace lies in the demonstration that only a single class of responses is sufficient under certain conditions. The word "error" is simply the name of one of two or more response classes defined by an experimenter; changes in the distribution of responses over the classes from moment to moment and from condition to condition are expected in any experiment. Ordinarily, at least two response classes are used with human subjects. But all responses to be considered must be observable since only emitted responses can be classified. In such tasks as the Air Force Discrimination Reaction Time unit (DRT) or the serial tracking of a target on an oscilloscope, the performance tends to be a continuous or serial one in which accurate observations of the relevant changes in the distribution of responses are extremely difficult to make. If the study of differential response distributions were of primary interest, single trial tasks with paced or self-paced features and with two or preferably three or more specific responses would seem more appropriate than continuous-movement tasks. In addition, it would seem desirable to equate the observed relative frequencies of the response classes under one common set of initial conditions before introducing changes in the experimental conditions since idiosyncratic initial-response tendencies are probably the norm. In the statistical analysis of the observations on successive trials, some technique other than the profile correlation suggested by Professor Holding and computed at two stages of practice probably would be necessary. While a correlation of 0.25 or even 0.50 is so low as to be of little if any explanatory value, the serious problem in the correlational method is that the correlations as computed do not reflect sensitively the tendency for given responses to specific stimuli to recur or to increase in frequency with successive trials, as would be the case if the error responses were learned responses.

If, as suggsted by Professor Holding, we were interested in determining whether certain responses, called "errors" at the moment, are less readily learned under prompting conditions than under direct reinforcement conditions, we would want to control very carefully for stimulus-and-response-generalization tendencies. To achieve such control and to maintain the observations of performance, an experimenter probably would have to use procedures and devices other than those represented in the several studies reported to date. Once having established a reasonable answer to the question of the relative efficiency of two training methods, we could then consider the extinction rates for the same responses acquired under the different procedures. Some of the previous work on the contiguity-noncontiguity issue, on overlearning effects, and on extinction rates of competing responses developed to different levels of habit strength should be of interest (Goldstein, Krantz, and Rains, 1965). With evidence of such relationships, the results of prompting as well as the analysis of responses called errors could be included in a limited but useful theory of learning. Of course, if the error functions are of interest only in connection with industrial, military, or educational training activities of an applied type, then these several suggestions for ways to improve the interpretability of the error data are irrelevant. In such pragmatic activities, the test of acceptability is whether the procedure works to the satisfaction of the sponsor; the interpretation of the relationship is of little consequence.

REFERENCES

Aiken, E. G., and Lau, A. W. Response prompting and response confirmation: a review of recent literature. *Psychological Bulletin*, 1967, *68*, 330-341.

Annett, J. Training for perceptual skills. *Ergonomics*, 1966, *9*, 459-468.

Bower, T. G. R. Slant perception and shape constancy in infants. *Science*, 1966, *151*, 832-834.

Gardner, R. A. and Gardner, B. T. Teaching sign language to a chimpanzee. *Science*, 1969, *165*, 664-672.

Goldstein, H., Krantz, D. L., and Rains, J. D. *Controversial issues in learning*, New York: Appleton-Century-Crofts, 1965.

Melton, A. W. Individual differences and theoretical process variables: general comments on the conference, 238-252. In Gagné, R. M. (Ed.), *Learning and individual differences,* Columbus: Charles E. Merrill, 1967.
Terrace, H. S. Stimulus control, 271-344. In Honig, W. K. (Ed.) *Operant behavior: areas of research and application,* New York: Appleton-Century-Crofts, 1966.

HOLDING'S REPLY TO
Bechtoldt's Critique

C. AMMONS. Perhaps we should give Dr. Holding an opportunity to comment on some of those remarks. Would you like to?

HOLDING: Well, if we are going to have time for any more questions I shall have to be very brief. I have noted a number of points here. Dr. Bechtoldt doesn't like my perceptual-motor distinction. There are a number of ways you can make this; I followed roughly the line of Poulton's distinction between closed and open skills, with which some of you might be familiar. This runs from closed skills, like shot putting in which you have very little traffic with the environment, to open skills like football in which you are modifying your performance all the time on the basis of external cues. Now, I have regarded this second form as more perceptual, the first form as more motor, but obviously there are a number of other ways you could divide things up. On hinting, well, it is a technique which is not forcing them and is not leaving them on their own. It is something in between forcing and leaving them to their own devices, so "hinting" seemed appropriate to us. Statistical points, very briefly. The problem of replications was mentioned. We did actually have a replication between experiment one and experiment two. There were differences in the amount of learning picked up from forced response under these conditions, and I can explain that. We modified the apparatus so that it moved in a jerk for the sake of the releasing movement (which we also wanted) and this modification effectively reduced the amount of training gains from forced response between experiment one and two. I don't know whether you noticed that. This emphasizes that you have to be very careful about the form a movement takes. There is no good taking a person's hand and going like that and saying, "look, he hasn't learned anything." The response demands (if I may be temporarily allowed to continue to follow that) do have to be taken notice of. Now, replications again, I am only too pleased (I should be only too pleased) to see some of this work replicated by somebody else. It is very tedious and laborious to do and I don't propose to replicate any more myself, but I should point out that I am happy about some of the lights and lever results, because, although this material is not being published, I have used the experiments as class exercises for about three successive years and have thus achieved informal replications. The transfer problem I had better skip or I shan't give you any more time. Yes, I was aware of Terrace's work and I cut out a section on it when I was cutting my paper down to what I thought was the right size. I think I touched on the problem involved here when I talked about the need for knowledge of alternatives to build up a discrimination. Now, as for the increased frequency of errors which should be predicted if subjects were learning their own errors—well, obviously it is not going to be like this. Nobody would ever learn anything if everytime he made an error he learned it. There would be more and more absolute frequency of errors as learning progressed—this would be ridiculous. Obviously I am not stating that this is the case, but merely that error learning is one of several factors. You must assume that in addition to this there are factors which make for learning rather than for deterioration. Well, I think I had better finish.

DISCUSSION OF HOLDING'S PAPER

C. AMMONS: Alright, but don't go away.

I think you [the audience] will have to buy a copy of the Proceedings when they are published because, obviously, important things have been left out. You may ask questions either of Dr. Holding or Dr. Bechtoldt if you like. Yes, Dr. Henry?

HENRY: I am rather happy that Dr. Bechtoldt is not going to comment on my paper, because he has some questions that he asks and I am not sure that I could field them. But he has opened up a can of worms this afternoon and I wonder just where they are going to squirm to. I refer to his suggestion that perhaps we would be well-advised to deal with what I would be willing to call the discrete-movement-type motor learning rather than continuous-task. One point I would mention here is that we may have a legitimate interest in the continuous thing and it can't be both discrete and continuous. Secondly, here is this question of massing and distribution of practice, while this is quite variable depending on the nature of the task—and we must expose our ignorance by saying we don't always know why this is. But in some tasks (and notoriously in the pursuit rotor) the effect of degree of massing is simply fantastic! Now, the minute you start using these discrete tasks you can just do your damnedest to have these tasks close together and you can't control their rate very well. At best they are going to be highly distributed, and there are many types of motor learning which tend to be the continuous rather than the discrete. So I am wondering if one would make this (or rather follow in this direction) if it won't force us into a very narrow direction of studying motor skills. This is the question I wish that Dr. Bechtoldt would react to. I might say that I, personally, have tended to be interested in some discrete tasks in theoretical ways, but then I see this other possibility.

BECHTOLDT: I agree, completely. Notice that I said—if we are interested in the distribution of responses, one class of which is called errors—then we had better watch for the specification. I happen to agree with you, the continuous movement, the obligatory movement—all of these are beautiful problems. But I don't think you will be talking in those situations about the distribution of errors.

C. AMMONS: Next? We could entertain at least one more question.

HOLDING: May I answer the last question before it has been asked? Has this work been applied to Physical Education? It has and with disastrous results as a matter of fact. I did do some teaching with physical education graduates, and one of them wanted to try guidance on a physical education problem. He chose balancing. So he took the task of balancing on a plank and in order to supply guidance, he propped the plank up so that the man just stood there—still. He said: "This guidance doesn't work!" Again, you have to pay attention to exactly what the "response demands" of the tasks are.

Feedback Mechanism of Athletic Skill and Learning

Karl U. Smith
Thomas J. Smith
University of Wisconsin

The following graduate assistants made this talk possible: Robert Arndt, Arthur Luedke, Rick Rubow, Michael Smith, Thomas J. Smith, Harvey Sussman

This chapter applies the concepts of action feedback and methods of *experimental feedback analysis* to the fields of athletic training, physical education, and sports medicine. The term experimental feedback analysis refers to the investigation of behavior as a self-governed, reciprocal motor-sensory process. The word *feedback* means the reciprocal interaction between motor function and sensory input, as mediated by neural processes (Fig. 1). In feedback research on athletic behavior, we are concerned with the reciprocal dynamic relationships between external neuromuscular response and sensory input, which serve not only to guide motion and to regulate learning and memory, but also to determine energy exchanges and physiological adjustments in physical conditioning.

The application of a systems feedback theory to behavior and learning has redefined the experimental foundations of physical behavioral sciences related to athletic training and sports medicine (Smith, 1967a; Smith & Henry, 1967; Smith & Smith, 1966). The crux of this approach and of the experimental facts underlying it is that direct, dynamic sensory effects of response, rather than homeostatic after-effects or reward reinforcements of response, govern physical conditioning, motor control, perception, and learning. The skeletal-motor system and its specialized receptor mechanisms are the dynamic focus of control of the external as well as the internal environment and of integration of all of these vital mechanisms. In the feedback view, the external neuromuscular component of exercise and athletic skill is not a centrifugal product of internal organic or drive determinants. Rather, it is a reciprocal regulator and integrator of all levels of physiological and internal vital organization.

The feedback concepts of athletic behavior proposed here contrast sharply with traditional lines of thinking about exercise, sports training, and physical conditioning. Up until recently (Smith, 1967a; Smith & Smith, 1966), the main trends in physiological (Falls, 1969), psychological (Clifton, 1968),

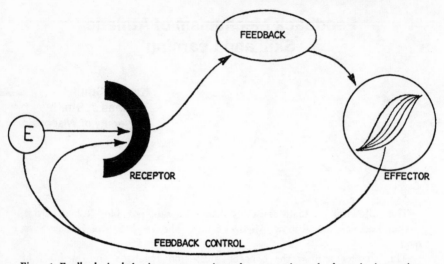

Fig. 1 Feedback in behavior systems pictured as a reciprocal, dynamic interaction between muscular action and sensory input that is mediated by the neural system.

and physical education (Cratty, 1968) theory identified athletic behavior as external motor of *psychomotor* behavior and referred its causation either to associative learning factors or to internal homeostatic mechanisms. In such thinking, various stimulus-response or S-R theories of learning were assumed to apply to athletic performance. These included the mental association, classical conditioning, and reinforcement theories, which assumed that separate discrete responses and their stimuli are linked for performance either by temporal association (Guthrie, 1952) or by reinforcement (Hull, 1943; Skinner, 1938, 1953).

The differences between a systems feedback theory and conventional homeostatic, associative, conditioning, and reinforcement doctrines lie in the fact that the traditional views assume that learning is determined by associative factors *between* different responses, whereas the feedback theory states that it is determined by the *direct sensory* or *stimulatory effects* of self-governed movement. The feedback theory questions the idea that reinforcing after-effects or associated reactions have primary or even significant meaning in learning of athletic performance. In fact, it is assumed that the traditional concepts of learning reinforcement and conditioning are incompatible with a feedback doctrine, because these past views stress open-loop factors of reward, punishment, anxiety reduction, and drive reduction as associated after-effects and contingencies of learned response, and do not recognize the significance of the direct sensory processes produced by response as a significant factor in determining learning.

The systems approach to be defined here identifies the human factors related to social interactions and to design of sports instruments in determining athletic learning. Most athletic skills rely upon various tools, instrumental devices and specialized objects which must be designed with exactness to fit the performer's body, as well as to execute particular sports functions. Traditional theories in both psychology and physiology have been quite incomplete in dealing with instrumental factors in athletic skill, and must be revised to incorporate action feedback and systems concepts which specify the relations between instrumental and human behavioral factors in acquisition of skill.

The point just made about instrumental factors in athletic performance applies also to social processes in sports. Most athletic performances involve social and group coordination in team play as well as critical interpersonal processes in coaching. Competition also constitutes a form of active social interplay in which contestants must read and follow as well as oppose one another in action. Traditional lines of thinking have been particularly limited in trying to describe the interpersonal and team processes in skilled performance. A systems theory has special value in creating a new scientific language which may be used to describe how individuals interact and are yoked together in integrated ways in group situations to produce both individual and team skill. We propose to use the terms *social tracking* and *social feedback regulation* to specify the ways in which individuals interact to affect team performance, coaching, and competition.

MOTION ORGANIZATION IN ATHLETIC PERFORMANCE

The challenge faced by any theory of athletic performance is twofold: (1) to explain the specialized details of articulated reactions and control functions characterizing specific performances in skill; and (2) to account for the overall integration and organization of behavior and physiological function which define particular athletic skills. Traditional theorists have not faced this challenge because they attribute causative factors to environmental events and therefore have no resources to specify modes of dynamic interaction between different specialized motor, sensory, autonomic, and physiological operations of the body. The main aim of the present chapter is to describe these interactions and thereby to disclose the systems factors in both specialization and organization of performances in athletic skill and exercise.

The foundation of a systems doctrine of athletic performance is that such activity is organized on a self-governed, continuous feedback basis, wherein active movements act reciprocally to control sensory input. Behavior is not a passive response to the environment; it is a process of self-generation and self-regulation of stimuli by movement to actively control both the external and the internal environment. Figure 2 illustrates five principal modes of movement control of sensory input. The figure indicates that in addition

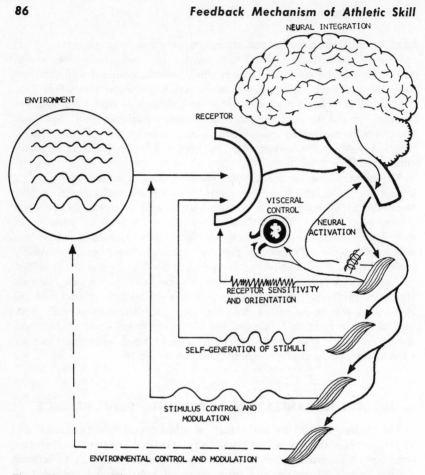

Fig. 2 Parameters of feedback regulation of neural activation, organic and metabolic function, receptor sensitivity, stimulus modulation and selection, and sources of environmental stimulation by motions of the skeletalmotor system.

to controlling sources of environmental stimulation and specific parameters of stimulation, the neuromuscular system also regulates and is reciprocally governed by the sensitivity and orientation of the receptors, the state of activation of the nervous system, and the magnitude and patterns of organic function. The purpose of experimental systems analysis of exercise and athletic skills is to clarify the features of specialization and organization of the reciprocal feedback interactions pictured in Figure 2. Results of experimental studies show that the movement systems of human behavior, including those used in athletic performance, are specialized in different ways—i.e., on the basis of functional anatomical specialization, and in relation to the space, time, and force feedback relations between movement and sensory input.

Anatomical-Functional Specialization Of Response

An action feedback concept suggests that a multidimensional theory of motion, rather than a generic concept of the reflex or a stimulus-response view, is needed to explain both motor performance and perception. Results of various studies on hand motion, locomotion, and speech have shown that these activities involve at least four levels of motorsensory feedback regulation, which correspond generally to postural, travel, manipulative, and articulated receptor movements. The division of labor and specialization of movements in control of sensory input in these four levels of motion are indicated in Figure 3.

The postural mechanism is the most primitive and generalized of the motorsensory systems of the body. Postural movements and their reciprocally related sensory-neural mechanisms maintain the body's position in space in relation to the pull of gravity while the individual is at rest or in motion. Postural movements also support the different parts of the body in various positions with reference to each other, and thus serve as a supporting base for the more specialized movements of the limbs, head, hands, eyes and other mobile parts of the body.

Transport or travel movements represent the second major movement system. Transport movements propel the legs in walking and the arms in moving the hands from one position to another. The transport movement system has dual representation on both sides of the midline to control the body's bilaterally-symmetrical parts. Its feedback circuits can control alternate movements of the right and left limbs, as in walking, and they also can control coordinate movements of corresponding parts, as the two legs in jumping or the two arms in pulling. This system is organized to define symmetrical motions that either parallel or mirror one another, and to integrate movements made in different directions.

The manipulative and articulated receptor feedback circuits of the body control the highly specialized and refined movements of the hands, feet, mouth, face, and the mobile receptors. Manipulative movements usually define the focal activities of the body, such as manual or verbal skills, so that detailed precise motions can be guided to perform highly precise stimulus control operations. Movements of the mobile receptors not only determine their sensitivity but also their orientation and special stimulus control functions.

Our view is that even the simplest response requires simultaneous coordinated control of receptor action and the postural, transport, and manipulative movement systems. Further, these neuromuscular responses must be governed against a background of internal organic activity, including breathing and heart action. Smooth coordination of these diverse bodily activities is possible only because of the closed-loop nature of the responding system. If external stimuli could control response directly in an open-loop fashion, as reflex theorists have claimed, behavior would break down into a chaotic mass of unrelated events. The built-in organized feedback circuits of the

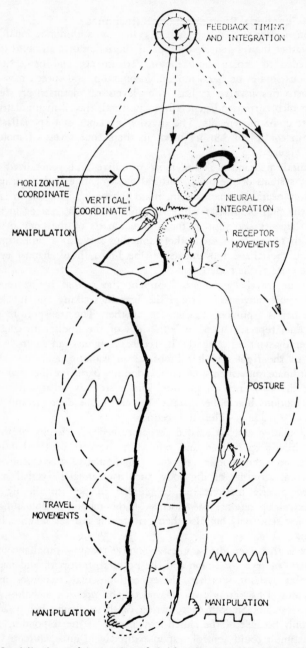

Fig. 3 Specialization and integration of the functional, spatial, and timing properties of postural, travel, manipulative, and articulated receptor movements of the body.

body not only locate the individual in space and guide his articulated movements; they also bring order, pattern, and continuity to receptor inputs and thereby organize motor and receptor functions in perception.

The concept of feedback control of different component movement levels defines a systems doctrine of motorsensory organization in motion, perception, learning, and physical conditioning. The theory states that the different postural, travel, manipulative, and articulated receptor movements are integrated on a space, time, and force feedback basis. Each component level is controlled by the reciprocal space and time feedback compliances between movement and sensory input, and as suggested in Figure 3, is specialized and integrated with other levels in terms of its space pattern and time characteristics. That is, the different levels of movement control, divide, stratify, and interlink their special functions in guidance of posture, dynamic motion, and articulated limb and receptor movements in terms of interacting space-time compliances. In general, one part of the body, such as the eye or head, can track movements of other parts in much the same way that the eye can track movements of external stimuli in the environment. This self-governed body tracking, which is prominently involved in all forms of athletic skill, has been found generally to be more accurate and to be learned more efficiently than tracking of environmental stimuli.

Experimental Substantiation Of The Systems Doctrine Of Athletic Skill

The experimental validation of this systems doctrine of motorsensory skill and exercise originated with investigations into three questions: (1) are postural, travel, and articulated movements actually distinctive in operation; (2) are self-governed modes of body tracking learned more efficiently than tracking of environmental stimuli; and (3) is dynamic movement integration involved in perception and learning as well as in motion regulation?

Specialization And Interaction Of Component Movements in Learning:

Special electronic behavior sensing and motion analysis systems were developed to test whether the different component postural, travel and manipulative movements are distinctively specialized. Such equipment was used to measure the changes in duration of manipulative and transport movements separately when the visual feedback of response was displaced or delayed by optical and laboratory television techniques, like those indicated in Figure 4. The results of many different studies (Smith & Smith, 1962) on panel control, handwriting, drawing, and other tasks indicated that the spatial and temporal characteristics of manipulative and travel movements are quite distinct and vary in different ways in relation to space displacement and delay of motorsensory feedback.

The results of this component movement research, which revised the prior generalized concepts of response in psychology (Smith & Smith, 1962), were applied specifically to formulating a new point of view regarding organization of behavior in learning, athletic skills, and physical education

(Smith, 1967a, 1968). This theory states that articulated manipulative, travel, and transport movements are affected differently by equivalent conditions of practice and reflect the specific space-time feedback properties in terms of which they are controlled. Additional research on the effects of space displacement and feedback delay of travel and manipulative move-

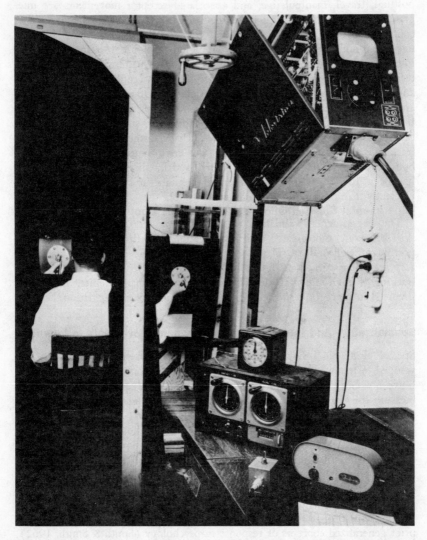

Fig. 4 Electronic behavior sensing techniques used to automatically measure and record separately the duration of component travel and manipulative movements in learning and performance (From Smith & Smith, 1962).

ments indicated that learning generally affects articulated and refined manipulative movements more than it changes travel movements. The initial and final levels of articulated movements were degraded more by altered and varied visual and auditory feedback than were travel movements. Both articulated and transport movements, however, displayed highly ordered, systematic practice effects during the massed and distributed learning conditions. The results confirmed the view that different components of motion and sensory activity are organized during learning by integration of the different levels of movement to achieve focal control of articulated manipulative and receptor activities, in relation to either self-generated or environmental stimuli.

Principle Of Dynamic Focal Guidance Of Motions

The general theory of organization of component postural, travel, manipulative, and articulated receptor movements is a cybernetic systems doctrine: it states that motion is organized primarily for spatial guidance of response and that all external responses are specialized and integrated to guide focal movements of limbs and head and the receptors in relation to self-generated and environmental stimuli. "Attention" and "perception" do not cause such guidance: they are products of the integration of different component levels of feedback control of stimulus selection, stimulus modulation, stimulus pattern formation, and receptor orientation control which are involved in the activities. Figure 5 describes eight levels of such dynamic control of sensory input which have been found to characterize common forms of visually guided behavior. The eight levels of feedback interaction consist of postural activation of the neural system, motor regulation of receptor sensitivity, stimulus pattern formation by the convergence and accommodation mechanisms of the eye, movement guidance of the receptor, self-generation of stimuli by voluntary movements, modulation of visual stimuli by the lid and pupil reactions of the eye, and control of sources of environmental visual stimuli by active movement.

The view presented in Figure 5 is that particular athletic skills are specialized dynamically and mainly organized in terms of the way that different components and levels of motorsensory control are timed and interrelated for precise focal control of the limbs and head to effect a tracking, throwing, holding, lifting, or striking action. The recognized practices of achieving a proper stance, follow through in throwing or swinging, proper rhythm of dynamic movements, and momentum in lifting or exerting force are meaningful as distinctive modes of self-regulation of posture or travel movements designed for precision of guidance and timing in performing articulated focal manipulative movements. In other words, the player must achieve specialized coordinations of the larger component postural and travel movements before he can hope to strike, hit, lift, throw, run, or hop with precision.

The results of a number of experiments have substantiated the view that

the component levels of postural, travel, manipulative, and articulated receptor movements operate to control sensory input dynamically as specified in
Figure 5. The idea that the movements of the eye actually control the sensitivity of the neural and receptor elements of vision was discovered nearly

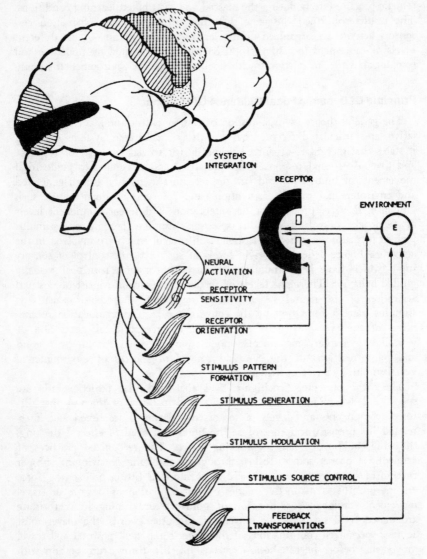

Fig.   5 The specialized levels of neural activation, receptor control, stimulus pattern
formation, stimulus modulation, stimulus selection, and environmental control involved in visually-guided behavior.

two decades ago by Ditchburn (1952) and Riggs *et al.* (1953). These investigators devised a method of stabilizing the retinal image so that no matter how a subject's eye moved the image always remained in the same place on the retina. This process of image stabilization, which eliminated the effects of flick movements in changing the position of the retinal image, caused observed light stimuli to disappear periodically for some period of time, after which the image of these stimuli would reappear. Image stabilization is known to affect the central visual mechanisms and possibly the retinal ganglion cells. The results prove, as specified in the general view outlined in Figure 5, that movements of the eye are required to maintain sensitivity of the visual system to continuous stimulation, and that when these movements are eliminated by image stabilization, the system quickly adapts to incident illumination.

Another experimental example can be cited which indicates that visual orientation is regulated by feedback control and that the tracking movements of the eye are also dynamically regulated. The experiment consisted of mounting a small dove prism on a scleral contact lens, which served to invert or reverse visual feedback of eyemovement itself. The effect of wearing such a prism was to cause *skittered vision,* or continual jumpy movements of the eyes, with corresponding unstable control of seeing. This effect persisted as long as wearing of the prism could be tolerated. The results suggest that movements of the eyes in a particular direction are essential to control the orientation of the retinal image, and that the ocular movements which perform this function cannot have their direction specificity and specialization altered experimentally and still control the orientation of the retinal image.

The investigations just described are a part of a larger spectrum of studies whose results show that every level of stimulus selection, sensory control, and neural activation pictured in Figure 5 is guided and integrated on a space-time basis by feedback regulation. The results of these investigations disprove the conventional psychophysical and stimulus-response dogmas that perception and motion can be separated and that reference to dissected neural mechanisms of perception and cognition can answer the many questions regarding dynamic specialization and organization of performance in different skills.

SYSTEMS BASIS OF PHYSICAL CONDITIONING

In the systems doctrine of athletic behavior which we are discussing here, physical conditioning represents the altering of the feedback interactions between external neuromuscular activity and autonomic-physiological regulation through exercise. Specifically, the effects of exercise are viewed as a main parameter of autonomic-physiological regulation by self-governed skeletal-motor action (Smith & Ansell, 1965). As shown in Figure 6, this feedback theory of behaviorally-guided autonomic interaction contains three main assumptions, namely: (1) that all levels of internal physiological and autonomic regulation have direct, reciprocal feedback links with skeletal-motor activity so that such activity alters the magnitude, pattern, and time characteristics of internal energy exchanges; (2) that external neuromuscular be-

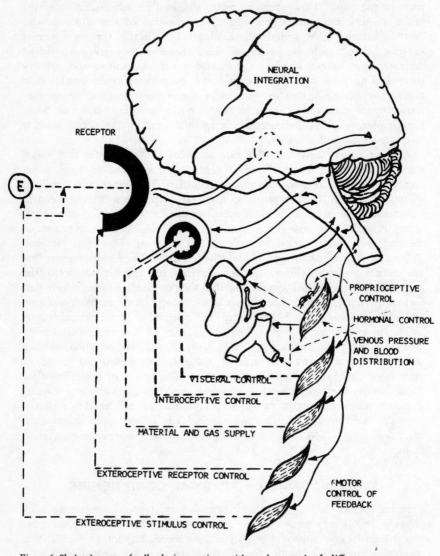

Fig. 6 Skeletal-motor feedback interaction with and control of different parameters of autonomic physiological function-in particular, circulatory function, material and gas intake, cellular energy exchange, hormonal processes, organic timing, interoceptive stimulation, and exteroceptive sensory processes related to the autonomic system. This theory of feedback control of autonomic-physiological function constitutes a system doctrine of physical conditioning.

havior, rather than being a centrifugal product of internal homeostatic processes, actually levels a dominant influence over the magnitude and pattern of organic, autonomic, physiological, and cellular function; and (3) that instead of reflecting homeostatic control by internal circulation, heart action and respiration, external motorsensory behavior acts kinetically to continually alter the state of internal metabolism and organic rhythms, not only to keep these systems sensitive but to specialize and integrate their operations for particular forms of adaptive behavior. As applied to the theory of physical conditioning, this third assumption states that a large part of the conditioning associated with particular skills is psychophysiological and not simply physiological or muscle-building processes. Physical conditioning is based on refinement and training of external behavior for specialization and integration of the spectrum of internal metabolism, endocrine function, organic rhythms, circulation, and energy exchanges to optimize accuracy and efficiency in a particular skill.

The classical view of autonomic and physiological regulation is Cannon's (1929) concept of homeostatsis. This view has been used along with the notion of reflex action to develop the idea that exercise has its main effects in directly improving homeostatic regulation in organic systems and by muscle building. In contrast to these ideas, a feedback view states that neuromuscular behavior, which Cannon (1929) himself believed could not be described under the rubric of homeostasis, operates as a primary determinant and integrator of internal autonomic function, cellular metabolism, organic rhythms, circulation, and oxygen and sugar energy exchanges. Physical conditioning is a process of building self-governed control over all levels of autonomic-physiological regulation by learning specific patterns of motorsensory skill and exercise, and is not limited to muscle building or to direct effects of exercise on organic processes. It involves more generally a wide spectrum of reciprocal feedback relationships between external motorsensory skill and the many levels and parameters of organic and metabolic mechanisms.

General Evidence For The Feedback Theory Of Physical Conditioning

General evidence for the systems doctrine of autonomic-physiological regulation pictured in Figure 6 consists of a number of facts about the role of the neuromuscular system and its self-regulated action in determining respiration, circulation, metabolic level, heart action, oxygen exchange and organic timing functions. The most relevant fact about external respiration is that its rate and depth can be varied over a wider range and more rapidly by so-called voluntary action and by exercise than it can by internal physiological influences, including drug effects. Respiratory control is yoked directly to the neuromuscular system, which in turn is a product of various levels of internal autonomic, organic, metabolic and cellular activities. The circulatory system also is directly subject to regulation by external neuromuscular function. Skeletal muscles are a main part of the circulatory system and have a specific function in regulating venous pressure. Skeletal muscles regulate blood supply by their marked variable capability for storing blood. They have a capacity not shared by other tissues and organs of the body in being able to anaerobically utilize their own stored carbohydrate resources for energy, thereby acquiring an oxygen debt that can be repaid later.

Motor activity has direct effects on hormonal exchanges in every part of the body, especially on catecholamine metabolism. Muscle activity serves as a direct means of activating some levels of brain activity and suppressing others. Skeletal-motor activity also is accompanied by changes in heart rate, which, like respiration, can be specialized and adjusted to different levels of activity. Skeletal-motor action can affect digestive interchanges and body temperature. It can influence the temporal patterns of circadian, temperature, and other organic rhythms.

Cellular and molecular levels of activity likewise are linked in specific feedback relationships with dynamic neuromuscular activity patterns. Striated muscles have the power to perform sustained, positive work by closely coupling energy production with energy utilization in a feedback manner, which regulates the level of work and thereby prevents fatigue. Through physical conditioning the efficiency of these diverse, reciprocal, feedback patterns of energy utilization and other systems functions in cellular energy exchange may be varied and altered to conform to particular patterns of athletic skill and exercise.

The concept of the neuromuscular function as one arm of a feedback control system which embodies reciprocal yokes to all levels of organic, autonomic, physiological and cellular activity constitutes a new psychophysiological systems doctrine of exercise, work, and physical conditioning. This theory emphasizes, not the homeostatic features, but the dynamic organizational characteristics of external and internal biological interaction. The theory is that the distinctive role of neuromuscular activity in reciprocally controlling the external and internal environments, as well as autonomic-physiological processes, also encompasses integration of these diverse internal mechanisms. The neuromuscular system, as the dominant engine of physiological regulation, is the most rapid, articulated, widespread, and specialized mechanism of the body in determining organization of internal organic and metabolic functions. It is the most highly integrated of vital mechanisms and is subject to a wider scope of adaptive alteration in evolution and development than any internal system. Its relations to the cerebral cortex are more direct and widespread than other body systems. And, by virtue of its compound levels of postural, travel, and articulated movement control of different parameters of stimulus selection, receptor function, and neural activation, the neuromuscular system is far more subject than internal organic mechanisms to direct self-regulated or voluntary control and to adaptive change through learning.

This feedback theory of neuromuscular integration of autonomic, physiological, and cellular function may be formulated as a theory of physical conditioning in athletic performance. Through processes of specialization of neuromuscular activity in specific skills and exercises, internal autonomic and physiological mechanisms also become specialized and integrated in distinctive ways. That is, physical conditioning involves specialization of the body as a compound behavioral-physiological system to affect particular organized patterns of feedback-linked muscular, sensory, organic, and metabolic operations.

Experimental Systems Analysis Of Behavioral-Physiological Interaction

The results of a series of experiments conducted over the last decade on feedback control and self-governed regulation of neural and organic function provide direct proof of the assumptions regarding skeletal-motor regulation which were defined above. These experiments were initiated with studies on the capability of subjects to acquire greater precision in respiratory regulation through training in respiratory tracking (Smith, 1966a; Smith, *et al.* 1965), and through self-governed feedback control of brain rhythms (Smith & Ansell, 1965) and heart action (Ansell, Waisbrot & Smith, 1967). The method and results of one of the initial experiments will show how com-

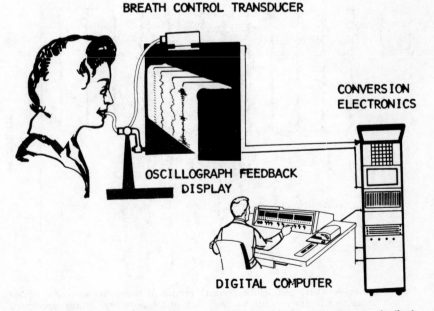

Fig. 7 Laboratory, hybrid, real-time computer system for investigating the feedback factors in self-regulation and learning of breath-pressure and ventilation movements in control of respiration.

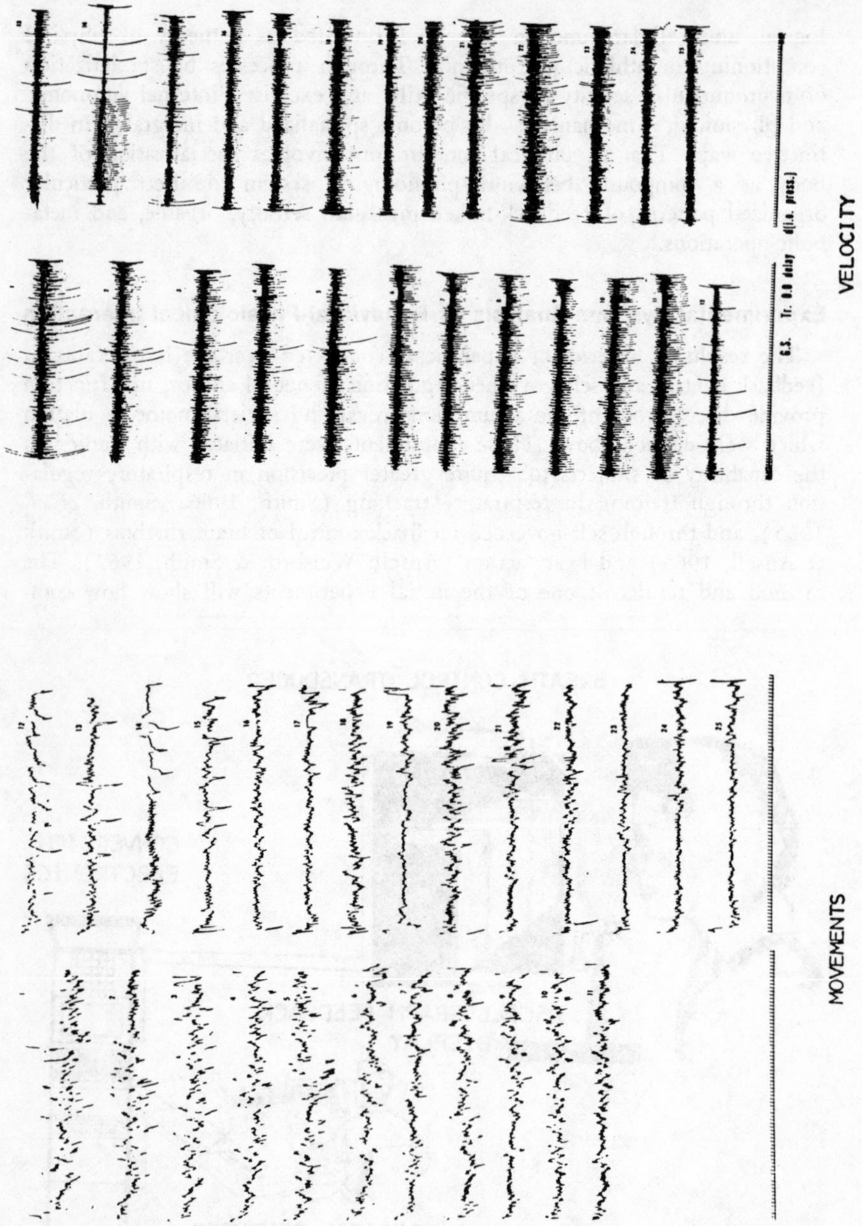

Fig. 8 Movement (left) and velocity (right) records of twenty-five successful trials in learning breath pressure tracking. Each of the movement records represents error in attempting to keep the feedback display indicator constant. If the performance had been perfect, the record for each trial would have been a straight line (Based on Smith & Henry, 1967).

puterized experimental laboratory methods were applied to the theoretical problem of self-governed autonomic-physiological control and to applied problems of physical conditioning in exercise therapy, rehabilitation, and athletics.

The first type of experiment, and one of the most informative for understanding self-governed and learned control of autonomic-physiological function, has been the investigation of the effects of training on breath-control tracking. Such tracking may consist of learning oral breath-pressure control, as in playing a musical instrument, or regulation of ventilation rate. Figure 7 illustrates the laboratory computer methods which were developed for such research (Smith, 1967a). The subject's task in these experiments was to maintain steady pressure in the mouth by watching a visual feedback display. The subject's breath-control movements were transduced and amplified (1), and then converted to digital form by means of a special analog-digital converter (Packard-Bell, Inc.), which sampled and measured the movement signal 128 times per second (2). The digital computer was programed to vary and perturb time, space, and signal characteristics of the movement-governed signal (3), and also to measure the accuracy of the subject in controlling his sensory input. After the experimental variations were made in the feedback signal, it was transmitted to a digital-analog converter (4) to be reconverted to dc form. This direct-current wave was then used to control the oscilloscope signal used by the subject to regulate his performance (5). In this study, the computer was programed to receive signals from a zero setting of the transducer and a feedback indicator, and to establish the voltage corresponding to these readings as zero. The computer then measured the magnitude of variations from this zero calibration.

The records in Figure 8 illustrate how a subject performed during twenty-five training trials in tracking a visual analog of his own oral breath-control movements. The records to the left show actual variations in pressure and thus represent the movements made by the subject, which have all the characteristics of self-generated, continuously-regulated, closed-loop reactions. They consist of uninterrupted oscillatory movements which display a dominant frequency pattern. As the subject continues to practice, the magnitude of the movements is reduced and the low-frequency movements tend to drop out. However, the subject never achieves a perfect performance, which would produce a straight line. The faster records to the right in Figure 8 represent the velocity of the breath-control tracking movements, as computed from the first derivative of the movement signal.

In these records, we see at first a number of very high velocity movements and also a repetitive variation which represents the effect of the heartbeat on the breath-control movements. As the trials progress, this *ballistocardiographic* effect on the movements decreases. It should be noted that there is no close correlation between velocity and movement magnitude over the training period. Also, the velocity of the movements does not decrease with practice in an orderly way.

Besides the effects of the cardiac rhythm, the breath-control reactions show variations related to postural shifts, the breathing cycle, and articulated movements of the lips, tongue, and jaw. Thus, movement control of breath pressure is a compound activity made up of a number of components which have variable relations with heart action, posture, and articulated activities

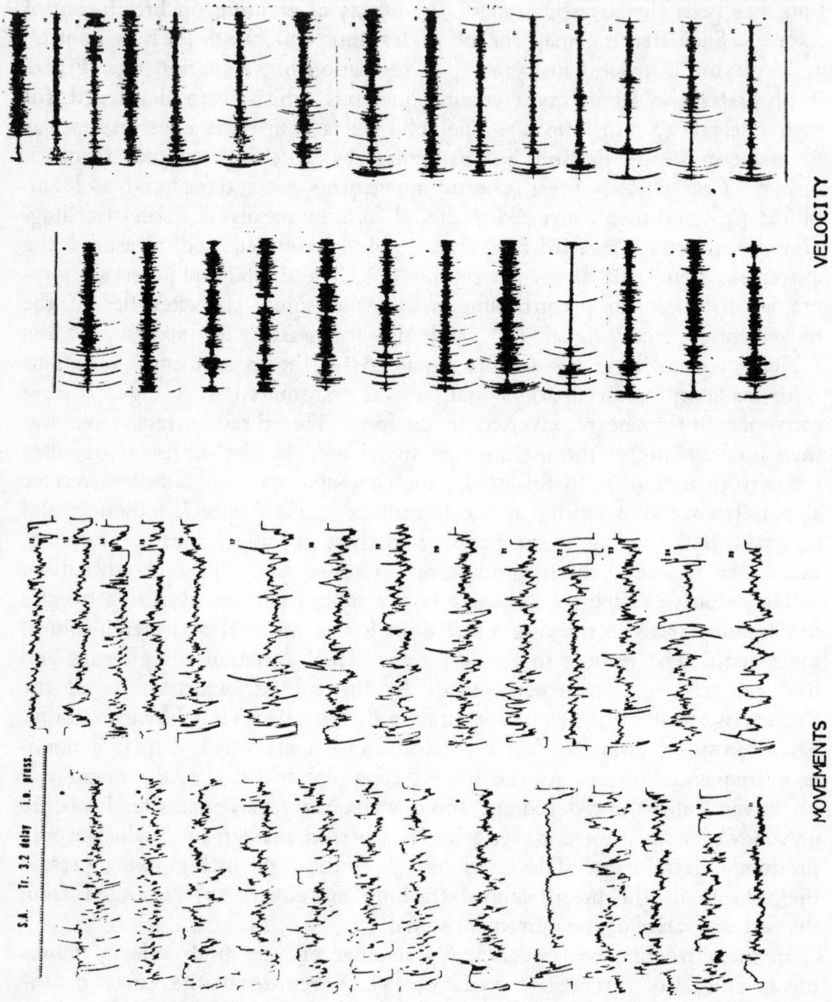

Fig. 9 Effects of a visual feedback delay of 3.2 seconds on self-governed breath pressure tracking. Movement control and error over twenty-five trials is indicated in the records to the left and movement velocity to the right. Movement velocity records were reduced somewhat more in photographic reproduction than the movement records (Based on Smith & Henry, 1967).

of mouth and head. These reciprocal interactions are neither accidental nor unimportant for respiratory control. As a matter of fact, they reflect a fact about neuromuscular regulation which has never been recognized in physiology or psychology: that the external respiratory mechanism is one of the ultra-precise tracking systems of the body and equals the eye in dynamic control of stimulation.

Results of several special experiments on delay of the visual feedback on ventilation and breath-pressure tracking have proven that these mechanisms are not simple stimulus-released reflex mechanisms, but depend continuously on reciprocal sensory feedback derived from actual movements. To produce delay of the feedback of respiratory tracking, the computer set-up shown in Figure 6 was programed to store the incoming signals of respiratory motion for a predetermined period of time and then to transmit these stored signals to the subject as a delayed feedback of the breath motions. The overall perceptual effect of such delay was to cause the subject to sense a discoordination between his breath movements and the sensory effects of these movements as observed on the oscillograph feedback display.

The effect of a 3.2 second feedback delay on learning of breath-pressure tracking over successive twenty-five trials of practice is shown in Figure 9. The records in this plate, comparable to those on the left in Figure 8, represent component activities which are continually integrated to determine, not only breath pressure, but the rate of air intake and expiration, the pressure of air in the lungs, and the rate of oxygen supply to pulmonary circulation. In the case of respiration, the regulatory interaction between internal organic and metabolic function and skeletal-motor activity is a natural one and does not depend initially on learning, because the driving muscles of external respiration are a part of the skeletal musculature. The results of the experiments on breath pressure and ventilation rate tracking suggest, however, that these different parameters of respiratory control can be changed with practice to effect improved control over all aspects of movement regulation affecting organic function, such as accuracy, velocity, and timing of respiratory motion.

These findings on feedback delay in breath-control tracking were reproduced in most respects by observations on ventilation-rate tracking. However, the ventilation tracking, which involved maintaining a constant rate of inspiration or expiration, was not affected by feedback delays as much as the breath-pressure tracking. Overall, the findings indicate that the process of external respiration, a skeletal-motor activity on which almost all levels of internal respiration and energy exchange depend, is regulated and learned in precise ways in relation to movement-controlled, sensory-feedback factors. The effects of feedback delays on breath control movements suggest in addition that the rhythmic timing and learning of external respiration can be altered by changing the temporal factors linking skeletal-motor activity and sensory inputs.

With visual feedback delay, the subject showed no real evidence of improvement with learning, and was just about as irregular in controlling his movements at the end of practice as he was in the first trial. The effect of the feedback delay was to cause gross irregularities in motion, decrease in the frequency and marked increase in the magnitude of movement, and distortion in control of velocity of breath-control motions. The results on the effects of feedback delays on learning breath control movements were extended by observations on the characteristics of performance with delays of different magnitude. The results of these observations confirmed the results on learning with feedback delay in showing that the motorsensory lags altered the regularity, accuracy, and velocity of different parameters of breath control. In addition, this study brought out that the frequency characteristics of the self-controlled tracking varied systematically with the different magnitudes of delay. The conclusion is that integration of different body movements with motions of the respiratory system depends on precise modes of feedback timing of movements and sensory stimulation of the respiratory system.

Self-Governed Control Of Organic Rhythms

Results of studies on self-governed regulation and feedback entraining of brain rhythms and cardiac rhythms provide further evidence regarding the role of external motorsensory activity in regulation of autonomic-physiological processes and their role in determining physical conditioning and exercise. In the original systematic experiments concerned with self-regulated feedback control of brain rhythms (Fig. 10), a real-time computer system was used to link the occurrence of short visual, auditory, and tactual signals to the occurrence of peak voltage values of the brain wave signal. The technique consisted of recording the electroencephalogram and causing the more prominent wave signals of the brain rhythm to key the occurrence of one type of sensory stimulus. The computer system was programed to detect peak values of the brain wave pattern, as recorded from the occipital region of the skull, and to generate discrete light, sound, or touch stimuli compliant with the frequency pattern of the electroencephalogram. The idea behind the experiment was to determine if the brainwave pattern would stabilize or vary in systematic ways with these brain-wave controlled sensory inputs. Although subjects could easily control the occurrence or suppression of alpha rhythms in the brain wave by relaxation or attention changes, the brain wave patterns of the same subject showed no noticeable variation in the frequency pattern of the electroencephalogram when the light, sound, or touch stimuli were linked in a feedback circuit with the prominent peak values of the brain wave. It was found also that introducing slight variations in frequency or delays between the occurrence of particular brain-wave peaks and the occurrence of the feedback yoked stimuli did not produce any greater effect of the feedback yoked stimuli on the frequency pattern of the brain rhythm than was found in the initial observations. The results thus suggested

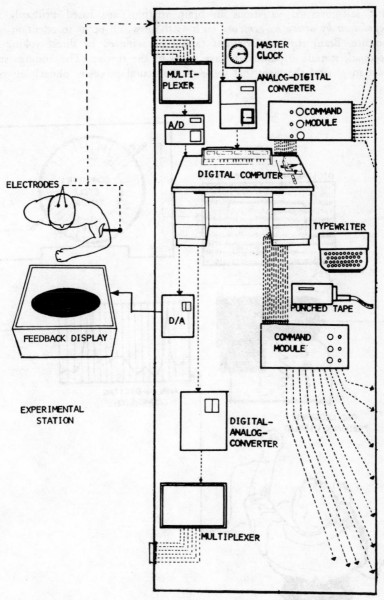

Fig. 10 Techniques of studying self-governed feedback of brain rhythms and the effects of entraining the brain wave pattern to variations in frequency of brain-wave linked visual, auditory, and tactual stimuli (From Smith & Ansell, 1965).

that self-governed variations in brain rhythms are based primarily on *regulation by active movements,* such as those which occur in attention and posture. Brain rhythm variations cannot be achieved by direct yoking of feedback stimuli to particular wave peaks of the rhythm. The findings support in general the view that some of the neural processes underlying per-

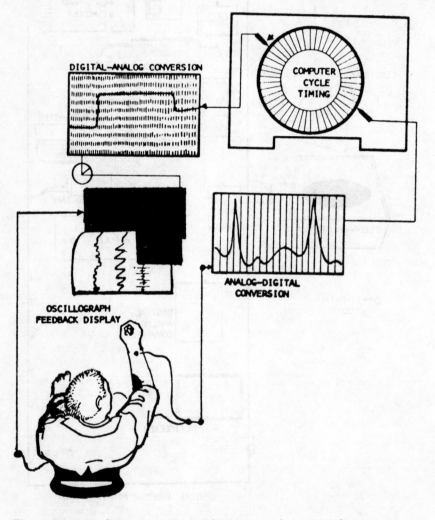

Fig. 11 Principle of measuring the heartbeat interval by means of the computer system. The real-time occurrence of heart peaks is stored in memory and the cycle time between these two events is measured by the computer (Based on Ansell, Waisbrot & Smith, 1967).

ception are feedback controlled through active movement and cannot be regulated directly by central neural events alone.

Studies comparable to the investigations of the brain-wave pattern have shown that to some degree the heart rate is subject to self-governed regulation involving control by external movements. The computer techniques used in this research (Ansell, Waisbrot & Smith, 1967) are illustrated in Figure 11. The subject sat before an oscillograph feedback display while his electrocardiogram and respiration were being recorded. The electrocardiogram signal was amplified and converted to digital form by an analog-digital converter. This digitized signal was then transmitted to the digital computer which was programed to select each peak of the QRS complex of the heart wave. The program used established a detection threshold for determining the exact time of occurrence of the peak of the QRS complex, and only the peak. In addition to detecting the peak value of successive heart waves, the computer program also initiated a counter upon the occurrence of a particular wave peak in real-time and measured the time interval between that wave and a succeeding peak by counting the intervening samples of the converted signal. This measurement gave the heart-rate interval, whose value was converted to a digital voltage value. The digital voltage representing the heart signal was deconverted to a step wave dc voltage and displayed on the oscillograph as a differential feedback display of variation in the heart rate. Since the sampling rate of the input signal was set at 1000 SPS, the number of samples between two QRS waves was equal to the time between beats in milliseconds. The nature of the step-wave produced by the time difference signal between succeeding heart beats is shown to the left on the oscillograph display in Figure 11. An increase in heart rate caused the record of this step signal to move to the right, while slowing of the heart rate caused it to move left.

Twelve subjects who saw their heart rates represented in the visual feedback display illustrated in Figure 11 learned to vary the rate to some extent at will. Fairly rapid changes in rate could be produced mainly by varying abdominal breathing and by head motions and tensing of the neck. These changes could be differentiated from slower variations which could be achieved by varying the degree of relaxation. Rapid changes typically were not as great as the slower variations. It was found that individuals could improve the extent of their control over the rapid changes with practice (Ansell, Waisbrot & Smith, 1967). Figure 12 gives the learning functions which were obtained on the twelve subjects. The two curves shown in the figure represent mean heart rate (solid curve) and variance of the heart beat interval (dotted curve). The measurement scale for the internal measure is given to the left, while the scale for the mean variance is shown to the right. As suggested by the heart-rate interval curve, it took the subjects some seven or eight trials to catch onto some technique of shifting their heart rate. The fact that the variance in the heart rate interval was reduced with practice suggests that the effects observed involved more than slowing the subject's heart rates with relaxation in the situation. The variations in heart-rate interval observed

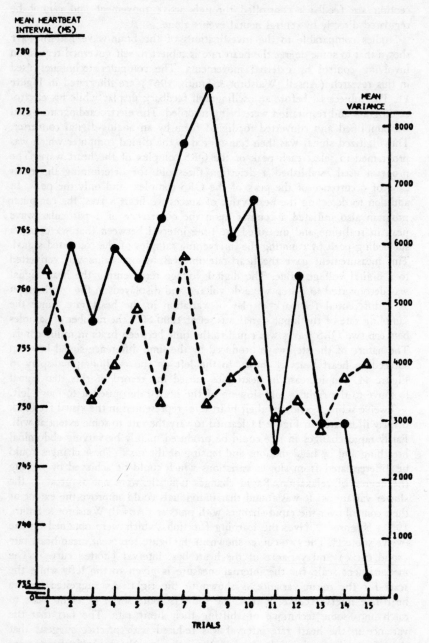

Fig. 12 Learning functions in self-governed control of the heart rhythm (From Ansell, Waisbrot & Smith, 1967).

in the twelve subjects with practice were found to be statistically significant.

Complete oscillograph records were obtained on all twelve subjects. Analysis of these records showed that subjects were actually controlling both increases and decreases in heart rate. In general, the most noticeable variations in heart interval accompanied irregularities in breathing. The most rapid adjustments of rate were made by controlling breathing. The fact that some subjects moved their heads and assumed tense positions of the neck suggested that they were controlling heart action by affecting circulation in the neck and possibly in the carotid sinuses. In general, subjects with slower heart rates seemed to be less able to vary their own heart rhythm than subjects who displayed faster heart rates.

Studies also were done on the feedback entraining of the heart rate by yoking short flashing light stimuli to the time of occurrence of the peak value of the electrocardiogram. Once this artificial cardiac stimulus feedback was established, computer programing was used to vary the time interval of the yoked visual stimulus above and below the measured heart rate of the subject. The aim was to determine if a slightly varying cardiac-yoked stimulus would cause the heart rhythm to follow this feedback stimulus. The findings, as in the case of the feedback-entrained brain rhythms, were inconclusive for a central theory of control of variations in organic rhythms. Changes in frequency of the cardiac-related stimulus had no systematic effect in increasing or decreasing the heart rate in the direction of the stimulus changes. The results confirm the interpretation stated above that variations in self-governed heart rate are achieved by *movement control* of circulatory mechanisms such as alteration of venous circulation by abdominal breathing.

Feedback Factors In Physical Conditioning

The experiments described above represent general theoretical studies which suggest that external motorsensory and internal autonomic-physiological processes may be linked by reciprocal feedback control and depend on dynamic movement for effective interaction. The experiments do not give detailed results however as to how external and internal activities are dynamically integrated in exercise and physical conditioning. The investigations to be described in the present section deal more directly with these interactions and show how systems feedback processes can determine physical conditioning. These investigations were designed to determine whether training in integration of visual-manual and respiratory interactions could be instrumented experimentally and whether efficient learning could occur in coordinating visual-manual and respiratory tasks. The experiments were set up to compare the efficiency of learning in respiration-related visual manual tracking and in tracking environmental targets. The hypothesis, as derived from the feedback concepts of physical conditioning described above, was that the respiration-related tracking would be more accurate than the environmental stimulus tracking, and that a fundamental factor in skeletal-motor, autonomic-physiological interaction is the highly precise nature of external respiration in tracking other self-generated body movements.

Relative Rate Of Learning Body Tracking And Stimulus Tracking: For purposes of this experiment, (Smith and Sussman, 1969b), processes of inter-relating respiratory activity and visual-manual activity shall be referred to as body tracking, while the comparable task of following an environmental target will be called stimulus tracking. The experiment consisted of comparing respiration-related body tracking and stimulus tracking under conditions in which the visual targets in the two modes of tracking were very nearly identical. In body tracking, the breathing movements of a subject were transduced by means of a pneumograph, and the electrical signal from these movements used to vary a visual target. The subject's task was to negate these respiration-produced target variations by moving a hand control device. If the subject performed perfectly, he performed hand movements which were identical to his respiratory movements except that they moved the target indicator in an opposite direction. The accuracy in performing this task was compared with tracking a computer-generated variation in the visual target which was approximately equal in frequency to the respiration-produced target variations. The study determined the relative rate at which the respiration-related and stimulus tracking were learned, the degree of transfer of learning between the two tasks, and the effects of feedback delay upon them.

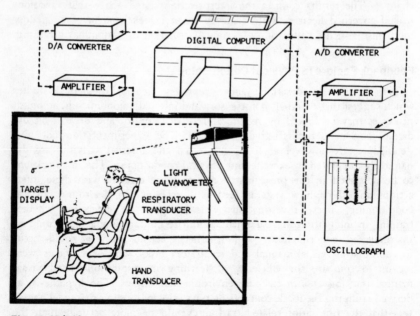

Fig. 13 Hybrid-computer system used for studying the interactions between external respiration and manual-visual tracking operations.

The subject's main task consisted of using a small spring-wand hand control to position a light target on a projection screen (Fig. 13). By moving the hand control, the subject could compensate any movement of this light spot from the center or zero point on the screen. In one experimental condition, the target light was caused to vary in position in relation to the subject's respiration, and the task was to correct for this respiration-perturbed variation in the target position. In a second condition, a hybrid-computer system was used to produce variations in movement of the target spot in a sine-wave pattern approximately equal to the rate and magnitude of the normal respiration rate. In this case also, the subject's task was to correct for the externally-controlled variation in the target position by using his hand control to keep the target on center. Using a controlled experimental design, the two conditions of performance were compared in regard to error level in tracking, the course and rate of learning the two tasks, the effects of feedback delays of several magnitudes on error level, and the extent of transfer from one task to another.

Twenty-four female college students were divided into two groups of twelve subjects each. The first was designated the Respiratory Group and the second the Stimulus Tracking Group. The Respiratory Group practiced for twenty-five trials with the respiratory-controlled target and then were tested in fifteen transfer trials with the stimulus tracking. The Stimulus Tracking Group practiced for twenty-five trials with the computer-generated target wave, and then were shifted to fifteen trials with the respiratory-related tracking. In both series of trials, feedback delay test trials were interspersed every five trials in the practice series and every three trials in the transfer series. Five feedback delay magnitudes between hand motion and action of the visual cursor were used, 0.0, 0.2, 0.4, 0.6, 0.8, and 1.5 seconds. The entire design of the experiment was based on the fact that the two modes of tracking—i.e., the respiratory-controlled and the stimulus-controlled tracking—were exactly comparable in terms of the calibration of the hand-motion-feedback display relationship and in terms of the relative degree that the computer and the respiratory waves perturbed the feedback display.

The main results of the experiment consited of: (1) learning functions for the initial training of the respiratory related and stimulus tracking groups; (2) transfer data for the two groups in shifting from the training tasks to stimulus tracking and respiratory-perturbed tracking respectively; (3) delay functions for the two training groups and the two transfer groups; and (4) a complete set of oscillograph records for the different conditions of learning and performance.

The first aspect of the observations consisted of twenty-five practice trials by the two experimental groups—the respiratory-perturbed and the stimulus tracking groups. The learning curves for the two groups in this practice are given in Figure 14. These curves indicate that the respiratory-related group was superior in tracking to the stimulus-tracking group throughout the twenty-five trials. The general form of the two curves is much the same, with that

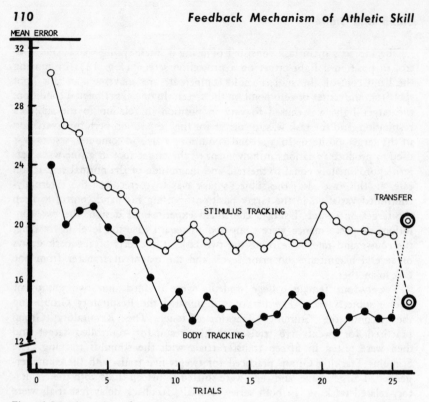

Fig. 14 Learning curves for stimulus tracking and respiratory-related tracking (Based
on Smith & Sussman, 1969b).

for the respiratory mode being somewhat more irregular. The learning of
both groups plateaued after 10-11 trials. Thereafter, the stimulus mode of
tracking on the average was twenty-five percent less precise than the respiratory tracking.

After the practice trials, the subjects in each training group were shifted
for fifteen test trials to the other tracking mode. The mean values of performance in the non-delay trials of the transfer tests are given by the
heavily circled points in Figure 15. These values indicate that transfer test
scores were typical of the training scores for the same tracking mode. Thus
the Respiratory-Tracking Group showed a marked negative transfer effect
with respect to their terminal learning scores before transfer, whereas the
stimulus tracking group showed a marked positive transfer effect. Relative to
initial learning scores, both training groups displayed positive transfer effects
in shifting to the other mode of tracking.

Effects of delay of the visual feedback of handmotion were determined by
delay trials interspersed in both the practice and transfer series. The delay

functions for the two modes of tracking in the two trial series are given in Figure 15. The two training series of delay trials are marked separately from the transfer series and indicated by five dotted lines. The performances affected most by delay were the respiratory transfer series and the stimulus learning series. The effects of the delay on the stimulus tracking training series and the respiratory transfer series were very similar, with the latter being consistently the least affected. The results indicate that only the target delay values of 0.8 and 1.5 second produced differentiative effects on performance, and that these effects were not consistent with regard to the conditions of practice and transfer.

The overall effects of delay were greatest for the Stimulus Tracking Group in the transfer series (Error = 60.5) and least for the Respiratory Tracking in the transfer series (Error = 35.5). The results indicate that self-governed and body-yoked modes of tracking may become less susceptible to effects of delay with practice, while stimulus tracking becomes more susceptible to the effects of delay.

Results of analyses of variance and associated range tests indicated that the means of the first four trials were significantly different from those of the last three trials for both the stimulus tracking and the respiratory-perturbed tracking. Findings of similar analyses on the delayed feedback data showed that the differences in performance related to delay magnitudes were not significant below the value of 0.6 second. Above that value, error increased significantly with each magnitude of delay.

Results of this experiment suggest that in athletic learning and exercise, body tracking in integrating external motorsensory and respiratory-related movements and functions is more rapid than, and therefore precedes, stimulus or environmental tracking tasks. This superiority of body tracking of self-generated, organically-related stimulus variations was found to persist in transfer tests. The results show that feedback delay affected processes of integration of movement and organic mechanism of body tracking in much the same way that it affects accuracy in stimulus tracking.

The findings give some definite ideas of how external motorsensory and autonomic-physiological mechanisms are coordinated in physical conditioning. In keeping with assumptions stated earlier, these two sectors of function were shown to be feedback yoked and to depend on precise conditions of closed-loop timing for coordination. Results also showed that feedback delay in an external motorsensory circuit may impair respiration. One main conclusion is that physical conditioning can be achieved in part by relating external motorsensory operations not only to improve smoothness and accuracy in performance but to reduce fatigue and to create more efficient organic function and behavior. A second conclusion is that the processes of integration of motorsensory and autonomic-physiological function precede learning of tracking of environmental stimuli, and that the patterns of such integration differ markedly in stimulus tracking and in body tracking essential for physical conditioning.

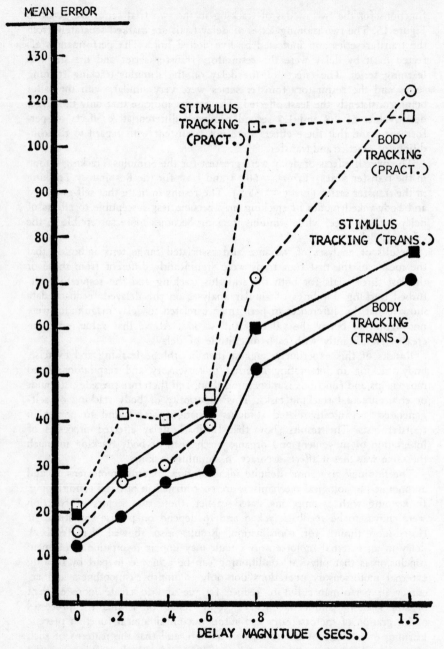

Fig. 15 Effects of feedback delay on environmental stimulus tracking and respiration related body tracking (Based on Smith & Sussman, 1969b).

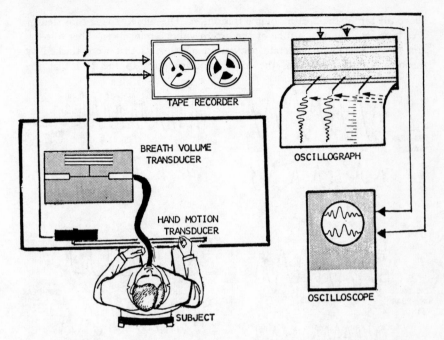

Fig. 16 Experimental set-up used to measure the difference between manual tracking of a visual display of respiration movements and respiratory tracking of a visual display of arm movements.

Analysis Of Respiration And Arm Movements Related To Swimming

In collaboration with Luedke (Smith & Luedke, 1969), several studies were conducted regarding the way respiratory movements and visually-guided arm movements are coordinated in tasks such as swimming. An initial investigation indicated that tracking of visual targets by control of breath volume was significantly more precise than manual tracking of comparable visual targets. Then in subsequent studies feedback control of arm and respiration integration was compared in two tracking modes, namely: (1) when changes in breathing served as a target indicator which was tracked non-visually by hand motions; and (2) when hand and arm movements served as an indicator which was tracked non-visually by control of breath volume. The experiment was designed to simulate to some degree the arm movements used in swimming and the coordination required in this skill between arm movements and breathing. The question of physical conditioning posed was: is it better to train the swimmer to make his breathing track his arm movements rather than the reverse?

The apparatus used in the experiment is illustrated in Figure 16. A breath volume transducer was constructed from the parts of a commercially sold metabulator. An arm transducer was devised and mounted some six inches

above the top of the breath-volume transducer. The subject's task consisted of
breathing into the mouth tube of the breath volume transducer either to track
arm movements or to generate respiration movements that were tracked by
the arm. In this situation, the term tracking refers to the fact that the

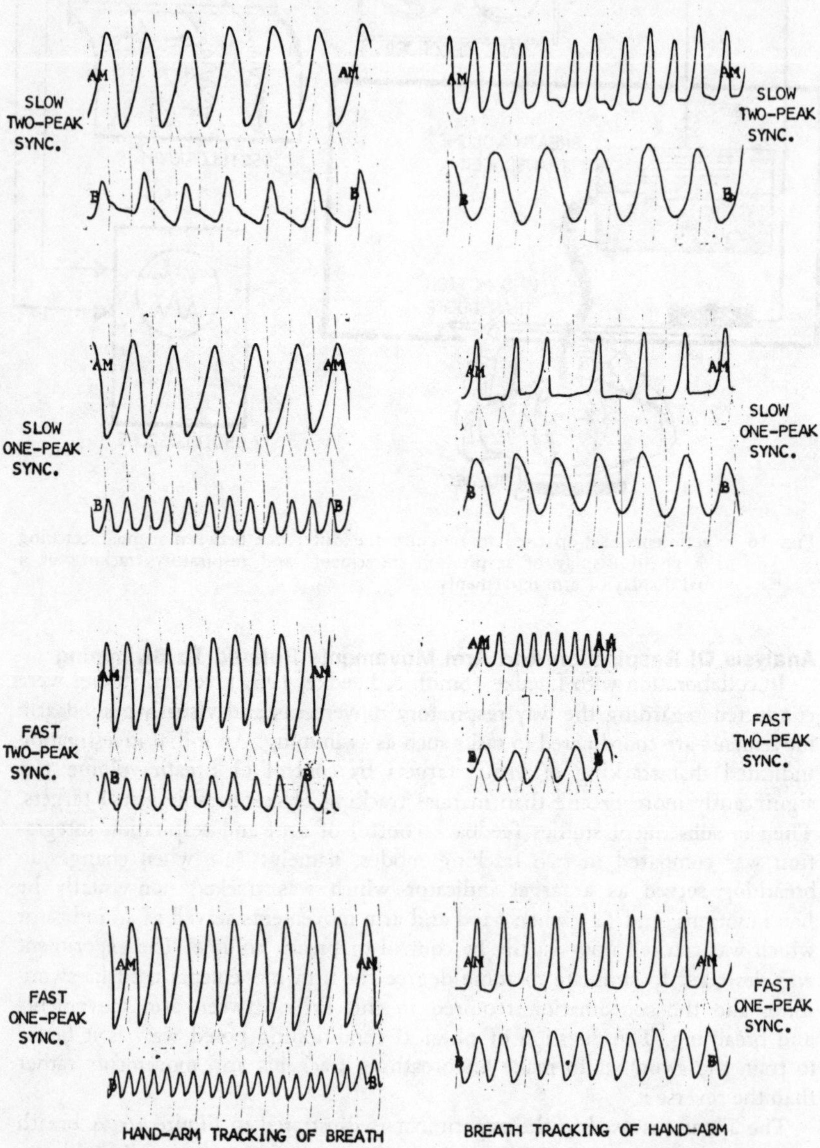

Fig. 17 Patterns of arm and respiration control of tracking used in the experiment on
hand-arm and respiration tracking.

respiration had to follow the pattern of hand motion or vice versa. The hand transducer consisted of a near-frictionless linear potentiometer. In doing the task, the subject's nose was closed by a nose clamp and vision was occluded by a pair of opaque goggles. The respiratory and hand-arm movements were recorded on an oscillograph and also on a magnetic tape recorder. These records were later measured in terms of timing errors between the respiratory and hand-arm motions. The error measures also were classified in terms of whether a given hand or breath movement led or dragged the indicator movement.

The study involved comparison between eight experimental conditions divided into two groups of four main conditions. In the first main condition the rate of the target-generating movement (either respiration or hand movement) and the timing of tracking motion had to be adjusted to every peak change in the target movement. In the second main condition the timing of the tracking motion had to be adjusted to every other peak change in the movement-generated target variations. Thus, as shown in the records in Figure 17, each of which illustrates a trace of arm movement (Top) and respiration movement (Bottom), there were eight conditions in which the two modes of tracking were varied in terms of the rate at which the target movement was generated and the timing of tracking motion with the wave peaks of the movement-generated target.

The subjects used in this study were eight expert swimmers. An experimental design was used in which each subject performed under all eight conditions in a given order. Four subjects performed the first trial with arm tracking of respiration-generated targets and the other four began with the breath tracking of the arm-generated targets. The trial length was kept at twenty seconds to prevent carbon-dioxide build-up in the breath-volume transducer from affecting the results.

The results of the experiment are indicated in Figure 18 in terms of a bar graph showing error level in the eight conditions. As the graph shows, all four conditions of breath tracking of hand-generated targets gave error values below those of hand tracking of breath-generated targets. The mean relative error for breath tracking was 6.56, while that for hand tracking was 11.99. Tracking was more precise when tracking movements were coordinated with every other peak of target motion.

The timing between the two movement systems was assessed by measuring the interval at which the tracking movements led or lagged the target generating motions. The results are summarized in Figure 19 in terms of the percentage by which the breath-tracking movements lagged arm motion. In both conditions, breath motions lagged arm motion and acted to follow the arm motions most of the time. Even when the arm was supposed to do the tracking, the arm led the breath-generated target a greater percentage of the time. These time data mean that in both modes of body tracking, the breath movements were coordinated with the arm movements. These time data thus confirm the error data in indicating that in physical conditioning

RELATIVE TIME ERROR

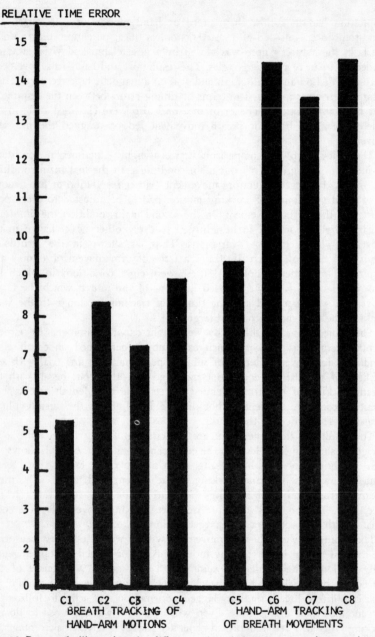

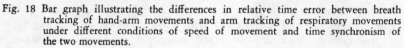

Fig. 18 Bar graph illustrating the differences in relative time error between breath
tracking of hand-arm movements and arm tracking of respiratory movements
under different conditions of speed of movement and time synchronism of
the two movements.

in swimming, breath control and respiratory function are feedback coordinated with, and do not determine, the rhythm of arm motion.

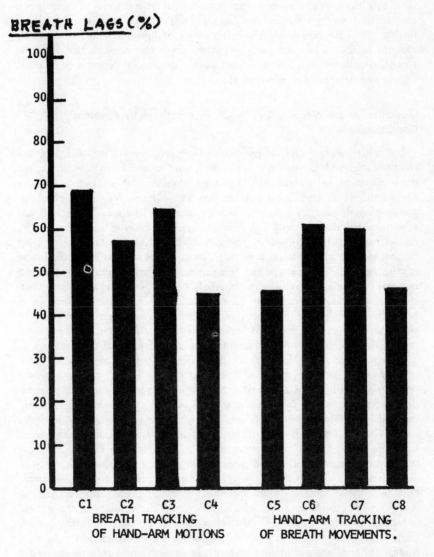

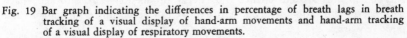

Fig. 19 Bar graph indicating the differences in percentage of breath lags in breath
tracking of a visual display of hand-arm movements and hand-arm tracking
of a visual display of respiratory movements.

The findings of this investigation agree with the results of the earlier behavioral-autonomic interaction studies suggesting that physical conditioning depends on processes of feedback-controlled body tracking which are integrated with the specialized closed-loop properties of the external neuromuscular movements concerned. The results suggest that the properties of time synchronisms between organically related movements of respiration and skeletal-motor activities are largely built-in mechanisms of feedback timing which are expressed in variable forms of breath tracking of dynamic motions of the limbs. There is no evidence from this research that the time synchronism between respiration and body movements depends on learned associations or operant reinforcement.

Muscular And Molecular Feedback Interactions In Physical Conditioning

Up until recently the overgeneralized ideas of psychoanalysis, operant conditioning, and homeostasis could be made plausible in describing the mechanisms of behavioral and autonomic-physiological interaction because few of the direct feedback effects of neuromuscular activity on internal organic, physiological, and cellular activity were understood. The traditional view persisted that the only significant reciprocal effects of muscular activity on internal function consist of the kinesthetic effects of movement. Over the last two decades, this situation has changed radically, with the disclosure of the existence of many direct reciprocal feedback interactions between external muscular activity and internal neural, interoceptive, and biochemical mechanisms regulating energy exchanges in cells and in the body generally. The data in this field of bioenergetics of exercise and skilled work can now be assembled to create a systems and action feedback concept of the molecular and biochemical correlates of physical conditioning.

A demonstration by Hill (1960) illustrates the general meaning of feedback processes in bioenergetics of music activity. In studies of nerve-muscle preparations, Hill found a marked difference in susceptibility of such preparation to fatigue when the muscle was required to do work while being shortened, considered *positive work,* and while being stretched, considered *negative work.* The finding was that there was rapid fatigue in positive work and little or no fatigue in negative work. As indicated in Figure 20, these recovery effects of positive and negative work were explained in terms of the differences in biochemical recovery of muscle under the two conditions. Positive work or contraction requires the accelerated expenditure of chemical energy in the muscle at a rate which far exceeds the capacity of the muscle to replenish energy supplies. On the other hand, the muscle performing work while undergoing stretch may act with nearly 100 percent efficiency, because energy demands are far smaller and energy production is able to keep pace with energy utilization. Thus, negative work can be sustained far longer than positive work.

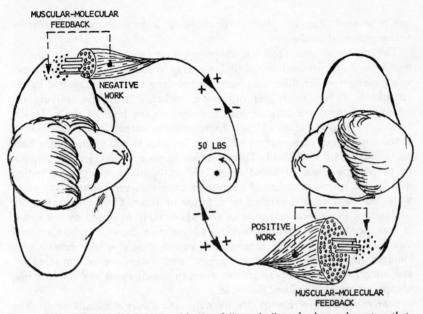

Fig. 20 The difference between "positive" and "negative" work. A muscle system that
must continuously shorten during contraction to do work fatigues much faster
than a muscle system that is stretched while in the process of doing an equal
amount of work in overcoming the tension imposed upon it (Based on
Hill, 1960).

Hill arranged an athletic demonstration of these reciprocal feedback
interactions of fatigue in positive and negative work. A tandem bicycle with
no brakes and with a common chain linking the two sets of pedals was fixed
with the drive wheel elevated off the ground. A strong young man sat in the
front seat pedaling forward, thus performing positive work, while a petite
young girl sat on the second seat and opposed the driving action of the man by
trying to pedal backward—i.e., doing negative work. If the efficiency of the
two types of work were identical, the two riders would tire at a rate corresponding to their relative strength, and the girl would tire first. Instead,
the girl remained fresh while the man was reduced to exhaustion in a short
time in trying to pedal against the opposition of the girl. The demonstration
thus confirmed the view that there are marked differences in the biochemical
feedback effects of different modes of muscular exercise.

The purpose of this section is to describe the variable feedback interactions
between muscle contraction, energy utilization, and hormonal regulation. The
major conclusion from this research is that the amount of chemical energy
utilized by action in muscle acts to feedback control the rate of production
of subsequent energy. This general finding means that energy-producing
metabolism may be yoked or coupled to energy expenditure in specialized

modes of work, exercise, physical conditioning, and the learning of skills involving physical conditioning.

The nature of the feedback coupling of dynamic activity patterns of muscle and cellular and supracellular energy metabolism has been known in a general way for three decades. This coupling was first suggested by the remarkable facility of higher organisms, including man, for varying the intensity of their metabolic activity according to the level of their physical behavior. Asmussen *et al.* (1939) determined the extent of this variation by measuring oxygen consumption of human leg muscle and of the entire body as a function of work load. There was an increase in oxygen consumption by the muscle tissue of about twentyfold in lightly working over resting muscle, and a further threefold increase in muscle oxygen consumption when work load was again increased by a factor of three. Over this same work load range, oxygen consumption in the whole body increased by ten times. It was estimated that with a work load variation between relaxation and maximum exertion, oxygen consumption in the muscle would increase one-hundred fold. These increases in oxygen consumption are accompanied by, and integrated with, temperature variations in muscle tissue and by dilatation of capillary vessels supplying the tissue.

Sources of Cellular Energy for Exercise And Physical Conditioning: The two fundamental questions posed by a systems doctrine of feedback regulation of energy metabolism and muscle performance are: (1) why does the metabolism of muscle proceed only rapidly enough to supply the energy required at any given time; and (2) how specifically are the different bio-energetic control mechanisms dynamically integrated during exercise to produce physical conditioning of the athlete. To answer these questions and to show how action feedback of exercise can reciprocally regulate internal vital interaction, it is necessary to explain the main features of molecular energy metabolism, which encompasses the mechanisms of ATP production, carbohydrate metabolism, and oxidative versus anaerobic metabolism (Fruton and Simmonds, 1960; White, *et al.,* 1964). Information regarding these phenomena indicates that energy metabolism is yoked to muscle action by both positive and negative feedback mechanisms, thus allowing the dynamic coupling of energy production to energy expenditure as specified above in the systems concept of physical conditioning.

Chemical energy production in cellular metabolism depends upon two major processes: the breakdown of carbohydrates and the consumption of oxygen. When we speak of chemical energy in the cell, we essentially mean one specific molecule, a compound called *adenosine triphosphate* or *ATP.* ATP can be considered as the end product of cellular energy production. It is essential for such activities as amino acid synthesis, protein synthesis, carbohydrate breakdown, muscle action, and production of body heat, as well as a host of other processes. Under *aerobic* (oxygen present) conditions, ATP is produced at the expense of sugar and oxygen. Cells also can produce ATP under *anaerobic* (oxygen absent) conditions, albeit in a more inefficient manner. It is the control of these processes that is our main concern here.

The primary site of ATP formation in cells of higher organisms is the

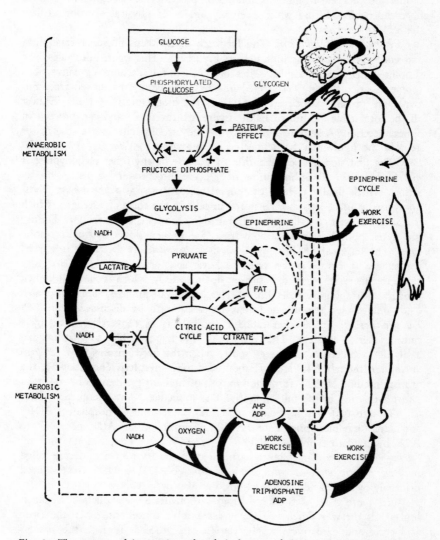

Fig. 21 The pattern of integration of carbohydrate catabolism and energy production in muscle, and the relationship to exercise and work by the body. Solid lines or broad arrows represent pathways of biosynthesis or catabolism. Dotted lines represent positive (+) or inhibitory (−) effects of the specified metabolic intermediates on the designated reactions or reaction sequences.

mitochondria, which are specialized organelles located in the cell cytoplasm. In muscles, carbohydrate (primarily glucose) and oxygen permeate into individual cells from capillary blood vessels supplying the tissue. Within the cells, carbohydrate *catabolism* (breakdown), oxygen consumption, and ATP production proceed in the mitochondria by processes described below. Muscle fiber contraction during work, exercise, and other physical exertion utilizes the ATP so produced.

Carbohydrate Metabolism: The feedback mechanisms of sugar catabolism and energy production is indicated in Figure 21. This figure illustrates in a simplified manner a complex series of biochemical reactions or conversions (some are not shown), each mediated by a different, specific enzyme. Enzymes are proteins which act as catalysts for biochemical reactions. Almost all the interactions indicated in the figure are reversible and can proceed in either direction. Assuming glucose to be the carbohydrate source, the major steps in the figure may be delineated as follows: (1) *Glucose phosphorylation.* The first step in the catabolism of glucose or any other carbohydrate is *phosphorylation.* Phosphorylation of glucose proceeds by a series of reactions which finally yield a compound called *fructose diphosphate.* Phosphorylated glucose also may be stored in cells in the form of glycogen, which is a large polymer containing many glucose molecules. (2) *Glycolysis.* During glycolysis, phosphorylated carbohydrates are broken down to smaller molecules. The terminal product of glycolysis is *pyruvate.* If the tissue is starved for oxygen, pyruvate is converted to lactic acid or *lactate.* (3) *Citric acid cycle.* In this cycle, pyruvate is broken down to CO_2, which is the well-known product of respiratory metabolism given off by all animals. This cycle proceeds only under aerobic conditions for reasons to be discussed later. (4) *Fat production.* Yet another fate for pyruvate is its conversion to fat by a complex series of steps. This process is readily reversible, so that fat can easily be mobilized as an energy source when the need arises. (5) *ATP production.* Although ATP is also produced during glycolysis (not shown), the primary method of ATP formation in cells of higher organisms is by *oxidative phosphorylation* in the mitochondria. The immediate, low energy precursors of ATP are two closely related molecules, adenosine diphosphate (ADP) and adenosine monophosphate (AMP). Conversion of ADP or AMP to ATP by oxidative phosphorylation requires oxygen (respiration) and *reducing power.* Reducing power is supplied in the form of a molecule called *reduced nicotinamide adenine dinucleotide* (NADH), which is produced primarily by citric acid cycle reactions, but also by glycolysis.

Much more ATP is produced from carbohydrate metabolism if sugar is broken all the way down to CO_2 under aerobic conditions, when the citric acid cycle and oxidative phosphorylation can proceed. In fact, the process of anaerobic glycolysis, when carbohydrate catabolism stops at lactate, releases only about seven percent of the energy obtained when glucose is broken down completely to CO_2. Therefore, the energy needs of the cell can be met with considerably less glucose under aerobic conditions. A further consideration is that fat can be mobilized for energy only if oxygen is available.

Pasteur Effect: The first observation on the functional relationship of respiration and carbohydrate metabolism was made over 100 years ago, when Louis Pasteur noted that yeast consumed a much greater quantity of sugar under anaerobic conditions than when oxygen was present (White, *et al.*, 1964; Fruton & Simmonds, 1960). This phenomenon, later termed the *Pasteur effect,* has subsequently been observed in a wide variety of animal tissue preparations and in microorganisms. The basic observation is that oxygen somehow decreases the rate of carbohydrate breakdown to pyruvate in glycolysis, so that glycolysis is much more rapid under anaerobic than under aerobic conditions. In trying to interpret the Pasteur effect, one is immediately struck by the fact discussed above that energy production is much more efficient under aerobic conditions. With oxygen present, glucose catabolism in glycolysis can proceed at a moderate pace and still produce a substantial amount of energy. The important inference of the Pasteur effect, however, is that cellular energy feedback controls the rate of its own production. As we shall see below, this has turned out to be exactly the case and to be the foundation of action feedback control of energy regulation by dynamic motor response.

Feedback Regulation of Energy Production: Experimental results from many sources have shown that ATP, and its precursors ADP and AMP, can exert multifaceted feedback control over the rate of carbohydrate catabolism, thereby regulating the rate of ATP production. This control seems to be achieved primarily through positive or negative modulation, by ATP, ADP, and AMP, of the activities of specific enzymes along the glycolytic pathway and in the citric acid cycle. Regulatory features of the system have been incorporated into a model termed the *adenylate control hypothesis,* recently reviewed by Atkinson (1965, 1966) and depicted generally in Figure 21. Dotted lines in the figure connect the regulatory metabolites to the metabolic steps which they modulate. Enhancement of a process is indicated by a heavy arrow, inhibition by a heavy cross. ATP controls its own production directly by inhibiting the enzyme which catalyzes the entry of pyruvate into the citric acid cycle, thereby restricting the operation of the cycle and the concomitant production of reducing power which is needed for energy production. ATP complements this process by also inhibiting one of the enzymes in the cycle. The action of ATP is reversed by that of AMP and ADP, which enhance the activity of another of the enzymes in the cycle to increase the production of energy. The general result is a coordinate control of the citric acid cycle: if the ATP concentration is high, the cycle is inhibited, but if it is low due to excessive energy expenditure, the resultant high concentrations of AMP and ADP tend to enhance NADH production.

ATP, ADP, and AMP also exert their effects at other points in the carbohydrate pathway to determine the Pasteur effect (Passonneau & Lowry, 1962, 1963). For example, under conditions of energy ·surplus, citrate and ATP would tend to accumulate, thus antagonizing the action of phosphofructo-kinase and thereby moderating the rate of glycolytic degradation of glucose. In addition to the discrete effects of ATP and its precursors on carbohydrate metabolism, further evidence exists that the rate of oxygen consumption is critically dependent on the supply of inorganic phosphate and ADP to mitochondria (Johnson, 1941; Lardy & Wellman, 1952; Lardy, 1956). The rate of carbohydrate oxidation in resting cells is slow because of the lack of inorganice phosphate and ADP precursors essential for oxidative phos-phorylation (energy surplus condition). Liberation of ADP and inorganic phosphate caused by ATP utilization with work accelerates carbohydrate catabolism. Moreover, oxidative phosphorylation can proceed at levels of in-organic phosphate too low to permit anaerobic ATP formation by glycolysis. When the rate of inorganice phosphate liberation exceeds the rate of oxidative phosphorylation (energy deficiency), the resultant accumulation of inorganic phosphate accelerates glycolytic phosphorylation.

The feedback relationships of ATP in Figure 21 allow multifaceted control of energy metabolism, including that resulting from the motor reactions of exercise. If the amount of energy in a cell or tissue drops due to any extra-ordinary exertion, the flow of carbohydrates and the production of NADH is augmented in a ramified manner. Glycogen breakdown increases, the pro-duction FDP is enhanced, and operations within the citric acid cycle are boosted. On the other hand, if the cell begins to accumulate excess energy in the form of ATP, this enhancement of carbohydrate flow is reversed due to ATP inhibition of fructose diphosphate and NADH production and the flow of pyruvate into the citric acid cycle.

Superimposed on the feedback control properties of ATP, ADP, and AMP on energy metabolism, summarized by the adenylate control hypothesis, are the influences of the body's endocrine system on carbohydrate metabolism, respiration, and energy production. In muscle, the most prominent such influence is that of *epinephrine,* the hormonal product of the adrenal glands (White *et al.,* 1964). Epinephrine secretion by the adrenal medulla is en-hanced by behavioral conditions of exercise, excitement, anxiety, exertion, or stress, apparently by direct stimulation of the adrenals by the nervous system. As illustrated in Figure 21, epinephrine promotes glucose production from glycogen (a process called *glycogenolysis*). Under aerobic conditions it also enhances energy production from fat by promoting fat breakdown. In addition to these effects, epinephrine also causes marked dilatation of capillary blood vessels feeding skeletal muscle. Therefore, epinephrine has a threefold positive effect on energy metabolism at times of tension or stress when the organism needs energy: (1) it enhances carbohydrate supply through glycogenolysis; (2) it provides an additional energy source through fat mobilization; and (3) it increases oxygen supply to muscle tissue by means of vasodilatation. This epinephrine cycle thus also constitutes a feed-back bridge between active motor response and vital regulation.

Variable Feedback Effects in Muscle Contraction And Work: The view that the muscle acts as a dynamic regulator and integrator of vital interactions in both cellular and organismic bioenergetic regulation has been validated further by the experimental studies of the mechanisms of contraction. This research has proven that the mechanism of contraction constitutes a physical-biochemical process for linking muscle action with control of ATP production and regulation, and has given rise to the *sliding filament theory* of striated muscle contraction, which Huxley (1969) reviewed recently. Muscle fibers are made up of a large number of individual filaments, bundled together along their longitudinal axes to form the fiber. Muscle filaments may contain one of two types of protein molecules, *actin* or *myosin,* and the actin and myosin filaments overlap each other in a highly precise manner within the fiber to form a characteristic lattice or array appearance when viewed in cross section. When the muscle changes length, during either contraction or stretch, the sliding filament model proposes that the length of the filaments themselves remains the same, but that the overlapping arrays of myosin and actin filaments slide past each other. Actin is drawn further into the array of myosin filaments as the muscle shortens, and withdrawn again as the muscle is stretched. During contraction, the traverse distance between the filaments increases considerably, accounting for the familiar muscle bulge caused by contraction. It is now fairly certain that the sliding of actin and myosin filaments along each other represents the energy-consuming stage of muscle action, and that ATP is directly required in the interfilament interactions which allow sliding to occur.

Using action feedback principles and some of the facts summarized above, we can correlate the molecular control features of muscle metabolism, and the energy demands of fiber contraction, with the more obvious, outward physiological manifestations of work or exercise for the different cases of resting muscle, short-term, intense exertion, and more prolonged exertion. At rest, energy demands of muscle tissue are slight and the rate of oxygen consumption is low (Asmussen *et al.,* 1939). Blood circulation is minimal—only one capillary of every hundred supplying the tissue may be open and carrying blood (Krogh, 1922). It is probable that the decreased blood supply is a physiological feedback response to the decreased demand of the tissue for oxygen (Lardy, 1956). In resting muscle, energy is derived primarily from fat oxidation, not carbohydrate oxidation (White *et al.,* 1964). Although other factors may be involved, the two major reasons for this mode of metabolism probably are that the low concentrations of inorganic phosphate and ADP limit the rate of glycolysis, and that the epinephrine-induced factors necessary for muscle glycogen breakdown to glucose are not available.

The "warmup" phenomena of exercise have a feedback basis in behavioral-molecular interaction. Violent exertion from a rest condition may cause adverse muscle effects, reflecting the inability of the tissue to convert instantaneously from a passive state to one of accelerated energy metabolism. Enhanced secretion of epinephrine caused by the activity (and, in the case of an athlete, also by anticipation of the pending contest) induces vasodilatation of capillaries feeding the muscle tissue, and oxygen supply to the tissue increases. Epinephrine also initiates a series of biochemical changes which ultimately stimulate glycogen breakdown, thereby raising glucose levels in the muscle. At the same time, the rate of oxygen consumption rises markedly, reflecting a higher energy demand due to muscle contraction. Inorganic phosphate and ADP levels increase the rates of glycolysis and oxidative phosphorylation become appreciably higher than their values in resting muscle.

Sudden violent bursts of muscle activity, such as occur in athletic sprints or similar intense, short-term exertions, introduce a profound shift in muscle metabolism. At near maximal work levels, ATP reservoirs in mammalian skeletal muscle become exhausted within a few seconds (White *et al.*, 1964). Furthermore, the maximal increase in ATP utilization for contraction is manyfold greater than the maximal increase in cellular oxygen consumption. Thus, neither the energy reservoir nor respiratory metabolism is adequate to meet the energy demands of muscle for intense activity, and the tissue switches to anaerobic glycolysis for ATP production. Note in Figure 21 that ADP, whose level is high because of energy expenditure, enhances glycolysis at a number of points. By catabolizing glucose at a high rate, the muscle is therefore able to keep pace with intense energy demands for an appreciable period of time by primarily anaerobic metabolism. This is why intense physical activity is always accompanied by the appearance of large quantities of lactic acid in the blood.

Although anaerobic metabolism can meet the needs of short-term muscle exertion, sustained muscle use over a longer period must be fueled by oxidative metabolism. This is because the carbohydrate reserves of muscle, in the form of glycogen, are limited and are rapidly depleted by anaerobic glycolysis. Over the long term, oxidative phosphorylation, which entails oxygen consumption and ATP production, must be able to keep pace with energy expenditure. A further feature of long-term muscle use is that the primary energy source is fat, not carbohydrate. Equating these effects with athletic performance, the 100-yard dash man relies almost entirely on his glycogen reservoirs, while the marathon runner consumes mainly fat for energy production.

"Oxygen debt" incurred in exertion has a closed basis in the direct feedback relationship between cellular metabolism and body respiration. The respiratory manifestations of this phenomenon are simply that oxygen consumption after intense physical activity continues to exceed the basal rate and is of greater magnitude than oxygen consumption during the activity. The metabolic and physiological basis of this oxygen debt is the necessity for the body to restore the energy balance of the muscle tissue by oxidative phosphorylation of ADP to ATP, catabolizing in the process some of the excess lactic acid produced by anaerobic glycolysis during the intense work. However, most of the excess lactic acid is used to restore the depleted glycogen reserves of the tissue, a synthetic process which requires energy and thus further prolongs enhanced oxygen consumption. The oxygen debt, therefore, is a direct manifestation of the intimate feedback relationship between external and internal respiration, energy balance, and catabolic and biosynthetic metabolism.

The various lines of experimental evidence concerning the reciprocal interactions between external neuromuscular activity and the various organic, physiological, autonomic, cellular, and molecular functions can be put together as a definitive systems interpretation of physical conditioning. Direct feedback effects of skeletal-motor activity are not focused solely on bioenergetic processes. As the results of different experiments show, these feedback effects also encompass sustained influences on organic timing, interoceptive control, material and gas supply, external respiration, circulation, and hormonal activities. Evidence from specific feedback studies described at the beginning of the section suggests that these feedback effects have adaptive characteristics—i.e., with practice and exercise, the conditions, modes and levels of feedback interchange are modified to effect more efficient patterns of regulation of the internal environment. It is these overall changes that constitute physical conditioning. We conclude that the athlete specializes and organizes all levels of vital interaction as a part of his skill acquisition in integrating different motions through both body tracking and environmental stimulus tracking.

In trying to understand the issues of autonomic and physiological changes in learning of athletic skill, we need no longer get involved in the tautologies and vague thinking of neoclassical associative learning, operant conditioning, and psychoanalytic reinforcement dogmas. The data on psychophysiological regulation of skill, described above, suggest that physical conditioning is the process of specialization and integration of all levels of vital interaction in work, exercise and skill acquisition. The feedback effects of neuromuscular activity are both regulatory and integrative, leading to enhanced specialization and organization of the body and of organs, cells, and molecular processes for particular patterns of activity and skill. As these patterns of activity are practiced, behavioral, muscular, and internal vital mechanisms have their most detailed, as well as their most highly organized, reciprocal interactions altered and adjusted to increase efficiency in movement, in use of the senses, and in bioenergetic regulation. The athlete may incorporate the effects of superficial rewards, medals, praise, and criticism by others into the diverse modes of skilled self-regulation of his body and his social and physical environment. Generally, however, these so-called "reinforcing" effects of skill activity are of far less significance in actually guiding the tracking activities of the athlete than specialized self-governed capabilities achieved in physical conditioning in detecting the direct psychophysiological effects of exercise and work.

Physical conditioning involves learning as well as regulatory behavioral-physiological effects and changes. The neuromuscular system is locked into the nervous system in the feedback adaptations of physical conditioning, and these closed links with neural function are changed as a part of the overall pattern of vital interaction in exercise. Thus, neural changes in reciprocal feedback control of movement parallel and accompany bioenergetic adaptations and their yoked neuromuscular alterations in physical conditioning. It is by differential, dynamic, reciprocal, neuromuscular adjustments of posture, travel, manipulative, and receptor movement that skilled motion self-regulates interrelated levels of skill and physical conditioning.

FEEDBACK FACTORS IN GUIDANCE OF MOTION IN ATHLETIC SKILL

The preceding section described the vital feedback components in athletic skill and suggested how autonomic-physiological-molecular processes could become specialized as part of skill development. The gist of the experimental findings was that particular skills involved distinctive differentiation and organization of internal levels of vital interaction through the feedback interplay between external neuromuscular activity and internal vital mechanisms. These processes of feedback control of differentiation and organization of vital interaction constitute the mechanisms of physical conditioning.

Athletes and athletic skills are specialized and integrated at other levels besides those related to internal processes. The neuromuscular motions making up performances are also organized in distinctive ways. In the systems view defined in the first section, motion specialization was said to be determined by the space, time, and force feedback compliances between particular patterns of movement and the sensory feedback patterns resulting from the movement. The main assumption of this systems doctrine of skilled motion is that movements are specialized and integrated primarily in terms of the dynamic expression of their anatomical components, which also define the differential properties of postural, travel, manipulative, and articulated receptor movements determining sensory input. Specifically, the guidance or spatial factors related to these components determine both their integration and differentiation. This view also assumes that time and force feedback properties are derivative and dependent on the guidance factors. Motions are developed in childhood and learned primarily in terms of their guidance feedback factors, and their time and force properties are adjusted to this guidance specialization through learning. According to this interpretation, the analysis of motions for improvement and training in athletic skills should initially emphasize guidance as a primary factor in designing practice, with more detailed attention being given later to development of timing and force characteristics.

Direction Specificity Of Motion In Learned Skills

Experimental evidence for a systems concept of directional specialization of response in skilled performance has been accumulated for the last quarter

of a century in tracking studies and in studies of space-displaced sensory feedback in behavior (Lincoln and Smith, 1952; Rhule and Smith, 1959; Smith
and Smith, 1962). Figure 22 illustrates two postulates of this theory—i.e., the

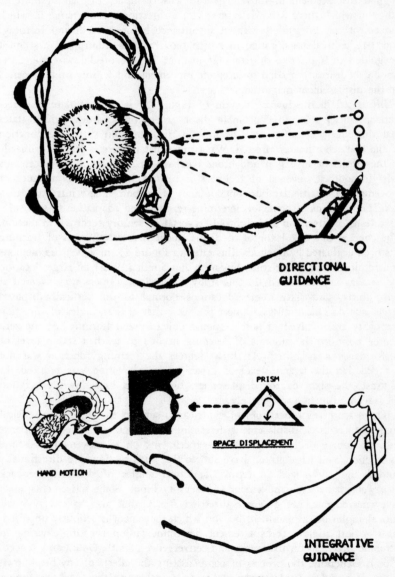

Fig. 22 The hypothesis of critical ranges of angular displacement and of coordinate
axes of space displacement of visual sensory feedback and behavior.

concepts of *critical ranges of angular displacement* in guidance of motion and of *directional specificity of axes of movement and receptor input.* The top diagram illustrates the concept that guidance of, and feedback compliance in, every motorsensory system depends on detection of three critical ranges of angular displacement of movement and sensory input: (1) an indifference range in which there is no detection; (2) a direction-specific range in which movement can be guided without disturbance before and during learning; and (3) a breakdown range in which movement is interrupted and must be guided in a discrete or irregular manner. In the breakdown range, the amount of learning needed to integrate movement and sensory input depends on the displacement magnitude.

Illustrated in the lower diagram of Figure 22 is the postulate of direction specificity through coordinate displacement of feedback, which states that the effects of different directions of disorientation vary as a function of the body coordinates affected. We assume that posture is related primarily to the effects of inversion and other feedback of the vertical displacements axis. In contrast, reversal of feedback is related to directional guidance of movements in particular horizontal planes of motion. These intrinsic direction specifications of behavior determine reaction and adaptation to particular conditions of inversion and right-left reversal of sensory feedback in motion. The concept of critical angles of displacement in determination of learning has been evaluated by methods illustrated in Figure 23, in which the methods and results of one major study by Smith and Smith (1962) on target location movements are illustrated. In this study, a television camera was oriented at zero, thirty, and sixty degree locations normal to the vertically-disposed target board. The findings support the view that critical angles of direction specificity are involved in both response guidance and learning. At the zero degree position, the amount of learning needed to reach a stable level of performance was limited. At thirty degrees the learning function was not changed, but the overall level of capability in adaptation was reduced. In contrast, the sixty degree displacement displayed a breakdown effect and the learning function was sharply elevated.

There are many other lines of evidence to support the theory that critical angles of feedback displacement determine directional guidance of response and the course of learning. Other experiments on eyemovement, posture, locomotion, and handmotion have shown that such motions are directionally guided and specialized in terms of critical angles of dynamic feedback displacement between movement and sensory input. Some movements, such as eyemovements, not only are direction specific but also have very small critical angles of displacement beyond which movement is seriously impaired. Such critical angles of displacement determine fusion for single vision in different directions of divergence and convergence (Smith, Gould and Wargo, 1963). Generally, the process of compensating the effects of any breakdown range of angular displacement also entails increasing the feedback timing of the motion.

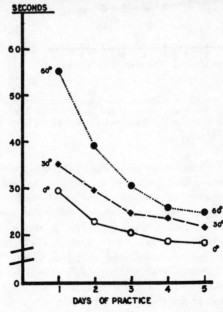

Fig. 23 Method and results of an experiment on the effects of different degrees of angular displacement of visual feedback of target location motions (Based on Smith & Smith, 1962).

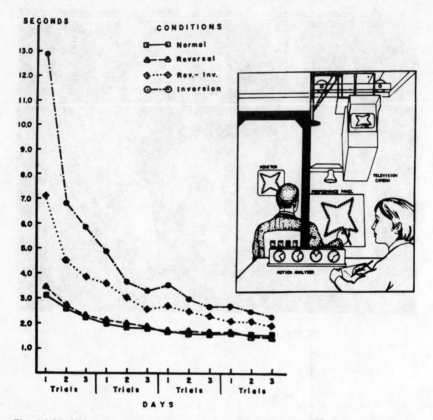

Fig. 24 Method and results of a quantitative comparison of the effects of reversal, inversion, and combined reversal and inversion of the visual feedback of star tracing motions on learning and performance (Based on Smith, Gould & Wargo, 1963).

As indicated in the lower diagram in Figure 22, the present systems view assumes that motions are also specialized in terms of the coordinate feedback displacement of sensory input of postural and travel movement systems. The experimental implication of this idea is that the effects of inversion, reversal, and combined inversion and reversal on particular motion systems will be significantly different. This experimental assumption was tested in at least ten different studies and was confirmed in all of them. The experiment described in Figure 24 shows how these three different modes of displacement of visual feedback—i.e., inversion, reversal, and combined inversion and reversal—were compared by means of cybernetic television methods. The task studied consisted of tracing a four-pointed star. The subject could not observe his own motions directly but had to guide his movements by watching the television monitor. The television camera used to view these movements was modified so that the orientation of the televised feedback of the subject's motions could be inverted, reversed, or both inverted and reversed by the flip of a switch. As shown by the learning curves in Figure 28, the effects of the inversion were more marked than either right-left reversal or combined inversion and reversal of feedback. These results agree with the assumption used to design the experiment, which was that inversion alone would have the most severe effect because the vertical postural mechanism is the most generalized of the integrative mechanisms of movement guidance. Also, inversion alone not only disturbs direct control by posture, but alters the normal coordinate relations between the postural and bilateral movement mechanisms and thus confuses the body tracking systems. Hence, inversion of feedback generally should cause more severe disturbance of guidance than combined inversion and reversal. This has been a consistent finding of additional studies carried out on other motion systems.

The learning curves in Figure 24 confirm another major assumption of the systems hypothesis of learning; namely, that the amount of learning needed to compensate a particular type of displacement will vary with the type and magnitude of the displacement. Not only does inversion of feedback cause the most perturbation in guidance of motion, it demands the greatest amount of learning to compensate for the breakdown effects. It will be noted that this compensation was not complete after several days of learning. This finding agrees with much longer studies on learning with inverted and reversed vision. These studies showed that subjects could never fully compensate inversion and reversal of feedback in drawing and writing even after twenty days of practice. These results agree with the objective studies of Ewert (1930), Peterson and Peterson (1938), and Snyder and Pronko (1952), in showing that human subjects, like animals, are never fully capable of compensating marked inversions of visual feedback of manual or body motions by learning.

Additional research on inversion of visual feedback has indicated that the extent to which individuals can adapt to and learn under displaced version depends entirely on the variable levels of movement control available to compensate the displacement. Thus, using the scleral contact-lens prism shown in Figure 25, the senior author (Smith, 1966a) studied to what extent the eye adapts to inversion of feedback of its own movements. When the eye was moved, the prism fixed to the scleral lens caused the retinal image to move in a direction opposite its normal orientation. As we mentioned earlier, this inversion of the feedback of eyemovement caused skittered vision. Although there was some reduction in the extent of this skittered vision after wearing the lens for as long as it could be tolerated (about forty-five minutes), it was still impossible to fixate objects at the end of the experimental period. These findings have been confirmed by studies of inversion of eyemovement feedback as produced by hybrid-computer control of an eye-yoked oscilloscope target. The findings indicate that the feedback of eyemovement cannot be inverted without impairing all the performance and learning functions of

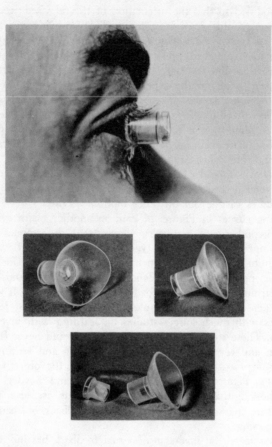

Fig. 25 Scleral contact lens used to invert eyemovement-retinal feedback (From Smith, 1966a).

vision, not only of the eye itself, but of all other parts of the body. Furthermore, there is little or no adaptation to this impairment.

The results of these space displacements can be accounted for in systems terms based on the understanding of the integration of the different components of posture and bilateral travel movements. The feedback mechanisms of these two movement systems create a coordinate up-down and right-left reference system for vertical and horizontal guidance of motion. Inversion of feedback affects this body reference system most because this mode of displacement disturbs the postural system and also disturbs the coordinate relations between the postural and travel components of the system. The learning functions of axial displacements of vision reflect these coordinate effects of inversion and other special distortions on motion. It may be noted parenthetically that these findings do not represent probings into the generalities of perception (Freedman, 1968), but apply specifically to many types of skilled performance, such as driving vehicles, altering the posture of the body in athletic skills like diving and jumping, using optical aids including ordinary spectacles, and performing with instruments of any sort, including athletic devices.

Additional meaning of spatial feedback factors in determining learning has been brought out in studies which showed that the ability to compensate inversion and reversals of visual-manual feedback develops late in childhood and corresponds roughly to the time that children develop a symbolic or conceptual sense of time. In these studies, boys from 9 to 15 years were tested for their ability to react to different conditions of televised inversion, reversal, and combined inversion and reversal of target location, writing, and drawing motions (Smith & Greene, 1963). The methods used were like those described in Figure 24. A very critical period of maturation at the age of about twelve years was found in the performance of the children, inasmuch as subjects younger than this age consistently failed to perform the drawing task with inverted visual feedback, whereas subjects older than this age showed few if any examples of complete failure. There was a fairly definite break at about age twelve between those who could do the tasks and those who could not. Of the boys aged 9, 10, and 11, there was only one who could perform under all conditions of feedback. Of the twenty-one boys aged twelve and thirteen years, there were eleven who could perform under all four conditions successfully and ten who could not. The difference between these two age groups was significant at the 5% level, using a corrected Chi square test for small frequencies.

The spatial feedback hypothesis of motion and learning assumes that the hundreds of thousands of distinct motions that the human individual can learn and perform in skilled athletic, tool-using, orientative, speech, musical, artistic, object-manipulation and social activities are specialized in ontogenetic development and adult learning as direction-specific responses. These movement patterns are based on detection of relative space-displacements of movement and of sensory input in bilateral activities. This view has been tested by measuring the number of significantly different direction-specific movements which are created by a combination of eight directions of movements in star tracing and four different conditions of inversion and reversal of feedback of these movements. Eight directions of movement were involved in the star-tracing task, and each of twenty-four subjects practiced four different axial displacement conditions. The actual experimental set-up used is illustrated in the laboratory television system diagrammed in Figure 26. Some of the main results are indicated by the lines of arrows in Figure 26. These lines represent results of Duncan (1955) range tests of the significance of differences for movement durations between the eight different directions of movements at each of the four displacement conditions. The results given represent the data for the last day of four practice days and indicate that over eighty, significantly different, direction-specific movements were produced by the different movement directions and displacement conditions.

Other results of this experiment confirmed the view that learning refines the directional-specificity of specialized motions, as produced by the relative space displacement and compliance between movement and sensory input. The critical findings were that the number of significantly-different, direction-specific movements increased by about thirty percent between the initial and final days of learning. The best interpretation of these findings is that the process of learning the nearly endless number of specialized movements which the body can perform is determined by the direction-specific feedback compliances in behavior and by the power to use such compliances not only to guide movements but to integrate them on a space-time-force basis.

DETERMINATION OF THE LEARNING
OF MOTIONS IN ATHLETIC SKILLS

As described previously, the systems theory of motor performance states that time and force factors in motion are derivative of or dependent on guidance factors. Stated formally, this idea represents a space-time doctrine which assumes that force and time feedback factors are relative and interdependent in the control and guidance of specialized skills. To shift the timing and force of motions it is necessary to alter their spatial feedback organization. This view also implies that dynamic space, time, and force feedback factors are more significant determinants of learning than static after-effects or reinforcements which arise after responses have taken place.

Dynamic Sensory-Feedback Factors As Determinants Of Learning

A primary issue raised by a sensory-feedback theory of learning is whether direct, closed-loop sensory effects of motor activity can induce learning. This issue was tested by Gould and Smith (1963), using cybernetic television methods to control the angular displacement of visual feedback of maze tracing and circle drawing motions. The design consisted of practicing twenty-four subjects in the two tasks. A direct view of the performance area was screened, while a television camera transmitted a substitute visual feedback image of the hand movements to the monitor screen in front of the subject. Different angular displacements were effected by placing a camera in different positions relative to the performance field. That is, changing the locus of the camera had the effect of altering the spatial relationships between the subject's motor and visual mechanisms. The subjects in this experiment were trained with displacements of 0, 20, 40, and 60 degrees.

The main point of design of this experiment was that the circle drawing task provided no significant means of feedback to the subject as to whether

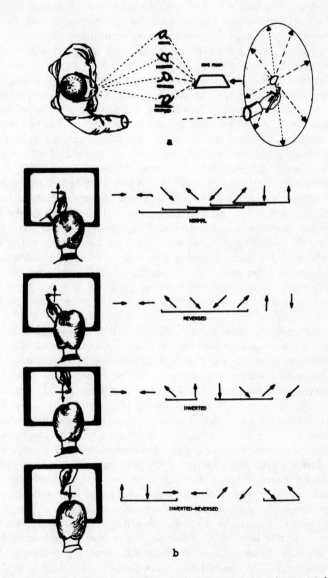

Fig. 26 An experimental demonstration illustrating that variations in spatial feedback compliance determine specialization of motion prior to and after learning. The arrows in the figure denote the number of statistically significant differences among eight different directions of movement in star tracing at four different conditions of feedback displacement of the motions. Common lines under different arrows specifying direction of movement denote means for movement directions that are not statistically significant from one another (Based on Smith & Smith, 1962).

he was drawing a true circle or not, since he had no means of knowing what the displacement angle happened to be in a particular trial. In contrast, by virtue of the markings defining the maze path, the maze task always gave a feedback indication of the precision of response independently of the angle of displacement.

The results of this experiment were very clear cut. No learning occurred with the circle-drawing task, in which sensory-feedback for specific movements could not be obtained. In contrast, learning occurred at all space displacements with the maze task, in which the subject obtained direct and immediate visual feedback of his movements. The conclusion from the study was that dynamic sensory feedback is not only an important factor in learning, but is a primary and essential determinant of learning.

The meaning of the experimental results just described above is that feedback determinants of learning may be either dynamic or static in nature. Dynamic feedback represents the continuous, real-time effect of the reactive, instrumental, and operational features of movement, whereas static feedback represents the persisting, delayed *after-effects* of a response on the environment. The static feedback of motion represents in part what traditional learning theorists have designated as *knowledge of results* and *reinforcement* in human learning. The term *informational feedback* also has been used to designate these static, operational after-effects of a given motion in learning (Bilodeau, 1966).

A major study was carried out (Smith, Ansell & Smith, 1963) to compare the relative advantages of dynamic feedback and static operational feedback in controlling performance and promoting learning. Television and videotape techniques were used to control separately the dynamic and static feedback of target location motions (See Fig. 4). The subject performed the task while observing a static image of the performance field in a television monitor. Meanwhile a televised image of performance was recorded on videotape. After the subject completed the dotting task, he was shown either a complete dynamic televised image of his movements or a static feedback image showing only the appearance of the target field at the end of his performance. Comparisons were made between the effectiveness of dynamic and static feedback with a normally oriented image and with an inverted-reversed image in determining performance accuracy and learning. The findings of this experiment indicated that the dynamic feedback condition was most effective in producing learning. Even the dynamic displaced condition was superior to the static conditions in determining level of learning and performance. The conclusion from this study is comparable to that from the angular displacement study: dynamic sensory feedback from movement itself is crucial for determining the course and level of learning.

Findings of this experiment should be interpreted in terms of the normal conditions of feedback obtained in learning situations. Normally, dynamic sensory effects of movement are not delayed, as they were in this study, whereas the static after-effects of the same movement are always delayed to some degree. This fact suggests that if dynamic and static effects of movement in learning were compared as they occur normally, the statistically significant differences in performance and learning observed in the experiment would be more marked. Dynamic sensory effects of movement are far more significant determinants of learning than the static after-effects or the so-called knowledge of results or informational feedback of performance. The results of the experiment, which represents just one example of several studies that have been done in this area, fully confirm the view that there are different sources of movement-controlled feedback in learning and that the immediate, dynamic sources are the most significant for determining acquisition.

Self-Generated Sensory Feedback As A Prime Determinant Of Learning

A principal assumption of the sensory feedback theory is that learning is determined primarily by the degree of self-regulated control of sensory input that the learner can impart to the learning situation. The greater the degree of self-determined control which the learner can impart to different parameters of feedback, the more rapid the learning and the greater its potential scope. Conversely, the more coercive and restrictive the learning situation and the greater the dependence of the learner on external environmental demands, the slower and narrower the scope of learning and the more unstable and inconsistent the learned response. This assumption is directly opposed to classical association and conditioning doctrines as well as to their current interpretation as stimulus-response reinforcement doctrines (Hull, 1943; Skinner, 1938, 1955).

Experiments on eye tracking (Colman, Huff & Smith, 1969; Smith, Putz & Molitor, 1966) have provided one source of information on the validity of the self-regulation hypothesis in the determination of learning. The experiment posed and answered the specific question as to whether closed-loop, self-generated stimuli are more decisive in determining performance and learning than the partially open-loop conditions of stimulus tracking, in which the individual is continually dependent on environmental stimulus variations to guide his movements.

The experiment was set up to compare the accuracy of eyemovement tracking when the subject's eye tracked an external computer-generated oscilloscope target (stimulus-tracking condition) and a hand-generated target path of the same pattern (self-regulated tracking condition). The subject wore a pair of transducing goggles fitted with photoresistors that sensed changes in eyemovement. The movements of one eye were recorded and the other eye was occluded. The computer diagram in Figure 27 illustrates in general how a hybrid analog-digital-analog computer system was arranged to yoke an oscillograph spot to eyemovements and thereafter to automate an experiment on comparing temporal proficiency in eyemovement tracking of self-generated and environmentally-produced visual targets. In these experiments the subject was fitted with an eyemovement transducer and the electrical signals from the transducer, eventually activated an oscilloscope target display.

The results of these feedback studies of eye-hand synchronism confirm the findings of a comparable type of study described earlier on reciprocal autonomic-physiological specialization through skilled motions. The results of both experiments show that learning is more rapid and performance more accurate with self-generated stimuli than with environmentally generated guidance. The experiments on eye-hand synchronism illustrate, in addition, that delay of feedback between hand and eye motion, which can occur in a variety of skills and athletic performances due to instrumental and environmental factors, can destroy the normal synchronisms of the eye in tracking the hand in the performance of common forms of steered or guided movements.

Role Of Feedback Timing In Learning

Earlier, the space-time relativity hypothesis of feedback theory was stated as being applicable to learning. Specifically, spatial factors in guidance of motion are primary in determining learning, while time factors are derivative and depend on the directional specialization of movements and sensory feedback of movements. A main corollary of this hypothesis is that time factors

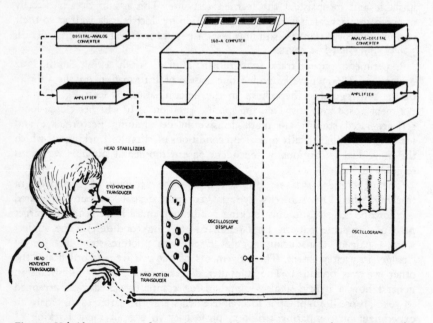

Fig. 27 Hybrid-computer and experimental vision station arranged to compare the time functions of eye tracking or self-generated and environmentally-generated targets.

in feedback are highly specific for control of particular movements and that feedback timing cannot be varied without disturbing both the performance and learning of motions.

Observations on the effects of feedback delay on learning of motions have confirmed the feedback relativity hypothesis. One example of these experimental observations was given in connection with Figures 8 and 9. Results of studies illustrated in those plates indicated that feedback delays of a few seconds or even a small part of a second severely impaired performance in breath-control tracking and prevented learning. These findings have been duplicated in other experiments on different motion patterns. The results show that particular motions and motorsensory interactions have built-in specialized feedback time characteristics and that these motorsensory patterns cannot be learned if their temporal characteristics are modified by even small parts of a second.

The results on feedback delay and learning represented a critical experimental turning point for learning theory, for these findings clarified for the first time the role of time factors in learning and memory processes. Classical theories related learning to time of *association between* responses or to *conditioning* and *reinforcement intervals,* which also referred to time relations between stimuli or responses. However, these theories never recognized the significance of the feedback interval—the interval between a movement and its sensory feedback—as a critical determinant of learning. Evidence for this statement rests on the fact that proponents of both associative and operant-conditioning stimulus-response theories hold that the conditioning and reinforcement intervals may be varied over seconds or even minutes without interfering with performance and learning (Hull, 1943; Spence, 1951). Equally important, stimulus-response theory contains no logical assumptions which would lead to the conclusion that variation in the interval between a movement and its generated stimuli would disturb performance as well as learning. Therefore, both classical and operant conditioning theories have professed to comprehend the stimulus-response determinants of learning but have formulated no ideas as to how the most important of the factors in the stimulus-response relationship can affect performance and learning.

A feedback doctrine is necessary to define the role of motorsensory time factors in learning and skill. Besides indicating that such timing is relatively fixed for a given spatial pattern of movement and cannot be varied without some alteration in the space pattern of a motion, other studies indicate that there are many parameters of such timing in addition to transmission delays. For example, there are many modes of variable delays and intermittency of feedback, as well as accelerations of closed-loop control, which can affect learning and memory. These findings suggest that feedback timing is a far more critical, diversified, and predictable determinant of human learning than anything thus far observed regarding reinforcement and conditioning time factors.

Feedback timing applies to receptor control and regulation of sensory

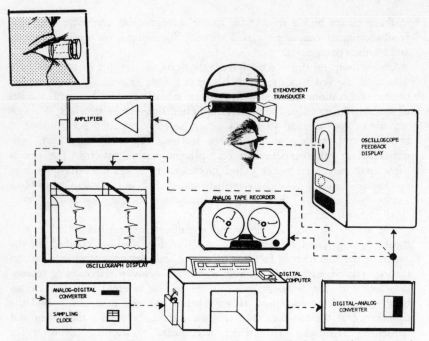

Fig. 28 Technique of producing eyemovement-retinal feedback delays by means of the hybrid-computer system (From Smith, Putz & Molitor, 1969).

processes as well as to governing of more general body movements. For example, the two eyes are not exactly conjugate in terms of the timing of their responses. One eye typically leads the other in visual response. Furthermore, these binocular time differences vary with the type of movement, whether pursuit or saccadic.

These results on time synchronism of the eyes in binocular vision correspond with other findings that accuracy of eyemovements and visual perception is very sensitive to delays between the action of external muscles in producing eyemovements and the occurrence of retinal stimulation resulting from such movements. Figure 28 illustrates the hybrid computer methods which have been used to produce feedback delays between ocular motion and retinal stimulation resulting from such motions. In the research conducted, the effects of feedback delay upon both compensatory or reversed eyemovement tracking and direct visual tracking were investigated. The experiments measured the effects of delay of retinal feedback of ocular movements. This feedback was experimentally controlled by yoking visual targets to the transduced electrical analog signals of eye motion by means of a hybrid-computer system. A photoelectronic eyemovement transducer and a real-time analog-digital-analog computer were set up to transduce a subject's eye position in viewing an oscilloscope target, to convert the electrical analog of sensed eye position to digital form, to program feedback delays into this digitized signal, and to deconvert the programed delayed signal back to analog form to actuate the oscilloscope feedback display which the subject viewed.

In this experiment, the oscilloscope target was yoked to the subject's eye-movements in a closed, dynamic relation by means of special experimental calibration and automation programs. The subject's head was fixed and eye-movements of one eye were transduced by photoelectric sensors mounted in a viewing device. At first the subject was required to fixate five successive target positions on the oscilloscope which were controlled by the computer system. During the successive fixations, the computer compared the respective eye and target positions and established a calibration of the proportionality of voltage values of ocular movements and target position. This calibration procedure was automated and performed at the beginning of each one-minute trial throughout the experiments. When the calibration was completed successfully, a computer program automatically locked the output control of the oscilloscope target to eye motions so that horizontal ocular motions thereafter caused the target to move in a compensatory way back and forth across the oscilloscope face.

The subject's task was to keep the oscilloscope target centered on a central zero mark of the display, while a computer program caused this spot to vary in a regular, smooth sine-wave pattern from this center position. Inasmuch as the target was yoked to the eyemovements in a reversed or compensatory feedback loop, the subject had to move his eyes in a direction opposite that of target action in order to bring the spot back to a center position. A precision magnetic tape record was made of the subject's eyemovement and eye tracking errors. This record was processed later by computer programing to measure the tracking error in keeping the oscilloscope target centered on the scope face.

In the second investigation of this experiment, the subject's eyemovements were yoked to a target cursor in a direct, positive feedback pursuit relation. Methods of experimental calibration and automated feedback-control programing similar to those described above were used, except for the fact that the yoke established between ocular motion and target movement was a positive one, so that when the subject moved his eyes the target spot moved compliantly in the same direction. In this investigation, the eyemovements actuated a light galvanometer which projected a target spot of 1-inch diameter on a cylindrical projection screen. A second light galvanometer actuated by a signal generator projected a second target spot on the projection screen. This spot moved in a sine-wave pattern back and forth across the screen. The subject's task was to keep his yoked target cursor matched in movement to the generated target motion. A precision FM tape recorder registered the voltage values of both the target signal generated and the subject's eyemovements. This record was processed later by computer programing methods to measure tracking error of the subject.

In both of these experiments, the computer was used as a variable time machine to vary the feedback delay interval between ocular motion and retinal input. The variable feedback delay was produced by "writing-in" and "reading-out" eyemovement signals at differentially spaced points in the memory cycle. In the first experiment, retinal feedback delays of 0.0, 0.1 and 0.2 second were used, while in the pursuit experiment delays of 0.0, 0.2 and 0.4 second were used.

The main results of the two studies consisted of the functions relating error in eyemovement tracking to delay magnitude. These two functions are shown in Figure 29, with results of the compensatory tracking given to the left. The curves indicate that the effects of the feedback delays were quite similar in the two types of eyemovement retinal interactions, and that delays of 0.1 to 0.2 second had a marked effect on vision and eyemovement control.

The results of this experiment on compensatory tracking confirm and add to observations made on wearing a miniature dove prism that was attached to a scleral contact lens and reversed the feedback of horizontal eyemovements. This contact-lens prism also caused very painful skittered vision. The results of both experiments negate repeated claims that complete adaptations can be made to reversed vision through learning. It may be possible to adapt hand, arm, head, and body motions to reversed vision, but not eyemovements themselves. The repeated statements of learning theorists from Helmholtz to the present that adaptation to reversed vision can be learned have been based on an experimental misconception and error that reversal of the visual effects of body and head movements is equivalent in every way

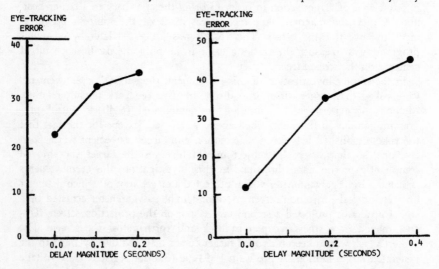

Fig. 29 Feedback delay functions for compensatory and pursuit eyemovement tracking (From Smith, Putz & Molitor, 1969).

to reversal of eyemovement-retinal interaction. When the retinal feedback of eyemovements is dynamically reversed, as it was in these studies, it is impossible for the eye to fixate images in an effective way.

In the present tracking task, the effects of retinal delay on the direct pursuit vision were insidious. Except for the fact that vision was persistently ineffective and inaccurate, the subject sensed no unusual visual or painful effects. Time-distorted retinal input was experienced, not as a timing defect, but as space-displaced vision which could not be controlled. The results give some clues to the significance of an heretofore unexplored sector of ocular dynamics in determining effective seeing in all types of visual tasks. To what extent are common defects of seeing the results of disturbed oculomotor, accommodative, and retinal timing, and to what extent are they purely optical defects? Overall, the results suggest that precise feedback timing is another one of the imperatives of effective seeing.

The findings of these timing studies on vision are particularly significant in comprehending the role of feedback delay in the motorsensory control of athletic skills. The evidence is that the limbs, head, and receptor systems are specialized both directionally and temporarily to perform distinctive guidance and positioning motions, not only to respond to environmental stimuli, but to track coordinately other parts of the body. (Shuenzel, Tait and Smith, 1969). The athlete's eyes and ears must be timed and exercised to refine time synchronism with body movements, and factors in body form and instrumental design must be adjusted to eliminate deleterious space displacements and feedback delays of receptor input which can impair coordination between receptor operations and body movements.

Learning And Memory As Dynamic Time Spanning Processes

The evidence that learning is controlled by dynamic, feedback timing factors has been complemented by results of several special studies which have shown that learning and memory are time-spanning processes that are determined by space-time factors in feedback. Learning occurs most efficiently when the pattern of response persists as a perceived, operational, sensory-feedback effect of movement, thus creating a spanned temporal memory record of past response. The more complete this persisting spatial feedback pattern of response, the more rapid and efficient the learning and the more complete the memory record.

The dynamic time-spanning functions of learning and memory have been investigated by Smith and Sussman (1969a) by means of tracking methods. Subjects were required to reproduce a tracked wave pattern much like that illustrated in Figure 30. Two conditions of tracking were compared, one in which subjects observed and tracked the wave pattern visually and a second in which the wave pattern was tracked both visually and manually. In addition, the extent to which the wave pattern persisted as a spatial pattern during the learning trials also was varied. As shown in Figure 31,

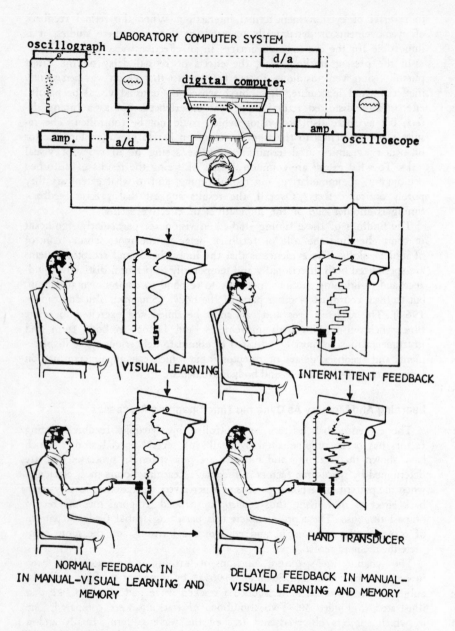

Fig. 30 Technique of using the hybrid-computer system to study learning and memory in visual and visual-manual tracking as dynamic, interrelated processes of motorsensory feedback and feedforward control of motion (Based on Smith & Sussman, 1969b).

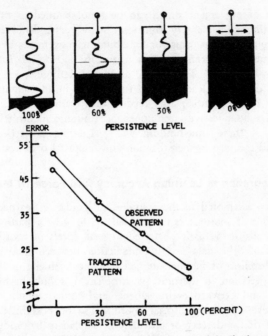

Fig. 31 Curve showing the effects of spatial persistence of feedback on memory under conditions of observational and visual-manual tracking of a stimulus pattern (From Smith & Sussman, 1969a).

the results indicated that the accuracy of memory reproduction varied directly in proportion to the spatial persistence of the wave pattern. No differences were found between the two conditions of observation by vision and by visual-manual tracking during learning.

The results of this study brought out the fact that memory is a dynamic time-spanning process which functions to do more than give a record of past movement and perception. In addition, it operates as a feedforward control process to project movement into the future. This conclusion was indicated in the memory tests used in the experiment, which were designed to require reproduction of the wave pattern by projecting this pattern in terms of both its time and space properties after it was observed for fifteen seconds. As tested in this way, memory was manifest as a dynamic capability of the subject to predict the course of a target as well as to recall the nature of past response and perceptions. The findings were that the accuracy of such memory prediction is a direct function of the space-time compliance and persistence of the dynamic sensory effects of movement.

The conclusion from these and other observations is that the primary determination of all aspects of learning and memory is related to the direct sensory effects of movement which can be time spanned to project future motion. Learning and memory function as interdependent feedback and feedforward control mechanisms for time-binding movements over particular space-time spans that permit prediction and projection of future motion and perception of objects. The factors of spatial, temporal, and force compliance which determine learning also function to build memory and make it into a predictive and anticipatory feedforward control process over future time spans. To be effective, techniques of training in athletics must be designed around these time-binding and space-time projection functions of learning and memory in specialization and temporal organization of skill.

Feedback Integration In Learning Accuracy And Force Of Motion

The evidence assembled in these studies of guidance, learned specialization, and timing of motions can be added up to give a partial picture of how athletic skills are actually perfected to peak levels of coordination and efficiency. Overall, the data on the interaction between guidance, timing, and time synchronism of motions suggest that most athletic motions involve extraordinary precision in dynamic synchronism, not only between the eye and the hand and between eyemovements and retinal input, but also between every level of neuromuscular coordination of posture, travel movement, manipulation and receptor articulation. The main by-products of such dynamic coordination are not simply guidance and timing. Included also is the regulation of the force of motion, which represents the effective combination of coordinate guidance and timing of the different components of motion to achieve power in the execution of a focal movement. When posture, travel manipulation, and receptor actions are accurately guided and timed, superior force occurs naturally and without special effort and strain.

Postural movements, with their coordinate mechanisms of gravitational and dynamic movement regulation, constitute an activation system for producing a stage or framework for particular travel movements of the head, limbs, and torso. As these members move to execute a motion, as in running or throwing, the postural mechanism tracks the flow of dynamic movement and compensates the effects of the motion on gravitational control. As the travel movement is initiated, its path is predetermined and projected by a quick burst of contraction. In addition, the manipulative movements and articulated receptor motions to be performed are also initiated and projected in a predictive way in relation to the pattern of the travel movement. For example, even before the travel movement of the arm in grasping or throwing reaches its termination, the hand and finger manipulations to be used are initiated in a predictive manner. Therefore, when the hand reaches the object to be grasped, the finger-hand pattern is formed to complete the grasping movement. As we noted above, in high precision manipulations, the travel movements defining the dynamic substrate of the finer movements must be carried out as a continuous motion with follow-through action in order for this predictive feedforward guidance and timing of manipulation to occur accurately and with maximum force. Much the same thing may be said for receptor functions and motions. For the eye to see accurately or the ear to hear with maximum precision, the head and eyes must adjust dynamically to larger travel movements of the limbs, head, and torso so that before these movements are completed, the head and eye initiate projected movements which establish a trajectory that predicts the occurrence of the finer manipulative movements of the task. When the focal manipulative movements finally occur, the head and ocular motions are appropriately oriented and adjusted for maximal guidance of the articulated movements of the hand or foot.

For a motion to execute effective force and power, the pattern of postural regulation and predictive feedforward guidance and timing of finer manipulative and receptor movements must be integrated in a unified pattern around the most rapid and dynamic phase of the travel movement. It is this feedback integration of the different component motions around the most rapid phase of the high-speed travel motion which makes possible execution of maximum power of the body near the focal point of the skilled action. The challenge faced by every athlete is to gain some insight into this pattern of dynamic coordination of different component movement mechanisms as it is related to his own distinctive body make-up and athletic activity.

Visual Versus Tactual Tracking In The Development Of Motion Skills

The common view in psychology is that motion skills are developed in the individual through progressive dominance of vision over the tactual and kinesthetic system during development. According to this view, visual control represents a superior form of guidance that is not equalled by tactual and kinesthetic reactions. Systems studies of interreceptor feedback control have suggested that these classical ideas about the comparative role of the visual and tactual receptors in particular motions represent a gross misconception which can be supported by only limited experimental facts. The results of these systems studies suggest, for example, that tactually guided tracking is far superior in many ways to visually guided tracking and that tactual modes of guidance are essential for developing smooth, continuously controlled tracking movements and smooth bilaterally coordinated motions.

Figure 32 illustrates the meaning of tactual tracking as it can be tested in a general way by finger and hand motions. The top diagram suggests that a blindfolded girl can follow movements of another person in an accurate way by light tactual contact with the fingers of the other person. When the girl tries to track the same movements with visual guidance, irregular inaccurate movements occur. This same superiority of tactual tracking occurs in any situation in which the two forms of guidance can be accurately compared. The results of these observations suggest that smooth uninterrupted movements, which are a requisite for most athletic skills, are not only developed in maturation, but also are perfected in learning and exercise by tactual tracking.

The experimental demonstration just given implies that body motions in skill, to be performed smoothly and accurately, need the support of tactual contact with other people or with other physical objects. Design of club handles and the surfaces of balls is very important in providing stimulus sources for such tactual control.

The significance of tactual tracking and its marked superiority over visual guidance may be demonstrated experimentally in terms of bimanual finger or hand dancing (Figure 33). The comparison in this figure indicates

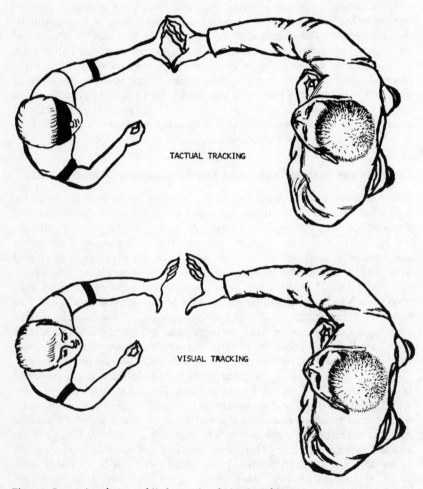

Fig. 32 Comparison between blind-tactual and visual tracking.

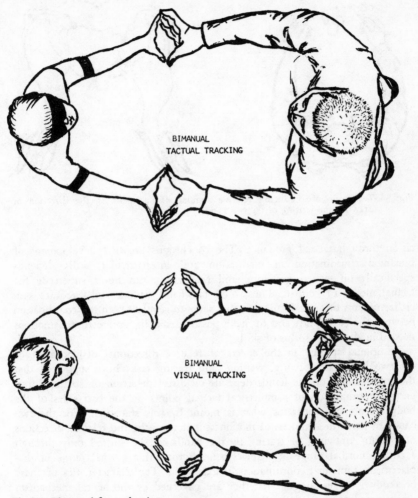

Fig. 33 Bimanual finger dancing.

that a blindfolded subject can tactually track hand movements of another person with smooth precise movements of both hands. These smooth movements can be made by the subject with either symmetrical or asymmetrical bimanual variations in the task. However, when required to perform the same simultaneous bimanual tracking with visual guidance only, the subject was completely lost, especially in performing tasks involving asymmetrical movements. Systematic observations of this sort have shown that bimanual tracking is nearly impossible with vision but can be developed to high pre-

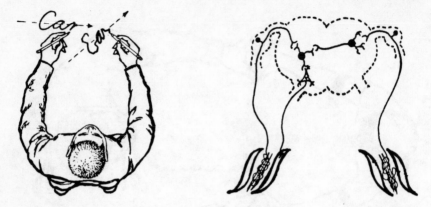

Fig. 34 Technique of producing relative angular displacement of the direction of
drawing and writing of the two hands.

cision through tactual guidance. The conclusions are that development of
bimanual coordination in maturation and in particular skills depends
specifically on tactual guidance, and that vision can never supercede the
tactual modes of control. Thus, most two-hand athletic skills require specialized forms of tactual guidance that serve to regulate both the coordination
between the two hands and to make possible smooth, uninterrupted motions
needed in almost all forms of skill.

Additional studies on the effects of relative directional displacement of
the two hands in drawing, writing, and tracing tasks have suggested that
the coordination of the hands depends on direct detection of spatial differences in stimulation of symmetrical tactual points on the two sides of the
body. Figure 34 illustrates what is meant by this statement. For the two
hands to perform symmetrical motions simultaneously, the relative directions
of writing, drawing, or tracing by the hands can be shifted only through
a critical normal range of displacement. Beyond this normal range of displacement, bimanual coordination breaks down. The characteristics of these
breakdown ranges suggest that they are governed by the neural mechanism
diagrammed to the left in the figure. Direction-specific neurons located at
different levels of the nervous system detect the spatial, tactual differences in
stimulation and guide movements within the normal ranges of bilateral displacement of feedback. When the angle of bilateral displacement exceeds
the critical range, these direction-specific feature detectors no longer sense
systematic differences from paired tactual points on the two sides of the
body and bimanual movement coordination disintegrates.

The overall meaning of these studies of tactual and bimanual tracking
for athletics is that tactual control cannot be dismissed as an incidental form
of guidance which is superceded by vision during the course of development.
The weaknesses of classical and current psychological thinking in depreciating

tactual control are based on the fact that these traditions have never comprehended or dealt with continuously controlled motions, as used in athletic skills. These stimulus-response or S-R theoretical traditions in psychology have been built exclusively around generic concepts of discrete response and have no resources to deal with continuously guided motions. The findings described here discredit the application of these outworn ideas in the analysis of athletic skills and suggest in addition that feedback and systems ideas are needed to specify the characteristics of uninterrupted smooth motions and their relations with tactual and visual tracking.

SOCIAL FEEDBACK IN ATHLETIC SKILL

The concept of social behavioral feedback is a new idea in psychology and social science, which may be used to describe the actual motor and sensory mechanisms that are involved in interpersonal and group interactions. The theory fills a great void in social psychology since it is the first to go beyond overgeneralized motivational and learning dogma to describe how performance and skill occur at the social level. Concepts and methods of studying social feedback mechanisms are particularly relevant to the fields of athletics and physical behavior science since they can be used to define a language for the design and exploration of the parameters and factors of organization and specialization of social performances in interpersonal coordination, competition, and team play.

One of the main challenges which has faced the development of sciences of athletic and work skill has been the understanding of the interactions between social, behavioral, and biological processes in determining specialization and organization of performance in biosocial and cultural adaptations. By being concerned mainly with motivation based on conflict and frustration, past psychoanalytic, classical conditioning, and reinforcement views of social processes have failed to deal with the positive factors in social interaction, as these occur in team play and interpersonal coordination of response and group patterns. Social feedback theory deals primarily with these positive factors in social interaction and with the development of a scientific language which can be used to describe the variable parameters and dimensions of both positive and competitive social interplay. This theory is applied in the present section to a description of principles of social tracking in athletics and sports.

The primary concept of a social systems interpretation of athletic skill is that of *social feedback control*. Generally, this term refers to the processes of active or dynamic motorsensory interaction between two or more people. The concept implies that when individuals interact socially or biosocially, they become locked together in an organized way that affects the physiological, autonomic, and organic mechanisms as well as neuromuscular-receptor mechanisms of performance. When individuals interact with one another in a sustained way, as in team play or competition, they become locked or yoked together through social tracking and thus achieve a level of organization and specialization of closed-loop control that is quite different from individual response. In biosocial tracking, two or more individuals productively generate movements and follow one another by means of linked and crossed motor-sensory feedback circuits. To be able to link their response and receptor systems in closed feedback arrangements with each other, two animals or individuals each must be able to produce movements that represent stimulus analogues of responses of the other organism, and vice versa (Fig. 35). In individual response, one person yokes his muscular movements to his own receptor action and orientation by feedback control of stimulus selection. In social tracking, the same type of motorsensory yokes occur, except that the motor activity of one person is locked as a stimulus source to response-controlled receptor input of the second person, and vice versa. Two individuals thus can continue to respond by each generating response-related sensory stimulation and analogues of the other's movement. Precision, efficiency, rhythm and compliance in all levels of social interplay are assumed to be related to the conditions and modes of social tracking.

Development Of Social Tracking Skills

One of the first questions posed by a systems feedback theory of social behavior was whether social tracking is important in development and matura-tion of motor, perceptual, and social skills in the child. The answer to this question was given indirectly in relation to the earlier description of the events of tactual tracking (Figs. 32 & 33). During infancy and childhood, tactual tracking, as governed by the abilities and habits of parents and sib-lings, is crucial to maturation of smooth, coordinated movements of limbs and receptors in the child. That is, other people constitute the primary re-source available to the baby and child for following and tracking environ-mental stimuli both tactually and visually, thereby promoting maturation of the graded neuromuscular and sensory mechanisms underlying athletic skills and social interaction.

Various special tactual, optical, electronic, and television techniques were devised to test maturation and learning of social tracking in young children. The main results of these investigations were that social, tactual, visual, and auditory tracking are present without special training in infants between six months and three years of age. Years before children can reproduce static forms in drawing and other movements, babies and young children can follow active movements of others in making distinctive forms that are later per-ceived as letters, numbers, and object forms. In other words, for several years before school age the child both develops smooth, graded, continuously-controlled movements and learns specific perceptions and motor functions by dynamically tracking the movements of others.

The different observations on social tracking in development have dis-closed that dynamic, self-governed feedback factors, as contrasted to en-

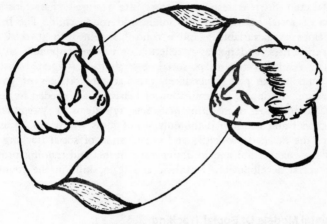

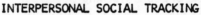

INTERPERSONAL SOCIAL TRACKING

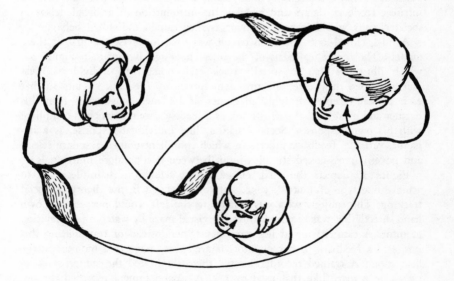

GROUP SOCIAL TRACKING

Fig. 35 The social tracking hypothesis. Interpersonal and group interactions are based on mutual, closed-loop, motorsensory feedback interaction. Top: Mutual yoked interpersonal feedback. Bottom: Yoked group social tracking (From Smith, 1967b)

vironmental and discrete response factors, are featured characteristics of maturation of social behavior in the infant and young child. The baby or child develops as a variable adaptive control system with marked social tracking capabilities, and not as a reflector or passive responder to social stimuli. The results of the infant social research have suggested that new concepts, quite unlike past generalized, mass action doctrines of environment, learning, and innate determination of behavior, are needed to describe these variable properties of maturing motorsensory systems. A systems concept of development and learning is the only set of ideas which can be used to account for the detailed properties and organization of social tracking capabilities of the young child and to design experiments and training programs related to social development of athletic and team skills in the young boy or girl.

Experimental Models Of Social Tracking

The theory of variable, dynamic, feedback control of social tracking has been substantiated by creating specific, experimental models of mutual, yoked tracking between two persons, and by delineating the variable feedback properties of such tracking. One of the first of such experiments tested whether particular social motorsensory interactions between two people may involve intrinsic feedback delays and whether the introduction of artificial delays in social circuits would impair behavior as they can in individual behavior.

A dual, closed-loop television circuit was used to devise the first of these models. The theoretical basis of the research design is shown in Figure 35, which illustrates that to socially track each other, two individuals must mutually yoke themselves in crossed motorsensory feedback circuits so that each person receives stimulus analogues of his own movements from his partner and must control such stimuli as a feedback source which is compliant with his own responses. Social tracking, like individual response, is a dynamic, variable, feedback process in which compliant mutual response selects and governs cross-yoked stimulus input between two or more individuals.

Figure 36 depicts the dual, closed circuit television chain designed to achieve one type of mutual, yoked interplay defined in the theory of social tracking. The subject, who was located to the left, could not see her own hand directly but was required to trace a visual maze by watching a television monitor. A camera viewed her movements, but instead of transmitting this image as a feedback to her monitor, relayed this image to a monitor in the next room. A trained recorder located there duplicated the subject's movements on a maze like that used by her. A second camera recorded the observer's movements and transmitted this mediated image back to the subject's monitor, who viewed it as a socially yoked feedback source.

The critical dynamic properties of the televised social yoke were studied systematically by having the trained observer-reproducer introduce feedback delays in the social loop. Results indicated that with the precautions used to

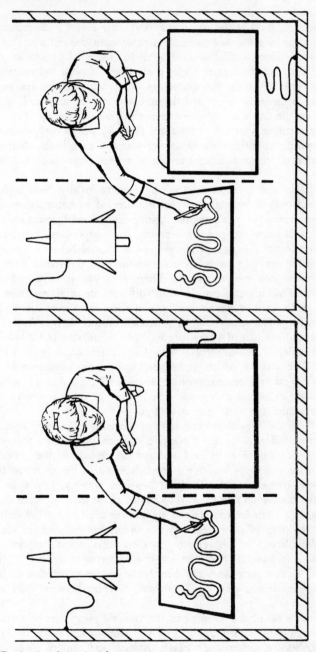

Fig. 36 Dual, closed-circuit laboratory television circuit used in one of the first experimental studies of social tracking in adults (Based on Smith & Smith, 1962).

prevent identification of the observer's hand, only 1 of 12 subjects suspected he was not tracking his own hand. The experiment showed also that, in the type of social loops described in Figure 36, there is a variable, intrinsic feedback delay which impairs tracking efficiency of both individuals in the loop. Figure 37 illustrates the differences between nondelayed tracing of the maze used in this experiment and the accuracy of four subjects in the social loop during the last trial of fifteen training trials. Generally, there was no significant learning with any of the three feedback delays used, including the shortest, which represented the fastest transmission time in the chained loop. Longer artificial delays reduced tracking to a level comparable to blind performance.

The finding that some social tracking circuits involve built-in feedback delays which impair learning and performance led to systematic exploration of the parameters of motorsensory yoking and interorganization between people that can lead to positive learning in interpersonal behavior. This analysis led to the discovery that interpersonal social behavior involves not one but many variable modes of cross connecting the motor and sensory mechanisms of two or more people. There are many positive and negative dimensions of yoking two people which differentiate imitation from mutual interplay, as in sexual behavior, and both of these from competitive play and warfare activity. The sensory signals generated by, and derived from, motions of one person in a pair of interacting individuals can vary and may represent either the analog of movement itself or some transformation of error in motor response. The way in which each individual in an interpersonal pattern relates to the external environment or situation affecting the two persons can vary, so that one person may act as a buffer for the other or the two people may react coordinately to the external stimuli.

Thus, there are many different modes of movement and error signaling, as well as many different modes of positive, compensatory, and complementary feedback regulation of individual and systems signals in the closed-circuit loop. A main finding of additional research was that the more the tracking arrangement between two individuals provides systems signals as an immediate feedback source to the two individuals, the more accurate the tracking. Also, when nondelayed systems signals are available to the individuals in social tracking, effective learning can occur, but only under such nondelayed conditions. In this research, systems social signals represent some combination or integration of the errors or movement signals of the two individuals so that each can sense directly the nature or accuracy of his own movements in determining the organized interplay between him and his partner.

Some indication of the meaning of the variable parameters of social tracking in athletic skill can be indicated by the diagram in Figure 38. This diagram describes the differences between chained, and bridged, linked motorsensory circuits in social tracking. The completely closed system shown at the top is comparable to that studied with the dual television setup described

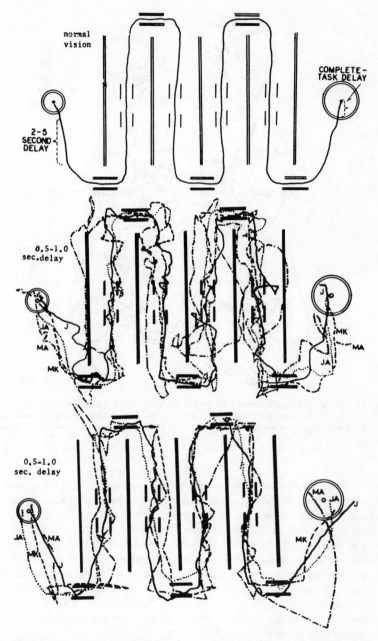

Fig. 37 Comparison between individual non-delayed tracing and the accuracy of four subjects in the first and in the fifteenth trials of training in social tracking involving linked social delays (Based on Smith & Smith, 1962).

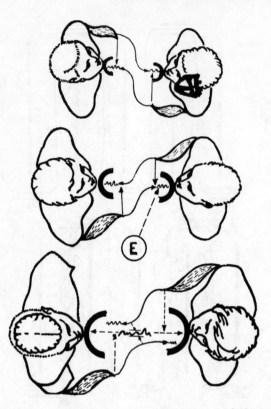

Fig. 38 Modes of systems control of social tracking. Top: Linked, closed-loop social circuit without systems error control. Middle: Linked social circuit with external perturbation but without a systems error control. Bottom: Combination of individual errors and/or movement indicators of the two individuals to create a systems feedback of social tracking (Based on Smith, 1967b).

earlier. It also models all forms of closed or intimate social behavior, such as that involved in sexual behavior, maternal activity, and forms of interpersonal communication such as therapeutic interviewing. The chained environmental control pattern is comparable to the television situation, except that the mutual social feedback is being perturbed in a variable way by a third source of dynamic activity in the environment. In this type of tracking, one of the partners must govern this source of stimulation while also tracking sensory information received from the other partner. This situation is comparable to the wife who must track her husband, who is adjusting to situations outside the home as well as to her, but who gives her only an indication of his errors as feedback.

In a bridged social circuit, each of the partners receives an indication of their combined error in reacting to each other besides getting an indication of their own individual error in tracking each other. This combined error is a systems measure and is necessary to eliminate the feedback delays due to chaining in social tracking. Normally, a bridging effect is achieved because one level of motor control is used to compare the mutual synchronism and rhythm and positions in body action and movement between the two partners, while individual sources of error are controlled by some other level of action.

Each of these basic types of social tracking can vary in terms of other parameters of social feedback control. As shown in Figure 39(a), the positivity or negativity of feedback regulation can vary to determine how the social interaction pattern may be specialized and organized. In one case, the two individuals can follow one another positively and thus duplicate the motions of one another as in mutual imitation. Or the two individuals may compensate or oppose the actions of each other, thus giving the basic pattern of competition. Other variations on this parameter of control includes complementary forms of response in which one individual produces a positive mode of response and the other generates the negative or compensatory pattern of this reaction. Such mutual complementary modes of adaptation define almost all forms of intimate sexual behavior as well as interpersonal and team coordination in athletic skill.

The diagrams in Figure 39(b) illustrate the difference between error tracking and movement tracking in social behavior. In responding to each other, one individual may sense and control the difference between his own motions and that of the other (error) or he may directly observe the sensory effects of the movements of the other (movement detection). These two modes of detection may be combined in various ways to give integrated modes of social error detection and movement tracking.

The bottom diagram in Figure 39(c) illustrates the variable dimensions of environmental control in social interaction. The main principle is that the social interplay is specialized and organized in terms of the individual who controls environmental or social stimuli external to the closed social circuit. In one basic mode of such control, called the *linked circuit,* one individual controls external environmental sources while also reacting to the other person. In this linked circuit, each person's response depends on his receiving prior information from his partner, thus creating an inherent delay in the social loop. In contrast to this linked pattern, both individuals in the pair may control external sources of stimulation while also reacting to one another. In this parallel circuit, the response to the environment is not delayed although each person may not get immediate feedback as to how the other is regulating the external source.

Experimental Social Feedback Analysis

To evaluate some of the detailed assumptions of the social tracking hypothesis, systems studies on the mechanisms of social tracking have been con-

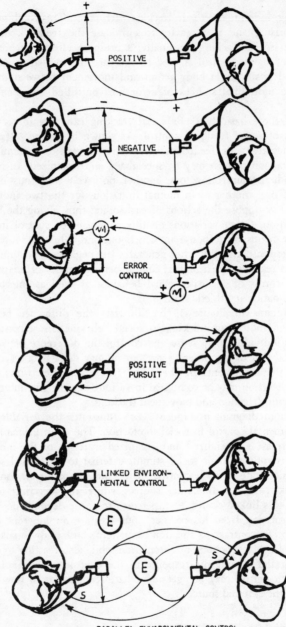

Fig. 39 General modes of feedback control of social tracking. a: Positive and nega-
    tive modes. b: Error detection and movement detection. c: Chained and parallel
    social tracking (Based on Smith, 1967b).

ducted. This research was based on use of hybrid-computer experimental methods, one example of which is described in Figure 40. The results of these studies provided scientific proof of the feedback regulation of social tracking and of the systems nature of behavior control in such tracking patterns. The studies substantiated directly that social behavior can be modelled as mutual, crossed, motorsensory circuits, as illustrated earlier in Figure 35.

The main issue raised in the experimental feedback study of social tracking was whether it could be shown that systems measures of error in tracking are different from individual sources of error, and whether a systems feedback effect will produce social coordination of a level superior to individual error. To conduct such studies, a hybrid-computer social behavior laboratory was developed to control the feedback parameters of yoked social tracking on a realtime basis (i.e., actual and continuous time basis) and to automate experiments in this area.

The diagram in Figure 40 shows how two subjects may be yoked together in a visual-manual tracking task by means of the hybrid-computer system so that each receives feedback that is mediated by the other. Numbers in the diagram indicate the sequence of steps involved in using the computer for variable feedback control of the social tracking: (1) manual movements of Subject 1 are transduced to an analog signal and transmitted to an amplifier; (2) this signal operates the oscillograph display used by Subject 2; (3) the tracking movements of Subject 2 are transduced, amplified, and sent to the analog-digital converter and to off-line recording devices; (4) the digitized signal is transmitted to the digital computer where it is programed for experimental variations, such as feedback intermittency, displacement, or delay; (5) this computer-controlled signal is relayed to a digital-analog converter and amplifier; and (6) the reconverted signal activates the oscillograph display unit of Subject 1 as a computer-controlled, yoked social feedback stimulus.

Results of social tracking experiments with the hybrid computer have indicated three ways in which feedback accuracy or error can be controlled in this type of experiment—i.e., systems error, individual error, and linked error. To get a systems error, error of the two subjects in tracking the input wave as transmitted to them from the computer is combined—i.e., added, integrated, or differentiated—and the combined error measure presented to each subject as a feedback source. In contrast, in individually linked social tracking each subject can receive only an error signal from his partner, or a linked error signal, and never knows what his error or the overall systems error may be. In this individual error situation, the subject gets an indication of his own error in controlling a movement or error signal received from his partner. He knows how effectively he is controlling the stimulus input coming to him but has no means of knowing whether he or the system is causing the error. By obtaining quantitative measures of systems and individual error in social tracking, we have been able to demonstrate for the

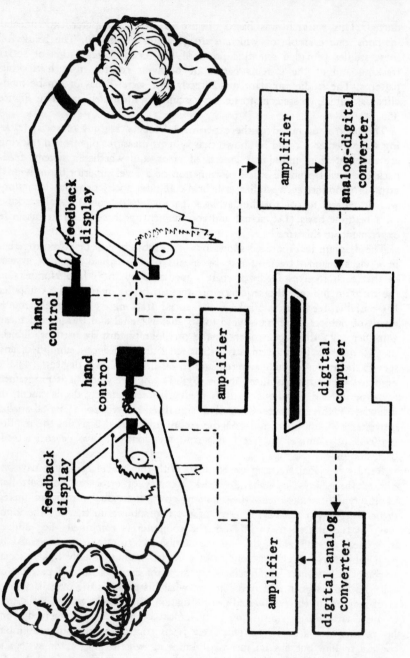

Fig. 40 Hybrid-computer system for the systems study of social tracking (Based on Smith, 1967b).

first time that social interactions between two human individuals in performance are organized most efficiently on a systems basis in which the two persons get a meaningful indication of the overall or combined performance of
the persons involved. The most efficient pattern of tracking is when a combined indication of individual error and synchronized systems error is obtained.

A main finding has been that when a systems error is not made available
to both subjects, subjects perform poorly, learn little, and quickly lose
motivation to respond. This is due to the fact that such non-systems tracking
introduces delays and poor information transfer in the interaction, thereby
segregating the persons involved and reducing their feeling of unity. In
series-linked social circuits, feedback delays operate to degrade tracking ability
below the level of individual performance. In parallel social circuits, which
lack an indication of a combined systems error, the two subjects never actually
know how they are synchronizing together. In contrast, combined systems
feedback error, which may be controlled by both subjects, eliminates errors,
provides critical target information, and greatly improves the precision of
tracking.

In keeping with assumptions stated earlier, it has been found that the
basic pattern of yoked social control of the environment can be varied in
systematic ways in closed social yokes. Instead of controlling the sensory
analogs of movement negatively or in a compensatory way, each member
can be made to control the sensory analogs of movements, errors, or transformations in a positive way by pursuit tracking. And instead of transmitting
either movement information or error, combinations of such information, or
integrations and differentiations of such information, can be transmitted.
Furthermore, the patterns of direct and compensatory control can be varied
between members, so that one follows the environment and the second attempts to compensate for errors made.

The fact that diverse experimental models of these yokes can be created
and studied gives a beginning substantiation of the theoretical systems-feed-
back assumptions regarding selective social tracking in terms of which the
experimental methods and procedures were designed. Social tracking, as
used in athletics and elsewhere, represents variable feedback control of both
the signals that are received and the mixture of the signals transmitted between individuals constituting interpersonal and group organizations. Such
organizations are not specialized in terms of the mass action effects of conflict motivation and reinforcement learning. Rather, their integration and
specialization depend on the variable parameters, dimensions, and patterns
of reciprocal closed motorsensory feedback control.

Social Tracking In Group And Team Organization

The main finding of the present experimental research with social tracking
has been to show that when a combined systems sensory signal or error is

provided to the two partners in a tracking loop, they can track with an efficiency which is elevated above the level of individualized errors in a social circuit. The research also indicated that there are many different patterns of linked and parallel modes of social tracking, each of which may be based on either positive or compensatory forms of feedback control. The principal conclusion is that it is the unification or merging of two or more people in unified compliant motorsensory loops that constitutes the real meaning and motivation of all major forms of social behavior, including the various interpersonal, group, and team patterns of athletic and sports behavior. Although controlled experiments are not extensive, it is possible to extend feedback theory and the results of experiments thus far described to the analysis of group and team behavior.

As suggested in Figure 41, group and team behavior typically involves three aspects of social tracking which have not been described in the closed interpersonal circuits thus far discussed. These patterns include social-interaction tracking (a), transformed social tracking (b), and individual-group tracking (c). The diagram of social-interaction tracking suggests that individuals not only track the movement and errors transmitted as signals by others; they also track the relations between two or more persons and act in terms of detected variations in such relationships. Such interaction tracking very likely is the basis of sophisticated social behavior and of all forms of effective team play. In it, a third individual reacts in one way when the relation of two or more other persons are in one state and responds in other ways as the interaction changes between the other people. A wife may disrobe when alone with her husband but would not think of such an action if both her sister and husband were present together. In team play, an effective player senses both the actions of other individual players and their interactions with one another. Many effective secret communications in team play can be developed in terms of subtle interplay between two or more members which act as signs only when the two persons are joined in a distinct way.

Most social behavior is self-generated and highly variable as a continuously changing activity which is guided and organized in the context of systems of customs, rules, language, and specialized tools and machines. The basis of this fluid activity is the fact that social interaction involves continuously transformed systems interactions as well as direct social tracking between the individuals concerned. Thus, two people may follow each other not only in a yoked motorsensory loop, but also talk in a continuously varied pattern of language. As a game proceeds, the specific actions may vary in the general context of team rules and procedures. Both interpersonal and team modes of variable, productive, social tracking depend on the fact that one segment of a social circuit can track what has been said or done by another and then transform this tracked pattern into a succeeding related pattern of action. Such dynamic transformations are based on memory and feedforward control of past and current social tracking and give continuity and general meaning to sustained interpersonal and group interactions. The transforma-

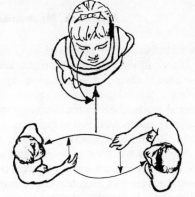

RELATIONAL SOCIAL TRACKING

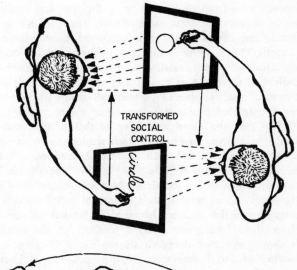

TRANSFORMED
SOCIAL
CONTROL

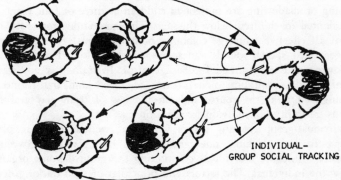

INDIVIDUAL-
GROUP SOCIAL TRACKING

Fig. 41 Patterns of group and team behavior. a: Social interaction tracking. b: Transformed social tracking. c: Individual group tracking patterns.

tions made in both verbal communication and nonverbal social interaction depend on systems factors in use of gestures, signs, language, and numbers which have meaning beyond their purely motorsensory functions.

Experimental evidence was obtained that speech and language, which serve as the most critical mechanisms to transform motorsensory social tracking for sustained variable and productive communication, are also based on social feedback control. Beginning about two decades ago, results of a series of experiments suggested that all forms of speech and sound communication in man are feedback controlled in a very direct way. In subjects fitted with protective earphones and exposed to magnetic-tape controlled feedback delays of their own speech sounds, Lee (1950, 1951) observed a definite slowing and blocking (artificial stutter) of speech. Since then, numerous experiments have been reported which indicate that the effects of delayed auditory feedback of speech arise from the specificity of the temporal feedback control, that all forms of sound production are affected, and that little or no learning in overcoming the effects of the delay occurred among subjects seriously affected (Smith, 1962). Other evidence has shown that feedback control of sound production and communication does not stop with closed-loop regulation of individual sounds. A special finding coming out of delayed auditory feedback research was the observation that individuals simultaneously follow and mimic one another by social following or sound tracking. Cherry and Sayres (1956) gave the name *shadowing* to this simultaneous mimicking. Yates (1965) and others investigated such shadowing in the retraining of stutterers, who were provided with slightly delayed normal feedback of their own speech by a shadower. In other studies (Smith, 1967b), various types of sound shadowing and its relationships with instrumentally-controlled, variable feedback factors were studied as mutual social tracking. Results of these studies showed that delayed shadowed speech has different effects on a speaker from those found with delayed feedback of the sound of an individual's own speech. Social speech shadowing or tracking is affected by visual tracking of facial expression of the speakers. Abilities in speech tracking or shadowing are present in children at three or four years, but are very limited in children below this age. The suggestion from such research is that all effective language combines both individual feedback control of self-generated speech sounds and social speech tracking based on language shadowing and transformed feedback control. In team play and group behavior, similar multidimensional forms of direct and transformed social tracking determine the course and effectiveness of team play and skill, as well as capabilities in individual competition.

Individual-group tracking occurs within, as well as between, organized groups. In such tracking, one person tracks the relations between group members, while the individuals constituting the group become organized to follow the individual. The factors and principles of such tracking define the conditions of leadership and team interaction under leadership. In all such cases, the captain or leader acts, not just as a symbol, but as a mediator or guidance tracking system for the whole team. Effective team play and skill depends primarily on optimizing such individual-group tracking and the use of special signals and codes to transform the tracking behavior into effective team action.

In athletics and sports, teams must be organized to reflect the fundamental modes of feedback organized behavior found in the individual. That is, the primary factor in coordinated action consists of spatial guidance and timing that can be socially tracked by different members. Execution of force and power depends on precision timing in team play in relation to the coordination of different members at the athletic moment of truth—i.e., the focal point at which a goal action or strike is to occur. Particular team members may be evaluated in terms of their individual characteristics as well as on the basis of their powers in tracking and transforming the actions of other team members.

Aside from the finding that specialized computer methods are essential for the experimental analysis of social feedback control, the most significant implication of social feedback research is that it has disclosed the actual motor and sensory mechanisms of mutual interpersonal interaction and social skills, are used in athletics as well as in all other areas of cultural behavior. Social behavior is not shaped by psychoanalytic affiliations and aggressions, or learned through reward or anxiety reinforcements. Rather, it is based on crossed motorsensory interactions between two or more people which can be learned effectively only on the basis of detection of true systems interaction between the persons involved. The main feature of social tracking in athletics and elsewhere is that it is one of the most precise, variable, and difficult motorsensory operations among all the behavioral skills performed by man, and can be developed in full only by extensive and continuous interaction with others in both visual and body contact. Social tracking and feedback control in team play constitutes a systems context or framework within which individual skills and their psychophysiological substrates are divided, specialized, stratified, and integrated to determine organized team functions.

HUMAN FACTORS IN INSTRUMENTATION IN SPORTS

Aside from such sports as swimming, wrestling, or running, most athletic performances involve the use of special equipment, tools, and vehicles which must be designed with precision to fit the athlete's body or to be compliant with his skilled actions. Even such instruments as a baseball bat, which individual batters select to correspond to their stance and style of swinging, must be constructed with great precision. Although heretofore of no concern to psychologists and physiologists as a problem of athletic skill and exercise, the human factors in design of sports objects and instruments represent a critical central aspect of specification and analysis of athletic skill and learning. A behavioral feedback concept is essential to deal with the problems of human factors in instrumentation in sports as well as in other fields, because it is the only scientific statement which can specify the principles of compliance and interaction between behavior, physiological function, and tool and machine design.

There have been two approaches to the feedback concept of instrumental behavior, the servomechanism and informational engineering analogies. The original views in this field were behavioral and were derived from direct experimental studies of visual-manual tracking during World War II and thereafter (Smith, 1945; Smith & Smith, 1962, Smith and Smith 1966). One of the first detailed behavioral systems specifications for design of machines was prepared by the senior author at the end of World War II and dealt with the human factors in design of fixed and flexible gun systems in high-speed aircraft (Smith, 1945).

The informational engineering or servomechanism model of instrumental behavior was given two related interpretations in the late forties, one by Craik (1947) and one by Wiener (1948). These two interpretations differed mainly in the extent to which machine (Craik) and mathematical (Wiener) analogies were used to describe the man-machine interaction in tracking behavior. These accounts of instrumental behavior have been most important in defining the foundations of the field of servomechanism and informational engineering, but have made no original contributions to the actual theoretical specification of the detailed behavioral-physical interactions which occur in the use of tools and machines.

As applied originally by Craik (1947) and Wiener (1948), and as used thereafter in the fields of informational engineering, the servomechanism analogy is equated to the concept of homeostasis (Cannon, 1929). As Davis (1958) pointed out, the term *homeostasis* has been used in two ways. First, it is a general descriptive term used to emphasize the relative constancy of physiological functions in the face of change. With this meaning, the term hasn't been very useful because it is circular or tautological. Relative constancy or stability is a feature of all physical and living systems, and identification of this stability offers no insight into the actual mechanisms involved. The second meaning of the term homeostasis implies the action of a specific mechanisms to restore equilibrium after it is removed. As used in the servomechanism model, homeostasis is equated with negative feedback control of zero error. This equating of negative feedback with mechanisms of maintaining equilibrium has served to give apparent scientific substantiation to both ideas, but in fact has provided no confirmation of the validity of either principle. Although many believe the homeostatic principle to have been experimentally confirmed in physiology, this confirmation has never achieved validity beyond that attained by other biological mass-action doctrines. Thus, it has not been possible to provide specific substantiation to principles such as homeostasis which contain no exact specifications of control actions or organizing mechanisms.

At the same time, there are many well known phenomena which contradicate use of the term homeostasis. Contrary to the principle of homeostatic equilibration, most of the productive behaviors of man, and especially those used in athletics, are necessarily productive and self-governed and follow none of the rules of equilibrium-seeking systems. This is especially true in athletic skills involving the use of special devices and instruments. Although it may be necessary for servomechanism and informational engineers to translate knowledge about man-machine interactions into servomechanism formulae and functions in order to build instruments that fit action of the human body, such interpretations of human behavior may add nothing at all to our knowledge of the feedback operations of the human machine itself or to the total requirements of what should be put into the servomechanism model.

Parameters Of Feedback Control In Tool Using

In behavioral feedback theory, tool and machine action represent transformations of dynamic action of closed-loop motorsensory mechanisms. The use of a tool not only adds to or modulates the action of an effector or receptor; it changes the feedback relations between the effector and the receptor surfaces of the body. The science of the human factors in tool and machine design deals with the specification of the types and variables of transformation of feedback control which normally occur in behavior and can be duplicated by tools or machines.

Figure 42 illustrates the human factors doctrine of tool-using behavior in action feedback theory. When an individual uses a tool or instrument or operates a machine, he multiplies the sources from which he can receive feedback information about his own responses. As shown in the figure, we identify three main sources of feedback in tool-using behavior. First, the individual receives feedback generated by his own bodily movements, as in unaided behavior, called *reactive feedback*. Second, the tool user receives feedback from the action of the tool or device, called *instrumental feedback*. Finally, the individual receives feedback from the dynamic and persisting static effects of the tool-using operation on objects or materials in the environment, called *operational feedback*. *Dynamic operational feedback* represents the active impact of the tool on the environment. *Static operational feedback* represents the persisting trace of the tool-using action on the environment.

These different classes of generation of feedback can be differentiated in all levels of tool-using and machine behavior, although there are some operations with tools which have no persisting after-effects. In using hand tools for example, the worker receives feedback from the movements of his hand and arm, instrumental feedback from movements of the instrument, and dynamic and static feedback from the tool-using action in marking, cutting, shearing, smashing, and piercing objects and materials. Similar types of feedback are generated in machine operations such as typing. In this task the typist receives reactive feedback from the movements of his hands and

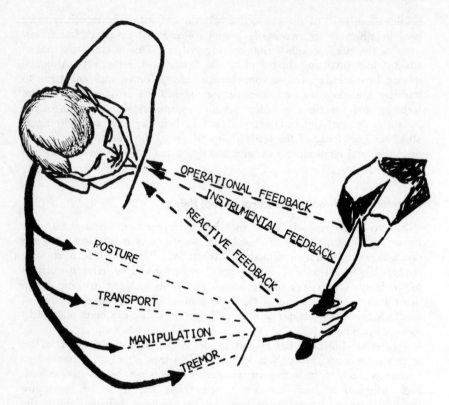

Fig. 42 Parameters of feedback control of instrumental behavior (From Smith & Henry, 1967).

arms, instrumental feedback from the movements of the keys and other parts of the typewriter, and operational feedback from the action of the keys in marking the paper. In driving a car, the same sources of feedback are generated, but there are no static operational after-effects of the steering and tracking.

The three kinds of feedback in tool-using and machine operation differ widely in their degree of correspondence or coherence with one another. In simple tool using, such as using a club, the three kinds of feedback are usually coherent: that is, movements of the instruments conform closely to movements executed by the hand, and the operational effects and trace of the instrumental action are patterned in much the same way as the movement. In typing, however, the space coherence between the reactive and instrumental feedback patterns is incomplete and there is but little correspondence between the persisting operational trace and the dynamic movements that produce it. The different letters of the alphabet are typed with similar striking movements of the hand that differ mainly in their spatial position.

With feedback from a number of different sources available to him, how does the tool user control his activity? Different kinds of tool-using operations involve many different relationships among the resulting feedback patterns, but the relationships are always systematic and not random or haphazard. In different operations, he may use one or two or three sources, perhaps shifting from one to another to check on different aspects of the performance. However, it has been shown experimentally that the instrumental performance is most efficient when it is controlled by dynamic feedback from the focal activity of the tool. A writer controls his writing by watching the moving point of the writing instrument, not by watching his hand or arm. A carpenter drives a nail by watching the hammer strike the nail. He operates a lathe by watching the action of the cutting tool on the object being turned. For the most efficient and accurate performance, the individual needs immediate, dynamic feedback from the focal activity.

Dimensions Of Man-Machine Compliance

The feedback concept of instrumental behavior constitutes a systems doctrine of the man-machine or man-tool interaction, which contains principles of both organization and specialization of response in the use of tools and implements. Tools and machines relate to the motor, sensory and neural integrative functions of behavior in systematic ways in terms of the structural and operational components of machines. These components are illustrated in Figure 43. Even the simplest of tools, such as a bat or racquet, is composed of three component parts or sectors—i.e., a *master-control,* an *actuator,* and a *slave* or *operational* sector. The master control is the part of the tool or machine which is directly related to the hand or other motor mechanism, and usually consists of hand control devices, steering mechanisms, or handles. The slave sector is the part of the tool or machine which does the work. Besides being capable of cutting, smashing, hitting, throwing, or performing other operations, the slave sector also must present a perceptual display to the operator, which can be seen, heard, or felt so that the operator can guide the tooling operation.

The actuator sectors of tools or machines perform amplifying or power converting functions. In the case of simple tools such as hammers, saws or bats, the actuator sector represents the mechanical or structural linkage between the handle and the working end of the device and thereby defines the mechanical advantage of the device. In power driven machines, the actuator sector is represented by the engine and gears which the operator can adjust to perform the machine functions. In complex machines such as television systems or computers, the actuator sectors represent the electronic systems which can make transformations of motor controlled sensory information, or "intellectual" or rational operations.

The primary feedback principle of design of tools and machines is that

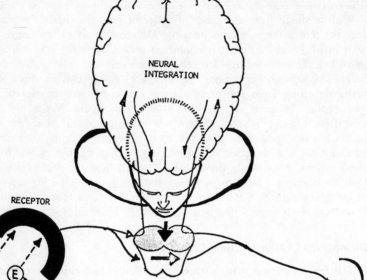

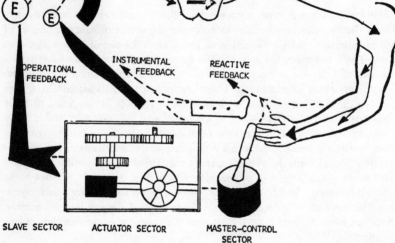

Fig. 43 Component sectors of machine operation.

the master-control, actuator, and slave components must possess systematic space, time, and force compliance with the motor, sensory and integrative behavior mechanisms of the operator. This does not mean that the tool components must duplicate exactly the space, time, and force operations of the body. Rather, it means that the instrument must systematically transform these space, time, and force functions of behavior.

The primary organizational principle of tool and machine design is that the master-control, actuator, and slave components of instruments must be differentially compliant with the motor, receptor and integrative mechanisms of the operator. The master-control sector must be patterned after the motor system (hand, foot or mouth) used to operate the controls of the implement. The slave operations of the machine must be compliant with the motorsensory mechanisms of the exteroceptors and action of the head in maintaining posture. When a machine controls power, sensing, or integrated operations, the actuator design must correlate with integrated motor and sensory operations which are linked together by the machine action.

The principle of integrative feedback compliance is that the more the space, time, and force factors of the different sectors of instrumental action are coherent structurally and dynamically with their respective levels of behavior, the lower the requirements for practice and learning in using the device. Conversely, the greater the non-coherence, the greater the demands for learning. The validity of this principle has been tested in a variety of actual design studies of cybernetic anthropomorphous, walking, manipulator, and force-amplifying exoskeleton machines (Mosher, 1965; Smith, 1966b). Such machines duplicate and follow coherently the walking, hand manipulations, and lifting operations of human operators. When machines of this type were designed and constructed according to principles of feedback compliance of their master-control, actuator, and slave components, operators required only short periods of practice to control the machines accurately.

Behavioral feedback compliance theory may be applied in detail to design of sports vehicles, such as racing cars, motor boats, racing boats, and aircraft. As explained in a number of experimental papers on this subject (Kao & Smith, 1969; Smith, Kaplan & Kao, 1969), the critical human factors in design of vehicles are related to the fact that these implements function as exoskeletons which affect the postural, travel, manipulative, and receptor movements of the operator in ways far different from stationary machines. The differences between such implements are described most directly by the contrasts between stimulus tracking (the pursuit or following of stimuli by local movements) and steering, in which tracking of self-generated feedback stimuli represents the main part of the task. Research has shown that steering movements in vehicles are not only affected by space-displacement and delay of sensory feedback, but that these effects vary as a function of the speed, momentum, and operating conditions of the vehicle.

The theory and results of the human factors analysis of the differences between steering and tracking behavior have application to sports other than those involving operation of vehicles. Running, swimming, and traveling games are also based primarily on unaided body steering and the principles of learning and physical conditioning of self-generated and self-integrated forms of body steering. Individuals learn and perfect such skills by appreciating how different components of motion and physiological function are integrated in their own distinctive modes of running, swimming, throwing, and striking, and by learning how to perfect their self-guided forms of body steering in relation to the manipulative tasks of the sport.

FEEDBACK DESIGNS IN PHYSICAL EDUCATION
AND ATHLETIC TRAINING

The feedback systems theory of skill and learning described previously defines a new spectrum of ideas for design of coaching, training, and physical conditioning procedures in physical education, rehabilitation and sports science. The designs of these procedures are based on the concepts of feedback regulation of motorsensory skills, as described in the sections above. Specifically, most of the tactual, social tracking, and television devices used to research feedback mechanisms can be adapted without modification to physical training, exercise therapy, and athletic training.

Physical Training In Children

Figure 44 illustrates some of the feedback techniques which have been developed to test and train dynamic motorsensory mechanisms in normal, retarded, and disabled infants and children. The diagram illustrates a rotating playpen and television display, child-actuated television displays, hand and voice actuated audiovisual mechanisms, small sand boxes for practicing preschool children in dynamic following of object and letter forms, tactual and visual finger dancing, and a visual social tracking device. In using the small sand trays, the parent or teacher moves his finger through the sand to produce an object or letter pattern and the child is required to follow. Periodically, the child is induced to generate a pattern on his own which the adult tries to follow. A small pen light also may be used with the sand trays to produce dynamic tracking patterns for the child to follow.

The letter and form visual tracking device is a very versatile instrument for pre-apprenticeship training in tracing, copying, drawing, and writing. A small vertical frame or table is made with a frosted glass panel in its top. A small pen light is used by the adult to trace various forms on the underside of the glass. The child must track these dynamic movements on a paper that is placed over the glass panel. Cutouts of large object and letter forms can be made and attached to the underside of the glass panel, and the child can practice actively tracking number and letter forms as the teacher or parent moves the light to make such dynamic forms. Also, using these forms the development in accuracy of such tracking can be measured. At periodic intervals the child is induced to produce his own forms, which the parent or teacher tries to follow.

Other types of visual social tracking apparatus may be devised to teach children head control of visual stimulus patterns, such as head flashlights and head-mounted sighting devices. It is now possible to construct electronic head movement and eyemovement transducers, the output of which can be yoked to calibrated projected targets to create improved techniques of coordinating eye and head movements.

The tactual tracking procedures illustrated in the figure can be elaborated to include training in blind following of letter, number, and object forms as

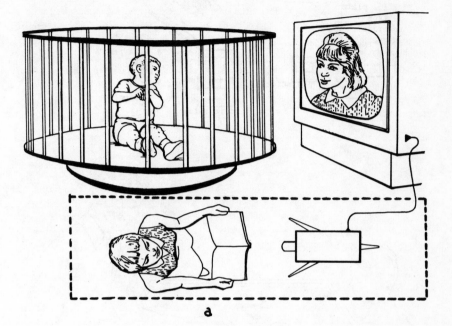

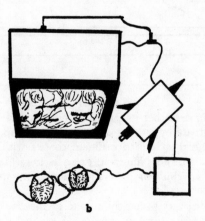

Fig. 44 Feedback designs used in training research in children. a: rotating playpen and television display. b: child-actuated television displays. c: hand and voice-actuated audiovisual mechanisms. d: small sand frames for relief visual tracking. e: tactual and finger dancing exercises. f: dynamic visual social tracking device for home and school preapprenticeship training in writing and drawing (Based on Smith, 1968).

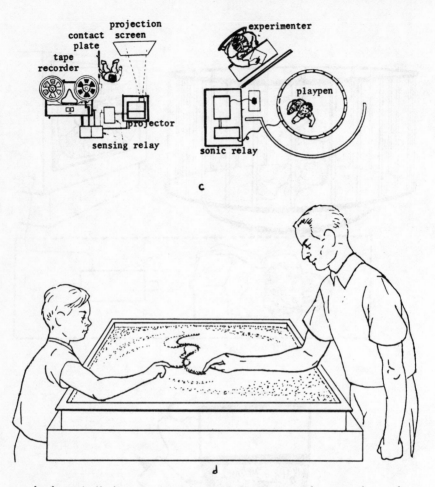

made dynamically by a teacher or parent. Similar procedures can be used to perfect tactual sensitivity by moving a small circular chip around on a cloth surface and requiring the child to maintain contact with the chip as letter and number forms are made. Numerous exercises in tactual following can be devised in which two children maintain contact with the ends of a stick while moving about.

Aid can be provided very young children to promote yoked visual tracking. The rotating playpen described in Figure 44 can be arranged as a visual tracking device for children between one and three years of age. The playpen, which is made to rotate at about two revolutions per minute, can be placed near the kitchen door, so the child must keep moving to keep his mother or others in the kitchen in view. The moving playpen also can be placed outdoors so that the baby can track other children at play, and can be modified

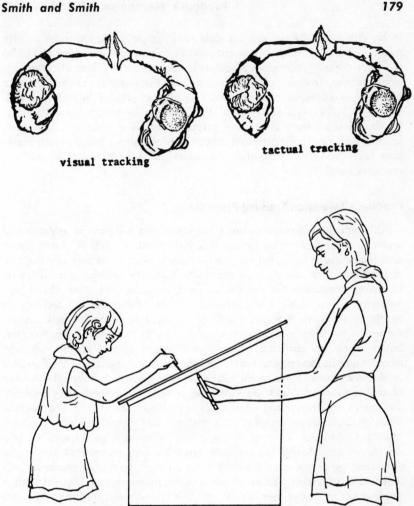

visual tracking

tactual tracking

and anchored to give designs for a variety of automated devices for visual training of young children.

Many different types of electronic infant-controlled and child-controlled devices have been designed which can be used as aids in developing visual tracking skills in children past two years of age. These devices contain a small, battery-operated transistor control relay which can be used to sense movements and speech of a child and to control tape recorders or slide projectors that will provide visual feedback effects to the child. These devices comprise a spectrum of self-stimulation devices, such as hand- or foot-controlled movie and slide projectors and tape recorders. Voice control devices of the same sort have been built. By speaking or by touching a large plate in his crib, the baby can cause a slide projector or movie projector to give pictures of himself or of his parents and brothers and sisters. The child also can control music and sounds of others in the same way. These electronic behavior sensing feedback procedures constitute the essential feature of design of all types of automated toys and training devices for infants and children.[2] Child-controlled relays of this sort can be used to activate social tracking devices, such as rotating playpens, television monitors, light projectors, and electrically-activated figures and displays. Sensing relays also have been used to activate slide projectors and tape recorders in teaching machines for children.

Feedback Television Training Procedures

Although the videotape recorder has come into wide use in athletics and sports as an instant replay device, this instrument, as well as closed circuit camera-monitor systems, has not always been applied to its best advantage in physical education. Research on use of the videotape recorder as a cybernetic laboratory instrument for controlling feedback delay and other closed-loop properties of visually-guided behavior (Smith, 1962; Smith, McCrary & Smith, 1960; Smith & Smith, 1966) has pointed up many feedback designs for use of the videotape recorder in education. These applications, however, hinge largely on instructor, student, and patient control of the videotape recorder and its images, and cannot be based on some centralized ETV control of the instrument. More recent research has suggested that the effective use of television circuits and the videotape recorder in rehabilitative training, training in educational and social skills in children, and athletic and machine training depends on making such systems into better-designed feedback control mechanisms. This can be done only by multiimage displays wherein the trainee can observe the feedback from his own movements and at the same time see or get social feedback from a parent, teacher or coach. In such multiimage television circuits, many training monitors may be used with a single coach or trainer monitor for effective use of social tracking and social feedback in the rehabilitative and training situation. Also, with multiimage feedback control, the videotape recorder may be used far more effectively than it is now for review and measurement of accuracy in individual, social and team performance.

Television systems have special application in teaching individuals the human factors involved in control of cycles, boats, aircraft, racing cars, and other exoskeleton devices. The basic idea in such methods is to interpose a camera-monitor or videotape system between the control movements of a

2. The claims of operant conditioning and reinforcement investigators for priority and originality in use of these electronic behavior sensing and television motion measurement techniques are misrepresentations (see Gelfand, D. M. Social Learning in childhood. Belmont California: Brooks-Cole 1969).

machine operator and the operational action of the machine. In the case of driver trainer devices, the driver must view a television monitor mounted on the windshield, and a camera mounted on the hood or top of the car views the operational action of the car as it moves on the road. The television camera can be directed giving different views of the road or can be located in different positions to test the most effective locus of operational vision from the automobile. The systems design of such methods also includes use of the videotape recorder, which is mounted in the trunk of the car, to record driver operational performance in guiding the car in relation to the road. The videotape recorder also can be used to record operational driving situations and to play these back to the driver in free-field driving to simulate real-life normal and emergency driving conditions. Such systems also may be used in different ways to measure accuracy of steering.

Several other main factors characterize use of cybernetic television and videotape methods in feedback controlling driving performance. Two or more cameras are located so as to give an operational view of the road ahead and of edge markers along the road. These two operational images are superimposed on the same videotape record, and thus can be used to relate in exact timing operational features of control of the car and a record of the car's tracking accuracy. Such records can be used not only to test driving accuracy, but to give drivers playback of control of the automobile in emergency driving situations.

Training Research In Physical Education: Analysis Of The Athlete As A Control System

The implication of the different feedback experiments on human performances thus far described in this paper is that even the simplest skilled response in man requires simultaneous coordinated feedback control of receptor action and the postural, transport, and manipulative movement systems. Further, these somatic responses are governed against a background of internal organic, autonomic, physiological activity, including breathing and heart action. Smooth coordination of these diverse bodily activities is possible only because of the closed-loop nature of the responding system, and its capability of integrating response. The built-in feedback circuits of the body not only locate the individual in space and guide his articulated movements; they also impart specialization, continuity, and organization to motor-sensory systems by focusing and combining different component levels of neuromuscular motions, receptor operations, and vital interactions for specific guided focused actions. Feedback training and research in physical education can be designed around these general systems principles. For example, the hybrid-computer and oscillographic experimental techniques for studying integration of respiration and arm movements could be simplified to provide a beginning line of physical conditioning and skill trainers for coordinating neuromuscular motions, breathing, and heart action.

Techniques comparable to physical conditioning trainers can be developed for research and training in postural coordination. A coordinate postural platform was designed to make possible diagnostic study and training of athletes, injured patients, dancers and others in developing postural control through tracking procedures.

Training in bilateral motor coordination has many applications for athletic and rehabilitative training. Such training is a fundamental technique for recapturing lost function in neuromuscular injury, because the matching of self-governed feedback from paired muscles on the two parts of the body can be used to bring one unpaired side back toward normal functioning. To achieve such training and to carry out research on it, a bimanual feedback system was set up to require a subject to track a visual, auditory, or tactual signal in terms of matching and synchronizing his two hands or other bilaterally symmetrical parts of the body. The subject's task in such bimanual tracking was not only that of compensating the action of a generated target variation, but also synchronizing the action of the two hands so that they work together in exact harmony. As indicated in Figure 45, the electrical analog from the two separate handmotion transducers was processed separately by the computer control system. In this operation, the digital computer was programed to measure the time synchronism between the two hands and to output this measure as an independently variable feature of the oscillograph

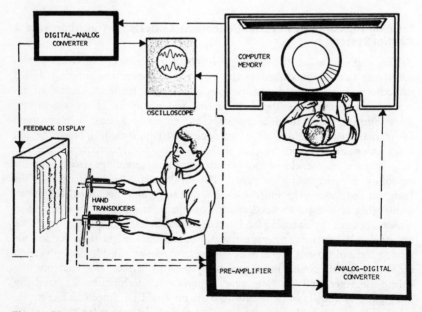

Fig. 45 Bimanual hand-motion transducer and laboratory computer system for systems measurement and feedback control of bimanual coordination.

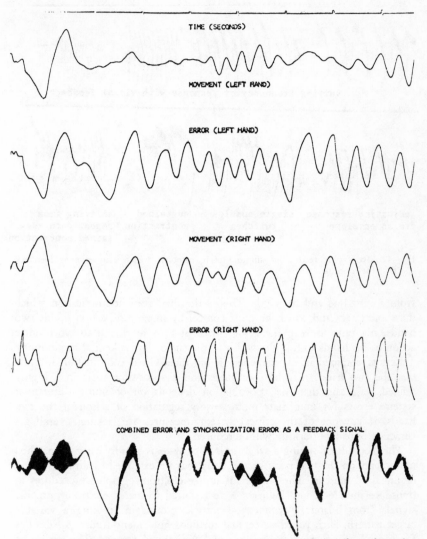

Fig. 46 Patterns of bimanual response which can be generated by a subject for training in two-handed coordination.

feedback indication which the subject sees. The subject watched and controlled the left channel of the oscillograph, and used dual indications of error and width of this error line to control his tracking. The oscillograph record in Figure 46 illustrates how these systems errors of bimanual tracking are combined. The record shown in this figure varies in terms of its deviation

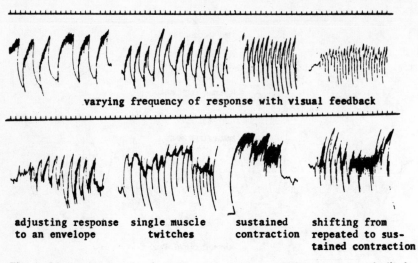

varying frequency of response with visual feedback

| adjusting response to an envelope | single muscle twitches | sustained contraction | shifting from repeated to sustained contraction |

Fig. 47 Myographic records of single muscle response which can serve as feedback for training.

from a zero line and in width. This is the dual feedback indication which the subject sees and which he must control by integrating action of his two hands, not only to keep the error cursor at zero level, but to synchronize action of his hands so that the width of the cursor line is kept at a minimum.

Results obtained in experiments on bimanual-visual coordination indicate that the two hands may be coordinated on a space-time basis in a highly refined way, and that this coordination depends on obtaining differential systems errors for immediate motorsensory regulation of action of the two hands. If any one of the critical systems measures are lacking, overall accuracy of bimanual tracking will be reduced.

The methods of yoking a synchronized or systems sensory error to matched movements on the two parts of the body may be extended to direct training of unpaired muscles. These methods utilize electromyographic procedures to transduce muscle action. Subjects were required to match electromyographic signals from bilaterally-symmetrical muscle groups in tracking a variable target pattern. Such yoked perceptual methods hold many future possibilities for control of neurological training of handicapped persons. The design of methods in this field is the employment of feedback control devices to automate control of training and computation of systems measures of error on which effective learning depends. The hybrid computer is used as an integrating device to obtain systems errors that the subject sees as feedback signals to control and modulate disturbed physiological functions that may be related to vision. Application of feedback techniques to muscle training illustrates how the above methods are used. In these procedures, muscle potentials are transduced by suction or silver cup electrodes placed over the critical muscle group to be studied. As shown in Figure 47, when the actions of only one muscle group are recorded, a direct hook-up between the muscle electrodes and an amplifier-oscillograph display is all that is needed to record muscle potentials and to control the training. The subject views the oscillograph feedback display and, following instructions or guiding signals, attempts to produce varying patterns of muscular contraction. Some of the possible dynamic patterns which can be trained are shown in the oscillograph records in the figure. These include varying frequencies of re-

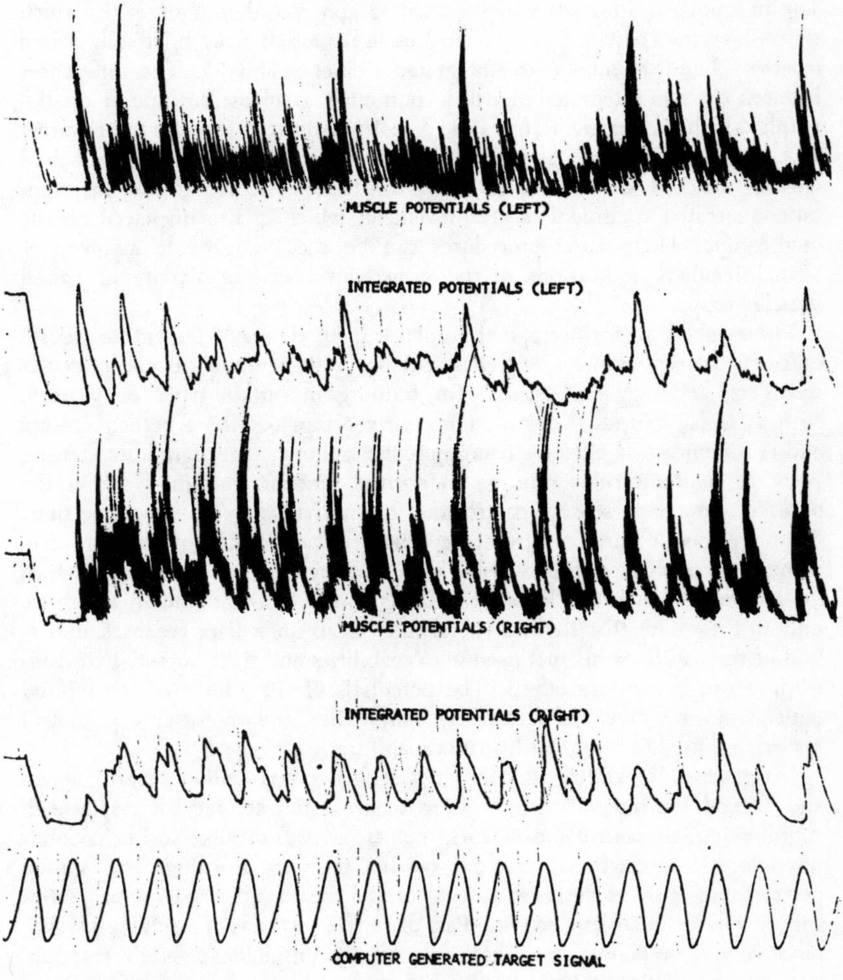

Fig. 48 Myographic records of paired bilateral muscles and integration of these movement signals to give a systems indication of bimanual neuromuscular coordination (From Smith, 1968).

sponse, adjusted wave envelopes of muscle contraction, production of single twitches, sustained contractions, and shifting patterns of contraction.

Using the hybrid-computer machine, systems measures of accuracy in paired muscle contraction from symmetrical points on the two sides of the body may be obtained. Electrical analogs from the two symmetrical points are transduced and the computer system is used to integrate and smooth both high-frequency muscle patterns. The computer also is programed to measure the difference between the two integrated signals which represent action of the symmetrical muscles and to output this signal as a feedback indication. The technique is illustrated in the oscillograph record in Figure 48, which shows how the frequency pattern of muscle potentials from bilaterally-paired muscles (Lines 2 and 4) are integrated (Lines 3 and 5). The differences between the two integrated signals is outputted to an oscilloscope or oscillograph, which the patient watches to control pursuit tracking of another target spot on the oscilloscope. As long as the subject can keep his bilaterally paired muscles matched at different levels of contraction, he can follow the computer-generated sinusoidal target movement, which is also displayed on the oscilloscope. These same procedures can be used to provide auditory or tactual feedback indications to the subject in matching activity in paired muscle groups.

These yoked, motor-perceptual feedback methods may have future significance for training athletes as well as persons with neurological and muscular disorders, and may be essential for training in certain types of injuries, such as facial injuries. Their design clearly brings out the cybernetic nature and requirements of effective neuromuscular training. One significant starting point of neuromuscular training in normal function and in injury is the positive resource of sensory control that the individual possesses at the time. Training doesn't start from some superficial reward or contingent reinforcement; it proceeds from the available motorsensory feedback capabilities which the individual can exert. Effective training can be built around this resource only to the extent that the individual can get an immediate feedback indication of the nature of his motorsensory capabilities and their potential for controlling specific sensory effects. The potentials of the athlete or the injured patient can be measured accurately only when the motorsensory control systems are used to bring out his full capabilities.

Inasmuch as the athlete functions as a self-governed, unified control system and depends on integrative indications of error and accuracy of response in coordinating component movements, motorsensory functions, and behavioral-physiological interactions, research on his training, learning, and skilled performance must be designed to control and measure the systems properties and operations in athletic activity. Past dissective methods of studying psychophysiological responses have been completely unsuited for such research, not only because they have been based on mass-action dogma of stimulus determination and associative learning, but also because they have been incapable of achieving measurement and control of systems interactions.

To do research on athletic skill and learning at any level requires more than examination of details of movement. As illustrated in every section of this chapter, investigation of different aspects of skill, the coordination of motor and sensory processes, the integration of different movements, the interaction between man and tools and between man and the environment, and the social interplay and organization of individuals demands the experimental capability of simultaneously measuring two or more functions or operations in real time and in presenting a systems measure of the interaction between these functions as a feedback indication of accuracy, error, or time to the subject.

The methods of experimental systems analysis, as just described, represent a new level of behavioral and physiological science in the study of performance, learning, memory, training, exercise, and work. Some of the main applications of this science to physical education and sports medicine have been outlined in this paper. The validity of the feedback and systems hypothesis, which guided the design of the many different experiments, is indicated by the success with which difficult systems studies were achieved and by the agreement between experimental results and hypotheses which was obtained in most of the studies.

An overall summary of the application of experimental systems analysis to athletic skill and training can be given in terms of the design of the computer laboratory which was constructed for systematic feedback research on human learning and performance. The overall lay-out of the real-time hybrid computer laboratory is shown in Figure 49. This laboratory does not represent simply an adventure in spending money on fancy equipment; it is absolutely essential for making systems measures on different response functions and operations in real time and for controlling feedback in terms of such measures. The term, real-time experimental methods, is more than appropriate in describing the overall design of this bimodal, hybrid computer system.

The laboratory apparatus diagrammed in Figure 49 is an analog-digital-analog computer implement arranged as a feedback control machine which can be used to automate research and training operations with such diverse activities as eyemovements, visual-manual tracking, muscle potentials, brain wave variations, head movements, posture, cardiac action, and respiration. In addition, the same control system can be used to automate feedback training in discrete or digital motion systems consisting of keyboard-light cell displays, electric typewriter units, panel control operations, object assembly work setups and locomotion. In each of these cases, the computer system senses, times, and measures accuracy and error of the discrete movements and their interactions and, in addition, controls feedback time, space, and signal variables which correspond to the particular response operations and their systems properties.

The hybrid computer system described in Figure 49 constitutes a bimodal, real-time machine, inasmuch as it can be applied to control of both analog

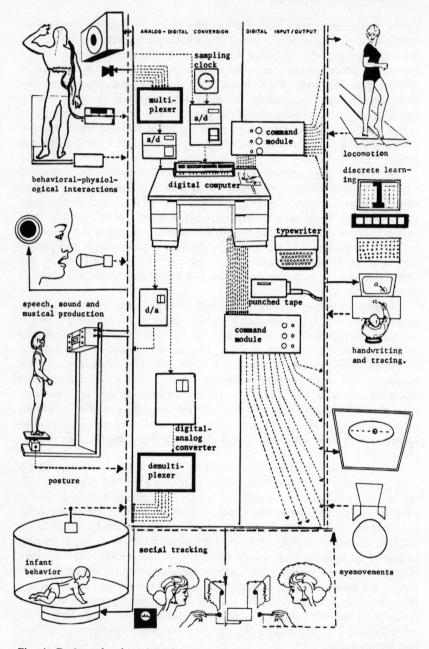

Fig. 49 Design of a bimodal laboratory computer system for learning research on skill, physical educational design, and sports medicine (Based on Smith, 1968).

and digital or discrete inputs and outputs. In developing this model automated laboratory, we have ignored time-sharing procedures and programing and have designed the system around flexible centralized switching circuits, which make possible the conducting of numerous, different, successively scheduled experiments and observations. Experimental design in use of such experimental automatic control is based on precise specification of every detail of experimental operation and on adaptation of special display and signal conditioning equipment for exact control and calibration of experiments. The most significant advances made by the use of the hybrid computer system as an automated laboratory instrument have been adaptation of its memory circuits as a time machine for experimental systems studies of all aspects of psychophysiological systems timing, such as closed-loop delays, intermittencies, temporal inversions, time distortion, and memory or memocontrol of current response functions. Other applications of the system include the analysis of the variable feedback factors which determine learning and systematic studies of automating rehabilitative training and neuropsychological training procedures.

The promise of experimental methods represented by the real-time laboratory computer system is the achievement of an experimental systems approach to understanding human skill and talent in terms of both its organized or integrative and its detailed specialized control properties. We stated at the beginning of this chapter that the real challenge of a theory of athletic skill and exercise is to encompass a scientific account of both of these aspects of behavior and physiological function. This same challenge faces those who would design laboratories and research on human skill and talent. We believe that the automated real-time laboratory diagrammed in Figure 49 meets many of the theoretical and methodological requirements of systems studies of the interrelation of specialization and organization of response in athletic as well as in many other levels of human skill.

SUMMARY

This paper surveys the feedback mechanisms of athletic skill and exercise in relation to a systems interpretation of physical conditioning, guidance of skilled motions, integration and time synchronism of motions, determination of skill learning and memory, social factors in interpersonal and team skills, instrumental factors in sports behavior, and feedback designs in athletic training and training research. The following points have been made:

1. A feedback doctrine of motor sensory organization states that athletic behavior is determined by: (a) reciprocal control of stimuli and sensory processes by movement; (b) reciprocal dynamic, closed-loop control of the internal environment and autonomic-physiological function by skilled motion; (c) guidance and organization of motion and physiological processes through feedback integration of postural, travel, manipulative, and articulated receptor movements.

2. Physical conditioning can be described as a detailed specialization and overall organization of the feedback interactions between distinctive patterns of motorsensory action and organic, autonomic, physiological, and molecular operations, which are differentially and reciprocally affected by the neuromuscular activities.

3. Experiments on respiratory tracking suggest that the breathing mechanism acts as a high-precision monitoring activity for interrelating neuromuscular responses and autonomic-physiological functions.

4. Respiratory tracking is the main mechanism for systems coordination of external respiration, limb movements, and energy metabolism in athletic skills such as swimming and running.

5. Systems experiments on integration between respiration and neuromuscular movements may be carried out by measurement of the time synchronism between the breathing and somatic mechanisms. Results of such studies suggest that all breathing patterns are exquisitely specialized as modes of respiratory tracking of particular body movements.

6. Externally, skilled motions are specialized and integrated anatomically and behaviorally in terms of four component levels of movement—i.e., posture, travel, manipulative, and receptor motions—each with distinctive patterns of sensory-feedback regulation which serve to interrelate these movements dynamically and operationally in particular skills. These somatic components of behavior also possess specialized, built-in feedback interactions with autonomic-physiological processes.

7. The main feedback effect of behavioral activity in exercise is reciprocally and dynamically to integrate and synchronize the diverse intracellular and supracellular molecular and hormonal functions which determine the bioenergetics of exercise.

8. The evidence for a systems feedback theory of physical conditioning covers results from many different types of studies of respiratory tracking, self-regulation and sensory feedback entraining, integration of somatic reactions, respiratory functions, and feedback interactions between muscular contraction and energy metabolism.

9. The experimental analysis of muscular contraction revises the classical view that muscle activity is a centrifugal product of biochemical events: such analysis indicates that the mode, level, and pattern of muscle contraction are reciprocally related to the molecular and biochemical events of cellular energy metabolism through feedback mechanisms. These interactions constitute the most fundamental substantiation of the feedback interpretation of behavioral-molecular systems interactions in physical conditioning.

10. Experimental results from many sources have shown that adenosine triphosphate and its precursors exert multifaceted feedback control over the rate of carbohydrate catabolism, thereby reciprocally regulating the rate of ATP production and the energy available for muscle contraction. This ATP control mechanism may be modulated by the modes and levels of contraction and activity of the muscle.

11. The sliding of muscle filaments in the contraction process represents the energy-consuming stage of contraction. Different modes of movement and exercise in the resting state, short-term contraction, intense exertion, and prolonged intense exercise feedback control the rate of energy utilization.

12. Athletic skills are organized at the behavioral level in terms of motion guidance which is governed by critical normal and breakdown ranges of angular displacement between movement and sensory input. Similarly, learning and integration of motion in athletic skill are determined by the direct sensory feedback effects of space-displaced motion and sensory input.

13. Directional specificity in guidance of motion is established in maturation of behavior in the child and serves as the basis of more refined specialization and organization of motion in learning.

14. One of the most decisive sources of evidence for a feedback theory and against a stimulus-response theory of athletic skill is that self-generated motions are learned more efficiently and performed more accurately than stimulus-released responses. The reinforcement and conditioning dogmas of learning theory not only lack relevance to specification of learning self-governed athletic activities; they have been proven false in general by systematic feedback studies of learning.

15. Feedback guidance by space-displaced motorsensory interactions during learning also involves regulation of feedback timing in terms of which different movements are synchronized and integrated.

16. Feedback timing is a regulatory factor not only in guidance of body motorsensory mechanisms; it is also fundamental to direct receptor control and synchronism of receptor mechanisms.

17. Learning and memory function to alter feedback timing in behavior by establishing a record of the pattern of receptor movements and body motion, and thus spanning time to project and predict the course and timing of motion in the future.

18. Tactual tracking and feedback control are critical in the development, maintenance, and guidance of smooth, continuous movements and in regulation of bilateral coordination of continuous movements.

19. Coordination of motions in interpersonal and team action is based on social tracking and feedback control.

20. Social tracking in athletic skills consists of mutual yoking of movements of one person to the sensory mechanisms of a second as an analog of sensory input of the motions of the second person, and vice versa.

21. Mutual social and tactual tracking are crucial to development of motorsensory skills and bilateral coordinations in infants and young children.

22. The theory of social tracking as the basis of interpersonal, group, and team behavior has been substantiated in social feedback experiments on development of young children, in studies of televised yoking of individuals in skilled tracing and tracking motions, and in investigations of different social tracking models by a hybrid-computer laboratory system.

23. The concepts of social tracking are essential to specify and describe

the parameters of yoked motorsensory interaction which are involved in positive, negative, linked, parallel, bridged, and systems-integrated patterns of social behavior.

24. The fundamental basis of learning in social tracking consists of occurrence of systems indications of error and accuracy of yoked movements, which serve as the only effective social feedback for sustained interpersonal and team behavior.

25. The variable parameters of social tracking are essential to specify the detailed motorsensory interactions which are involved in group behavior, group skills, cultural patterns of transformed social interaction, and variable patterns of social control of the environment.

26. Feedback theory is fundamental to specification and analysis of the human factors in instrumenal learning and performance in athletics and sports.

27. The main feature of systems control of instrumental behavior consists of the variable nature of space, time, and force compliances between the different levels of reactive, instrumental, and operational feedback involved in use of tools and machines.

28. All machines and tools involve variable design factors related to their master control, actuator, and slave or operational sectors, which must have certain definite space, time, and force compliances with the properties and components of movements and receptor action, as well as with the integrative characteristics of postural, travel, manipulative, and receptor movements.

29. The feedback behavioral and psychophysiological designs developed in experimental systems research on skill, motion, and learning may be applied with only slight modification as flexible training and training research instruments in athletics, physical education, and exercise therapy.

30. A real-time hybrid-computer system is an essential instrument for future research on training designs, physical conditioning, and social learning in athletics and sports medicine.

REFERENCES

Ansell, S. D., Waisbrot, A. J., and Smith, K. U. Real-time hybrid computer analysis of self-regulated feedback control of cardiac activity. Proceedings of 1st Institute of Science and Technology in Criminology, New York: Thompson Book Co., 1967, pp. 403-418.

Asmussen, E., Christensen, E. H., and Nielsen, M. Die O_2-aufnahme der ruhenden und der arbeitenden skelettmuskeln. Skand. Arch. Physiol., 1939, 82, 212-220.

Atkinson, D. E. Biological feedback control at the molecular level. Science, 1965, 150, 851-862.

Atkinson, D. E. Regulation of enzyme activity. Annual Review of Biochemistry, 1966, 35, 85-124.

Bartz, A. E. Eye and head movements in peripheral vision. Science, 1966, 152, 1644-1645.

Bilodeau, E. (Ed.) Acquisition of skill. New York: Academic Press, 1966.

Cannon, W. B. Organization for physiological homeostasis. Physiological Review, 1929, 9, 399-468.

Cherry, C., and Sayers, B. McA. Experiments on total inhibition of stammering by external control and some clinical results. Journal Psychosomatic Research, 1956, *1*, 233-246.

Clifton, M. Pertinent theories of motor learning. Report of the 1968 N.A.P.E.C.W. Workshop. (Ed. by E. A. Gorton). 1968, pp. 5-17.

Coleman, P., Huff, C., and Smith, K. U. Effects of feedback delay on hand-eye coordination in steering and tracking behavior. Journal Applied Psychology, 1969 (In press).

Craik, K. J. W. Theory of the human operator in control systems: I. The operator as an engineering system. British Journal Psychology, 1947, *38*, 56-66.

Cratty, B. J. Perception, motion and thought. Report of the 1968 NAPECW Workshop (Ed. by A. E. Gorton), 1968. pp. 18-33.

Davis, R. C. The domain of homeostasis. Psychological Review, 1958, *65*, 8-13.

Ditchburn, R. W. Vision with a stabilized image. Nature, 1952, *170*, 36-37.

Duncan, D. B. Multiple range and multiple F tests. Biometrics, 1955, *11*, 1-42.

Ewert, P. H. A study of the effect of inverted retinal stimulation upon spatially coordinated behavior. Genetic Psychology Monographs, 1930, *7*, 177-363.

Falls, H. B. (Ed.) Exercise physiology. New York: Academic Press, 1969.

Freedman, S. J. Neuropsychology of spatially oriented behavior. Homewood, Illinois: Dorsey Press, 1968.

Fruton, J. S., and Simmonds, S. General biochemistry. New York: Wiley & Sons, 1960.

Gould, J., and Smith, K. U. Angular displacement of the visual feedback of motion. Science, 1963, *137*, 619-620.

Guthrie, E. R. The psychology of learning (Rev. Ed). New York: Harper & Row, 1952.

Helmholtz, H.L.F. von. Treatise on physiological optics (Trans. from the 3rd German edition [Ed by J.P.C. Southall]). 3 Vols: Rochester, N. Y.: Optical Society of America, 1924-25.

Hill, A. V. Production and absorption of work by muscle. Science, 1960, *131*, 297-307.

Hull, C. L. Principles of behavior: an introduction to behavior theory. New York: Appleton-Century, 1943.

Huxley, H. E. The mechanisms of muscular contraction. Science, 1969, *64*, 1356-1366.

Johnson, M. J. The role of aerobic phosphorylation in the Pasteur effect. Science, 1941, *94*, 200-202.

Kao, H., and Smith, K. U. Cybernetic television methods applied to feedback analysis of automobile safety. Nature, 1969, *222*, 299-300.

Krogh, A. The anatomy and physiology of capillaries. New Haven, Conn.: Yale University Press, 1922.

Lardy, H. A. Energetic coupling and the regulation of metabolic rates. (In C. Liebecq [Ed.] Proceedings). Third International Congress Biochemistry, Brussels, New York: Academic Press, 1956, pp. 287-294.

Lardy, H., and Wellman, H. Oxidative phosphorylations: role of inorganic phosphate and acceptor systems in control of metabolic rates. Journal Biological Chemistry, 1952, *195*, 215-224.

Lee, B. S. Some effects of side-tone delay. Journal Acoustical Society America, 1950, *22*, 639-640.

Lee, B. S. Artificial stutter. Journal Speech and Hearing Diseases, 1951, *16*, 53-55.

Lincoln, R. S., and Smith, K. U. Systematic analysis of factors determining accuracy in visual tracking. Science, 1952, *116*, 183-187.

Mosher, R. S. Exoskeleton prototype: Technical Proposal. Department of the Navy, Office of Navy Research. Schenectady, New York: General Electric Company, 1965.

Passonneau, J. V., and Lowry, O. H. Phosphofructokinase and the Pasteur effect. Biochemical, Biophysical Research Communication, 1962, *7*, 10-15.

Passonneau, J. V., and Lowry, O. H. P-fructokinase and the control of the citric acid cycle. Biochemical, Biophysical Research Communication, 1963, *13*, 372-379.

Peterson, J., and Peterson, J. K. Does practice with inverting lenses make vision normal? Psychology Monographs, 1938, *50* (No. 5), 12-37.

Rhule, W., and Smith, K. U. Effects of inversion of the visual field on human motions. Journal Experimental Psychology, 1959, *57*, 338-343.

Riggs, L., Ratliff, F., Cornsweet, J. C., and Cornsweet, T. N. The disappearance of steadily fixated test objects. Journal Optical Society America, 1953, *43*, 495-501.

Schuenzel, R., Tait, C. A., and Smith, K. U. Feedback delay of middle-ear response in hearing. Journal Speech and Hearing Research (Submitted). 1969.

Skinner, B. F. Behavior of organisms: an experimental analysis. New York: Appleton-Century, 1938.

Skinner, B. F. Science and human behavior. New York: Macmillan Company, 1953.

Smith, K. U. Analysis of aircraft gun systems: Special report to the Air Force Air Material Command. Project AC-94: NDRC University of Wisconsin, 1945.

Smith, K. U. Delayed sensory feedback and behavior. Philadelphia: Saunders, 1962.

Smith, K. U. Cybernetic theory and analysis of learning. (In E. Bilodeau [Ed.] Acquisition of skill). New York: Academic Press, 1966a.

Smith, K. U. Review of principles of human factors in design of the exoskeleton and four-legged pedipulator. Madison, Wisconsin: University of Wisconsin Behavioral Cybernetics Laboratory, 1966b.

Smith, K. U. Cybernetic foundations of physical behavioral science. Quest, 167a, 8, 26-82.

Smith, K. U. Social tracking: the educational bond between parent and child. Madison, Wisconsin: University of Wisconsin Behavioral Cybernetics Laboratory, 1967b.

Smith, K. U. Educational feedback designs. Madison, Wisconsin: University of Wisconsin Behavioral Cybernetics Laboratory, 1968.

Smith, K. U., and Ansell, S. Closed-loop digital computer system for study of sensory feedback effects of brain rhythms. American Journal of Physical Medicine, 1965, 44, 125-137.

Smith, K. U., Ansell, S., and Smith, W. M., Sensory feedback in medical research. Delayed sensory feedback in behavior and neural systems. American Journal of Physical Medicine, 1963, 44, 228-262.

Smith, K. U., Gould, J., and Wargo, L. Sensory feedback analysis of visual behavior: a new theoretical-experimental foundation for physiological optics. American Journal of Optometry, 1963, 40, 365-417.

Smith, K. U., and Greene, P. A critical period in maturation of performance with space-displaced vision. Perceptual and Motor Skills, 1936, 17, 627-639.

Smith, K.. U., and Henry, J. P. Cybernetic foundations for rehabilitation. American Journal Physical Medicine. 1967, 46, 379-467.

Smith, K. U., Henry, J. P., Junas, R., and Ansell, S. Remote experimental cybernetic analysis of delayed feedback of oral breath pressure control in normal and emphysema patients: applications to space medicine. (In Proceedings (IV) of the Manned Space Flight Meeting, St. Louis, 1965). New York: American Institute of Aeronautics and Astronautics, 1965, 326-337.

Smith, K. U., Kaplan, R., and Kao, H. Human factors analysis of driver behavior by experimental systems methods. Accident Analysis and Prevention, 1969, 1, 1-10.

Smith, K. U., and Luedke, A. F. Experimental feedback analysis of external respiration and behavior. Madison, Wisconsin: University of Wisconsin Behavioral Cybernetics Laboratory, 1969.

Smith, K. U., Putz, V., and Molitor, K. Experimental systems analysis of yoked vision: cybernetic foundations of visual rehabilitation. Madison, Wisconsin: University of Wisconsin Behavioral Cybernetics Laboratory, 1966.

Smith, K. U., Putz, V., and Molitor, K. Eyemovement-retinal delayed feedback. Science, 1969, 166, 1542-1544.

Smith, K. U., Putz, V., and Schmidt, J. Theory of yoked vision (Presented before the Eastern States Optometric Congress, 1968). Madison, Wisconsin: University of Wisconsin Behavioral Cybernetics Laboratory, 1968.

Smith, K. U., and Smith, W. M. Perception and motion: an analysis of space-structured behavior. Philadelphia: Sanders, 1962.

Smith, K. U., and Smith, M. F. Cybernetic principles of learning and educational design. New York: Holt, Rinehart and Winston, 1966.

Smith, K. U., and Sussman, H. Cybernetic theory and analysis of motor learning and memory. (In Bilodeau, I. and Bilodeau, E. [Eds.] Acquisition of skill). New York: Academic Press, 1969a, pp. 103-139.

Smith, K. U. and Sussman, H. Feedback analysis of steering function in motorsensory learning and performance. Journal Applied Psychology, 1969.

Smith, K. U., and Wehrkamp, R. A universal motion analyzer applied to psychomotor performance. Science, 1951, 113, 242-244.

Smith, W. M., McCrary, J. W., and Smith, K. U. Delayed visual feedback and behavior. Science, 1960, *132*, 1013-1014.
Snyder, F. W., and Pronko, N. H. Vision with spatial inversion. Wichita, Kansas: University of Wichita Press, 1952.
Spence, K. W. Theoretical interpretations of learning. (In S. S. Stevens [Ed.] Handbook of Experimental Psychology). New York: Wiley & Sons, 1951, pp. 690-729.
White, A., Handler, P., and Smith, E. L. Principles of biochemistry. New York: McGraw-Hill, 1964.
Wiener, N. Cybernetics. New York: Wiley and Sons, 1948.
Winer, B. Statistical principles in experimental design. New York: McGraw-Hill, 1962.
Yarbus, A. L. Eye movements and vision. New York: Plenum Press, 1967.
Yates, A. J. Delayed auditory feedback and shadowing. Quarterly Journal of Experimental Psychology, 1965, *17*, 125-131.
Young, L. R., and Stark, L. Variable feedback experiments testing a sampled data model for eye tracking movements. Institute of Electrical and Electronic Engineering. Human Factors Engineering, 1963, *HFE-4*, 38-51.

FEEDBACK ON THE SMITHS' FEEDBACK[1]
by Carol H. Ammons

No comments from me on the work described in the paper, "Feedback mechanisms of athletic skill and learning," which K. U. Smith and his son, Thomas J. Smith, have prepared could enhance the excellent conception of Karl Smith's research program, or embroider the obvious elegance of the technology which supports the various facets of this work, or add to the essential interest-value of the many data from parallel and interlocking studies which are well conceived and beautifully executed. His talk, which dealt with only a portion of the material treated in his longer paper, gives pleasure in several ways: gut level sensory awareness of the humming shiny equipment and delight in the abstract task of trying to trace the origins of his predictions toward their consequent assured confirmation.

For me, and perhaps some of you, research life occurs on a simpler, less grand level for reasons other than simply lack of comparable monetary support. It *could* be maternal instinct—but I find there is meaning and pleasure in studying the behavior of humans as they work and play in the world. Designing studies to improve our comprehension of how various skills are learned, how high levels of skill are maintained, etc., for me seems most effectively to rise from familiarity with a variety of learners who are themselves concerned with acquisition of a skill and interested in their proficiency, and also, from personal awareness of that which characterizes performance and change for the skill in question.

In case certain of these remarks should sound a bit too reinforcement-oriented, this should not be interpreted as any lack of sympathy for Dr.

[1]The preparation of this paper was generously supported by the silence of those seven who went to bed quietly and on time for several evenings this September, 1969.

viction that Edward Titchener was gilded took time to crystallize into recognition that his research was elegant and systematic. The remnants of such youthful illusions would, of course, be slow to depart since I've had such great fun for years living with a reinforcement theorist and experimentalist. I do hold a willingness to ask learners what they observe themselves doing and how they feel, being concerned to check the strategies and hypotheses learners develop in the process of learning. These often seem relevant to the motivating aspects of learning. In short, *I'd* tap into Dr. Smith's self-generated feedback loops.

Just now, let us take a look at some characteristics of Dr. Smith's research. There are several important strengths, about which a number of observations can be made. Then, too, there are some problems. Let's look at a few of both.

Strengths of This Research Program

(1) The first point to be made is most obvious from reading the long manuscript but may not be so sharply clear from this afternoon's talk. A search of the literature will show that the research reported here is part of one of the few long-term, systematic programs in the field of motor skills.

The focus of Dr. Smith's paper has been on feedback mechanisms in athletic skill and exercise as related to "a systems interpretation of physical conditioning, guidance of skilled motions, integration and time synchronism of motions, determination of skill learning and memory, social factors in interpersonal and team skills, instrumental factors in sports behavior, and feedback designs in athletic training and training research" (p. 189). This focus does not effectively ensure listeners' appreciation of the wide variety of experiments efficiently done with relatively few subjects of varying ages, differing proficiencies in skill, etc. From a solid base of fundamental research, Dr. Smith has extended his work to include maturational changes in tactual tracking and feedback control in the guidance of movements during childhood and adolescence, application of basic principles of social tracking in interpersonal interactions occurring in team sports, in teaching specific movements to young, handicapped or mentally retarded persons, in marital relationships, etc.

New experiments grow out of completed ones, mend prior experimental errors, and extend application of confirmed results. Such a systematic program is a strong one, albeit not a popular approach among psychologists even in 1969.

(2) A second observation concerns the design and development of computerized instrumentation for the conduct of the experimentation in his laboratory. Dr. Smith says: "A real-time hybrid-computer system is an essential instrument for future research on training designs, physical conditioning, and social learning in athletics and sports medicine" (p. 192). In yet another place, Dr. Smith writes, "specialized computer methods are essential for the experimental analysis of social feedback control . . ." (p. 169).

These new devices are complex and make excellent use of modern techno-logical know-how. Further, their availability makes possible the investigation of old problems with advanced technological skill and of new problems, conceived through the shaping of the experimenter's thinking by the gadgetry with which he may now work.

It is very exciting therefore to read about Dr. Smith's experiments on respiratory tracking. To study the changes over a brief time in a subject's breathing movements which he makes in response to varied signals generated by a computer program as a visual analog of the subject's own breathing movements means the experimenter has posed a new problem. Application of such study to tracking of cardiac-generated output and eyemovement-determined motion may subsequently appear both obvious and appropriate.

"Feedback systems theory of skill and learning . . . defines a new spectrum of ideas for the design of coaching, training, and physical conditioning pro-cedures . . ." (p. 176), e. g., use of video tape recorder during training sessions.

Reports of experimental work give ample descriptions of the design of this instrumentation and those modifications suitable for the study of drawing, changes in posture, speech, etc. The computerized design remains novel al-though Dr. Smith's laboratory has been in operation for quite a few years.

(3) The next observation is related to the preceding one: this research program has yielded ingenious experiments concerned with *human* activities. One may draw attention to only two of the possible illustrations. Use of a rotating playpen and a televised display actuated by hand or voice to study social tracking in infants is certainly *not* the usual means of investigating the effect of amount of work done (Smith & Green, 1963; Smith, Zwerg, & Smith, 1963). Also, inversion of visual feedback by means of a scleral contact-lens prism (p. 93)[2] which causes the retinal image to move in a direction opposite to its normal orientation yields results different from those described by Ivo Kohler (1953) who used inverting spectacles: performance was grossly disturbed and showed little or no adaptation. Dr. Smith has also tested competent swimmers to check the coordination of respiratory move-ments and visually guided arm movements designed to simulate [swimming] to some degree" (p. 113).

(4) A new language is demanded and introduced. "Concepts and methods of studying social feedback mechanisms are . . . relevant to . . . athletics . . . since they can be used to define a language for the design and exploration of the parameters and factors of organization and specialization of social performances in interpersonal coordination, competition, and team play" (p. 153).

"The primary concept of a social systems interpretation of athletic skill is that of *social feedback control* . . . processes of active or dynamic motor-sensory interaction between two or more people . . . who become locked or

[2]References are to pages in the article by the Drs. Smith.

yoked together through social tracking and thus achieve a level of organization and specialization of closed-loop control that is quite different from individual response" (pp. 153-154).

"The captain or leader [of a team] acts, not just as a symbol, but as a ... guidance tracking system for the whole team" (pp. 168-169).

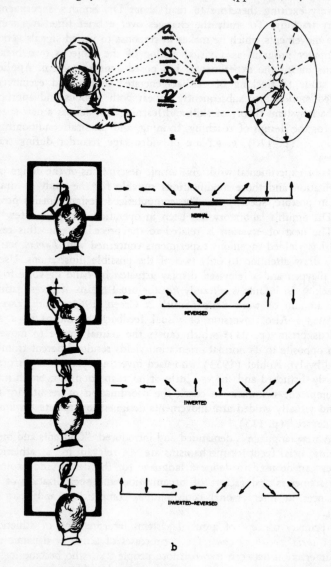

Fig. 1. Dr. Smith's Fig. 26, a McLuhan-cool summary of procedure and data from a study of feedback in angular motions.

"A behavioral feedback concept is essential to deal with the problems of human factors in instrumentation in sports . . . because it is the only scientific statement which can specify the principles of compliance and interaction between behavior, physiological function, and tool and machine design" (pp. 169-170).

"This general finding means that energy-producing metabolism may be yoked or coupled to energy expenditure [in] . . . work, exercise, physical conditioning, and the learning of skills involving physical conditioning" (pp. 119-120).

(5) Consonant with a new language is a novel means of presenting (in tidy juxtaposition) information about apparatus-task demands and experimental results. Dr. Smith has worked out ingenious ways of summarizing for the reader as may be illustrated in his Figure 26 (below).

In this figure it is possible to see that S tracks an angular drawing (a star maze such as Tom Cook and I have also used). Dr. Smith says that the main results are indicated by the arrows in Fig. 26[b]. These lines denote the number of statistically significant differences among 8 different directions of movement in star tracing at 4 conditions of feedback displacement of the motions (p. 137). Unfortunately I am so rigid, having been brought up in the traditional manner, that Dr. Smith's McLuhan-cool summary does not always answer enough questions for me, such as the effects of having only 24 Ss in a complex design. But, perhaps the impact would be greater had Dr. Smith gone all out with juxtaposition of color, use of pressure sensitive inks, etc. He has made the medium the message in this case.

(6) Dr. Smith's reports of experimentation, the present one included, yield a rich array of conceptual innovations, such as "self-governed body tracking" (p. 89) and "dynamic focal guidance of motions" (p. 91).

However, consider also, that "physical conditioning is a process of building self-governed control over all levels of autonomic-physiological regulation by learning specific patterns of motorsensory skill and exercise, and is not limited to muscle building or to direct effects of exercise on organic processes" (p. 95), or that the "external respiratory mechanism is one of the ultra-precise tracking systems of the body and equals the eye in dynamic control of stimulation" (p. 101).

"The common view in psychology is that motion skills are developed in the individual through progressive dominance of vision over the tactual and kinesthetic system" (p. 149).

"Direction-specific neurons located at different levels of the nervous system detect the spatial and tactual differences in stimulation and guide movements within the normal range of bilateral displacement of feedback" (p. 152).

The " . . . vertical postural mechanism is the most generalized of the integrative mechanisms of movement guidance" (p. 133).

"The athlete's eyes and ears must be timed and exercised to refine time synchronism with body movements, and factors in body form and instrumental design must be adjusted to eliminate deleterious space displacements and feedback delays of receptor input which can impair coordination between receptor operations and body movements" (p. 145).

Social behavior "is based on crossed motorsensory interactions between two or more people which can be learned effectively only on the basis of the detection of true systems interaction between the persons involved" (p. 169).

"Even the simplest skilled response in man requires simultaneous coordinated feedback control of receptor action and the postural, transport, and manipulative movement systems" (p. 181).

Problems

Some, despite their positive response to Dr. Smith's enthusiasm and ingenuity, will have reservations about the looseness of the organization of his written ideas, for often the free quick flow from one point to another omits logical steps needed by the reader. This looseness of language may on occasion trip even the cautious reader who may fail to distinguish between assumptions, "facts," proofs, conclusions, etc. In fact, one is often so swept up into the reading, that he may require a very sharp sensitivity or the ghost of Harry M. Johnson[3] to detect occasional lapses into proof by proclamation.

Perhaps a few may be concerned that none of the research reported here has even approached actual "field" situations. That is, no studies reported so far have come close to approximating assessment of self-regulated feedback controls of, say, two *judokas* in *rondori* or of the backstroker swimming a 200-meter race. Nor have any experimental conditions directly involved the procedures or time typically required for physical conditioning or groups varying in their levels of physical conditioning despite the fact that generalizations to such conditions may be found. Of course, Dr. Smith would no doubt agree that appropriate cross-validation in the field needs to be undertaken for the coach who is training cross-country trackmen who normally run, say, 12 miles or more at one stretch during a day's workout or swimmers who work out on schedules requiring two hours a day to cover 7000 yards.

One further matter may be noted. This unusual laboratory undoubtedly has the services of a knowledgeable electronics expert, for one may not always successfully ace the bugs in such a setup with scotch tape or chewing gum. Excellent financial support is thus mandatory, which means that most of us will, without envy, like Ebbinghaus, perform simpler studies.

With all due apologies to Japanese writers of *haiku,* I have one final set of reactions:

> Digitized cardiac
> Signals guide self-generated
> aerobic skill.

[3]Dr. Johnson taught many of us at Tulane University about the logical fallacies which trap one less than compulsive in his thinking.

Or,

       Self-generated—
       Visual cardiac-peaks
       Drive a touchdown pass.

Or,

       Light astride my breath
       Creeps across the screen, programmed
       Errant wanderer!

Or,

       The light's in motion—
       Cardiac-peaked movements now
       Bounce away from me.[4]

One thing is clear: K. U. Smith may not be 16 years old or wear long hair, but he *is* doing his thing.

REFERENCES

Kohler, I. Rehabilitation in perception. *Die Pyramide,* 1953, Parts 5, 6, and 7.
Smith, K. U., & Greene, P. A critical period in maturation of performance with space-displaced vision. *Perceptual and Motor Skills,* 1963, 17, 627-639.
Smith, K. U., Zwerg, C., & Smith, N. J. Sensory-feedback analysis of infant control of the behavioral environment. *Perceptual and Motor Skills,* 1963, 16, 725-732.

Summary. Brief comments on the strengths of Dr. K. U. Smith's research program (it is systematic; has generated new apparatus, new language, and novel devices for reporting results from ingenious experiments; and has yielded a rich array of conceptual innovations) were made and certain problems were noted.

K. U. SMITH'S REPLY TO
Carol H. Ammons' Critique

I would like to comment, very briefly; let me say that through long years of experience I have learned that if you get tied up or yoked to female feedback circuits your vast deportment is one of retiring modesty—preparation to give even further grounds than one wanted to do at first.

CAROL AMMONS: You defend yourself nobly. Are there any questions that you would like to direct to Dr. Smith—or to me—but not to my poetry!

KLOTZ: I would like to apologize to somebody: I am Don Klotz—University of Iowa. I have heard throughout the day a great deal said about details in motor performance. Dr. Smith has made a couple of comments today which I was hoping he would explain further. There is no question that we have in this human body one of the most refined mechanisms of the world. We have, it is true, a complicated system of muscles, levers,

---

[4]It may be noted that these poems, being written in quick succession, provide an illustration of a feedback loop.

and so on, but it is adequately controlled by an equally complex nervous system. I was trained in both graduate and undergraduate study to present a great many details to my pupils in motor learning. One thing that didn't add up to me after being out in the teaching field was that these many details seemed to get my students confused. So it would seem obvious that I was going to have to cut down on the number of details that I presented to my youngsters.

K. U. SMITH: I think those are good points; I would go even further to encompass the hopes and expectations of people in science for the past 100 years who tried to follow the Helmholtz tradition of dissecting out particular mechanisms of the body so that they can be observed more or less in isolation. The tendency of psychologists to try to follow this tradition of simplification is not yet dead although the ideas are inadequate for the goals that were initially set—namely, that through such dissected research never really arrives at principles that will tell you how different parts of one system are tied together and what the principles of organization are.

Now, the real meaning of the feedback concept as it was initially developed in psychological work with machines, was not simply to point out details of control, but to study the principles of the locking together—the integration, the stratification and ordering and interplay of different parts of the system as distinctive phenomena. In other words, organization itself is not only a proper object of scientific study, it is an essential. The fact that it hasn't been studied by traditional methods doesn't reduce the importance of the study. However you are talking about another thing: your capabilities as a teacher or a coach to absorb and to reduce and integrate whatever sources of information there may be for an athlete or a group of athletes. Now, my point of view is that the coach today must, like the advertiser or the medical man or the teacher himself, utilize whatever information is available. Not only must he be able to sense the limitations of overworked detail which is often misleading in its purity, you might say. He doesn't dare limit himself to his own ways of understanding these details, ideas and theories, but must appreciate the ways in which an individual or a sport is tied together. The gist of my talk—without going into a lot of details—is that you've got to have systems, research methods, to study athletic skills.

We haven't looked at athletic skills in their real manifestation—which I might say is often beyond controlled methods—we have, however, looked at the functional processes that are directly involved in such skills. We studied human beings as systems methods. Now these systems methods are very plain (as far as we are concerned). If you want to study how the eye works you just can't throw stimuli into it as psychophysicists have done in the past. You've got to study how the eye relates to the head, how the eye controls its own stimulus as a systems mechanism, how the eye relates to the rest of the body. And making a lot of overgeneralized statements about the refinements of the brain isn't going to solve these problems. Now, to get methods to do that, what I've told you is simple: *you've got to invest in equipment that will enable you to measure the time relations, the space. relationships between the movements of the eye or the head, and visual stimuli from other parts of the body.* Some 25 years ago we were studying in Laredo, Texas, the B-29 computer system that guided the external guns for that newly developed plane and we happened on to the phenomenon of delayed feedback for the first time. And since that time, I have struggled to get equipment to both *space displace,* that is to invert or reverse, and delay the retinal feedback of eye movements, and we accomplished that for the first time about four or five years ago. And to do that, we not only had to get a lot of money, we had to battle everybody who had any relationships to our work at the University of Wisconsin. Just survival to do this was a critical thing. You are not talking to a pansy here (seeking ideas to do the kind of work that we do) we not only have had to do a little thinking, but we have had to really battle for equipment, and *you don't dare give up.* If you want to study the human individual, from now on you are going to have to battle for computer systems. If you don't, you are going to be out of the swim of things. *You're done for if you don't.*

KLOTZ: I think Dr. Smith has explained what he is doing perhaps a little better than I understood it, but I go back to my original point. Are we going to do a study in motor learning on how we can get the results we want in the least possible time presenting as few details as possible, not how many? *My definition of a good teacher is one who can get the job done,* saying as little as possible, using key or cue words. I would suggest that someone else do this, I haven't been doing what is commonly known as scholarly research but I have been doing day-by-day practical reasearch for 34 years. My research results emphasize simplicity. On this basis I wonder if someone somewhere along the line would like to do a study on how to get the job done in motor learning with the use of key words, key movements, with as little detail as possible.

SMITH: Permit me again, will you? Scientists, including those with whom one disagrees, although spoken of with some degree of contempt at least are respected for their efforts; the redundancy of science is something that the teacher is never going to change. Redundancy of science is a part of the evolution of man. Leonardo produced drawings of machines that weren't used for hundreds of years and if you thought of his details as redundant and superfluous in the 16th century you would have made a great mistake. The scientist who uses conventional methods to push them to their limits, with all the detail, is doing you just as much a favor as sensationalists like myself. I like to do novel things, but I have perhaps more respect for the guy that will get in and *dig* and *dig* and *dig* at something—at details that ought to at least be identified as limited—than I do for myself. *You're the guy that has to do the selecting.*

Decremental and Related Processes in Skilled Performance[1]

R. B. Ammons
C. H. Ammons
University of Montana

We started out in 1946 with the idea that if we worked persistently, we would develop sufficient facts within 10 years to construct an excellent, comprehensive, rigorous theory of motor skills learning and performance. Of this 10 years, we allocated roughly six or seven years to developing a thorough knowledge of the phenomena of rotary pursuit, followed by a three- or four-year period during which we would check out the basic laws derived from study of rotary pursuit on a variety of other skills. The resulting extensions and generalizations of the basic laws to all important skills then could form the basis for a theoretical formulation. After five or six years of vigorous research effort, we revised our estimate of the time needed for the research and theoretical program to between 15 and 20 years.

It is now 23 years since the start of our overly ambitious and impractical program, and there is a notable absence of comprehensive laws, let alone a general theory of skilled motor behavior, at least from our quarter. We can honestly say that we know essentially nothing relative to what we can see that we should know, i. e., what is likely knowable by application of present methods. A good example of an important gap in our knowledge is that we know practically nothing about the relationships of warmup decrement to the nature of the task and subject (task and subject variables).

In the face of the personally rather unsatisfactory situation outlined above, we have two consolations: First, we know a great deal more than we did 23 years ago. Our attempts to include in the following paper even a small fraction of the facts already developed have shown us just how much *more* we

[1] I would like to take this opportunity to thank the people of Iowa, and the administration and faculty of this University, for making possible my study here. I arrived in 1940 without a penny and left in 1946 with the professional's greatest friend, a fine education. It is a pleasure to acknowledge the important contributions to my personal and intellectual growth made by John A. McGeoch, Kenneth Spence, and Don Lewis, as well as the particularly great influence exerted by Gustav Bergmann, E. F. Lindquist, Wendell Johnson, and J. B. Stroud. This mention provides but a weak recognition of these men's contributions to my development as a scientist, scholar, and person. Perhaps the better parts of the following paper will acknowledge their contributions in a more effective and meaningful way.

know now than then. Second, as we have carried out more than 100 studies, discovering, describing and measuring a great many phenomena, we have never found a dearth of interesting problems calling for further research. No matter how much we find out, there is always a great deal more to find out, and the search remains exciting.

We began preparation of this paper with a goal of reviewing in it all important rotary pursuit studies in the literature. After all, 90 minutes seems a long time when compared with the 3 or 5 or even 12 minutes generously allotted at meetings these days. We soon found that we would have to limit ourselves to a coverage of our own work and that we would not be able even to cover that in detail. *We will report primarily rotary pursuit work, with some mention where extensions of this work to other skills have been made or are underway.*

Our goals in preparing the present paper were several: (a) to make this an "ideas" paper—we like to play with ideas; (b) to pull together our own major published and unpublished studies, to give an overview—selfishly, this should provide *us* with a good picture of where we have been and where we might go, while supplying the listener with some potentially useful information about our unpublished, or published but unread research; (c) to point out some relatively neglected but important issues in skills and related research; (d) to relate our findings to persistent problems in the field of learning; (e) to mention and discuss some "new" quantitative indexes of skilled behavior—some measures and methods of measurement; (f) to make some observations on apparatus problems based on systematic studies conducted by us in conjunction with investigation of effects of other variables; (g) to note some thinking about the design of studies in several skills areas; (h) to report some results of formal and informal study of methodological difficulties; (i) to indicate briefly the nature of the research we now have underway in our laboratory; and, finally, (j) to put on record some conceptual extensions of our thinking about problems of skills learning and performance, extensions motivated by considerations of social relevance of our research going back at least as far as our undergraduate days.

Only to a limited extent is it possible to take up these points separately. Practically every study was designed to throw light on several, frequently quite different, problems. Most sets of data have been reanalyzed several times, often to extend their application to problems not foreseen years before at the time of designing the study and collecting the data. This complexity has been increased further by our deliberate building into later studies tests of earlier findings, quite independently of the primary purposes of the later studies. We have planned our research program so that every major finding is independently checked by different experimenters at different times and, if at all possible, in quite different basic experimental contexts. Two results of this procedure (other than the inordinate complexity of our over-all program just mentioned) are long delays in reporting of findings and that, as far as we know, none of our more significant findings reported in the literature have been found to be incorrect, although several have been temporarily challenged.

OVERVIEW OF EXPERIMENTAL, OBSERVATIONAL AND THEORETICAL WORK

Perhaps the best place to start on this overview of the work of our group would be with bread-and-butter issues of general methodology, apparatus characteristics, and subject variables.

General Methodology

A rather basic question often put to us, is *Why use the rotary pursuit task in research at all?* This task, particularly to the person who only reads about it, sees the equipment waiting to be used, or watches others practicing without doing so himself, seems trivial, unrelated to any important real-life activity except perhaps "trying to read the label on a phonograph record while it is rotating." In weak moments, we ourselves have had our doubts. But, there are some excellent reasons for studying rotary pursuit: it is intrinsically interesting to almost all subjects; the subject does not find it difficult to improve, but to achieve perfect performance on the task is nearly impossible; variations in important task dimensions such as speed and accuracy, and duration and temporal distribution of practice, are easy to achieve; performance level is quite sensitive to these and other significant learning and performance variables; and, last, we know a great deal about rotary pursuit, so that considerably more precise formulations of problems are possible as a rule than in the case of most other skill tasks. In addition, experience has shown that findings from studies of rotary pursuit can be generalized to other tasks with encouraging frequency.

Reasonably satisfied with the task, we can raise the question as to *How many subjects need to be run to obtain stable results?*—differential performance levels, trends, differences in trends, and curves from which parameters can be estimated with some accuracy. As in all research, answers to this question must depend on sensitivity of task performance to easily producible changes in the variable, in relation to consistency and stability of task performance by the individual subject. Practically all the effects we have studied could have been detected, on a gross scale, with 25 or 30 subjects in each of a few groups. However, if one wishes to extrapolate parts of single curves in order to estimate the effect of one variable independent of effects of other variables (e. g., warmup decrement independent of reminiscence over rest in rotary pursuit), it is necessary to have a minimum of 50 and better 100 or even 200 subjects in a group. We have arrived at these figures by playing games with computers, using data from very large groups. The procedure in each case has been randomly to assign subjects to subgroups of small size, compute mean curves, then inspect and attempt to use the curves to make the desired estimates. Next, either subgroups were combined to make larger subgroups, or subjects were randomly assigned to larger groups, and the process repeated. Our smallest subgroups in each case have been in the range of 8 to 12, and combinations have been explored up to the range of 400 to 600. Gross differences in performance between male and female college students can be detected easily with groups of 25. Fine differences can be detected adequately only with groups of 100 or more (R. B. Ammons & C. H. Ammons, 1965; see Fig. 1). If one wishes to study the microstructure of rotary pursuit behavior (e. g., durations of "resting" responses; R. B. Ammons, C. H. Ammons, & Morgan, 1958), one will need more subjects than in cases where only cumulated time on target is studied; 50 subjects a group is probably a minimum. Study of one subject at a time presents a different set of problems, partially soluble by running the subject more times and longer.

We have found another quite different reason for running several times as many subjects per group as are really needed to accomplish the purposes of the immediate study. Over a period of years, new methods of analysis

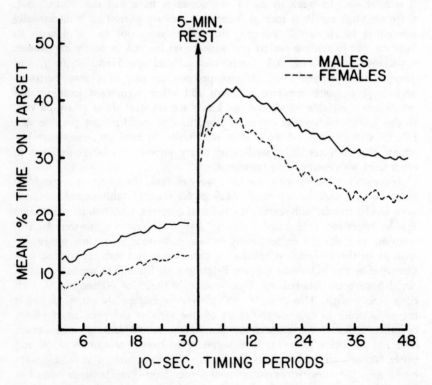

Fig. 1. Mean rotary pursuit performance, male $(N=370)$ and female $(N=210)$ college groups (R. B. Ammons & C. H. Ammons, 1965)

have been developed, and new aspects of performance have been seen to be important. We have no major study in our files, the data from which have not been reanalyzed at least once to obtain information not even guessed at when the study was originally conducted. A large initial surplus of subjects has been very helpful where we wished to fractionate the data (e. g., according to sex, age, or initial proficiency of subject) or to use relatively unstable or insensitive statistical procedures (e. g., correlations).

From the above information and experiences, we have concluded that one should run as many subjects as possible, ordinarily several times more than the minimum, and never run the minimum except perhaps in preliminary explorations where the data bear on a highly specific problem and will for various reasons not be reusable (e. g., known apparatus malfunction or peculiar characteristics of experimenters).

This brings us to a delightful topic, *degree of experimenter bias,* or *experimenter effect,* to be a little less evaluative. Dr. Robert Rosenthal has found a number of experimental situations in which such bias can be demonstrated or, better, produced. Clearly, a task the performance of which can be and is easily influenced by silly or scientifically insane hypotheses or values of experimenters, is one to be avoided unless one is deliberately studying experimenter bias. We have a very considerable amount of information about the susceptibility of rotary pursuit performance to "illicit" experimenter effects. My interest (RBA) was probably first aroused in 1947, when a research assistant (handsome, young, ex-navy-officer) commented that he seemed to be able to motivate young female college students to better performance by holding out dates (half humorously) as incentives. I was unable to follow up this particular lead, as I found it impossible to vary the incentive value in a clean and socially acceptable way. However, we have incorporated the experimenter as an orthogonal variable in practically every large study carried out in our laboratory from 1948 until the present. For example, complete replications with different experimenters were run in such early studies as those by R. B. Ammons (1951b); R. B. Ammons (1958), R. B. Ammons, Alprin, & C. H. Ammons (1955); and R. B. Ammons & Willig (1956).

What have we discovered about experimenter effect in rotary pursuit studies? In most studies, we have found statistically significant differences in subject performance associated with experimenters, but almost never have we found a statistically significant interaction between experimenters and other important variables whose effects were being studied. In no study have we been able to assign subjects completely randomly to experimenters and both subjects and experimenters completely and randomly to times (neither subject nor experimenter has or can reasonably be expected to have all hours, days, weeks, and months free for this kind of assignment during a major investigation). Although we have seldom been able to discover any systematic bias in assignment, we have regularly found significant (although absolutely small) differences between groups run by different experimenters. Where careful study of the groups has been possible, we were able to conclude that the differences were most likely due to minor differences in composition of the groups. These differences arose from use of different although apparently equivalent subject pools or sources and were usually related to differential availability of subject groups over hours of day, days of week, or times of school quarter or year. Experimenter effects deserve continuing study. We provide for such study in most of our designs, particularly where new variables or new ranges of variables are being examined.

Since the experimenter variable has been found to be at least potentially important in our studies, we have worked out a number of simple precautionary measures which seem to minimize experimenter bias: (a) the experiment is replicated by several experimenters (five or more if possible) at different times, with experimenters aware of our policy of replication, and independent consistency of results made into a challenging game; (b) the project director is known to be thoroughly familiar with the task and situation (of course, we have run thousands of subjects ourselves); (c) experimenters are carefully checked out for proficiency in standardized data collection procedures; (d) experimenters are encouraged to discuss problems encountered in their conduct of the experiment with the project director and actively to look for and report possible artifacts related to method, as well as any sort of peculiar or unusual behavior by a subject; (e) experimenters simply *never* "know" how the study "should" come out or set out to "prove" something. They are cautioned that we "know" from earlier studies what outcomes to expect but have good reason to anticipate some differences in the present study; and that it is perfectly all right, in fact an excellent idea, to watch what is going on, but to have real respect for the typically found large differences among subjects. Above all, experimenters are to discard questionably obtained data and to conduct themselves as if being watched by all scientists to come in the future; they simply cannot and must not put any but "absolutely correct" information on record. We only want to know "how it is" and "what makes it that way."

Now Dr. Rosenthal has done important work on experimenter bias, and we hope and believe he is a good friend of ours. But we do not find appreciable experimenter *bias*. Perhaps this is because skills behavior and particularly rotary pursuit behavior is robust, little affected by bias on the part of the experimenter. However, we strongly suspect that Dr. Rosenthal would find little experimenter bias in his experiments if he took the above precautions. His work seems to us to show that experimenter bias is possible, especially with relatively unsophisticated experimenters, but we have found that it is definitely not necessary, at least within studies of rotary pursuit and several other skills.

Methodology seems to be a weak point in psychology. It is interesting to note that there are no standard procedures for administration of the rotary pursuit task or standard reference conditions to run to "calibrate" new studies. Fortunately, although standardization of rotary pursuit apparatus is important and has not been achieved, we do know a great deal about its functioning and the effects of variations in apparatus on subject performance.

Apparatus Characteristics

It is nice to be able to begin a discussion on a positive note. With pleasure we report that the basic rotary pursuit apparatus, going back to Wilhelmina Koerth and presumably Carl Emil Seashore, "lives" and still manages to produce quite adequate results for most purposes. By some sort of small miracle, this ridiculous equipment, the phonograph turntable revolving clockwise, the metal target, and the simple hinged stylus, have turned out to give the best (most clear-cut) results in the study of many imporant learning and performance variables. Unfortunately for our present hard-nosed, empirical stance, this fortunate combination was arrived at by intuition with some luck thrown in, since no systematic, objective studies of apparatus variables were then given serious consideration.

In 1955, after several years of gathering and analyzing data, we published a review on reporting of apparatus variables in the published rotary pursuit literature (R. B. Ammons, 1955b). We had found that investigators often forgot or did not think it worthwhile to put on record, and apparently had felt quite free to vary, such important apparatus characteristics as size of target, rate of rotation of turntable, weight on stylus tip, etc. It is perhaps even more significant that our review almost was not published because of its "lack of importance" to the editors of prestigious journals—it was rescued at the last moment through the intervention of Dr. Arthur Melton who saw some significance in the problems raised. By direct investigation, we have since found that rate of rotation (from 30 to 90 rpm), size of target (from $\frac{1}{4}$ in. to 1 in.), distance of target from center of rotation (approximately 3 in. to 8 in.), weight on stylus tip (approximately 1 oz. to 5 oz.), and shape of stylus tip (flat, through rounded, to pointed), all have significant effects on one or more important aspects of rotary pursuit performance. On the other hand, we have found that length of hinged section of stylus (approximately 2 in. through 12 in.), material used for target and stylus tip (brass and various alloys of silver), voltage through the stylus-target circuit (12v DC vs 110v AC), and height of turntable surface (hip through shoulder), may have small, often undetectable, absolute effects, but their effects *relative* to those of the variables included above in the first set are quite minor.

Two other apparatus issues have given us real concern: use of photoelectric stylus-target devices and use of extremely sensitive condenser-type timers. As early as 1949 (Hullett, Eckles, & R. B. Ammons, 1952), we tried out various arrangements of photo-electric cells and lights for use as stylus-target combinations. We found repeatedly that such devices were relatively unreliable, demanding frequent servicing and recalibration, since their functioning was inevitably related to such things as changes in cell sensitivity, changes in apparatus light intensity, changes in light-transmitting surfaces as they were abraded in use, and intensity of ambient illumination. It took the part-time services of one lab technician to keep the equipment running (we tried a number of designs with aiming, linear pursuit, and rotary pursuit tasks). Our conclusion, after several years of experimentation with design and continuing frustration, was that photo-electric systems were a very poor bet for ordinary laboratory use. With considerable interest, then, we noted several years ago that an equipment manufacturer was producing a photo-electric-type pursuit device. We purchased one. In months of trials, we found that it was subject to all the problems we had noted earlier in our own equipment, plus a tendency to speed up greatly as some part heated up. We contacted the responsible production engineer, who stated that we were the "first and only customers to complain," but suggested several changes (which did not work). We then requested and received an "improved" version of their device, for testing and a special report in *Perceptual and Motor Skills*. Those of you who read PMS will not have seen the report, and because of the following: malfunctions of the "improved" equipment were nearly identical to those of the earlier version; the production engineer moved to another company; at least that one new company and yet another one started producing equipment which appeared to be essentially the same; we could not afford to buy equipment from the new producers and they did not feel like giving us equipment to use and report on; and we finally were able to correct the major malfunctions by drastic changes in the rather flimsy circuits of the two pieces of equipment which we already had on hand. About all we can say, albeit with considerable feeling, is BEWARE! It should also be noted that the very nature of the equipment (use of stencil arrangements to make pursuit paths) is such as to impose some very interesting rate variations on the basic task, unless an absolutely circular path is used.

The story of our use of the vacuum-tube-and-condenser timing system is more cheerful. By using a vacuum tube for a relay, cumulating a charge with a condenser, reading this charge at the end of each trial, then discharging the condenser, we were able quite adequately to time rotary pursuit performance. In principle this arrangement is much less expensive than one with electromagnetic relays and Standard Electric timers, and it is far more accurate in an absolute sense, giving score increases when the Standard Electric timer would just be chattering wildly as the subject's stylus tip skittered around on the target. Our photographic studies as well as direct observations of subject and clock behavior have indicated that the condenser arrangement gives a very nearly perfect record of the time the stylus is in contact (including moving contact) with the target. But, don't throw away your old "Air Force"-type equipment, even though it does not give comparable absolute values. In several different ways, we have compared sets of scores, and each time we have come up with correlations in the high .90s. So, unless absolute values are of real significance to your research (and this has almost never been the case in our work), the old design, dependent on an electromagnetic clutch, will be satisfactory. However, a word of caution is in order. Check your timers against each other and balance them when they are used in alternating banks. We have regularly found large differences in the performance of new Standard Electric timers checked in the same circuit, and these differences seem to increase with use.

Having remarked on general methodology and apparatus characteristics, we now come to our last bread-and-butter area, subject variables.

Subject Variables

Ultimately, our research goal is "complete" specification of the effects of subject variables, that is, how subjects behave under what circumstances. All we propose to do in the present section is to note a few behavior-related differences among subjects which have often been disregarded in the design and conduct of research, but which we have found to have practically significant effects. Since each of the following will be covered in detail elsewhere in this paper, we will simply point out some findings with a few of their implications for research. Specifically, we have noted significant differences in rotary pursuit behavior related to sex, age, laterality, initial level of ability, and motivation of subjects.

Sex-related behavior differences have been studied repeatedly. Prior to our first research in 1945 (R. B. Ammons, 1947b), several investigators had already observed, evaluated and reported significant superiority of college men over college women in time on target. We found that marked sex differences appeared only after the third grade (R. B. Ammons, Alprin, & C. H. Ammons, 1955). In that same study, it was also observed that, when proficiency was held constant, little or no difference appeared between male and female subjects in warmup decrement or temporary work decrement. (See Fig. 2.) We have subsequently found far more subtle differences between male and female subject performance at the college level. Sex-related variables are of sufficient magnitude that we must control for sex of subject in most rotary pursuit studies.

As noted above, there are complex relationships between age and sex of subjects and their rotary pursuit performances. We have found that performance: increases with age from CA 6 through about CA 16 or 17 (C. H. Ammons & R. B. Ammons, 1967; R. B. Ammons, Alprin, & C. H. Ammons, 1955); remains fairly constant through college and until about CA 30 or 35 (all our college studies; unpublished age study of males in a state prison); then declines slowly to age 70 (same prison study). One should certainly specify the age of his subjects and might well, for most purposes, restrict his samples to young adults (CAs 18 through 30) unless he is specifically studying age-related effects.

Strength of laterality has been found in several minor studies to be related to performance, and, happily, just as folk-beliefs suggest. Right-handed subjects do achieve higher time-on-target scores with their right hands than with their left (several unpublished analyses of performance of "discarded" LH

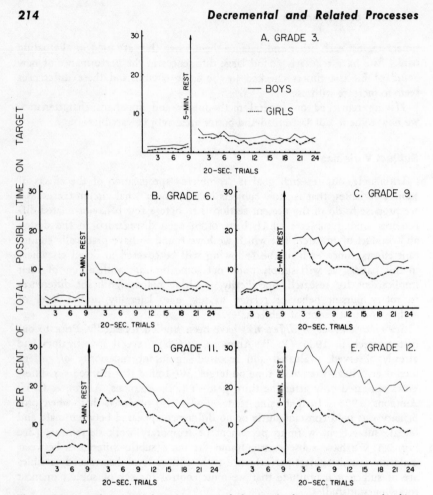

Fig. 2. Mean performance of rotary pursuit before and after a 5-min. rest for boys and girls of different grade levels. N = 35 at each point. [R. B. Ammons, Alprin, & C. H. Ammons, 1955; Adapted, copyright 1955 by the American Psychological Association, and reproduced by permission.]

subjects in relation to "accepted" RH subjects). Subjects also tend to be right- or left-footed, and this preference is reflected in higher scores (C. H. Ammons & R. B. Ammons, 1958; R. B. Ammons & C. H. Ammons, 1962). Thus the investigator should certainly control for the laterality of his subjects. Strangely, there seem to be no well-validated or even conceptually adequate laterality scales; so such control becomes somewhat difficult, although one can at least ask the subject to indicate his own evaluation of his laterality, or which hand he writes with, or which foot he uses to kick a ball. More of this later.

Every investigator of motor skills learning in his right mind (behaviorists please pardon the language) "knows" that *subjects differ greatly in motivation* and that these differences are "of course" reflected in performance. We will dispute this "knowledge" to some extent later. Here we simply note that with a physically satisfactory laboratory situation, and an even half-humane experimenter, it turns out be difficult to alter the typical subject's fairly strong positive motivation to perform the rotary pursuit task. We have had only a few subjects out of many thousands actually quit in the middle of a session, and only a few more fail to continue to attempt to perform the task following some verbal encouragement, this in the face of frequently reported headaches, dizziness, nausea, double vision, aching arms and backs, etc. So motivation is probably not an important subject variable in rotary pursuit. But *level of proficiency* is. Wide individual differences in performance typically appear in the first seconds of practice. These differences persist and are remarkably stable, making the pursuit rotor a psychometrically excellent instrument, with odd-even and test-retest reliabilities of total scores comfortably in the .90s. Several of our recent studies have uncovered large interactions between various indexes of proficiency and other aspects of rotary pursuit behavior. It appears that we *must,* even if only statistically, control for subject proficiency. We should also investigate the development of differences in proficiency.

In studying rotary pursuit, is there much chance that we will develop a "psychology of the sophomore" (freshman, in the case of the University of Montana)? That is, are our results specific to college students at the freshman or sophomore level, as in so many other fields of psychological research? We think not. Evidence already presented plus much to be presented later in this paper supports our position. If we can just prevent college entrance committees and officers from using rotary pursuit performance as an entrance criterion (and this shouldn't really be too difficult), college students will continue to be fairly representative of all physically able young adults (at least in rotary pursuit). Further age studies should continue to show, as we have already found, that college students' performance is part of a continuous developmental sequence from early childhood to late maturity.

We seem to have come to a "natural discontinuity" in the discussion at this point, a time for a brief look at what we have already covered, where we are, and where we propose to go in the remainder of this paper. So far, you have been slightly introduced to the value systems of two rotary pursuit investigators and have been given a quick summary of issues related to general methodology, apparatus characteristics, and subject variables as we have investigated and thought about their effects and significance. Several of our early, pre-meeting, "trial" readers asked what we meant by "bread and butter" issues. We had nothing sinister in mind—just that any investigator who disregards these issues is likely to find himself deprived of bread and butter!

The remainder of our paper will be taken up with: a review of some of our completed but mostly unpublished research in a number of specific areas; brief comments on our theoretical work; some indication of the research projects which we have underway; and a discussion of general issues related to our research, mainly within the context of "social relevance."

First let us address ourselves to those areas in which we have done most of our research: decremental processes, classical transfer, cross-limb transfer, age-related phenomena, initial proficiency, motivation, generality of originality, nature of the learning process, and properties of measures used. In this section and those following it, all we can hope to do is to sample from the large amount of information which we have developed, introducing you to the general outlines of most of our major studies. It is only reasonable that we start with decremental processes, in view of the title of this paper and the fundamental nature of the research.

Decremental Processes

Temporary work decrement.—Kenneth Spence used to say it was inevitable that graduate students in psychology would decide that they should do research on fatigue and sleep, considering how tired and sleepy they soon became in the process of working toward advanced degrees. There seems to be no reason to limit this observation to graduate students. Tired and sleepy we were, tired and sleepy we are, and tired and sleepy we are going to be, in spite of already having completed our graduate work.

My first introduction to the study of work decrement was via an exciting thesis by Leo Reyna (1944). My first actual research was that forming a part of my dissertation (R. B. Ammons, 1947b). From that time on, my constant interest has been in the when, where, and why of various sorts of decremental processes, and Dr. Carol has joined me in this interest.

To make the following discussion more intelligible, I would like to propose as I did 23 years ago that: (a) the basic unit of skills practice is the work-rest-work cycle; (b) relatively independent estimates can be obtained, by analyzing performance during such a cycle, of proficiency, temporary work decrement (Hull's, Kimble's, and Eysenck's reactive inhibition, I_R), permanent work decrement (Hull's, Kimble's, and Eysenck's conditioned inhibition, $_sI_R$), and warmup decrement. You may already have noticed in earlier figures that the curve of mean performance with continuous practice after a rest several minutes in duration almost always shows a sharp rise, a plateau, a relatively declining section, and then a resumption of increase if practice is continued much beyond eight minutes. Fig. 3 pictures such a "standard" curve, and shows how we obtain our estimates of work decrement and warmup decrement, as well as an number of other variables. Computation is based on the assumption that increase in mean performance over a rest of some minutes will take place in exact proportion to the amount of temporary work decrement present just before the start of the rest, providing that there is no decrement at the start of postrest practice due to need

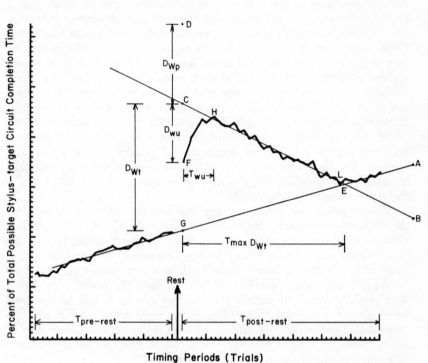

Timing Periods (Trials)

Fig. 3. Schematic drawing of work-rest-work rotary pursuit mean performance curve, showing methods for estimating numerical values of variables. Following are definitions of the points and terms shown on the graph: A—extrapolation of pre-rest performance curve; B—straight line fitted to the relatively decremental segment of the post-rest performance curve; C—level of line B at first post-rest trial, estimated performance level if there were no D_{wu}; D—'true' level of learning, performance level if there were no D_{wp}, D_{wt}, or D_{wu}; E—intersection of B and A, estimated point at which maximum post-rest D_{wt} is reached; F—actual performance level on first post-rest trial; G—predicted level of performance on first post-rest trial if there had been no rest; H—relative high point reached early in post-rest performance; L—relative low point in post-rest performance at the end of the 'decremental' segment; $T_{pre-rest}$—time spent practicing before rest; $T_{post-rest}$—time spent practicing after rest; D_{wp}—permanent work decrement on first post-rest trial, $D - C$ where all temporary work decrement has dissipated over rest; D_{wt}—amount of temporary work decrement dissipated over rest; $T_{max} D_{wt}$—time to reach a maximum level of temporary work decrement after rest; D_{wu}—initial decrement in post-rest performance curve due to necessity for subject to 'warm up' after rest; T_{wu}—time to overcome 'warm-up' decrement after rest. [Redrawn from R. B. Ammons, 1947a, copyright 1947 by the American Psychological Association and reproduced with permission. Actual data points taken from R. B. Ammons & C. H. Ammons, 1967.]

to warm up. It is further assumed that warming up, if present, will be rapid (nearly complete in two or three minutes at most) and that, by backward extrapolation of the following section of the curve to the beginning of postrest practice, one can estimate performance free of warmup decrement. We can then define as follows: *proficiency* as actual performance level at any given point in practice; *warmup decrement* (D_{wu}) as the difference at the start of postrest practice between actual level of performance and the warmup-free estimate based upon backward extrapolation of the later curve (usually the section between three and six or seven minutes after rest); *temporary work decrement* (D_{Wt}) as the corrected gain-over-rest at any point in practice; and *permanent work decrement* (D_{Wp}) as the amount the estimated initial level of postrest performance free of D_{wu} falls below performance under ideal conditions of distribution of practice and rests. It can be seen that D_{Wt} is similar in properties to reactive inhibition (I_R) and D_{Wp} to conditioned inhibition ($_sI_R$) as these terms have been used within Hull's theory and many of its later variants.

Without going into detail, we note that our research strongly supports the following conclusions about *temporary work decrement*: (a) it appears during the performance of many or perhaps all motor skills; (b) its net accumulation seems to be related to the homogeneity of the skill; (c) it transfers across closely related skills (such as rotary pursuit at 50 and 60 rpm); (d) it transfers from limb to limb "within" the subject; (e) it is at least partially central in nature; (f) it is not due to fatigue in the usual sense; (g) it is not due to boredom in the usual sense; (h) it seems to affect skilled performance by causing a partial distortion or disintegration of habits, through a kind of filtering process; (i) its effect on the development of a skill is mostly or perhaps completely transitory.

Although we have carried out a great deal of related research, we will not go into the controversy as to whether there really is any *permanent work decrement* due to massing of practice. We simply note that: D_{Wp} is difficult to find and small in amount, if there is any at all (R. B. Ammons, 1950, 1952; R. B. Ammons & Willig, 1956); D_{Wp} is certainly *not* due to development of resting responses (R. B. Ammons, C. H. Ammons, & Morgan, 1958) even though this hypothesis seems to have 9 x 9 lives[2]; and we have been able to demonstrate D_{Wp} most clearly not in rotary pursuit but in practice of reversal of perspective (unpublished study).

The skills investigator must eventually answer one very important question about learning under conditions of massed and distributed practice: why does the subject who has practiced under a no-rest condition and never done very well, quickly (within a few minutes) catch up with a subject who has been doing extremely well under a distributed practice condition when the me-

---

[2] Its latest reincarnation (if it was ever dead) seems to be in an article by Eysenck, *et al.* (1969). We should add at this point that much of our enjoyment in researching and theorizing about rotary pursuit has arisen from studying and reacting (mostly privately) to many provocative reports by Eysenck and his co-workers.

diocre performer is switched to the distributed condition? He has not been practicing efficient skills and the high-level performer has been. Our guess is that the skills he *has* been practicing are similar enough to the efficient skills that very rapid and almost complete transfer takes place. In other words, it is fine to mass your practice, if you practice the right things.

Study of perceptual distortions has probably given us the most useful clues to the nature of temporary work decrement. Some years ago, we realized that there were at last superficial similarities between reports of figural after-effects and figural breakdown by investigators of both visual and kinesthetic perception, and reports by our subjects practicing rotary pursuit when they were asked to describe any peculiar phenomena experienced. Repeatedly, our rotor subjects reported peculiar phenomena ranging from simple slowing and speeding up of the turntable (and target), through ellipsoidal and other regular but non-circular patterns of target movement, through detached seemingly autonomous hand-and-arm movements, to grossly erratic movements of the target and unpredictable movements of the whole apparatus toward and away from the subject. It occurred to us that visual perceptual processes might well lie behind these rotor phenomena and that we could throw some light on the rotor phenomena by obtaining reports of their experiences from naive subjects who simply viewed a light rotating in the dark (by removing the structured visual field, we hoped to intensify the central perceptual phenomena).

In this "rotor-target-in-the-dark" study (unpublished), subjects viewed a visually unstructured round spot of light under massed or distributed conditions. Each subject was assigned to one of the several spot-size and rate-of-rotation conditions. The spot of light was positioned in exactly the same physical location and followed the same clockwise path for the standing subject that a standard rotor target would. The subject then made a continuous verbal report of what he was "seeing" during periods of movement by the light (it was only visible to the subject during periods of rotation). Although target (light) sizes and different rates of rotation had no detectable differential effect, subjects "saw" a fantastic variety of visual movements. Movement was often in three dimensions and almost never in a simple circle or a nearly circular elipse. I myself viewed the light spot, knowing the exact structure of the apparatus; yet I experienced vividly the rotation of a moon in which the moon kept one face to its parent body. The percept was vivid and intense, especially so to an amateur astronomer. Examination of subject reports repeatedly reinforced the initial impression that these experiences were, as predicted, intensified ones of the same kind experienced by regular rotor subjects.

Warmup decrement.—Performance deficit due to need to warm up at the start of a new practice period is the second decremental process which we have studied intensively. It is probably the most controversial of the distribution-of-practice phenomena in skilled performance. At least one major investigator at one time affirmed the null hypothesis after an experiment and insisted that D_{wu} did not exist in rotary pursuit. D_{wu} has been handled theoretically in a variety of ways, including its use as evidence of conditioned inhibition (permanent work decrement), its being due to extinction of competing habits which have spontaneously recovered strength during a no-practice period, and as being a kind of physical (physiological) process necessary at the beginning of any motor-skilled activity after a period of "rest" (no related activity).

In our own rotary pursuit research, we have found that the following statements about D_{wu} hold fairly generally: (a) proficiency must be developed before D_{wu} appears; (b) more D_{wu} is found following massed (especially continuous) practice than following distributed practice; (c) using fairly gross performance measures, no D_{wu} is found after highly distributed practice, but it quickly appears (reappears?) if blocks of highly massed practice are undertaken; (d) pre-practice of rotary pursuit motor components does not eliminate D_{wu}, although it may decrease D_{wu} somewhat; (e) D_{wu} transfers from limb to limb and usually from level to level along task dimensions such as speed and target size.

Briefly, our theoretical account of D_{wu} phenomena (R. B. Ammons, 1959) is based on an analysis of the stimulus complex during acquisition and further practice of rotary pursuit skill. As proficiency increases toward an asymptote, motor behavior of all kinds (gross postural; ocular; hand, arm, and shoulder) becomes quite stable and increasingly uniform ("homogeneous"?) with an increasing uniformity of stimulus complex. At the very start of a practice period following considerable rest (five minutes or more), the subject has just been engaging in motor behavior quite different from rotary pursuit, so the stimulus complex is quite different from that during almost all of the prior rotary pursuit practice. As practice continues, traces of rest-related stimuli drop out as do traces from the somewhat erratic behavior engaged in early in the practice period, and an increasingly stable stimulus complex emerges after one to three minutes. We further assume that the motor behaviors associated with highly proficient performance become increasingly likely to be elicited by a stimulus complex, the longer these behaviors are engaged in, in the presence of that stimulus complex. Work decrement can be assumed to be loading of inhibition on perceptual patterns as a function of the time they are present, with transfer from pattern to pattern along similarity dimensions.

There is really not enough time to state this theoretical formulation adequately, let alone trace out the many predictions that can be made from it. Intuitively, you may feel that the theory can account rigorously for most of the stable D_{wu} phenomena which we have observed and summarized earlier in this section, as indeed is the case. One simple, unexpected prediction following from the theory is that D_{wu} as evidenced by a sharp rise in time on target should not be present within short trials during distributed practice. An analysis of hits within 1-min. trials separated by 30-sec. rests was made by 10-sec. periods (R. B. Ammons, 1955a). When subjects had achieved some proficiency after a few minutes of practice, the curves based on the mean durations of hits during the six successive 10-sec. intervals in each 1-min. trial uniformly showed a sharp drop, as predicted. Prior analysis of performance by 1-min. periods had simply obscured the phenomenon (e. g., R. B. Ammons & Willig, 1956).

We are pleased to note that this theory is in part an extension of ideas worked out jointly with Dr. Kenneth Spence in 1944 or 1945.

Classical Transfer

By classical transfer, we mean, roughly, transfer along dimensions of tasks using similar sets of muscle-bone-joint units. In our rotary pursuit research, we have determined degree of transfer of skill and decremental components along task dimensions of speed of rotation, accuracy required (target size), and stylus length, among many. We have given up this line of research, at least temporarily, even though much effort has been expended (typically more than 1000 subjects in each study), because of the great amount of time and effort required, the small amount of information developed, and the apparent impossibility of meaningfully generalizing or applying that information to tasks other than rotary pursuit, or for that matter, to other variations of the rotary pursuit task.

We have drawn the following conclusions from our research findings: (a) within-task transfer of proficiency and temporary work decrement is generally quite high, as is transfer of warmup decrement if it is independently found in both versions of the task; (b) amount of transfer is *not* a simple function of degree of physical difference in task versions; (c) the obviously great complexity of behavioral effects deserves extensive study using motion picture or videotape recordings; (d) current theories of transfer are so oversimplified that they are almost completely useless in the face of real behavioral changes as in rotary pursuit; (e) further work by us should be delayed until a far more adequate and comprehensive theory is constructed.

Cross-limb Transfer

By cross-limb transfer, we mean, roughly, improvement of performance of a skill using one limb due to practice of the "same" skill with a different limb. Whereas we developed a sense of frustration over our disproportionately unproductive research with classical transfer designs, we early formed a strong conviction that cross-limb transfer studies would throw important light on all transfer phenomena. This conviction has persisted and has been accompanied by an increasing excitement as we have gone from study to study and theoretical analysis to theoretical analysis. We firmly believe that our paper (R. B. Ammons, 1958) summarizing cross-limb transfer phenomena and suggesting a tremendous number and variety of experimental approaches, measurement procedures, lines along which theory might well develop, and fragments of actual theory, is easily the most original and creative we have ever written, and certainly the most neglected, if infrequencies of citation and/or use of the ideas mean anything.

We became interested in the phenomena of cross-limb transfer very early in our research careers, very likely because of some of Robert Woodworth's remarks (1938, especially pp. 181-189). In 1949 we conducted a cross-hand transfer study (R. B. Ammons, 1958) in the earliest attempt as far as we are aware to determine the extent to which temporary work decrement is a phenomenon of central or peripheral origin. We found marked cross-hand transfer of temporary work decrement, warmup decrement, and proficiency, consistent with a central or a mixed central-peripheral interpretation of these phenomena. By 1958 (C. H. Ammons & R. B. Ammons, 1958), we had established that the same sorts of transfer of proficiency and decremental effects took place from foot to foot. In these studies, we used a "full" transfer design, with two separate periods of practice and all four combinations of limb sequences (RR, RL, LR, LL), a practice not encouraged by the magnitude-of-transfer indices then in vogue. In order to measure transfer of warmup and temporary work decrement, we ran a group with a short rest (20 sec.) and a separate group with a long rest (20 min.) through each of the four limb sequences. Failure to use this "full" design has frequently limited the analyses possible in subsequent studies of cross-limb transfer.

By 1962, we had completed a "full-design" study of cross-limb transfer including both hands and both feet, as well as short- and long-rest conditions (R. B. Ammons & C. H. Ammons, 1962). Over 2,000 subjects were distributed randomly into 32 conditions, providing all 16 possible limb sequences and short or long rest (20 sec. or 5 min.) between the two practice periods. Subsequently (unpublished), by dropping out subjects we matched means and variances of scores during the first practice period for all groups using the same limb and analyzed the resulting data for transfer both by classical methods and by our own curve-comparison methods developed in the course of the earlier studies. Again, we found clear-cut evidence of transfer from each limb to each other limb of proficiency, temporary work decrement, and warmup decrement. A new correlational method for evaluation of transfer of proficiency was tried out and worked well, giving even more consistent' results than the classical and curve-comparison methods. Results are summarized in Table 1.

It can be seen that over-all transfer of proficiency is greatest to the same type of limb (H to H or F to F) and to the other limb on the same side of the body (RH to RF or LF to LH). We note with mixed feelings that this same correlational approach had earlier been used with equal success to evaluate the degree of retention of skills across intervals of up to two years (R. B. Ammons, Farr, Bloch, Neumann, Dey, Marion and C. H. Ammons, 1958) but that the report of the results so obtained was removed from the journal version of the report at the request of the editor. We believed the approach worthwhile and still do, particularly where many subjects are run in each group, or where large individual differences in the transfer or retention processes are suspected, and an over-all test of the interactions of these individual-difference variables ("within-group" variance) and the major manipulated variables is needed.

You might be interested in an apparently new design we have been playing

TABLE 1

PRODUCT-MOMENT CORRELATION COEFFICIENTS BETWEEN TIME-ON-TARGET TOTALS FOR TWO SUCCESSIVE 8-MIN. PERIODS OF CONTINUOUS ROTARY PURSUIT PRACTICE SEPARATED BY 20-SEC. OR 5-MIN. RESTS (32 GROUPS, $N = 71$ OR 73 IN EACH), "FULL" TRANSFER DESIGN INCLUDING BOTH HANDS AND BOTH FEET

Limb Used During First 8-min. Practice Period	Limb Used During Second 8-min. Practice Period			
	RH	LH	RF	LF
Groups With 20-sec. Rest				
RH	.828	.856	.691	.750
LH	.732	.911	.522	.626
RF	.626	.652	.847	.688
LF	.457	.561	.809	.945
Groups With 5-min. Rest				
RH	.800	.778	.787	.455
LH	.774	.829	.687	.587
RF	.636	.545	.749	.663
LF	.439	.573	.814	.860

with since completing the large cross-limb transfer study. This design permits study of both classical (between task) and cross-limb (between subject-components) transfer. We call it an "alternating" design and feel that it more closely approximates a larger proportion of real-life transfer situations than do the more standard transfer designs used heretofore in the laboratory. Basically, the subject alternates repeatedly between or among tasks, being given relatively short periods of practice on each. The following are some of the variables which can be introduced and controlled within the design: number of different tasks; time spent practicing each of the tasks during each alternation cycle; mastery of each of the tasks at any given time in the total alternation sequence; and durations of rest periods. This design allows one to observe cumulative transfer of proficiency, temporary work decrement, and warmup decrement (or any other identifiable and measurable skills components) between or among tasks, and *reciprocally* among all skills being alternated in the study within each single subject, which latter analysis is not possible with conventional designs (e. g., we can observe and measure not only RH to LH transfer for a given subject, but also LH to RH for that same subject, with the subject serving as his own control in several different ways). This alternating design quickly becomes very complex, particularly as one adds all the desirable control groups and control variations within subjects. Although it appears to have exciting prospects, we have not carried this approach beyond the first few feasibility studies (e. g., R. B. Ammons & C. H. Ammons, 1959), because in principle almost all transfer studies done to date, using other designs, apparently could be meaningfully duplicated. Such a program has remained slightly beyond our means and facilities.

Age-related Phenomena

We initiated a research program in 1952 to determine relationships between age and rotary pursuit performance variables including proficiency, temporary work decrement, and warmup decrement. Our first study (R. B. Ammons, Alprin, & C. H. Ammons, 1955) covered the age range from CA 9 through CA 18, including equal numbers of boys and girls at each of five school grade levels (3, 6, 9, 11, 12). Mean performance curves are shown in Fig. 2. We observed that proficiency increased with age, at least until CA 16, that amount of temporary work decrement built up was greater with increase in age (but unfortunately this effect was not independent of proficiency which also increased), and that warmup decrement increased with age (but the increase was positively related to increases in proficiency and temporary work decrement). In interpreting our results, we proposed that warmup decrement might be due at least in part to spontaneous recovery of competing habits within a rest period and made two further predictions about age-related performance: that less warmup decrement would be found in younger children's performance, even with extensive practice, and that

increasing amounts of warmup decrement would be found in the performance of increasingly older subject-groups. These predictions were based
on the assumption that the younger the child, the fewer the habits already
learned, including competing ones, and the older the adult, the more the
habits, already learned, including competing ones.

Pursuing this line of research, we gave 30 kindergarten children extensive
rotary pursuit training (C. H. Ammons & R. B. Ammons, 1967). As predicted, they showed no warmup decrement during two final 4-min. periods
of continuous practice, even though their proficiency had reached a respectable
level. Unfortunately, in order to bring them to a point where they could perform continuously at 60 rpm with some proficiency, we had to use lower
target speeds, short practice periods, and highly distributed practice. When
we ran 30 college students, each yoked exactly to one kindergarten child's
pattern of rotor speeds, practice periods, and distribution of practice, they
also showed no warmup decrement. We had simply discovered a method for
preventing the development of warmup decrement in adults, and perhaps
also in children. We did observe that the kindergartners were primarily
learning how to attend to, concentrate on, and persist in the task, a set of
skills which had presumably already been learned in other situations by the
college students and were easily transferred by them to rotary pursuit.
Actually, we already knew from earlier studies (R. B. Ammons, 1950; R. B.
Ammons & Willig, 1956) that distribution of practice would decrease or
eliminate warmup decrement but had expected it to show up in the second
continuous-practice "test" period as it had in those studies.

In another attack on the same problem, we gave 30 male and female 9-
year-olds eight 6-min., 60-rpm practice periods scattered over five days. These
subjects showed much less warmup decrement than college students, consistent with our competing-habits prediction.

We then turned to older subjects. With the cooperation of the Kentucky
state prison, we trained 30 male prisoners in each age group, 20-29, 30-39,
40-49, 50-59, and 60-69 yr. (unpublished study). Two periods of continuous
practice were given, separated by a rest. Although there was no appreciable
increase in *amount* of warmup decrement with increasing age, there was a
statistically significant increase in the time to overcome the warmup decrement, consistent with the competing habits prediction. We also found a
steady decrease in proficiency after age 39, with an accompanying and
probably functionally related decrease in temporary work decrement. We
subsequently attempted to duplicate this study in the Montana prison system
but were unable to run more than a few subjects over CA 40. There was
some sort of "disagreement" between prison administration and older con-
victs, and the latter were resisting passively by refusing to serve as subjects
in a number of experiments. Many older men approached the experimenter
with apologies for not participating but felt that as a matter of principle
they really could not.

We have developed little information about the performance of females beyond college age. Representative groups are almost impossible to find and study in the community, and there are relatively few females in either Kentucky or Montana prisons. We have speculated as to whether women are just better-behaved than men or get away with more. It might appear that if one "needed" to commit a crime, "he" should be sure to be a clearly identifiable female!

The studies outlined above suggest that more intensive study of age changes in motor skill would be productive. Unfortunately, there are two practically insurmountable problems. If one follows the same subjects over the years and repeatedly trains them, one will produce a large, uncontrolled practice effect. If, on the other hand, one carries out cross-sectional studies with a different group at each age level, how can one possibly assure comparability of groups from age to age? Obviously the more physically fit and the more highly motivated persons will survive longer on the average. We will simply have to work around these problems, looking for data bearing on pertinent problems and hoping to find new methods for controlling the built-in contaminating variables.

Proficiency

As already mentioned, in our study of school-age subjects (R. B. Ammons, Alprin, & C. H. Ammons, 1955), we found that proficiency increased with increases in age. In that study and in many others with college students, we have found that initial proficiency, final proficiency, total proficiency, gain in proficiency with practice, magnitude of recovery from temporary work decrement over a rest, and amount of warmup decrement are all positively related. This has been the case whether subjects were of homogeneous or heterogeneous ages. You have already seen the curves associated with different age levels in Fig. 2. Fig. 4 shows these relationships for a group of 370 college males, stratified into proficiency fifths by total scores (R. B. Ammons & C. H. Ammons, 1967).

An interpretation of these findings which we presently favor is as follows: (a) initial proficiency is due to net positive transfer from related skills already learned; (b) with increase in age to CA 16 or 17, there is an increase in number and variety of skills already learned, so initial proficiency increases, due to greater total positive transfer; (c) the more proficient subjects at any age are more proficient because they have learned a greater variety of skills, including skills transferring later in practice (e. g., task persistence, methods for making fine behavioral adjustments); (d) so, initially more proficient subjects at any age will show greater increase in proficiency during prolonged practice; (e) not only are positively transferring skill components learned better and in greater variety as one lives longer, but so are negatively transferring components; (f) thus, if warmup decrement arises from recovery during rest of competing habits "unlearned" during earlier practice, we should find greater warmup decrement associated with age-related

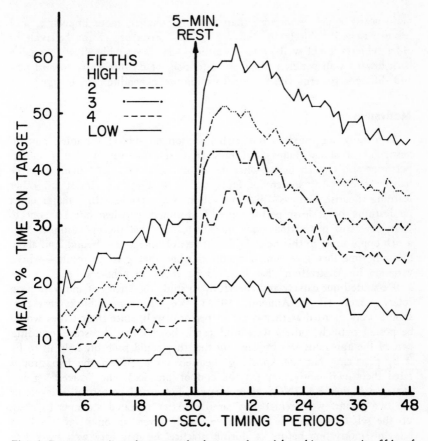

Fig. 4. Rotary pursuit performance of subgroups formed by taking successive fifths of a male college group ($N = 370$), based on level of post-rest proficiency. $N = 74$ at each point. (R. B. Ammons & C. H. Ammons, 1967)

increases in proficiency, as well as with greater initial proficiency within an age level (and this is just what we do find).

An interesting confirmation of these ideas appears in data from the first prison study. The post-39-year-old men show a decrease in mean proficiency. Could this decline simply be due to physical changes with ageing, or might it be a matter of learning responses of slowing down, moving less rapidly, avoiding "unnecessary" activity, expending less energy, as a response to the physical changes? To the extent that we are dealing with a learning process, we may be able to slow down, arrest, or even reverse the decline in skills performance frequently found with increasing age. Perhaps Welford's older subjects (Welford, 1958) took longer to make discriminative responses because they had learned to consider more alternatives and to assign them more nearly equal importance than had his younger, more impulsive, and less-experienced subjects. A study of the microstructure of the behavior of older subjects might well prove rewarding—do they simply show regression back toward skill patterns found in childhood, or do they move toward new and different patterns functioning to minimize expenditure of energy?

Motivation

As already suggested in our earlier section on subject variables, any investigator of skills "knows," if only from self-observation, that a subject performs skills much better when he is optimally motivated than when he hardly "tries." Any student of Hull, or, for that matter, almost any other learning theorist, "knows" that motivation is a variable with a major effect on learning or at least performance. Unfortunately, when one sets out to "vary levels of motivation," one quickly realizes that the operationists have a rich opportunity in this field. Different sets of operations abound, and about the only time they give similar results is when they give no results—where variation in "motivation" has little or no effect on behavior.

We started out naively and cheerfully to study the effects of motivation on rotary pursuit (R. B. Ammons, 1952). We told some subjects that they should work as hard as they could to perform well, since their scores would be posted publicly; others were told (and shown) that the score-recording part of the apparatus was broken, but that they could probably help us to fix it by practicing but not knocking themselves out. When the two groups rated their own motivation (at the end of practice), the "correct" group averaged higher RATINGS of motivation, but actual performance levels of the two groups were remarkably similar. After repeated attempts to clean up the self-rating approach, we have simply given up on it: if a subject rates his motivation before or during practice, he may very well work less or more in order to behave consistently with his self-rating; if he rates himself *after* practice, he may simply be reporting his feelings about having already performed more or less well.

In a different attack (unpublished study) on the possible effects of motivation on rotary pursuit performance, we bent the canons of Watsonian Behaviorism by using trained subjects and even trusting them. Ten graduate students with considerable prior experience and proficiency at rotary pursuit served as subjects. Each practiced continuously for seven 8-min. periods, separated by 10-min. rests. During either periods 1, 3, 5, and 7 or periods 2, 4, and 6, the subject went all-out to perform the very best he could, while during the alternate trials, he relaxed and performed minimally (just as poorly as possible while still performing the basic task). Two mean 8-min. curves by 20-sec. trials were computed for each subject, one for his low-motivation periods and one for his high-motivation periods. Practice effects were thus balanced fairly well within subjects; they were further balanced across subjects by assigning the high motivation role to periods 1, 3, 5, and 7 for five subjects, and to periods 2, 4, and 6 for the other five subjects. Each of the ten subjects performed at a significantly higher level when "more highly motivated" (by this definition). An 8-min. high-motivation mean curve by 20-sec. trials was computed for all subjects, as was a comparable low-motivation curve. Both curves showed the typical sharp initial rise to a plateau followed by a steady decrease. The "high motivation" mean curve was appreciably higher at all 24 points, and the two curves ALMOST EX-ACTLY PARALLELED EACH OTHER. So much for a multiplicative theory of effect of motivation level on rotary pursuit habits!

Several years later, our motivation-studying habits showed spontaneous recovery, and we tried another approach (R. B. Ammons, Adams, and C. H. Ammons, 1966; R. B. Ammons, Adams, Leuthold, and C. H. Ammons, 1965). We reasoned that persons required to serve as subjects for a considerable period of time (several hours) would find it rewarding to progress toward being allowed to leave early with full time-credit and would quickly develop a high level of motivation. By suitable manipulation of reported scores, we

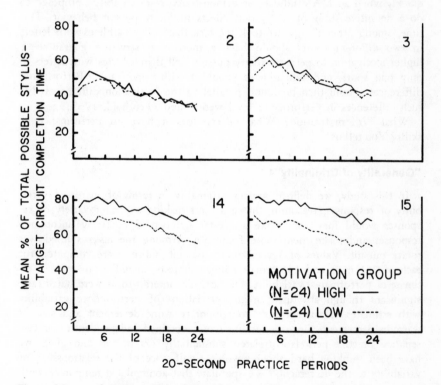

Fig. 5. Mean performance early and late in practice (8-min. practice periods 2, 3, 14, 15) as a function of differential motivation. $N = 24$ college males at each point. (R. B. Ammons, Adams, & C. H. Ammons, 1966)

produced a group of 24 subjects who were obviously highly motivated as they anticipated leaving and left quite early, and another group of 24 whose motivation was rather low, moving to lower levels as they stayed through the whole experimental session, watching "better" subjects leave. Initially the mean performances of these groups were almost identical. By the fourth 8-min. practice period, the high-motivation group was drawing ahead. Their superiority was clear during the last 12 of the 15 8-min. continuous practice periods. So we had produced rotary pursuit performance differences associated with an intuitively acceptable set of motivating operations. Fig. 5 shows mean performances during periods 2, 3, 14, and 15. It is clear that the only differences were in over-all performance; there were no consistent differences in warmup decrement, temporary work decrement, or recovery over rest (reminiscence) associated with the demonstrated differences in motivation. These findings agree with those in the study of assumed motivation roles described earlier.

Again our motivation-studying responses extinguished, only to recover quickly when an MA candidate of demonstrated research ability proposed to do a definitive study of motivation effects in rotary pursuit behavior. This time, among other things, we took the tack that college athletes with letters in two different sports should have a motivation structure guaranteeing' higher motivation to perform rotary pursuit well than athletes with letters in only one sport, and non-athletes should be least motivated. Performance differences should then be found paralleling the motivation differences. No such differences in performance level were found (Leuthold, 1965).

What "*is*" motivation? What effects does it have on performance of skills? You tell us!

"Generality of Originality"[3]

In this study, we defined greater originality in terms of increased variability of responses, reasoning that a subject making a greater variety of responses would inevitably make a greater number of relatively uncommon responses and make them more frequently. Among the tasks studied was rotary pursuit. Values of several rotary pursuit indices were computed for each of 261 male and 136 female college subjects, including an over-all estimate of performance variability. Of particular interest to us were statistically significant though absolutely small correlations of performance variability with estimates of susceptibility to temporary work decrement and size of warmup decrement. Since variability scores obtained independently for two separate practice periods correlated substantially (*r*s of .38 and .48), we have been thinking hard about possible significance of the relationships of variability to the decrements. We speculate that accumulated temporary work

[3] This research was supported in part by Grant HD00939 from NIH, Public Health Service, to R. B. Ammons.

decrement loading a well-established response can increase the likelihood of occurrence of a less common (more original) and therefore a possibly more creative response. There is no time to trace it out here, but this line of reasoning seems to throw light on a wide variety of problem-solving behaviors (and, of course, we consider rotary pursuit practice to be a form of problem solving).

Nature of the Rotary Pursuit Learning Process

Refusing to spend time on the "learning" vs "performance" controversy, we would like to point out that certain relatively basic, stable, permanent changes in rotary pursuit behavior take place with continued practice, and these changes are what we mean by "learning," a useful although vague term.

We have attempted to gain better understanding of the learning of rotary pursuit skill(s) in several ways. An early study (unpublished) utilized photographic time exposures, 5 to 10 sec. in duration, of the path of a light on the stylus tip or on the hand of the subject. In a later study (R. B. Ammons, C. H. Ammons, & Morgan, 1958), motion pictures of rotary pursuit under a variety of standard conditions were used to carry out a detailed motion analysis. Both studies indicated that learning consists of dropping out of inadequate behaviors (e. g., rapid irregular circling movements) which are incompatible with highly efficient behaviors and of making closer approximations to the smooth, continuous, swinging, circular movements which lead to high scores.

Rotary pursuit is clearly a highly integrated skill. Separate practice of visual or motor components, or "mental" practice of components or the whole task (R. B. Ammons, 1951b; unpublished extension of first study; unpublished "rivet" study) has little effect either on total score or on aspects of performance which "should" be directly influenced (e. g., no decrease was found in postrest warmup decrement following mental practice of the task during a rest period).

Properties of Measures Used

As any good operationist, neo-operationist, general semanticist, or for that matter probably any sensible person who has given thought to the problem, realizes, definitions of relationships within measuring scales and of measurement units, as well as determination of the phenomena to which they are to apply, are arbitrary.

Rotary pursuit units were defined by default, defined by investigators deferring to the physical characteristics of counters, commutators, and clocks. Even a kind of sand clock was used in one simple pursuit device, and such a clock could be used to measure rotary pursuit performance. Time-on-target was the obvious behavior-characteristic to measure. It did not seem to matter that there were discriminably different kinds of times on target or that they resulted from a myriad of different behaviors. Non-psychologist scorers in our motion picture studies (e. g., R. B. Ammons, C. H. Ammons, & Morgan, 1958) were fascinated and confused by the wealth of behavior variations, and concluded one by one that time-on-target was a thin, pale, unrevealing indicator of the total behavior pattern. We have mentioned elsewhere in this paper that absolute values of time-on-target obtained through different sets of measurement operations do not agree at all well, even though relative values are nearly perfectly correlated (vindicating a hard-nosed operationist dictum).

Once we accept the arbitrariness of measurement units, we are free to play with measurement operations, seeking those which make analysis and/or interpretation of data easier for us or which give mathematically simpler laws, or forms of laws, more to our liking in some other way (Bergmann & Spence, 1944, especially p. 10; Lindquist, 1953, especially p. 151). In our laboratory, we have confined ourselves to two kinds of measurement-oriented research, effects of transformations on outcomes of statistical tests, and effects of transformations on forms of simple functional relations.

Most of our common statistical tests making simultaneous multiple inter-group comparisons assume normality of distributions of scores, homogeneity of variances, and independence of means and variances. Rotary pursuit scores are typically badly skewed, showing extreme "floor" and "ceiling" effects, and means are usually correlated with variances. Now, one might routinely transform scores mathematically to minimize skew, heterogeneity of variance, and variance-mean correlation. Two important objections to this are: that unless one uses a computer the transforming of hundreds of thousands of scores is a gruesome, forbidding task, and that the resulting scores may much better meet the assumptions of the statistical model than do the "raw" scores but are often an affront psychologically (e. g., a simple square-root transformation makes a score of 64% time-on-target only twice as good as a score of 16% time-on-target, .8 vs .4).

In an unpublished study to find out if we could perhaps avoid both the gruesomeness and the affront by using raw scores, and yet trust the results of our analyses of variance, we transformed scores in two common ways— $\sqrt{X+1}$, $\log_{10}(X+1)$—for a great many distributions in several studies (e. g., R. B. Ammons, C. H. Ammons, & Morgan, 1956). We then analyzed the variances of raw scores and both kinds of transformed scores. The results were interesting. Hypotheses of normality of distribution, homogeneity of variance, and zero correlations of means and variances of *raw scores* could be rejected at all points, usually at fantastic levels of confidence. With both types of *transformed scores*, practically no sets of related distributions showed statistically significant departure from within-groups normality of distribution or homogeneity of variance, while variance-mean correlations became much smaller. Of more practical importance was the finding that in no single case was there appreciable disagreement between the results of analysis of variance of raw scores and analysis of variance of transformed scores. So, after a cautious look for large interactions, we have used raw scores forever after, with no reason not to be happy.

Another practical motivation for exploring various transformations of raw scores is to find one or more methods for appreciably reducing the heterogeneity of the forms of rotary pursuit performance curves obtained under a variety of conditions. By shortcut methods, we investigated (R. B. Ammons & C. H. Ammons, 1963) the effects of several transformations on median performance curves for subjects practicing continuously for 8 min. with right hand, left hand, right foot, or left foot (400 in each group). Although the following transformations produced wide variations in absolute numerical values and in shapes of curves, none produced a set of curves judged to be simpler or more meaningful: $\sqrt{X+1}$, $\log_{10}(X+1)$, arc sin, $1 - \left(\dfrac{1}{X}\right)$, T-score. We had hoped for a better outcome, but expected no worse.

Research and Work on Theories Now Underway

Before discussing two general problems and drawing some conclusions, we would like to make mention of the more extensive theoretical work related to motor skills undertaken in our laboratory and to outline very briefly the lines of skills research in which we are now engaged.

In addition to a great many partially stated hypotheses and fragmentary essays toward theory to account for some set of phenomena or other (a few of which have been included in this paper), we have come up with a number of more rigorously and more fully stated theoretical formulations, some of which you may not be aware of and which might be of interest to you: (a) formulation of relationships among proficiency, temporary work decrement, permanent work decrement, reminiscence, warmup decrement, duration of practice, duration of rests between practice periods (R. B. Ammons, 1947a); (b) effects of motivation on rotary pursuit behavior (Wing & R. B. Ammons, 1950; Leuthold, 1965); (c) effects of knowledge of performance, including by implication a simple explanation for findings that rewarding a rotor subject for hits of long duration by sounding a buzzer leads to increased time on target—the subject believes that the experimenter will reward him and the experimenter does reward him for long hits, so he concentrates on developing behavior patterns allowing long hits, which patterns also lead to much higher overall time-on-target scores (R. B. Ammons, 1956; R. B. Ammons & C. H. Ammons, 1956); (d) relationships of cross-limb transfer phenomena to many major problems in the study of learning, especially the nature of task-task transfer (R. B. Ammons, 1958); (e) what to measure and how to measure it, including smoothing of performance curves of individual subjects to allow estimation of constants (R. B. Ammons, Adams, Leuthold, & C. H. Ammons, 1965; Leuthold, 1965), and effects of transformations of units on forms of families of curves (problem shown clearly in: R. B. Ammons & C. H. Ammons, 1963; R. B. Ammons & C. H. Ammons, 1968); (f) warmup decrement as a stimulus generalization phenomenon (R. B. Ammons, 1959); and (g) the nature and conditions of occurrence of "permanent" work decrement (R. B. Ammons, 1947a, 1950, 1952; R. B. Ammons & Willig, 1956).

As usual for the last twenty years, we have so many lines of skills research in progress that it is hard even for us to keep them in mind. Research areas include: differences between subjects showing large amounts of temporary work decrement or warmup decrement and subjects not showing any such decrement; photographic studies in two and three dimensions of actual behavior changes as subjects become proficient at a skill; relations of "limbedness" to cross-limb and task-task transfer; physiological learning—"fitness" as a learning phenomenon; perceptual changes during acquisition of skills; age-related changes in skills, skills acquisition, and skills performance; empirical characteristics of various measures of proficiency, warmup decrement, and temporary work decrement—what are their psychometric properties, how stable (reliable) are they under various conditions; methods for producing and removing permanent work decrement; and, finally, theoretical and empirical relationships of aspects of skills acquisition and performance to formally recognized research and thought about problem solving, with special reference to occurrence and generality of originality and creativity.

DISCUSSION

There are two further matters which we would like to discuss before concluding this paper. First, *why, with all the information we have gathered quite systematically, and with our bent toward theory construction, haven't we constructed a comprehensive, rigorous theory?* In part, this failure is due to a general social problem. There is no social support for thinking. No grants are given for thinking *per se*. Institutes, agencies, and other similar groups with the means for supporting theory construction are simply not interested in skills theory. Then, in addition to lack of interest and concrete support of our theory construction effort, there is the "Lehmann effect." As we get older ungracefully, we have less time for creative activity because of a seemingly inevitable increase in number and demands of irrelevant obligations. *Psychological Reports* and *Perceptual and Motor Skills* have come to be our most time and energy consuming obligation. Although our editorial and related activities have always been highly rewarding both intellectually and personally, this "obligation" has gradually come to seem somewhat incompatible with our creative activities as individual scientists. There have been no practical suggestions from any source as to how we can preserve and increase the social value of these journals, yet cut down their interference with *our* creative scientific lives.

The second more general matter which we would like to discuss is the *social relevance of our work with the pursuit rotor.* One's first reaction when thinking about time spent watching people chase a little brass target around may be: Well, I guess it doesn't have any social relevance. But then, one remembers that basic science needs no justification in terms of immediate, obvious application of findings. However, understanding of efficiency in learning and performing motor skills just may turn out to be enormously socially relevant. In any case, our rotor research has achieved social relevance in another way, leading to an intensive research attack by us on the nature, incidence, and correlates of anti-intellectual and therefore anti-scientific attitudes and behavior. We have easily done as much research on the variables related to anti-intellectualism as on rotary pursuit. We are willing and pleased to discuss this research either in public or in private in any appropriate setting. Several of our findings seem directly relevant to the present report and to motor skills research in general: (a) We, Robert Bruce Ammons and Carol Hamrick Ammons, turn out to be distinctly anti-intellectual on an absolute basis, even though relative to the general population we place extremely high value on intellectual activity. (b) Using a variety of approaches, we have repeatedly found that our present society is basically and almost completely anti-intellectual and anti-scientific—our freedom as scientists apparently exists *only* because the rest of the population does not understand the nature of what we are doing, how we are doing it, or its continually revolutionary implications. Our whole personal research program has repeatedly and materially suffered as we have been forced by some new observation or finding to realize sharply the precariousness of our intellectual and scientific position. (c) Results of several independently conducted and large studies have been consistent in indicating that there is essentially no relationship between college major field and value placed on intellectual activity. Physical education majors are not any *more* anti-intellectual than students with other majors, and neither are prospective teachers any *less* anti-intellectual.

We would like to propose some highly socially relevant hypotheses about the present "state of things" in our science(s) of human behavior, hypotheses growing out of our research findings in many fields (a few of which have been reported here), plus our experiences of many years as teachers, journal editors, and small-scale psychopoliticians[4]: (1) With increased use of computer retrieval of scientific information, (a) the stupidity of problems researched will increase notably, (b) the organization of any field will decrease (exit unplanned cross-articulation of ideas), (c) the ultimate form of journal publication will be one copy of each issue of each journal which must be treated like the platinum meter bar in the vault of the Bureau of Standards. (2) There will be increased reward and therefore increased incidence of unitized, modular research—the stand-alone, no-significance driblet. (3) Continued unintentional reward of originality should

---

[4] I slightly acknowledge my professional and intellectual indebtedness to Frank du Mas in borrowing this delightful word from him.

preserve the present situation in psychology, where we are so original that we cannot understand each other or even successfully replicate each other's research. (4) We seem doomed to remain in the straitjacket of probability. The work of Skinner and his followers with individual organisms was and is hopeful, but its influence seems to have reached a plateau far below a level dangerous to probability reasoning. Let us suggest that acceptance of probability thinking is equivalent to acceptance of ignorance. Nothing is really the matter with being ignorant except when you don't know you are and don't take steps to replace that ignorance with information. For example, the randomness of events assumed in the mathematical model for the analysis of variance is known not to exist in our correlated world, but we get by in practice because most inter-event correlations are quite small. What teacher of statistics points this out or develops its implications? (5) The bubble-heads are likely to take over and we will be *forced* in one way or another to work on socially relevant problems *as defined by them!* The ideologically blindfolded are likely to displace the tough-minded social engineers (as if a Gresham's law of the mind were at work, weeding out high-quality thinkers). We are afraid that research based upon disregard of variables and arbitrary assumptions about methodology, no matter how great the face validity of its social relevance, can only be useless or worse.

CONCLUSION

We remarked early in this paper that we know almost nothing about skills decremental processes relative to what we could know by simple extensions of present research techniques and designs. But, we feel that our research program has accomplished something worthwhile. We and our students have been forced repeatedly to realize that knowledge about motor skills shares a characteristic with other scientific knowledge—the more you know, the less you know. We have developed a great deal of concrete information, capable of meaningful integration within a formal theory. We have achieved many insights, exciting to us, to try out for generality in other fields. For example, we have already found that many relations among variables discovered in the field of motor learning appear also in the field of visual perceptual learning. We feel that psychology is extremely unlikely to become an integrated science until researchers are given sponsored time to think and are prepared to use it well in theory construction. Intuitively, we are certain that there are major insights and integrations waiting to be achieved with the data you have glimpsed today.[5]

5 I must acknowledge one more intellectual debt. Were it not for a truly great paper on "The methodology of experimental studies of human learning and retention," published in 1936 in the *Psychological Bulletin* by Arthur Melton, we would not have been conceptually or methodologically capable of the research program reported in our paper or of making the report itself. The sheer intellectual power and great elegance of conceptual grasp still to be recognized throughout Melton's near-definitive paper now more than thirty years after its publication should indicate to you why a graduate stu-

REFERENCES

Ammons, C. H., & Ammons, R. B. Bilateral transfer of leg-and-foot rotary pursuit skill. *Proceedings of the Montana Academy of Sciences,* 1958, 18, 95.

Ammons, C. H., & Ammons, R. B. Rotary pursuit performance by kindergarten children: learning to learn? Paper presented at the annual meeting of the Montana Psychological Association, April, 1967.

Ammons, R. B. Acquisition of motor skill: I. Quantitative analysis and theoretical formulation. *Psychological Review,* 1947, 54, 263-281. (a)

Ammons, R. B. Acquisition of motor skill: II. Rotary pursuit performance with continuous practice before and after a single rest. *Journal of Experimental Psychology,* 1947, 37, 393-411. (b)

Ammons, R. B. Acquisition of motor skill: III. Effects of initially distributed practice on rotary pursuit performance. *Journal of Experimental Psychology,* 1950, 40, 777-787.

Ammons, R. B. Effect of distribution of practice on rotary pursuit "hits." *Journal of Experimental Psychology,* 1951, 41, 17-22. (a)

Ammons, R. B. Effects of pre-practice activities on rotary pursuit performance. *Journal of Experimental Psychology,* 1951, 41, 187-191. (b)

Ammons, R. B. Relationship of motivation and method of testing to distribution of practice phenomena in rotary pursuit. *Quarterly Journal of Experimental Psychology,* 1952, 4, 155-164.

Ammons, R. B. An analysis of "hits" in continuous rotary pursuit before and after a single rest. *Journal of General Psychology,* 1953, 48, 3-10.

Ammons, R. B. Performance within short practice periods as affected by warm-up decrement and temporary work decrement. *Year Book of the American Philosophical Society,* 1955, 181-185. (a)

Ammons, R. B. Rotary pursuit apparatus: I. Survey of variables. *Psychological Bulletin,* 1955, 52, 69-76. (b)

Ammons, R. B. Effects of knowledge of performance: a survey and tentative theoretical formulation. *Journal of General Psychology,* 1956, 54, 279-299.

Ammons, R. B. "Le Mouvement." In G. H. Seward & J. P. Seward (Eds.), *Current psychological issues.* New York: Holt, 1958. Pp. 146-183.

Ammons, R. B. "Warming-up" in the performance of a simple skill. Paper presented at meeting of University of Montana chapter, Society of Sigma Xi, October 29, 1959.

Ammons, R. B., Adams, E., & Ammons, C. H. Relationships of motivation and proficiency to components of simple skill performance. Paper presented at the annual meeting of the Rocky Mountain Psychological Association, May, 1966.

Ammons, R. B., Adams, E., Leuthold, B., & Ammons, C. H. Evaluation of some methods for fitting rotary pursuit performance curves for individual subjects. Paper presented at the annual meeting of the Montana Psychological Association, April, 1965.

Ammons, R. B., Alprin, S. I., & Ammons, C. H. Rotary pursuit performance as related to sex and age of pre-adult subjects. *Journal of Experimental Psychology,* 1955, 49, 127-133.

Ammons, R. B., & Ammons, C. H. Some "knowledge of performance" concepts. *Psychological Reports,* 1956, 2, 65-66.

Ammons, R. B., & Ammons, C. H. Alternation design for studying learning and transfer. Paper presented at the annual meeting of the Montana Psychological Association, April, 1959.

Ammons, R. B., & Ammons, C. H. Cross-limb transfer. Paper presented at the annual meeting of the Rocky Mountain Psychological Association, May, 1962.

Ammons, R. B., & Ammons, C. H. Speculations on the equalization of units for measurement of rotary pursuit performance. *Proceedings of the Montana Academy of Sciences,* 1963, 23, 280-286.

dent in the field of skills learning would read this paper with excitement and admiration in 1940, would continue to reread it throughout his professional life, and would hold it up in 1969 as a model of intellectual achievement in the field of behavioral science, capable of emulation but not of being surpassed (cf., Melton, 1936).

Ammons, R. B., & Ammons, C. H. Learning and performance of rotary pursuit and reversal of perspective with continuous practice and a single rest. Paper presented at the annual meeting of the Rocky Mountain Psychological Association, May, 1965.

Ammons, R. B., & Ammons, C. H. Relationships of rotary pursuit proficiency, warm-up decrement, and temporary work decrement. Paper presented at the annual meeting of the Rocky Mountain Psychological Association, May, 1967.

Ammons, R. B., & Ammons, C. H. A comparison of correlational and graphic methods for exploring relationships among rotary pursuit performance indices. Paper presented at the annual meeting of the Rocky Mountain Psychological Association, May, 1968.

Ammons, R. B., Ammons, C. H., & Morgan, R. L. Transfer of skill and decremental factors along the speed dimension in rotary pursuit. *Perceptual and Motor Skills,* 1956, 6, 43.

Ammons, R. B., Ammons, C. H., & Morgan, R. L. Subskills in rotary pursuit as affected by rate and accuracy requirements and by distribution of practice. *Journal of General Psychology,* 1958, 58, 259-279.

Ammons, R. B., Farr, R. G., Bloch, E., Neumann, E., Dey, M., Marion, R., & Ammons, C. H. Long-term retention of perceptual-motor skills. *Journal of Experimental Psychology,* 1958, 55, 318-328.

Ammons, R. B., & Willig, L. Acquisition of motor skill: IV. Effects of repeated periods of massed practice. *Journal of Experimental Psychology,* 1956, 51, 118-126.

Bergmann, G., & Spence, K. W. The logic of psychophysical measurement. *Psychological Review,* 1944, 51, 1-24.

Eysenck, H. J., Iseler, A., Star, K., & Willet, R. A. Post-rest upswing and downswing in pursuit rotor learning after distributed practice as a function of length of practice. *British Journal of Psychology,* 1969, 60, 373-384.

Hullett, E., Eckles, A. J., & Ammons, R. B. Effects of practice conditions on aiming skill. Paper presented at the annual meeting of the Southern Society for Philosophy and Psychology, April, 1952.

Leuthold, B. L. Effects of motivation on rotary pursuit performance. Unpublished Master of Arts thesis, University of Montana, 1965.

Lindquist, E. F. *Design and analysis of experiments in psychology and education.* New York: Houghton Mifflin, 1953.

Melton, A. W. The methodology of experimental studies of human learning and retention: I. The functions of a methodology and the available criteria for evaluating different experimental methods. *Psychological Bulletin,* 1936, 33, 305-394.

Reyna, L. J. An experimental study of work inhibition in motor learning. Unpublished Master of Arts thesis, University of Iowa, 1944.

Welford, A. T. *Ageing and human skill.* London: Oxford Univer. Press, 1958.

Wing, C. W., & Ammons, R. B. A theoretical formulation of the effects of motivation on rotary pursuit performance. *Motor Skills Research Exchange,* 1950, 2, 44-47.

Woodworth, R. S. *Experimental psychology.* New York: Holt, 1938.

CRITIQUE OF THE AMMONS' PAPER
by K. U. Smith

To recast the presentation of Professors' Ammons: their paper summarizes the results of over two decades of research on the decremental events of motor skill as measured by pursuit-rotor performance. The term decrement is used to describe events involving reduced accuracy, efficiency, or increased time of performance in such things as inhibition, fatigue, decline of performance in warm-up periods, interference, forgetting, extinction, etc. However, in this paper, the main decremental events studied were temporary or transient work decrement in the pursuit-rotor task. Before going into the description of these main subjects, information is given about design of experiments with the rotary-pursuit task, experimenter error in studies with this device, the effects of subject variables on performance, and characteristics of the apparatus to be used. In the research on transfer of reduced accuracy due to continued performance, limited studies were done on the effects of stimulus factors (target speed, target size, etc.) and on crossed-limb transfer. The last section of the paper deals with phenomena of age and motivational factors in determining work decrement and proficiency in rotary-pursuit performance.

Although the Ammons claim to have achieved and learned little in twenty-three years of research and in the more than a hundred studies covered by their paper, I think this is more an expression of modesty than it is a true overall characterization of the information presented. However, I do think that the dedication to a single limited method of study which predates most of the significant advanced experimental technology of the last two decades would almost of necessity lead to limited experiences in advancing the basic theoretical and factual framework of behavior. It is also my opinion that the theoretical context of this research—i.e., the stimulus-response views of motor skill—almost by necessity leads to only limited experience in understanding any really meaningful aspects of human behavior.

The main findings of the Ammons are of value in defining the limitations of traditional thinking about response decrements. I found the section on the effects of age and variations in task content on warm-up and work decrement to be a particularly interesting part of the work inasmuch as the results suggest that the degree of variable self-control which the subject brings to the task will determine the occurrence of decrement in proficiency with sustained performance. Rather than supporting the traditional S-R view in terms of which the research was conducted, however, these results point to the need for a revised point of view.

The theme of my evaluation of this research on rotary-pursuit performance from here on deals less with the Ammons' specific work and more with the meaning of tracking and motor-skill research on response decrement and inhibition. Although the Ammons do not commit themselves to a specific position, their research brings out the gross limitations of stimulus and environmentally-oriented styles of theorizing not only in interpreting experimental results but in planning and designing experiments. In past S-R and informational engineering traditions, the true meaning of behavioral control of environmental stimuli and the effects of such self-governed feedback control on performance have never been recognized. In the context of such theorizing, the nature and origins of response decrements, such as negative transfer of learning, fatigue work decrement and inhibition, are particularly mysterious and can be discussed only in terms of interference between stimuli and responses or as a reduction in the drive states motivating specific reactions. These neo-classical, mass-action environmental theories of behavior provide absolutely no latitude for considering the role of self-regulated and self-generated stimuli and sensory factors in determining performance characteristics, learning and response decrements. The Ammons' paper reflects the inability to be able to delineate the significant features of response decrements when trying to discuss these events in general environmental terms.

Basically, the Ammons' research deals with the events of learning and response decrements in manual-visual tracking, inasmuch as the pursuit-rotor represents one of the early devices and methods arranged for such study. However, their paper fails to align events of warm-up decrement, work decrement and transfer processes with detailed findings and more recent levels of theoretical study of these events in visual tracking systems which were better designed and controlled than the pursuit rotor. For example, in preparing an analytic survey on the behavioral factors in design of aircraft gun tracking systems at the end of World War II (Smith, 1945), most of the then existing research findings on learning, learning theory, and transfer in tracking with the pursuit rotor were reviewed in the hope of obtaining data which would be critical in making recommendations about behavioral design in the tracking systems concerned. The conclusion reached then, which can be restated here, is that experimental results on and stimulus-response theoretical ideas about the pursuit rotor seem to have relevance to nothing but the pursuit rotor and even fail to give any really critical suggestions about how people operate and learn this instrument. The research of the Ammons does not seem to change this general picture of pursuit-rotor research as far as practice- and theory-related concepts of motor skill in human factors science and physical education are concerned.

Reaction decrements in performance represent one of the few phenomena of behavior which have not been considered theoretically in the context of a control or feedback interpretation of response and physiological function. One of the few exceptions to this statement occurs in a recent paper by Békésey (1969), who found it necessary to introduce a highly speculative account of sensory inhibition with consideration of a limited machine model of neural feedback, which he proposed as a possible basis of complex inhibitory relations in the neural mechanisms of vision and audition.

According to the view just stated, most of the response decrements studied in learning and performance by S-R learning psychologists would be reduced or would disappear altogether if performance situations and training procedures were designed to be compliant with the modes of self-governed modes of performance and acquisition by individuals. When put in the context of feedback theory, this statement implies that different types of response decrements, from sensory inhibition to mental fatigue, may represent at base organized ways which the organism has for selectively self-regulating stimulus, sensory, neural, and physiological inputs by coordinated movement and of maintaining a sustained level of reaction with available sources of stimulation. From what we know presently about feedback control of stimulus, sensory, neural, and neurohormonal and molecular selection by movement' and muscular contraction, we can speculate that each of these levels of psychophysiological and motor control of systems input and integration involves specific negative feedback processes for closing, desensitizing and redirecting input channels to maintain effective integration of the responding system in dealing with specific and general sources of stimulation for guiding and timing activity.

In a behavioral-physiological feedback view, any condition of stimulation or performance which perturbs or alters the normal space, time, force, and signal feedback compliances between motor response and sensory input constitutes a source and cause of response decrement as compared to unperturbed conditions of motorsensory operation. A main function of learning is to compensate these sources of perturbation of the normal self-governed modes of behavior and thus make possible adaptation to various sources of displaced, delayed, force-altered and signal-distorted conditions of feedback. The observed positive course of learning typically represents the rate and extent of such compensatory adaptation. A major cause of what has been called sensory inhibition, reactive inhibition, fatigue, and work decrement is the extent to which the organism can maintain the energy expenditure and modes of response necessary to effect the difficult compensatory reactions initially induced by the situation and required to effect some degree of self-regulated control over the source of perturbing stimulation. According to this view, many of the mysterious conditions of fatigue, response decrement, reactive inhibition and transfer of response decrement represent little more than reinstitution of some perturbing non-compliance between self-governed movement and sensory input that initially disturbed existing organized patterns of behavior and induced the beginning course of learning.

As Békésey (1969) suggested in a limited way, the types of sensory inhibition studied in classical psychophysics and sensory physiology are not simply sensory and neural, but represent the operation of dynamic feedback-regulated receptor and movement processes in acting selectively on sensory input and thereby determining the pattern of perception. Bekesey's example of not feeling vibrations in any of the surfaces and joints of the body except the soles of the feet while standing on a vibrating platform represents a common pattern of feedback regulated inhibition which occurs during the course of learning and is associated with focalizing articulated movements and sensory orientation (attention) in motor skill. To perform or sense in a guided directed way, it is essential that all levels of movement control be integrated to focus on a restricted articulated motion of the eyes, head, hands or feet in performing some specialized task in relation to environmental stimuli or objects. This focusing or focalizing movement operation entails enhancing sensory input of the articulated movements while reducing or degrading the prominence of background stimuli related to larger orienting movements and posture. Initially, in learning, these sensory effects of these larger movements are prominent but are reduced in significance as learning proceeds. This learned inhibition represents a type of response decrement for the particular motorsensory systems affected. From a feedback point of view, the best way to think of these sensory inhibitive effects is to consider the brain as a ramified system of space, time, and signal feature detections whose differential detection ability can be learned on and off in a direct way by dynamics of receptor reactions or by the feedback effects of postural, travel, or articulated manipulative movements. In this view, a main aspect of sensory feature detection of the space, time, and signal characteristics of receptor input is the capability of eliminating the differential dendrite inputs on which all neural feature detection depends. If these assumptions are true, most of the events of inhibition and response decrement are not due to some mysterious inhibitory substances in the brain; rather, they represent a controlled elimination of positive detection of sensory input by nerve cells that depend on differential movement-controlled sensory inputs for their operation.

When viewed on these more recent theoretical feedback terms, Ammons' dedication to studying response decrement by a 1930 instrumental model of stimulus-response psychology should be viewed as a milestone, for the researcher in this case has had the modesty and the courage to take note of the fact that his methods and theories are not up to the challenge of pushing experimental efforts into new avenues and sectors, while still paying high respect to those who defined a past partly successful era of study of motor functions and learning but who now represent only the past in the study of motor skill.

BIBLIOGRAPHY

Bekesey, G. von. Similarities of inhibition in the different sense organs. *American Psychologist,* 1969, 24, 707-719.

Smith, K. U. Special report to the Air Forces on design of aircraft gun tracking systems. Project AC-94, (University of Wisconsin) 1945.

R. B. AMMONS REPLY TO K. U. SMITH'S CRITIQUE

Dr. Smith's comments are interesting and provocative as usual, but seem relevant to some larger context, rather than to our *specific* work as reported here. In the last analysis, the listener (and later the reader) will have to decide to what extent our concepts, methods, findings, and miniature theoretical formulations are useful to him. We certainly *would not* grant that we "had the modesty and the courage to take note of the fact that [our] . . . methods and theories are not up to the challenge of pushing experimental efforts into new avenues and sectors. . . ." We believe we have in fact done a great deal of this pushing.

Individual Differences in Motor Learning and Performance

Franklin M. Henry
University of California, Berkeley

The concept of individual differences in performance is of great interest to the field of physical education as well as to education in general. It is quite obvious to all who have performed in activities where a degree of motor skill is required, that individuals differ among each other. In addition, individuals are consistent or inconsistent in their own series of performances from time to time.

However, the concept of individual differences in performance and learning tasks has often been misinterpreted. Many researchers (and most statistics texts) have not devoted enough consideration to the fact that observable differences among individual scores do not constitute proof of the existence of individual differences. Indeed, other factors could well cause the observed differences between scores, with only a small portion actually caused by real individual differences. For example, the existence of large random experimental errors could account for most of the score differences. Then the magnitude of differences among individual *scores* would mostly come from the large error factor and a smaller amount would be due to real individual differences. However, there is another portion which is contained in this total variation quantity; it has been called *intra*-individual variance. It consists of the variation of an individual's scores about his own mean score. This latter part is a measure of the consistency or inconsistency of successive performance scores for each individual in a particular sample. Thus, the total variance that is observed in a sample of performances consists of *inter*-individual (true score) differences, *intra*-individual variance and error variance. True-score variance is the variance of true scores (defined as the scores that would be obtained if each subject had been given an infinite number of trials under constant conditions, so that his score contained no sampling error). While "true-scores" cannot be observed directly in a rigorous mathematical sense, it is often possible to average many trials per individual, in which case the difference between true scores and observed scores is trivial. It is self-evident that the variance of such a set of scores also differs by only a trivial amount from the true score variance calculated from statistical theory. It is more convenient, however, to state the operational definition of individual differences as total variance (S_x^2) minus the average of the variances of each individual about his own mean (S_w^2). Note that the latter term includes some of the variance that arises from any secular trend in the data—this can be handled statistically, but in the interest of simplicity we may assume plateau conditions for the present, so that this source of variance as a main effect will be zero.

The "error variance" in a set of scores has usually been defined as the difference between the true score variance (S_t^2, the individual differences) and the total variance of the scores. "Error," under this definition, is a combination of the sampling error of individual true scores and the actual variable error in the experiment; it will be designated S_w^2. However, the variable error *per se* (S_e^2) in any carefully conducted research comes from the variable functioning of the instruments, error in reading and recording scores, and possibly uncontrolled environmental influences. Few have recognized that the real *intra*-individual variance (S_i^2) is biological in nature and reflects the status of the individual from time to time rather than constituting a kind of error. In fact, in some circumstances the actual error variance can be considered negligible in comparison to the *intra*-individual variance (F. Henry, 1959a, 1959b; C. Taylor, 1944).

Error variance is often confused with sampling error, which can be computed for any set of scores. A distinction should be made between intrinsic error (technological error) and sampling error. Even the true score variance (which is necessarily free of error) *can* be thought of as error, because if one uses the mean score of a group of individuals to estimate the population mean, the sampling error of this estimate involves the true score variance and may even be largely determined by it. If one is interested in the *individuals* themselves, however, (rather than the estimation of a group mean) then the *inter*-individual variance (S_t^2) is not sampling error. In fact, it *is* the individual differences. Similarly, (S_i^2) or *intra*-individual variance estimates the variance of the performances of the average or typical subject about the mean of his own scores. It can serve in computing the sampling error of an individual's score without necessarily being an error variance in itself. It may even constitute the appropriate error term to use in testing hypotheses about individual differences. Similarly, the real error variance—what is here called S_e^2 (intrinsic error)—is the appropriate term for testing hypotheses that for a given individual there are no genuine differences from one set of performances to another set, within that individual. Thus the three variances can be visualized as the basis for a "hierarchy of error estimates," even though it is only the third (S_e^2) that is caused by and is a measure of experimental error *per se* in a basic sense (Henry, 1961).

It is necessary to consider all of these kinds of variance in order to conclude whether there are or are not individual differences in the performance of a motor learning task, and to estimate how large these differences may be. For instance, if the size of the within-individual variance (including S_e^2) is large as compared to the true score or *inter*-individual variance, one cannot emphasize the importance of individual differences, although they are present. Some writers have erroneously used the standard deviations of a group of performances as a measure of individual differences, but this is in reality the total variance. Only when the reliability coefficient approaches unity, can one use the standard deviation in this way.

The reliability coefficient yields a relative measure of individual differences, since under a simple model it may be shown to be the ratio of the true score variance to the total variance ($r = S_t^2/S_x^2$). The true score variance is then expressed as the proportion of the total variance that is accounted for by individual differences. The numerator of the reliability coefficient is the co-variance team (mean of the sum of the cross products) and also the true score variance S_t^2 when the calculation is done for pairs of trial performances. Total variance (S_x^2), composed of the three component variances $S_t^2 + S_i^2 + S_e^2$ is the denominator of the reliability coefficient.

The single trial reliability coefficient is the most meaningful measure of individual differences because it is based upon single performances, rather than constituting a variable measure reflecting whatever number of trials may have been used, as well as the amount of individual differences. The conventional reliability coefficient, using k trials, is therefore apt to be misleading. In fact, if there is even a small amount of real individual differences, then as the number of trials sampled (k) approaches infinity the reliability coefficient will approach unity. (The scores are approaching true scores themselves and the reliability of true scores is necessarily unity.) Reliability coefficients refer to individual differences elicited by the test—not to the test itself or to the instruments used in the test.

At this point, it will be well to go back to the definition of individual differences and develop it more rigorously before discussing further the practical method of calculation, and before giving examples of research findings.

Consider a set of N "honest" dice, honestly thrown. There are no individual differences; the probability of turning up a 1, 2, 3, . . . 6 is exactly 1/6 for one throw, for each of the N individual cubes (which are numbered from 1 to N for identification). Make one throw per cube with each of the N individuals. The resultant data will consist of a series of random numbers ranging from 1 to 6. A second throw will produce a comparable series of random numbers. Now, compute the correlation coefficient between the individual Test 1 and Test 2 scores of the N cubes. It will of course be zero within the limits of sampling error, since there are no individual differences among the N cubes. This outcome establishes that the mere existence of differences in scores from throwing a set of cubes does not imply that there are individual differences among the cubes.

Next, let us create individual differences among the cubes by loading each cube (for example, in each set of six, progressively put a small weight on face 1 of the first, on face 2 of the second, on face 3 of the third, and so on). Now, repeat the experiment described in the preceding paragraph. The results will no longer be random, since there are now individual differences among the cubes—individual cube #1 will consistently tend to turn up a 6 (i.e. face 1 down), individual cube #2 will consistently tend to turn up a 5, and so on. In consequence of the individual differences in cubes, there will now be a correlation between the first and second throws (i.e. tests)—in fact, if the loading is heavy enough (i.e. if the individual differences are large), the test-retest correlation will approach $r = 1.00$.

It may be well to reiterate that if one accepts the concept that it is meaningful to define a population mean as being estimated by a sample mean, one has in principle accepted the concept of true score variance (i.e. the individual differences) as a population parameter that can also be estimated empirically —in both cases, the closeness of the estimate is dependent upon the number of individuals N that can be tested, and the number of trials k that can be given, within practical limits. Furthermore, if one is willing to rely on statistical theory, the accuracy of σ_t^2 depends on $\sqrt{N}$ rather than $\sqrt{k}$, although there is the restriction that $k > 1$ in order to make our estimate.

Perhaps the method of calculating S_w^2 (i.e. $S_i^2 + S_e^2$) and S_t^2 can best be approached both correlationally and by variance analysis. Consider the data from N subjects, each tested by k trials. (For the moment, we will specify that the data are secured under plateau conditions, so that the possible influence of such secular trends as learning and fatigue are small or trivial.) It is possible to compute the single trial reliability coefficient as a product-moment correlation, *viz* $r_{ab} = \Sigma_{ab}/N)S_x^2$ where a and b are deviation scores in some pairs of trials A and B, and S_x^2 is the arithmetic average of two estimates of σ_x^2, namely $(S_a^2 + S_b^2)/2$. Note that the usual product-moment correlation uses the geometric average as a parametric estimate, i.e. $\sigma_x^2 = S_a S_b$. In the case of reliability coefficients, S_a and S_b are similar in magnitude, so the differences as between the two methods tend to be trivial.

There are $j = (k-1) + (k-2) + \ldots + (k-k)$ correlations among the k trials. One way to secure a mean value is to average S_t^2 (i.e. $\Sigma ab/N$) for the j sets of pairs of scores, and average the k values obtained for S_x^2. Then $r = S_t^2/S_x^2$ based on these values may be considered an average single trial reliability for the experiment and will in fact be the same as calculated in a rows x columns (i.e. subjects x trials) variance analysis.

To demonstrate this, compute in the usual way the variance sums of squares. Divide each of these by Nk to convert them to variances. Then S_t^2 as obtained above is S^2 total minus S^2 residual/$k-1$, and S^2 total minus S^2 trials is identical with the mean S_x^2 as well as $S_t^2 + S_w^2$ where S_w^2 is calculated as S^2 residual multiplied by $k/(k-1)$. It may also be noted that, in consequence, the reliability coefficient for scores consisting of k trials averaged is $r = S_t^2/[(S_t^2 + S_w^2)/k]$, which is the same as the well known Spearman-Brown relation $R_{kk} = \frac{kr}{1 + (k-1)r}$. This may be a convenient place to mention that the reverse of this formula, which may be used to calculate the single trial reliability from estimations using the mean of k scores per trial, is $r = 1/\{k[(1/R) -] + 1\}$.

It should be explicitly noted that the product-moment correlation excludes the main effect "trials" (i.e. learning or fatigue trends) as a factor in the relationship and assigns the interaction "subjects x trials" to the within-subject variance S_w^2 and thus contaminates it to some extent. This is illustrated by the fact that S_w^2, computed as $S_x^2 - S_t^2$, can also be computed as $S_{A \cdot B}^2 / 2$. It is self-evident that the presence of individual differences in learning or fatigue, as well as the irregular biological variation and error variance, will contribute to the variance among the individual scores of between-trial differences.

Fortunately, it can be shown that the reliability of the between-trial score changes (for adjacent trials) is in general rather low, except sometimes during the first few trials in a learning task. Thus while this factor cannot be excluded, it is a second-order effect in the case of adjacent trial correlations. This is not the case when reliability coefficients and intravariances are computed from variance analysis data—in that method, if there is a secular trend, it would seem necessary to fit individual trend curves and measure the deviations from these curves. Such an approach is easy to recommend from the comfort of one's armchair, but when one deals with actual data, various problems become evident. One of the first that comes up is the rather involved question of whether one type of mathematical curve is to be used, or whether different individuals do not require different curve forms in order to properly fit their trends.

The above is of particular importance when the possibility of individual differences in intravariance scores is examined. The commonly used statistical models assume S_w^2 to be a random variate, because it has been considered error variance. However, since $S_w^2 = S_i^2 + S_e^2$, there is good reason to question that assumption, because S_i^2 is usually much larger than S_e^2. If it represents the normal biological variation within a complex living organism, it should occasion no surprise to discover that there are individual differences in the amount of variation from moment-to-moment in the functioning of indivdual organisms. (It should be mentioned, however, that the absence of individual differences would not establish that S_i^2 was not of biological origin.)

In recent years, ample evidence has been obtained as to the reality of widespread individual differences in S_i^2 in the area of motor performance (Henry, 1967a). In the experiments herein reported, the standard deviations of serial performance scores of each individual about his own mean constitute individual scores of intra-individual variability (including of course the random error variance S_e^2). The reliability coefficients of these variability scores indicate the relative amounts of individual differences in intra-variability.

In these results, the first reliability coefficient of each pair was computed by the odd-even technique, while the second made use of the first and second serial halves. (These coefficients have *not* been corrected by the Spearman-Brown formula.) In all cases there was preliminary practice—the performances scores over the range of trials analyzed showed horizontal regression without slope or secular trend. Fifty to 60 subjects (college males) were tested in each series (new sample for each except where noted). The number of serial trials used in the computations ranged from 30 to 36.

The reliability coefficients were: Reaction time r = .75 and .49, movement time (same subjects) .65 and .50, pursuit rotor .61 and .46 in one sample, .66 and .47 in another, peg shifting coordination .44 and .36 in one sample and .40 and .35 in another under different conditions. In four experiments on rate of work output on a rotating arm ergometer, using 30 serial trials under steady-state (fatigued) conditions, the reliability coefficients were r = .83 and .85, in a retest under a different work schedule, .77 and .77; in another sample .78 and .47 and in a retest under different conditions .90 and .47.

All coefficients in the ten experiments were significant at the 1% level; while some were small, others were substantial. Granted that there may be many types of performance in which there are little or no individual differences in the intra-individual variability, it is clear that there are also many in which there *are* individual differences (Henry, 1967b).

Individual intra-variance scores tend to be correlated with individual mean scores. This suggests that the relatively large individual differences in performance scores may cause the individual differences in S_w^2. The present study examines this question by computing the intra-variance reliability as a second order partial correlation, holding statistically constant the influence of individual differences in performance in both the test and retest.

The first set of data consists of 62 trials on the stabilometer, performed by 100 male subjects. While the amount of improvement is largest in the early trials on this task, there is still some learning (14%) in the last 20 trials. Both individual differences (S_t^2) and intra-variance (S_w^2) are found to decrease, paralleling the decrease (improvement) in performance scores.

The second set of data (obtained by Dr. Kenneth Lersten on 60 male subjects) consists of 60 trials during the sixth day of practice on the pursuit rotor task. After the first two trials, there is no further appreciable change in performance scores, or in either S_t^2 or S_w^2, as a result of practice.

Two methods have been used to compute the reliability coefficients: Correlation between individual S_w and M from (A) adjacent blocks of trials, and (B) using odd-numbered trials *vs.* even-numbered trials. The number of trials per block has been systematically varied from 4 to 28, yielding coefficients for each of 10 block sizes. Depending on block size, the first 6 to 16 trials have been discarded, and the coefficients from several blocks of a particular size have been averaged.

Using odd-even trials, the reliability coefficients for intra-variation scores range from r = .36 (4 trials) to .87 (28 trials) in the case of the stabilometer. With the influence of performance level partialled out, these coefficients become r = .24 and .72. For the pursuit rotor, the corresponding r's are .38 and .68 and drop to .19 and .59 in the partial correlation form.

The reliability coefficients are of course smaller when the adjacent block estimates are used. The highest values for the stabilometer occur with blocks of 13 to 20 trials, reaching r = .60 for 15 trials, which drops to .29 in partial r form. For the pursuit rotor, the 15-trial reliability is .50 and drops to .38. The 17-trial value is .50 and is not reduced in the partial correlation form.

It is concluded that the subjects in both of these tasks are characterized by substantial amounts of individual differences in their intra-variance. While a considerable proportion of the reliability in this aspect of behavior is related to individual differences in performance level, approximately half is independent.

The size of the reliability coefficients is dependent on the number of trials per block in accord with the Spearman-Brown relationship, over the range 4 to 20 trials.

In the following list of reliability coefficients, the values in parentheses represent the estimates made by the Spearman-Brown method from the 6-trial coefficient. Reliabilities were obtained directly for 4, 6, 10, 14, and 20 trials averaged per score on an adjacent block basis. Where the available numbers of trials permitted, several coefficients were calculated and averaged. For the stabilometer, the observed and S-B estimated values were: 4 trials, r = .37 (.36); 6, r = .46 (.46); 10, r = .59 (.59); 14, r = .68 (.67); 20, r = .75 (.74). The estimated values for 2 and 1 trial scores were r = .22 and .15. In the case of the ladder climb task, the agreement between observed and predicted was not as close, but both followed the same trend. The results were: 4 trials, r = .29 (.27); 6, r = .36 (.36); 10, r = .50 (.48); 14, r = .53 (.56); 20, r = .62 (.65); for 2 and 1 trials per score, the estimates were r = .17 and .11 (Henry, 1969).

It is both reassuring and convenient to find that (at least within the limits justified by the available data), the intravariance scores can be handled by elementary sampling theory. Great importance must be attached to the strong indication that individual differences in the intravariance of single track and 2-trial scores are trivial in magnitude. It follows from this that the treatment of intravariance as a random variate in our conventional statistical models, while unjustified theoretically, probably does not lead to serious error in the case of single trial scores, although it can certainly be expected to be troublesome when the score of an individual is constituted by averaging a large number of trials per subject. (I leave this problem to the tender mercy of mathematical statisticians.)

It was shown above that application of sampling theory to individual scores as well as to the mean scores of subjects leads to the Spearman-Brown formula. Sometimes, of course, this formula is applied to inappropriate situations in which it may or may not be dependable. Perhaps the most important of the implicit assumptions underlying its legitimate use is the requirement that both S_t^2 and S_w^2 be unchanging among the various trials that are averaged to constitute an individual score. (This is more restrictive than the assumption that the correlations between the trials are equal.) As is always true of the assumptions underlying the statistical models, departure from them may have a small or a large impact. Thus there is concern as to

the robustness (i.e. the lack of sensitivity to the assumptions) that characterizes a particular statistical measure or procedure that the scientist may need
to use.

The Spearman-Brown relationship (or more accurately, the principles
that underly it) is particularly important in estimating the reliability in
learning tasks. Consider the problem of determining the amount of relation
between individual differences in kinesthetic ability (A) and motor learning
ability (B). The occurrence of a low correlation might be the consequence
of either a low intrinsic relation between A and B, or a low reliability of
the scores in A or in B or in both. It becomes necessary to correct for the
attenuation caused by unreliability. This correction requires consideration of
the reliability coefficients for A and B. If they are very small, the correction
cannot be dependable. Ideally, one should secure scores approximating true
scores, but that is usually not practical. From the Spearman-Brown relation,
one has some basis to make some rational decision as to how many trials to
use, as well as to estimate the reliability for the full-test scores (rather than
half-scores). Unfortunately, in the case of learning scores (or other difference scores) the reliability coefficients are apt to be rather low.

In a learning situation, the initial performance scores are rapidly increasing
(or decreasing). It would be hazardous to simply assume that the Spearman-
Brown relationship would apply. Some trend may well be present in the
final or post-learning scores, since an asymptote is seldom approached very
closely. While the reliability of the difference score (i.e. learning score)
can be calculated from the reliabilities of the initial and final scores and
the initial *vs.* final correlation, this is not very helpful if one remembers
that this latter correlation is a *result* rather than a *cause* of the dynamics of
the situation. There are two conflicting factors that influence the reliability of
learning gains or fatigue decrements. Both initial and final scores become
more reliable as an increasing number of trials are averaged.

In contrast, the magnitude of the difference score becomes smaller as more
trials are averaged, since the mean initial score approaches more closely the
mean final score. The consequent restriction in range or variability of the
difference scores may be thought of as a factor tending to reduce the reliability
of the different scores. In fact, it has been found that in the case of Stabilometer scores, the true-score variation S_t is a linear function of the decreasing
size of the learning score, as an increasing number of trials are averaged. On
the other hand (the intravariation S_w decreases curvilinearly at a declining
rate, rather than according to the predictions of classical sampling theory. In
consequence, the reliability coefficients of the difference scores fail to increase
in accord with the Spearman-Brown formula, and in fact pass through a
maximum for scores based on the average of 8 trials (Henry, 1967c). The
results are given in the table which follows.

Another problem of interest centers on the question of whether, and to
what extent, practice of a motor task influences individual differences in
performance and influences the within-individual variation. Observations

TABLE 1.

RELIABILITY INCREASES WHEN SEVERAL
TRIALS ARE AVERAGED (STABILOMETER)

k TRIALS AVERAGED	INITIAL Obs.	Sp-B	FINAL Obs.	Sp-B	GAINS Obs.	Sp-B
1	.724	—	.733	—	.671	—
2	.840	.841	.846	.846	.803	.804
4	.908	.913	.913	.916	.875	.891
6	.933	.940	.950	.943	.900	.924
8	.955	.955	.964	.957	.928	.942
10	.956	.963	.969	.965	.922	.953
12	.967	.969	.972	.971	.908	.961
Av. error	—	.003	—	.003	—	.020

limited to changes in score variability (i.e. S_x^2 rather than its components S_t^2 and S_w^2), as in the older studies, are inadequate. The same can be said for observations of the effects of practice on the reliability coefficient, since changes in the coefficient might reflect changes in either S_t^2 or S_w^2. Moreover, there can be changes in *both* of these variances in the absence of changes in the coefficient.

Weighing various considerations that have been discussed earlier in this paper, one is led to the conclusion that the estimation of S_t^2 and S_w^2 on the basis of adjacent trial relationships constitutes an effective approach. Having available the adjacent trial correlations and S_x^2 for each trial, $S_t^2 = rS_x^2$ and $S_w^2 = S_x^2 - S_t^2$. The main effects "trials" has automatically been removed (although not discarded, since it is used to construct the practice curve or the fatigue curve for trial-by-trial performance). The influence of the second order effect, of individual differences in learning or fatigue, is minimal, and the influence of individual differences in intravariance is trivial.

The instrumental and other variable errors S_e^2 may be assumed to be the same in each of two adjacent trials, and ordinarily would not be expected to change appreciably in a systematic way during the course of an experiment—to the extent that this is true, observed trends in the effect of practice on S_i^2 (the net biological variance) should parallel the observed changes in S_w^2. Without question, it would be desirable to know the values of S_e^2 for each experiment and each trial, but usually that is impractical or impossible. As mentioned earlier, a method for evaluating S_e^2 is available for certain tasks (Henry, 1959a, 1959b)—in brief, it involves duplicate instrumentation and reliance on the fact that only the largest one or two of the error sources is quantitatively important (Henry, 1949). In the case of reaction time, speed of movement, muscle strength and jumping performance measurements, S_e^2 has been found to be very much smaller than S_i^2 (Henry, 1959a, 1959b). More recently, the writer has also found this to hold true for Stabilometer data. This constitutes another reason for the belief that trends in S_i^2 do in general parallel trends in S_w^2. An additional practical point is that variance form skewed distributions—this can usually be avoided by using the square roots (i.e. variabilities) wherever the operations permit doing so.

Turning now to the experiment on the effect of practice on S_i^2 and S_t^2, the writer has been of the opinion that the identification of S_i^2 with biological rather than error variance leads to the *a priori* hypothesis that it should ordinarily not be influenced by practice. There is some justification for hedging a bit, since it is conceivable that in some types of discrimination response, the feedback loops may operate more precisely in consequence of practice. It is anticipated that such cases will be exceptional.

With respect to the effects of practice on individual differences (S_t^2), there seems to be little basis for *a priori* theorizing, other than the vague expectation that the index of variability ($S_t/\bar{x}$) may tend to remain constant. If one feels that all individuals have equal ultimate motor capability, individual differences should tend to decrease with practice—this would also be true if the nature of the scoring were such as to cause a ceiling effect. This should also result in a skewing of the true scores, but it is not clear how this could be examined—possibly something could be done in the case of tasks characterized by extremely slow learning, which would permit many trials within each of several stages of practice. One could of course take the point of view that if the initial trials did not indeed represent a zero stage of learning (or an approximation of this stage), it should be self-evident that there would be no individual differences until they developed in consequence of practice—thus practice should increase the individual differences. In harsh reality, it is probably a rare situation that a subject starts at a stage approximating zero, although it may be that some tasks are much closer than others in this respect. These considerations are complicated by the likelihood that performance in most (and probably all) motor tasks is in part dependent on built-in motor coordinations that are there and functioning *before* practice. Summing up these arguments, the writer is forced to the eclectic position: Try it out and see what happens.

Data on the effects of motor skill practice on variability components are available on nine tasks. In some cases, several independent experiments are available for a particular task. The writer carried out some of these experiments; others were performed by doctoral students under his direction. In all cases, the number of subjects was at least 50 or 60; in a few cases N= 100. Discrete movement tasks have employed 60 trials, all in one experimental period. In the continuous performance tasks (pursuit, rotor, stabilometer, ladder climb etc.), there usually has been a 30 sec. practice followed by 30 sec. inter-trial rest (15 sec. periods were used for the pursuit rotor). The continuous tasks were performed on the basis of 10 or 12 trials per day on each of six days (60 per day in the case of the rotor). In all experiments except the simple RT and MT measurements, large amounts of learning occurred—in some cases, trend curves were fitted and found to be of the one or two component exponential type. The detailed trial-by-trial influence on performance as well as S_t and S_w are shown on the slides—in the paragraphs which follow, the results are summarized.

Practice evidently has essentially no effect on the intravariance in any of the speed tasks, namely simple RT, simple forward movement, the circular and linear phases of the Rho test, or the peg-shifting task. There is consistent and considerable downward drop during the first 3 or 4 trials, which may well be caused by the subjects-by-trials interaction during this short period of extremely large improvement. Subsequently the trend is horizontal (for the remaining 55 or so trials), although there is sometimes a suggestion of a slight upward or a slight downward drift. In no case does this drift parallel the relatively large improvements from learning. The same findings characterize two of the continuous tasks—the Leavitt stilt-balance task (scored as time in balance per attempt), and the Bachman Ladder Climb task. In contrast, the Pursuit Rotor data show a relatively large and steady upward trend for the first 60 days (Day 1). Thereafter, the trend is substantially horizontal, although large changes in the practice curve are occurring. The Stabilometer data exhibit an exponential downward trend that seems to parallel the performance level trend although it does not do so exactly, since the relative variation ($S_w/\bar{x}$) shows an S-shaped upward trend. Another sample of subjects performed continuously—the results are approximately the same, although $S_w/\bar{x}$ remains constant after the first 10 or 12 of the 60 trials. In one of the ladder experiments and one of the stabilometer experiments, the subjects were retested for 40 trials after a one year lay-off. The intravariance had not changed, and remained independent of the performance changes during relearning.

It is of course difficult to generalize from the above findings. An overall evaluation might be that the intravariance level is largely independent of practice, the exception being the very first few practice trials (or a somewhat larger number in the case of the pursuit rotor.) This generalization definitely does not apply to stabilometer performances—for this task, the intravariance is definitely reduced throughout practice until learning has been completed, although it apparently does not reflect relearning changes in performance.

A cautionary statement was made earlier in the paper, to the effect that the intra-variability computed by the adjacent trial method was contaminated somewhat by an inter-action that included individual differences in adjacent trial score gains or decreases (i.e. Δ learning). It was anticipated that this influence would be small and largely confined to the first few trials.

Its magnitude can be estimated by partitioning the variance of the individual Δ scores into individual differences and intra-individual variation. To avoid redundancy, the pairs of individual scores are calculated as trial 1 minus 2 (i.e. Δ_1), trial 3 minus 4 (i.e. Δ_2) and so on. The correlations and variances are then calculated as in the adjacent trial situation, to obtain $S_{t\Delta}$ and $S_{w\Delta}$. Note that $S_{w\Delta}$ does not contain the learning interaction term present in S_w, and is accordingly somewhat smaller.

For comparison, S_t and S_w are also calculated for performance scores (trial 1 *vs* 2 and 3 *vs* 4), with the variances averaged for the first set, and so on. It is found that for the first set of Δ scores for the stabilometer, $S_{w\Delta}$ is only 5.1 percent smaller than S_w. For the second and later sets of scores, it is from 1.7 to 1.2 percent smaller. In the case of the ladder climb, it is 7.1 percent smaller for the first set, for the second set it is 3.0 percent smaller, and for the later sets it is approximately 1.0 percent smaller. It seems evident that the expectation has been realized. The contamination from individual differences is small and after the first few trials it becomes trivial. This is confirmed by examining the reliability coefficients for the Δ scores—they are very low, ranging from $r = .14$ to $.11$ for the stabilometer and from $r = .12$ to $.06$ for the ladder task.

Individual differences (S_t) are, in general, influenced by practice—the exceptions are simple movement time (where there is very little change in performance) and the stilt-balance task scored as time-in-balance per trial (where there are large changes in performance). Surprisingly, S_t for simple reaction time decreases noticeably during the first few trials, paralleling the decrease in performance level. Thereafter, it steadily increases, although the performance level is no longer changing. In the linear component of the Rho speed task, a mirror image of this trend is seen—S_t increases for the first 8 or 10 trials, then decreases to level off after 25 trials; performance time scores are exponentially decreasing during the entire practice period, as they are for the circular component. On the other hand, S_w declines exponentially (paralleling the performance trend). In the other speed task (peg shift), S_t approximately parallels the declining performance time as practice progresses.

In the continuous performance tasks (ladder, stabilometer, pursuit rotor) where the practice is divided among 6 days, individual differences consistently increase or decrease during the first day, depending on whether the performance scores increase or decrease with practice. Thereafter, S_t is independent of performance trends in both samples of ladder data, and in the rotor data—performance scores continue to improve with practice, but the individual differences exhibit a horizontal trend. For some reason this finding does not hold for the stabilometer data; in both samples of subjects, S_t continues to decrease in proportion to the decrease in performance scores throughout the entire practice period. In one sample the relative variation ($S_t / \bar{x}$) remains constant in middle practice and increases in the late stages of practice. In the other sample, where the number of trials and inter-trial rest is the same as the other, but there are no between-day rests, the relative variation remains constant throughout the last 80 percent of practice. In the case of the stilts task (inter-trial rests, but no between-day rests), performance improves greatly with practice but the trend for S_t is horizontal.

In attempting to generalize from these findings, there seems to be considerable basis for concluding that in the early stages of practice, individual difference trends usually tend to parallel the performance score trends, although not in exact proportion since the relative variation is not constant. There are exceptions, the most notable being simple reaction time. In middle and late practice, although performance continues to improve, individual differences seem to remain constant (i.e. exhibit a horizontal trend). A striking exception is evident in the stabilometer task, where the individual differences continue to decrease with practice.

It should be noted that the data summarized above offer several examples of large trends upward or downward in the amount of individual differences, accompanied by corresponding trends in intra-variance and consequently no change in the reliability coefficient. They also offer examples where there are changes in S_t that are independent of the trend in S_w, and changes in S_w that are not paralleled by the changes in S_t, thus demonstrating the invalidity of the standard deviation S_x as a measure of individual differences.

In bringing this paper to a close, it hardly seems necessary to point out that there has been no attempt to review the literature. My underlying theoretical position probably traces back to a course in differential psychology taken in 1934 with Professor R. C. Tryon. The required reading included the 1904, 1907 and 1913 papers of Charles Spearman and selections from the 1911 and 1921 editions of "The Essentials of Mental Measurement" by William Brown. Subsequently, Tryon's continued interest in individual differences led him into the area of intra-domain reliability, whereas my own direction was increasingly toward problems that chiefly involved repeated measurement data. As I reflect on what in retrospect seems to have been the naiveté of psychologists of that period, I must confess that some of my publications on rat psychology exhibited the common misconception of the time that reliability was chiefly a function of the instruments or the methods. Somewhere during the next 10 years my thinking became clearer—I recall conversations with my friend Craig Taylor (a physiologist at Stanford) on the necessity of using duplicate instrumentation if one wished to measure the accuracy of a method. By 1948 I was thinking of the standard deviation as

$$S = \sqrt{S_i^2 + (S_i^2 + S_{e_1}^2 + S_{e_2}^2 \cdots)}$$ and indeed in 1949 formally stated that

"σ_i represents the true variation *within* an individual" and that, in attempting to reduce errors, "nothing can be done about σ_i since . . . it is an inherent part of the situation and must so be accepted." These concepts were subsequently worked into a number of my reports of research, a few of which are given as references in this paper.

In the meantime I had noticed, in the course of recording the resting heart rates of many individuals, that some of them were characterized by high variability, while others exhibited very little deviation from moment to moment. It seemed to me that motor performances of various types might well exhibit individual differences in intravariability, and from time to time I worked up data that supported this notion (this work was not extensive, since the calculation of hundreds of within-individual SD's was a tedious task in the pre-computer culture). I was not aware, until considerably later, that Lovell (1941) had approached this problem, although his results are probably not very meaningful because of inadequacies of method. Later Fiske and Rice (1955) discussed the topic. It is my impression that they took the existence of individual differences in intravariance for granted and offered little or no firm evidence of a quantitative nature. A paper by Ghiselli (1956) should also be mentioned.

With the event of the electronic computer, it has become practical to work with this type of problem, and a number of papers have appeared in the last year or two. One of the recent investigators is Richard Schmidt, who has the task of commenting critically on my paper.

REFERENCES

Fiske, D. W. and Rice, L. Intra-individual response variability. *Psych. Bull.* 1955, *52*, 217-250.

Ghiselli, E. E. Differentiation of individuals in terms of their predictability. *Jour. Applied Psychol.* 1956, *40*, 374-377.

Henry, F. M. Errors in measurement. In: *Research Methods,* G. Scott (ed.) Washington, D.C.: Am. Assn. Hlth., Phys. Educ. and Rec., 1949.

Henry, F. M. Reliability, measurement error and intra-individual difference. *Res. Quart.* 1959a, *30*, 21-24.

Henry, F. M. Influence of measurement error and intra-individual variation. *Res. Quart.* 1959b, *30*, 155-159.

Henry, F. M. Stimulus complexity, movement complexity, age and sex in relation to reaction latency and speed in limb movements. *Res. Quart.* 1961, *32*, 353-366.

Henry, F. M. Best *vs.* average individual scores. *Res. Quart.* 1967a, *38*, 317-320.

Henry, F. M. Individual differences in intra-individual variability. (Abstract). Paper presented at Research Section, Annual Conference, Am. Assn. Hlth., Phys. Educ. and Rec., Las Vegas, Nevada, March, 1967b.

Henry, F. M. Inter-relation of factors involved in maximum learning score reliability. (Abstract). Paper presented at Research Section, Annual Conference, Calif. Assn. Hlth., Phys. Educ. and Rec., Los Angeles, Calif., March, 1967c.

Henry, F. M. Within-individual variability. (Abstract). Paper presented at Research Section, Annual Conference, S.W. District, Am. Assn. Hlth., Phys. Educ. and Rec., Sacramento, Calif., March, 1969.

Lovell, C. A study of personal variation in hand-arm steadiness. *Am. Jour. Psychol.* 1941, *54*, 230-236.

Taylor, C. Some properties of maximal and submaximal exercise. *Am. Jour. Physiol.* 1944, *142*, 200-212.

CRITIQUE OF HENRY'S PAPER
by Richard A. Schmidt*

The official reaction to Professor Henry's presentation must be one of general agreement, as his arguments have been carefully thought out over the years and much evidence is available to support his points of view. Thus, the position taken in the present paper will take the form of answering some common criticisms, some of which have been heard in the past and some of which are, as far as is known, new.

*Now at the University of Michigan.

Individual Differences

First, data from the writer's laboratory at the University of Maryland is entirely in support of Professor Henry's findings that there are individual differences in within-S subject variability. Using a discrete task in which S had to lift his finger from a microswitch, move the right hand and arm to knock down four barriers in order, and move back to a microswitch as quickly as possible, the reliabilities of within-S variability (computed as the correlation between the SD of the odd trials about S's subjects odd trial mean versus the SD of the even trials about S's even trial mean) ranged from .40 to .73 (mean $r = .57$) for four slightly different variations of the same task (Schmidt, 1969b). In a task requiring S to move a slide with a pointer attached so that the pointer "hit" a moving target, the reliabilities ranged from .27 to .81 (mean $r = .52$) for 8 different variations of the basic task (Schmidt, 1969b). Finally, data from Lois Williams (1969) using a simplified barrier knock-down task for the right and left limbs, both for hands and for feet, showed reliabilities ranging from .44 to .70 (mean $r = .66$). Thus there is strong support for the notion that within-S variability is not random, but is systematic and shows individual differences.

There is also support from Maryland for Henry's contention that within-S variability (the SD of S's responses about his own mean) behaves similarly to traditional mean performance scores as the number of trials per S is increased. Williams' (1969) data showed that the reliability of within-S variability increased markedly as the number of trials per S used to compute the score was increased. She found that the reliabilities were .07, .21, .29, .39, and .66 when the number of trials per S was 4, 8, 16, 28, and 54, respectively, following closely the predictions from the Spearman-Brown "Prophesy" formula which is known to hold for mean performance scores.

Finally, the data from Maryland agrees with the Henry findings with respect to the specificity of within-S variability, with the correlations among very similar timing tasks (Schmidt, 1969b) averaging .30, among very similar discrete barrier knock-down tasks (Schmidt, 1969b) averaging .57, and among very simple barrier knock-down tasks (Williams, 1969) averaging .12. Thus there appears to be a weak general factor of within-S variability, with Ss who are inconsistent on one task tending to be inconsistent on other tasks, but the correlations are small and do not offer much hope of any kind of useful predictive relationships.

Rationale for partition of "error"

It is certainly a simple matter for Professor Henry to divide conceptually that which is traditionally termed "error" (the difference between the true score and the observed score) into within-S variability and what he calls "technological error." Alternatively, one could divide "error" into three components, dealing with variability in machinery and measuring devices, variability in the central decision processes, and variability in the local effectors of the response. However, science has always demanded parsimony, and complications of theoretical and statistical models must have sound justification. What is the justification for the partition of error presented by Professor Henry?

One intuitively satisfying justification might be the fact that the two classes of variability come from difference sources, one coming from non-living machinery and the other coming from living individuals. But such a justification does not seem entirely sound, since it must be shown that the two sources of variability are not merely different members of a common class of variabilities (with common properties), but are members of a common class of variabilities with each class having different sources and behaving in fundamentally different ways. Otherwise, little will be gained by such a division.

One justification worth considering is as follows: If a source of variability shows reliable individual differences across Ss, then it should not be labelled "random error;" if it does not show reliable individual differences, then it should be labelled "random error." The first of these contentions is relatively easy to see. If there are individual differences in the SD of S's rsponses about his own mean, then the within-S variability cannot be considered *random*, i.e., a source of variability which has a value randomly assigned for each trial. If it were truly random, the reliability of within-S variabilty could be greater than zero only by chance, and a great deal of evidence has already been presented showing that the reliability is indeed greater than zero.

The converse of the above proposal is not so obvious. If there are no individual differences in the SD of S's responses, then the variability is not systematic and should probably be properly labelled "random error." In speaking with Professor Henry personally before the symposium, he denied that the converse was true, and provided body temperature as a counter-example for which there would be systematic biological variability but no individual differences, each S having nearly the same body temperature. However, if a very large number of trials per S were administered using a very sensitive thermometer, there would almost certainly be reliabilities of body temperature greater than zero (and thus individual differences), although the magnitude of the individual differences would doubtless be very small.

Thus, whether or not there are reliable individual differences in a source of variability might be a criterion for determining whether or not a source of variability was random. Having determined that two sources of variability are fundamentally different (e.g., technological error and within-S variability), it would seem unwise to lump random and non-random sources of variability into one measure called "error." Thus, the conclusion is that Professor Henry's division of error into its components is not unwarranted, and should lead to modifications in statistical models which make the assumption that the differences between the true score and the observed score is *random* error. Such an assumption is not in keeping with the evidence, at least for some motor responses.

Within-S consistency as a criterion

A number of investigators (e.g., Williams, 1969; Schmidt, 1969a, 1969b) have indicated that within-S variability is an aspect of responding which is not captured by traditional measures of performance such as mean algebraic or absolute error. If so, what does within-S variability represent, and to what extent do other measures contain information concerning within-S variability?

It has been shown (e.g., Gottsdanker;[1] Marteniuk, 1969) that absolute error and within-S variability are correlated, with the correlations in some cases being as high as .80. Using a timing task in which S had to "hit" a moving target by moving a slide with a pointer attached, Schmidt (1969b) found that the correlations between mean absolute error and within-S consistency were around .60 for various tasks, which might indicate that within-S consistency does not represent a unique component of responding not captured by mean error scores.

Also, the standard method for computing the absolute error,

$$\text{Absolute Error} = \frac{\sum_{t=1}^{N} |X_t - C|}{N}$$

is really the expression for the average deviation (AD), in which t is the trial number, N is the total number of trials, X_t is S's score on Trial t, and C is some specified "correct" score. In addition, the usual method for computing the within-S variability,

$$\text{Within-S variability} = \sqrt{\frac{\sum_{t=1}^{N} (X_t - \overline{X})^2}{N}}$$

is really the SD of S's responses about his own mean, where N, t, and X_t are defined as before, but X is the mean of S's own responses. In many tasks X and C are nearly equal; in a timing task (Schmidt, 1967), the algebraic (constant) error (the difference between X and C) was only 3 msec. If X and C are very nearly equal for some Ss, then the absolute error and the within-S variability for those Ss will only be as different as are the AD and the SD. Thus, it is not surprising that absolute error and within-S variability are sometimes very highly correlated.

In addition, there is evidence that the absolute error and within-S variability scores behave very similarly as a function of independent variables. For example, Schmidt (1968a, 1968b, 1969a, 1969c) studied the effects of movement speed, movement distance, and movement load using a timing task. He found that increased speed of movement decreased both absolute error and within-S variability, that increased movement distance increased them both, and that the added load did not affect either of them. This prob-

---

[1] R. M. Gottsdanker, Department of Psychology, University of California, Santa Barbara, Personal Communication, 1968.

ably reflected the fact that for this task the X and C were very nearly equal, and that absolute error and within-S consistency were correlated.

These three lines of reasoning lead one to suspect that the within-S variability and absolute error scores are really not measures of independent components, and that we are not really obtaining separate and non-overlapping information from them. That this was the case was pointed out to the writer by Professor Henry[2] when he demonstrated that, for performances demanding accuracy, the total variance of a set of responses about the correct response (within a single S) could be partitioned into two statistically independent components, one being the constant error (sometimes called the algebraic or arithmetic error) which gives the average error of Ss responses with respect to direction (sign), and the other being the within-S variability (sometimes called the variable error) which is the standard deviation of S's responses about his own mean constant error.[3] Henry showed that the use of the absolute error (the AD of the S's responses about the specified correct score) confounds information from the constant error and the variable error. Thus, these lines of evidence would suggest that two measures of error should be used in accuracy situations, the constant error and the variable error. However, using the absolute error seems justified in cases where there are few trials per subject, in which case the reliability of the absolute error will be higher than that for the variable error, or in cases where there is only one trial per subject, in which case the variable error is undefined.

REFERENCES

Marteniuk, R. G. Individual differences in intra-individual variability and the prediction of motor performance. *Journal of Motor Behavior,* 1969, 1, 307-316.

Schmidt, R. A. Motor factors in coincident timing. Doctoral dissertation, University of Illinois, 1967.

Schmidt, R. A. Anticipation and timing in human motor performance. *Psychological Bulletin,* 1968, 70, 631-646. (a)

Schmidt, R. A. Unpublished data, University of Maryland, 1968. (b)

Schmidt, R. A. Consistency of response as a function of selected motor variables. *Research Quarterly,* 1969, 40, 561-566. (a)

Schmidt, R. A. Intra-limb specificity of motor response consistency. *Journal of Motor Behavior,* 1969, 1, 89-99. (b)

Schmidt, R. A. Movement time as a determiner of timing accuracy. *Journal of Experimental Psychology,* 1969, 79, 43-47 (c)

Williams, L. A. Specificity versus generality of motor response consistency. *Journal of Motor Behavior,* 1969, 1, 45-52.

[2]F. M. Henry, Department of Physical Education, University of California, Berkeley, Personal Communication, 1969.

[3]A proof of this contention is available from the writer.

Microcosmic Learning Single Nerve-Cell Training[1]

J. B. Basmajian
Emory University

Microcosmic Learning: Single Nerve-cell Training

A recently developed technique, motor unit training, offers a useful approach to studies of the conscious control over spinal motoneurons, of the neurophysiological processes underlying proprioception and feed-back, and of many related psychophysiological phenomena. It is based on the auditory and visual display to human subjects of individual myoelectric potentials recorded from fine-wire intra-muscular electrodes. The cues provide the subject with an awareness of the twitching of individual motor units. They learn quickly to control this activity and can give many bizarre responses with only the artificial feedback cues as a guide.

Many sets of experiments are discussed which bear upon the factors that influence motor unit controls. Local factors in the limb in which a single motor unit is being activated obviously have an effect; however, subjects can be trained to control a unit in spite of competing local movements. Even massive contractions of the same muscle induced by electrical stimulation of the motor nerve do not block the controlled firing of a well-trained unit.

Previous training and skills appear to be a deterrent rather than a help when the time for isolating the activity of single units is the criterion of success. Handedness plays a role, but its importance emerges only during repeated training sessions when isolation is much quicker during the second session if the preferred hand was the one previously used. Factors of age and intelligence have only broad influences and no clear-cut conclusions have been made.

Practical applications in the field of rehabilitation training, design of myoelectric artificial aids to the physically handicapped and the application of the technique to psychological research all underline its importance in neuropsychophysiology.

In the search for ultra-models of the learning process, motor-unit training

[1] The research efforts of many colleagues and assistants provided the material for this article, the principal ones being recorded in the references. Continued financial assistance from the Medical Research Council of Canada and the Muscular Dystrophy Association of Canada facilitated the bulk of our work at Queen's University upon which much of this article is based.

emerges as an important frontier demanding widespread exploration. Whilst it is not the molecular basis of learning (if such exists) it certainly provides a microcosmic model for neuromuscular training, operant conditioning, and conscious control over spinal motoneurons. If these become thoroughly charted and understood, we will have taken a major stride forward in the investigation of motor learning.

This new approach to an old problem owes its origins to the improvements in electromyography during the past two decades. Although in the 1930's Smith (1934) and Lindsley (1935) gave brief accounts of man's ability to discharge single motor units and to vary their rates, electromyographers tended to take this phenomenon for granted and performed no systematic studies of it. Thus the significant history of motor-unit training dates back to 1960 when Harrison and Mortensen became interested in their finding that subjects of kinesiologic studies on the tibialis anterior muscle could recruit a number of isolated motor units one after another. Urging them to publish their results (Harrison and Mortensen, 1962), I set about studying motor-unit isolation and control in earnest.

A company of many colleagues and assistants have helped me in a series of explorations following my first report (Basmajian, 1963). In addition, our coincidental development of an elegant intramuscular electrode provided us with a superb vehicle for rapid progress (Basmajian and Stecko, 1962). Meanwhile, scientists in other centers have taken up the study of conscious control of single motor units, both from the inherent physiological point of view, and the point of view of the experimental psychologist who uses motor units as a device to be manipulated. Perhaps the most dramatic application has been the use of motor-unit controls to operate myoelectric prostheses and orthoses; this in turn has demanded greater depth in our understanding of the physiologic and psychologic phenomena.

A motor unit includes only one motor neuron (motoneuron) in the spinal cord—or in the case of cranial nerves, in the brainstem. Thus, the activity of the motor unit is a reflection of the activity of the motoneuron. From the cell-body of a motoneuron a single axon runs in a nerve to a small group of striated muscle fibers. Collectively, the motoneuron (cell-body and axon) plus the muscle fibers it supplies, constitute the motor unit. A twitch-like contraction of the muscle fibers of the unit is detected by a recordable myoelectric potential and indicates an activation of the neuron.

Obviously, in man it is much easier to place an electrode in or near the muscle fibers rather than in his spinal cord. Thus refined electromyography provides us with a simple way to record the activity of the motoneurons. In other words, we exploit the fact that the electromyogram can be made an accurate reflection of the electroneurogram with none of the overwhelming technical problems. As early as 1921 when electromyography first became a practical research tool, Gasser and Newcomer suggested just this, to be echoed eight years later by Adrian and Bronk (1929)—to no avail! Electromyography was used for kinesiology and clinical diagnosis and little, if any, for studies of motoneuronal activity; an exception to this was the work of Gilson and Mills (1940-41) who reported that discrete brief voluntary effort resulted in the discrete twitching of a single motor unit.

ELECTROMYOGRAPHY

To avoid confusion, we must first clarify the basis of electromyography. Although the structural unit of a gross contraction is the muscle fiber, the functional unit (for the purpose of electromyography) is the motor unit, which is a group of fibers supplied by a single nerve cell. A contraction of a motor unit is a twitch lasting a few milliseconds. Immediately after each twitch the fibers of the motor unit relax completely and they only twitch again when an impulse arrives along the nerve fiber.

Individual muscles of the body consist of many hundreds of such motor units and it is their summated activity that develops the tension in the whole muscle. The motor units twitch repetitively and asynchronously. It is this very randomized activity that causes the smooth tension of the whole muscle rather than a jerky one.

The amount of work produced by a single motor unit is quite small. In a living human being it is usually insufficient to show any etxernal movement of a joint spanned by the whole muscle of which it is a part. Even in the case of small joints, such as those of the thumb, at least two or three motor units are needed to give a visible movement.

Under normal conditions small motor units are recruited early and, as the force is automatically or consciously increased, larger and larger motor units are recruited (Henneman *et al.*, 1965) while all the motor units also increase their frequency of twitching. The upper limit in man is about 50 per second, but rates much slower than this are the rule. There is no single, set frequency; individual motor units can fire very slowly and will increase their frequency of response on demand.

MOTOR UNIT POTENTIALS

The motor unit potential has a brief duration (with a median of 9 msec) and a total amplitude measured in microvolts or millivolts. When displayed on the cathode-ray oscilloscope, most motor units recorded by conventional techniques are sharp triphasic or biphasic spikes; from fine-wire electrodes, the potentials are much more complex and recognizable as individuals. Generally, the larger the motor-unit potential involved, the larger is the motor unit that produced it. However, distance from the electrode, the type of electrodes and equipment used (and many other factors) influence the final size and shape.

Electrodes

Probably the most disagreement in electromyography since its beginnings has centered around the types of electrodes. There are a multitude of special electrodes (wires or needles). Because kinesiology is often performed by investigators who are not medically qualified, surface electrodes have been used widely. However, for the excellent recordings required in motor-unit training, the difficulties rising from surface electrodes are prohibitive. Moreover, inserted electrodes are no longer as forbidding as they once were. Our fine-wire electrodes are as easy to use and as easy to tolerate as are skin electrodes. They are (1) extremely fine and, therefore, painless, (2) easily injected and withdrawn, (3) as broad in pick-up from a specific muscle as the best surface electrodes, and (4) give excellent sharp motor-unit spikes with fidelity. With one millimeter of their tip exposed, such electrodes record the voltage from a muscle much better than surface electrodes (Sutton, 1962). Bipolar fine-wire electrodes isolate their pick-up either to the whole muscle being studied or to the confines of the compartment within a muscle if it has a multi-pennate structure. Barriers of fibrous connective tissue within a muscle or around it act as insulation. Thus, one can record all the activity as far as such a barrier without the interfering pick-up from beyond the barrier (such as there always is with surface electrodes).

Bipolar fine-wire electrodes are made from a nylon-insulated Karma alloy wire only 25 or 75 microns in diameter, or any other similar material. They are very simple to make and their preparation is described by us in detail in the literature (Basmajian and Stecko, 1962; Basmajian, 1967).

Apparatus

Electromyographs are high-gain amplifiers with a preference for frequencies from about ten to several thousand cycles per sec. An upper limit of 1,000 cycles per sec is satisfactory. Ideally, the recording device should either be photographic, or employ electromagnetic tape-recording. In recent years, multi-track tape-recorders have provided a relatively cheap method of storing EMG signals, especially for motor-unit training studies.

MOTOR UNIT TRAINING

Techniques

Fundamentally the technique consists of providing human subjects with the best possible feed-back of the activity of his motoneurons through the monitoring of electromyographic signals. No magic surrounds the general experimental approach and different laboratories have already devised their own routines. The following is a general design.

Following the implantation of fine-wire electrodes and routine testing, a subject needs only to be given general instructions. He is asked to make contractions of the muscle under study while listening to and seeing the motor unit potentials on the monitors (fig. 1). A period of up to 15 minutes

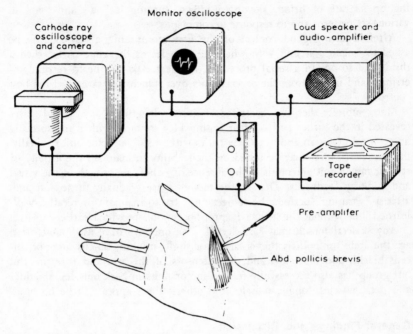

Fig. 1. Diagrammatic example of motor-unit training set-up.

is sufficient to familiarize him with the response of the apparatus to a range of movements and postures.

Subjects are invariably amazed at the responsiveness of the loudspeaker and cathode-ray tube to their slightest efforts, and they accept these as a new form of "proprioception" without difficulty. It is not necessary for subjects to have any knowledge of electromyography. After getting a general explanation they need only to concentrate their attention on the obvious response of the electromyograph. With encouragement and guidance, even the most naive subject is soon able to maintain various levels of activity in a muscle on the sensory basis provided by the monitors. Indeed, most of the procedures he carries out involve such gentle contractions that his only awareness of them is through the apparatus. Following a period of orientation, the subject can be put through a series of tests for many hours.

Several basic tests may be employed. Since people show a considerable difference in their responses, adoption of a set routine is difficult. In general, they are required to perform a series of tasks. Usually the first is to isolate and maintain the regular firing of a single motor unit from among the 100 or so that a normal person can recruit and display with this technique. When he has learned to suppress all the neighboring motor units completely, he is asked to put the unit under control through a series of tricks including speeding up its rate of firing, slowing it down, turning it "off" and "on" in various set patterns and in response to commands.

After acquiring good control of the first motor unit, a subject may be asked to isolate a second with which he then learns the same tricks; then a third, and so on. In a serial procedure, his next task may be to recruit, unerringly and in isolation, the several units over which he has gained the best control.

Many subjects then can be tested at greater length on any special skills revealed in the earlier part of their testing (for example, either an especially fine control of, or an ability to play tricks with, a single motor unit). Finally, the best performers may be tested on their ability to maintain the activity of specific motor-unit potentials in the absence of either one or both of the visual and auditory feedbacks. That is, the monitors are gradually turned off and, after a "weaning" period, the subject must try to maintain or recall a well-learned unit without the artificial "proprioception" provided earlier.

Any skeletal muscle may be selected. The ones we have used most often are the abductor pollicis brevis, abductor digiti minimi, tibialis anterior, biceps brachii and brachialis and the extensors of the arm and forearm. But our group has also successfully trained motor units in back muscles, shoulder and neck muscles, tongue muscles and others; there appears to be no limit.

General Findings and Discussion

Ability to Isolate Motor Units. Almost all subjects (among many hundreds) have been able to produce well-isolated contractions of at least one motor unit, turning it off and on without any interference from neighboring units. Only a few people fail completely to perform this basic trick. Analysis of poor and very poor performers reveals no common characteristic that separates them from better performers (Basmajian, Baeza and Fabrigar, 1965).

Most people are able to isolate and master one or two units readily; some can isolate and master three units, four units and even six units or many more. This last level of control is of the highest order, for the subject must be able to give an instant response to an order to produce contractions of a specified unit without interfering activity of neighbors; he also must be able to turn the unit "off" and "on" at will.

Control of Firing-Rates and Special Rhythms. Once a person has gained control of a spinal motoneuron, it is possible for him to learn to vary its rate of firing. This rate can be deliberately changed in immediate response to a command. The lowest limit of the range of frequencies is zero, i.e., one can start from neuromuscular silence and then give single isolated contractions at regular rates as low as one per second and at increasingly faster rates. When the more able subjects are asked to produce special repetitive rhythms and imitations of drum beats, almost all are successful (some strikingly so) in producing subtle shades and coloring of internal rhythms. When tape-recorded and replayed, these rhythms provide striking proof of the fineness of the control (Basmajian, 1963).

Individual motor units appear to have upper limits to their rates beyond which they cannot be fired in isolation; that is, overflow occurs and neighbors are recruited. These maximum frequencies range from 9 to 25 per second (when the maximum rates are recorded with an electronic digital spike-counter). Almost all lie in the range of 9 to 16 per second. However, one must not infer that individual motor units are restricted to these rates when many units are recruited. Indeed, the upper limit of 50 per second generally accepted for human muscle is probably correct, with perhaps some higher rates in other species.

Reliance on Visual or Aural Feedback. Some persons can be trained to gain control of isolated motor units to a level where, with both visual and aural cues shut off, they can recall any one of three favorite units on command and in any sequence (Basmajian, 1963). They can keep such units firing without any conscious awareness other than the assurance (after the fact) that they have succeeded. In spite of considerable introspection, they cannot explain their success except to state they "thought about" a motor unit as they had seen and heard it personally. This type of training may underlie some facets of ordinary motor skills.

Variables Which Might Affect Performance. We have found no clear-cut personal characteristics that reveal reasons for the quality of performance (Basmajian, Baeza and Fabrigar, 1965). The best performers are found at different ages, among both sexes, and among both the manually skilled and unskilled, the educated and uneducated, and the bright and the dull personalities. Some "nervous" persons do not perform well—but neither do some very calm persons.

Local Factors. Moving a neighboring joint while a motor unit is firing is a distracting influence but most subjects can keep right on doing it in spite of the distraction (Simard and Basmajian, 1967; Basmajian and Simard, 1967). We tend to agree with Wagman and his colleagues (1965) who believe that subjects require our form of motor unit training before they can fire isolated specific motor units with the limb or joints in varying positions. Their subjects reported that "activation depended on recall of the original position and contraction effort necessary for activation." This apparently is a form of proprioceptive memory, and although in the past I proposed that it is integrated in the spinal cord, the problem of localization is unsolved. Carsloo and Edfeldt (1963) also concluded that: "Proprioception can be assisted greatly by exeroceptive auxiliary stimuli in achieving motor precision."

Our observations on trained units in the tibialis anterior of 32 young adults showed that motor unit activity under conscious control can be easily maintained despite the distraction produced by voluntary movements elsewhere in the body (head and neck, upper limbs and contralateral limb). The control of isolation and the control of the easiest and fastest frequencies of discharge of a single motor unit were not affected by those movements (Basmajian and Simard, 1967).

Turning to the effect of movements of the same limb, we found that in some persons a motor unit can be trained to remain active in isolation at different positions of a "proximal" (i.e., hip or knee), "crossed" (ankle) and "distal" joints of a limb. In order to maintain or recall a motor unit at different positions, the subject must keep the motor unit active during the performance of the movements; and, therefore, preliminary training is undeniably necessary. Boyd and Roberts (1953) suggested that there are slowly adaptive end organs of proprioception, which are active during movements of a limb. They observed that the common sustained discharge of the end organs in movements lasted for several seconds after attainment of a new position. This might explain why a trained single motor unit's activity can be maintained during movements.

The control of the maintenance of a single motor unit activity during "proximal," "crossed" and "distal" joint movements in the same limb has been proved to be possible providing that the technique of assistance offered by the trainer is adequate. The control over the discharge of a motor unit during proximal and distal joint movements requires a great mental concentration on the motor activity. The same control during a "crossed" joint movement provides even greater difficulties for obvious reasons.

The Level of Activity of Synergistic Muscles. The problem of what happens to the synergistic muscles while motor units are being isolated and controlled has been taken into consideration only in a preliminary way. The level of activity appears to be individualistic. Active inhibition of synergists occurs only after training of the motor unit in the prime mover is well established (Basmajian and Simard, 1967).

Effect of Competitive Nerve Stimulation. Any changes in the action potentials of trained motor units as a result of electrical stimulation of the motor nerve supplying the whole muscle must reflect neurophysiologic changes of the single neuron supplying the motor unit. We, therefore, investigated the influence of competing strong contractions in a muscle while a discrete motor unit in it was being driven consciously (Scully and Basmajian, 1969).

Each of a series of subjects sat with his forearm resting comfortably on a table top. The stimulator cathode was applied to the region of the ulnar nerve above the elbow. The effective stimuli were 0.1 msec square-wave pulses of 70 to 100 V, delivered at a frequency of 90 per minute. Because stimuli of this order are not maximal, all axons in the ulnar nerve were not shocked and slight variation must have existed in axons actually stimulated by each successive shock.

Contrary to expectation, the superimposing of a massive contraction in a muscle by electrical stimulation of its motor nerve does not significantly alter the regular conscious firing of a motor unit in that muscle. Our experiments leave little if any doubt that well-trained motor units are not "blocked"

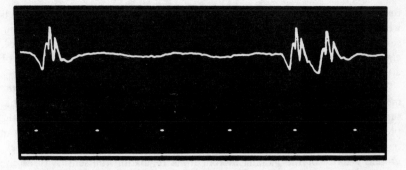

Fig. 2. Electromyogram illustrating normal doublet action potentials of a motor unit. Time marker: 10 msec. intervals. (From Simard, Basmajian and Janda, 1968).

in most persons. Even the coinciding of the motor unit potential with elements of the electrically induced massive contraction does not abolish the motor unit potential.

Effect of Ischemia. A study of a series of subjects in whom ischemia of the limb in which a motor unit was under control (Simard, Basmajian and Janda, 1968) showed that experimental ischemia greatly influences the control of a motor unit's activity, probably because a diminution in perception by sensory receptors and a decrement of motor nerve conduction suppress motor responses. In general, the amplitude of action potentials increases during ischemia and decreases in the post-ischemic stage.

The evocation of doublets (fig. 2) at commands before and during ischemia demonstrates clearly the influence of the central nervous system. In healthy human subjects, the production of doublet potentials during different stages of ischemia probably rises from hyperirritation within the motor unit. This is similar to that previously described in tetany. Its occurrence in two athletic subjects might depend on biochemical changes in their well-exercised motor units.

Effects of Previous Training and Skills. Our earliest studies, even though they included hundreds of subjects, failed to reveal any correlation between the ability of subjects to isolate and train individual motor units and such variables as sex, age, academic record, athletic ability, handedness and general personality traits (Basmajian *et al.,* 1965). The purpose of a new study completed recently was to discover whether in fact there are any differences in the performance between subjects with special manual skills and those without, using the time required for training of motor units in one of the hand muscles as the criterion (Scully and Basmajian, 1969).

Twenty-five subjects in this series were successful in consciously isolating and maintaining single motor units in regular, isolated activity, and in varying the rate of isolated activity on command. The median training time was 20 minutes. As noted before, all required more time to train their motor units than to isolate them. The training times of only two manually skilled subjects were faster than the median; one, equal to it; and the remaining seven, slower. Of the fourteen manually unskilled subjects who were successful, eight required less than 20 minutes for training; two, the median time of 20 minutes; and only four, more than 20 minutes.

The training time of most of the manually skilled subjects was above the median, although one might expect the opposite. Henderson (1952) has suggested that the constant repetition of a specific motor skill increases the probability of its correct recurrence by the learning and consolidation of an optimal anticipatory tension. Perhaps this involves an increase in the background activity of the gamma motoneurons regulating the sensitivity of the muscle-spindles of the muscles involved in performing that skill. Wilkins (1964) postulated that the acquisition of a new motor skill leads to the learning of a certain "position memory" for it. If anticipatory tensions and/ or position memory are learned, whether they are integrated at the cerebral level, at the spinal level, or both, these or some other cerebral or spinal mechanisms may be acting temporarily to block the initial learning of new skills. In a sense, perhaps some neuromuscular pathways acquire a habit of responding in certain ways, and it is not until that habit is broken that a new skill can be learned.

Effects of Handedness. When a long series of subjects were studied on two occasions using a different hand each time, Powers (1969) found that they always isolated a unit more quickly in the second hand. Isolation was twice as rapid when the second hand was the preferred hand; it was almost five times as rapid when the second hand was the non-preferred one. The time required to train a subject to control a previously isolated unit was shortened significantly only when the preferred hand was the second hand. (W. R. Powers and W. J. Forrest are preparing a series of publications on this research which also include consideration of the contralateral effects of contraction in homologous muscles.)

Other Related Investigations

The microcosm of the spinal motoneuron suggested its counterpart in the cerebral cortex to Fetz (1969) whose ingenious application of the basic idea to the conditioning of cortical cells is worthy of special note and adaptation. His work suggests that all parts of the central nervous system may be controlled by adequate artificial feedbacks provided electronically.

In the area of applied research, much recent effort has gone into the use of trained motor units for the control of myoelectric devices such as artificial limbs and orthoses. In addition to my associates and myself, other groups in various centers have been exploiting the possibilities. At this time it is safe to say that normal persons can adequately control several motor units connected through appropriate electronics to electric motors for which they act as switching devices. With appropriate stepping motors, the control of the rate and strength of contraction can be made variable. Many practical design problems have been met but there is no question of the feasibility of using individual motor units to drive separate channels of mechanical devices.

Another practical use of motor unit training has come in the form of retraining of muscles and in teaching patients to relax specific muscles. In the latter application, Jacobs and Felton (1969) have shown patients with painful traumatic neck spasms how to relax the spasm, thus effecting relief from the pain. Hardyk, Petrinovich and Ellsworth (1966) have used similar techniques to abolish laryngeal muscular activity in certain types of reading problems where the speed of silent reading is impeded by subvocalization. These and other practical ideas are obvious to specialists and need to be exploited by them in the field. There is no limit to the novel applications in research and in technology that are possible from the basic knowledge that, given electronic feedbacks, man can consciously control individual motoneurons with exquisite precision.

REFERENCES

Adrian, E. D. & Bronk, D. W. The discharge of impulses in motor nerve fibres. Part II: The frequency of discharge in reflex and voluntary contractions. *Journal of Physiology*, 1929, 67, 119-151.

Basmajian, J. V. Control and training of individual motor units. *Science*, 1963, *141*, 440-441.

Basmajian, J. V. *Muscles alive: their functions revealed by electromyography.* (2nd ed.) Baltimore: Williams & Wilkins, 1967.

Basmajian, J. V., Baeza, M. & Fabrigar, C. Conscious control and training of individual spinal motor neurons in normal human subjects. *Journal of New Drugs*, 1965, *5*, 78-85.

Basmajian, J. V. & Simard, T. G. Effects of distracting movements on the control of trained motor units. *American Journal of Physical Medicine*, 1967, *46*, 1427-1449.

Basmajian, J. V. & Stecko, G. A new bi-polar indwelling electrode for electromyography. *Journal of Applied Physiology*, 1962, *17*, 849.

Boyd, I. A. & Roberts, T. D. M. Proprioceptive discharges from stretch-receptors in the knee-joint of the cat. *Journal of Physiology*, 1953, *122*, 38-58.

Carsloo, S. & Edfeldt, A. W. Attempts at muscle control with visual and auditory impulses and auxiliary stimuli. *Scandinavian Journal of Psychology*, 1963, *4*, 231-235.

Fetz, E. E. Operant conditioning of cortical unit activity. *Science*, 1969, 955-958.

Gasser, H. S. & Newcomer, H. S. Physiological action current in the phrenic nerve. An application of the thermionic vacuum tube to nerve physiology. *American Journal of Physiology*, 1921, *57*, 1-26.

Gilson, A. S. & Mills, W. D. Single responses of motor units in consequence of volitional effort. *Proceedings of the Society of Experimental Biology and Medicine*, 1940, *45*, 650-652.

Gilson, A. S. & Mills, W. D. Activities of single motor units in man during slight voluntary efforts. *American Journal of Physiology*, 1941, *133*, 658-669.

Hardyk, C. D., Petrinovich, L. F. & Ellsworth, D. W. Feedback of speech muscle activity during silent reading: rapid extinction. *Science*, 1966, *154*, 1467-1468.

Harrison, V. F. & Mortensen, O. A. Identification and voluntary control of single motor unit activity in the tibialis anterior muscle. *Anatomical Record*, 1962, *144*, 109-116.

Henderson, R. L. Remote action potentials at the moment of response in a simple reaction-time situation. *Journal of Experimental Psychology*, 1952, *44*, 238-241.

Henneman, E., Somjen, G., & Carpenter, D. O. Excitability and inhibitibility of motoneurons of different sizes. *Journal of Neurophysiology*, 1965, *28*, 599-620.

Jacobs, A. & Felton, G. S. Visual feedback of myoelectric output to facilitate muscle relaxation in normal persons and patients with neck injuries. *Archives of Physical Medicine & Rehabilitation,* 1969, *50,* 34-39.

Lindsley, D. P. Electrical activity of human motor units during voluntary contraction. *American Journal of Physiology,* 1935, *114,* 90-99.

Powers, W. R. Conscious control of single motor units in the preferred and non-preferred hand: An electromyographic study. *Ph.D. Thesis. Queen's University,* Kingston, Ontario, Canada. 1969.

Scully, H. E. & Basmajian, J. V. Effect of nerve stimulation on trained motor unit' control. *Archives of Physical Medicine & Rehabilitation,* 1969, *50,* 32-33.

Simard, T. G. & Basmajian, J. V. Methods in training the conscious control of motor units. *Archives of Physical Medicine & Rehabilitation,* 1967, *48,* 12-19.

Simard, T. G., Basmajian, J. V., & Janda, V. Effect of ischemia on trained motor units. *American Journal of Physical Medicine,* 1968, *47,* 64-71.

Smith, O. C. Action potentials from single motor units in voluntary contraction. *American Journal of Physiology,* 1934, *108,* 629-638.

Sutton, D. L. Surface and needle electrodes in electromyography. *Dental Progress,* 1962, *2,* 127-131.

Wagman, I. H., Pierce, D. S., and Burger, R. E. Proprioceptive influence in volitional control of individual motor units. *Nature,* 1965, *207,* 957-958.

Wilkins, B. R. A. A theory of position memory. *Journal of Theoretical Biology,* 1964, *7,* 374-387.

CRITIQUE OF BASMAJIAN'S PAPER
by Joan C. Waterland

Dr. J. V. Basmajian has provided us with an excellent review and a wealth of information in the area of individual motor unit isolation and control. His paper contains a summary of the many contributions that he and his colleagues have made in order to better enhance the understanding of motor unit behavior. Dr. Basmajian has investigated this area so extensively that his name has almost become synonymous with the term "individual motor unit control." In his paper, he has provided us with a survey of the instrumentation used in motor unit studies, the basic anatomy and physiology of the motor unit, action potential characteristics, procedures and techniques necessary for first isolating and then controlling individual motor unit activity, and the general research findings on this topic. Therefore, this paper is recommended for those researchers who want to review the instrumentation, theory and procedural bases upon which to build foundations in the area of microcosmic motor learning.

The instrumentation section of the paper represents many years of experimentation in order to find the most effective and efficient electromyographic techniques to use while investigating various parameters of individual motor unit control. The fine wire electrodes and the basic electronic equipment which he has described illustrate the most expedient methods currently used to obtain accurate action potential recordings with a minimum of artefact and the necessary amount of sensitivity. An excellent supplement to this section is the book *Motor Function in the Lower Extremity—Analysis by Electronic Instrumentation* by J. R. Close, M.D. (1964). This text includes a thorough evaluation of the fundamental electronics used in the electromyographic method, and also a detailed description of available recording equipment. Close's book emphasizes the view that the physiological characteristics of the motor unit action potential dictates the basic requirements of the recording equipment including the type of electrode, amplification system and the recorder used.

Dr. Basmajian's discussion on the techniques used to teach individuals to first isolate and then to control motor unit activity is cogently and concisely presented and one can understand why his method has been so widely accepted in kinesiology laboratories throughout the world. In addition to using Dr. Basmajian's training procedures, we in the Motor Learning Research Laboratory at the University of Wisconsin have also found it helpful, prior to the initial stages of learning, to show each subject electromyograms illustrating the picket fence patterns characteristic of individual motor unit firing. In addition, subjects who have never been exposed to the electromyographic method are asked to listen to previously taped recordings of action potential sounds from an audio-amplifier. Thus, the subject has an orientation into the type of motor task that he will eventually be expected to perform. Dr. Basmajian states that an individual's personality characteristics, sex, age, academic achievement, athletic ability and hand dominance do not seem to influence his ability to learn motor unit control. However, we have found that athletes who have had previous specialized training in sports activities which emphasize isometric or "static" types of muscle contraction, *i.e.,* gymnastics or weight lifting, are usually able to initially isolate and then to train their individual motor units faster than the majority of other subjects with whom we have worked.

An interesting point that Dr. Basmajian made in his paper was that individual motor unit firing can be maintained by trained subjects in spite of movements occurring in other parts of the body. This finding has been supported and expanded by experimentations conducted in our laboratory. We found that individual motor unit firing in the triceps muscle of normal man was not only maintained during head rotations but that it also increased in firing rate when the head was turned to the ipsilateral side and decreased in rate during contralateral head rotation. This intriguing observation was also made in 1953 by Eldred, Granit and Merton in anesthetized cats with intact nervous systems. They demonstrated that head manipulations evoked spontaneous extrafusal muscle contractions and these findings were attributed to the influence of the classical tonic neck reflexes. We are currently describing the vestiges of this reflex phenomenon observed in children and adults as the "head-shoulder linkage."

Recently, Ashworth, Grimby and Kugelburg (1967) have reported that motor units are recruited in the same order regardless of whether the movement task is willed or is initiated reflexly. These researchers claimed that the motor units recorded during both types of movements are of the low threshold tonic classification. They concluded that the "inherent properties of the motor neurons are the most important factor in determining the order of recruitment of motor units." However, it was demonstrated that cortical intervention could override otherwise stereotyped or natural motor responses since the subjects of this study could will to reverse or change the order of motor neuron recruitment.

I was particularly interested in Dr. Basmajian's finding that some of his subjects could be trained to control any one of three units without the aid of visual or auditory feedback. He stated that "they can keep such units firing without any conscious awareness other than the assurance (after the fact) that they have had success. In spite of considerable introspection, they cannot explain their success except to state that they thought about a motor unit as they had seen and heard it previously." It must be remembered that in this series of experiments, the sensory receptors from the muscles, joints and skin were still intact even though vision and hearing had been eliminated. Thus, proprioceptive information from the periphery was still being transmitted back to the central nervous system in spite of the fact that the subjects were not consciously aware of it. Since all of Basmajian's subjects' had previous training in the ability to both isolate and to regulate motor unit activity, it is possible that the sensorimotor coordination necessary for the task was coded and then engrammed within the higher levels of the central nervous system. Later when the subjects were asked to recruit previously trained units, the engram repertoire was triggered releasing a sequence of muscle contractions of the desired amplitude and timing in a given muscle. Merton in 1964 experimentally demonstrated the engram theory or as he called it, the "sense of effort" phenomenon when he selectively blocked the sensory nerves subserving joint position sense in the thumb. Merton observed that active joint motions in previously trained subjects could still be "executed quite accurately" during the time of joint anesthesia, and he attributed his findings to the subjects' knowing through the "sense of effort" how far they had moved their thumbs, even when position sense was eliminated.

In conclusion, I believe that Dr. Basmajian's paper will contribute significantly to the existing body of knowledge in the area of "single nerve-cell training." However, in discussing the applicability of conscious motor unit control to various areas of research and technology, Dr. Basmajian neglected to mention the importance of this type of motor skill in the realm of music. He touched on the subject of musical artistry when he stated that "when the more able subjects are asked to produce special repetitive rhythms and imitations of drum beats, almost all are successful (some strikingly so) in producing subtle shades and coloring of internal rhythms. When tape-recorded and replayed, these rhythms provide striking proof of the fineness of the control." Since individuals have the ability to rhythmically vary motor unit firing patterns and to produce the slight nuances necessary for eliciting different tonal qualities, Dr. Basmajian or one of his colleagues should think of composing a musical score entitled, "Concerto for Four Individual Motor Units and Tape Recorder." The key to this composition would be motor units firing in varying spatial and temporal patterns which is the phenomenon underlying the neuromuscular patterning of skilled movement.

REFERENCES

Ashworth, B, Grimby, L., and Kugelberg, E. Comparison of voluntary and reflex activation of motor units: Functional organization of motor neurones. *J. Neurol. Neurosurg. Psychiat.*, 1967, 30:91-98.
Close, J. R. *Motor Function in the Lower Extremity: Analysis by Electronic Instrumentation.* Springfield, Illinois: Charles C. Thomas, 1964.
Eldred, E., Granit, R., and Merton, P. A. Supraspinal control of the muscle spindle and its significance. *J. Physiol.*, 1953, 122:-498-523.
Merton, P. A. Human position sense and sense of effort. *Symp. Soc. Exper. Biol.*, 1964, 18:387-400.

BASMAJIAN'S REPLY TO
Waterland's Critique

BILODEAU: I think that at least I have learned that Dr. Basmajian was being excessively modest in telling us how easy it was. He didn't tell us quite how it got to be that easy. Would you first care to reply to Dr. Waterland's comments?

BASMAJIAN: This is going to sound like a mutual admiration society because you are going to find that my remarks about Dr. Waterland's paper are effusive as well. But we didn't work it out that way; I must thank her for the very, very kind way she let me off the hook. I expected at least a few chiding remarks about technology. Her last part interests me a great deal and this might be the title of the next talk I give, that is, Concerto for Three Motor Units & Tape Recorder. She was not anticipated in time, but at least it got to me sooner than her remarks because Emily Stevens, a music therapist in Atlanta, has been bugging me to do a study of tones with mentally retarded children and to provide them with various tonal feedbacks, rhythms and so on. She did a study for her Masters some years ago on changing the rhythm of head banging. Now some of you are aware that retarded children very often sit all day long hitting their heads against something in a specific rhythm. She was able to change that rhythm by techniques of music therapy and so she is bugging me to do some similar studies together on this and I don't know where it will lead.

Now, to turn to another matter, I like the idea of engrams; it may not be good science, but that's the way we have been thinking, too—that there are patterns developing internally. And along this line—if I may take a moment to develop another idea that I didn't have time for—which has been developing in the minds of my colleagues and myself—particularly, perhaps, in my own mind because I have less to risk. (I should explain that remark, too. Sometimes, in this business, when you are as old and grey as I am you can take chances and make crazy statements, and you have nothing much to lose except your reputation. Younger colleagues have their jobs to lose as well.) But, I have been developing the idea that, in fact, all motor learning is based upon the indoctrination of specific motor units for specific tasks. I am now mustering enough nerve to announce publicly my belief—not absolutely scientifically sound and underpinned that every movement is determined by patterns of motor unit training that have been imposed in the individual from the first time that he moves a muscle. That by trial and error, he refines this to the point where he can produce a perfect pitch—pitch of a baseball let's say, or the perfect swing of the golfer's club. He has developed a pattern of sequences and frequencies of motor units which, if the pitch is absolutely perfect or the swing absolutely perfect, have been determined by the proper sequencing. The reason that some people aren't good at it is that they can't reproduce the sequence in that perfect timing. Now, how does one prove this? I have no way, but I just feel that it is so. In motor-unit control, our finest controllers are our finest performers, and thus perfection comes with this improvement of training, until the motor units come in at their proper time —their proper sequence, that is, in the right amount of spurt.

Your motor units can be changed in frequency; individual units can be given faster or slower frequencies, and therein lies the justification for my calling it the microcosm of learning. The question of recruitment patterns is an interesting one. Have you noticed that when a person makes a moderate contraction during our movie it starts out with small motor unit potentials and they get bigger, bigger, and bigger? Henniman, Ashworth and others have shown that there is this patterning. Small motor units in a muscle are recruited first—that is in an ordinary movement without special instructions. In reflexes the small motor units are recruited first. Henniman, in particular, who is a neurophysiologist in Boston, was almost annoyed with me for stating that one could reverse this pattern and train people to recruit big motor patterns instead of small motor units first. It took a lot of convincing but he is now convinced it can be done. But, of course, as good neurophysiologists we have agreed that he is right and I am right because we are talking about two different phenomena. He now agrees that one can recruit large motor units voluntarily but one can't do it if the movement made is fast or untrained and certainly not if it is a reflex. This is a very interesting area. For example, we will pick out very large motor units on the scope deliberately, simply because it is more convenient to work with them, to record them, to take pictures of them, and so on. And we asked the subjects to suppress the little motor units because they are hard to record.

Dr. Waterland raised a point when she was speaking about the different qualities of training and the factors which influence it. We have done a lot of studies on different types of people with different levels of intelligence. We have published a report on children which indicates one can train children down to the age of about three and a half to drive single motor units voluntarily; the limitation there is boredom. Little boys are all right; they are intrigued with the gadgetry and so on. Little girls aren't interested in that, and therefore, are bored a little bit sooner by the process. You can train kids as long as they will listen to you and work with you down to the age of three and a half and get them to drive single motor units voluntarily, easily. I think that answers all the points that were raised.

DISCUSSION OF BASMAJIAN PAPER

BILODEAU: Are there questions from the audience?

DICK SCHMIDT FROM THE UNIVERSITY OF MARYLAND: I have first a question and then a small quibble. The question: subjectively speaking, how much attention is required to perform this trick, so called? Does the subject have to spend a lot of time attending to exactly what he is doing or can he do other things at the same time?

BASMAJIAN: The answer to that is that it is rather like any skill that one acquires. For example, the first time you drive a car (a very massive skill to acquire) you have to devote your entire attention to it. Pretty soon, though, you can fight with your wife, or look at the pretty girls going by and fight with your wife at the same time, and continue to drive. The answer is as simple as that; it is a learning procedure with all the inherent, well understood, controlled mechanisms of learning.

SCHMIDT: The second point I had relates to your statement concerning withdrawal of visual and auditory cues. I believe you said it was obviously due to some sort of internal proprioceptive feedback mechanism. I don't think that necessarily follows; it could be the tricks are executed in an open loop with absolutely no feedback control. I think this will be an interesting question to try to dig out, to see exactly how these things are being done.

BASMAJIAN: This has been suggested to us before, but we don't know how to dig it out. The limitations are our own, and we have temporarily stopped working with this particular series of experiments. We haven't, for example, done a single experiment in the last year on why people can drive motor units without feedbacks. I think we reached the point where we found it could be done and then were afraid of the technological problems involved. It becomes very subjective after awhile you see; the subject says, "I don't know how I am doing it," but he is doing it. And how do you even get a person to verbalize this—what he feels inside. Now you see between Wagmann's work and ours, dozens and dozens of subjects have been trained to do this, but not one of them has said, "I do it clearly because of this." (Wagmann's observation was that they were doing it by moving the thumb into different places and holding it there.) When it was there, this was the set which allowed them to bring out one factor in the set. That is what led us, as I said, to moving the thumb around while doing the motor unit. There is a lot of superstitious behavior in our subjects. And there seems to be some superstitious behavior in the observers too. You think to make this motor unit go, you must put your thumb—if it's a thumb—in a particular place. And at first this works, but you can quickly unlock that one and put it anywhere. Some subjects, until you force them to give up their superstitious behavior, do this.

The first subject to work with the removal of cues was myself and one of my colleagues acted as the Director. I too felt I had put my thumb in one place for one motor unit and moved it for another motor unit—having nothing to do with the primary action of the muscle that was involved. Now that's important:—having nothing to do with the primary action of the muscle involved. It was just putting the muscle, I suppose, into a (if you will pardon the use of this term) "set." And then pulling out what you wanted. I don't know how we would go about that, but I have heard rumors that a couple of graduate students elsewhere are working on it. And this is an ironic thing; there is an awful lot of motor unit training going on all over the U.S.A. and I don't hear about it until their Ph. D. theses are published.

K. U. SMITH—WISCONSIN: I would like to make one or two comments. The first one that I would like to point out is that these controlled reactions have very many of the elements of recorded responses that a gamma afferent system and probably muscle spindle activity have. I think the solution of some of the real questions of what's going on here both externally and internally is going to rest on developing ways of differentiating to what extent some of these specific responses are alpha-gamma reaction mechanisms. I am not too sure from all I have heard about the subject that the differences being attributed to psychological factors aren't dependent upon placement of electrodes near the muscle spindle of a motor unit. And whether the ability of some subjects and the variations in the same subjects at different times to do this aren't dependent on that. And I would like to comment too, on what I have always thought is a very sloppy use of terminology—that is, borrowing of feedback terminology by Skinnerian operant conditioners in describing what's going on here. I am convinced that the phenomena in this field are just as clearly feedback as the gamma-afferent system represents a fundamental physiological feedback control system of muscle systems of the body. It is never dispensed with whether you are training single motor units or musicians or symphony conductors or college teachers. The use of this outworn rat-pressing terminology is confusing the field rather than leading to experiments that really get at the basic mechanisms. Consider that a question.

BASMAJIAN: Well, all I can say is that I am proud to be able to respond by saying that we thought of the same things Dr. Smith thought of and were working, (I think work is the wrong word) we're running in circles on this problem of the gamma system. Literally three persons in my group are devoting their time to elaborating this idea, two of them being full time professors of neuroanatomy-neurophysiology and the other a poor graduate student who will probably do all the work. It is definite that the responses we are recording are alpha motor neurons. What we have not been able to prove conclusively is that mixed in with these are not some spindle reactions.

The difficulty is that the spindle contains somewhere between four and seven muscle fibers; their peculiar and propagated potentials have never been recorded from them in vitro. In about four of the fibers—you know that there are two types of fibers in a spindle—one type has never recorded a propagating potential. Therefore, theoretically it will never register a spike potential, in vivo.

Here you are left with two or three muscle fibers that might produce potentials which are slow propagating potentials. So we have come to the con- and they are slow propagating potentials. So we have come to the conclusion that, although we may have on occasion recorded from muscle spindles, from their contraction there is no way of our proving it. On the other hand, the kind of responses—the mass of multiple EMG potentials—that we start with—that is, the ones we want to train (and we pick each one deliberately not just one that is convenient)—are all alphas and are all regular motor units.

BASMAJIAN: We are worried about it and we are working on it now. Maybe in a couple of years we will have some answers on the gamma system. We have done some studies on fast extension of the elbow while recording motor units in biceps, and there is a recordable period of silence and then the recovery of the motor unit. We think this is spindle response. But slow movements, no. Yes, sir?

VOICE UNIDENTIFIED: Sir, are you getting any bilateral transfer effects or is it specific?

BASMAJIAN: There is transfer effect, and in the written paper I describe the work of Whitney Powers in our group. Some of you know Whitney Powers who is in Boston. He did his doctoral thesis on transfer, cross transfer. He trained motor units on one side and then by tricks and so on he had subjects activate motor units with movements of the opposite side and then turn them off and on and bring them up over a threshold. He has gone on to study hemiplegic subjects. There is a practical application, you see, and in the field of medicine involving patients who have had strokes. There will be half a million Americans who will have strokes this year so if you can do something for them . . . he is working on that. Yet, there is cross transfer. There is something that goes on in cross effect but we aren't sure exactly about the details.

LEWIS ANDERSON—UNIVERSITY OF MINNESOTA: Dr. Basmajian, would you be willing to speculate with respect to the individuals who have had this type of training, their either increased or decreased ability to make motor movements of a gross nature or a fine nature? That is, would you be willing to say that this kind of simple motor unit training would enhance an individual's ability to make gross or fine motor movement?

BASMAJIAN: That's a little difficult to answer.

ANDERSON: Just speculate if you will.

BASMAJIAN: I don't think I can say in good conscience that training people to drive single motor units, in itself, will make a better performer in even a coarse movement. The reason that I say this, is by inverting the question, or inverting the matter, and telling you that in our experience (and we have published a paper on this particular experience) that highly trained people are somewhat slower than the median in acquiring motor unit training. Now, we are talking of minutes, mind you, but, as I recall, the median of this particular type of training (we are imposing a specific type of training) was either 15 or 20 minutes, and all of the highly trained people but one or two took longer to train a motor unit while all the people who had no special skills, didn't play the piano, were not athletes—were faster than the median. So, I think if there is any inference we can take, it's that. Now, from the point of view of training, you remember that I am in a Rehabilitation Research and Training Center. We do hope to apply the training of motor units to the major training of handicapped people and it is largely by demonstrating to them—the you-can-do-it sort of thing. And you heard yesterday someone comment how patients could (by demonstration of facial muscular activity, now innervated by, "the wrong nerve," so to speak), achieve this transfer faster by the use of EMG techniques, and that, of course, is part of our mission in a Rehabilitation Center.

There are some interesting things; people have put electrodes on and around the larynx and have improved the reading speed of people who subvocalize. A group in California have applied motor unit training techniques, but again they are concerned with coarse movements, not in training single motor units. If you demonstrate to the subject that he is using his larynx while he is reading silently so very slowly—that is, show him that this is happening and then tell him you don't want it—you may cut it down and remove it. They claimed in a published paper that their patients enormously increased their reading speed. And there have been other such practical applications of this technique, but usually at the coarse level. You don't start with training motor units and then do something else.

ANDERSON: Would it be inappropriate for Dr. Bilodeau to comment on that with respect to the pursuit rotor?

BILODEAU: I don't think it would be appropriate. I have never gone beneath the subject's skin, and I think I would get lost very fast.

ANDERSON: I don't think you would. Dr. Bilodeau could do the needling. I am only asking if you think that subjects that have had this kind of training would handle a pursuit rotor device more efficiently, or effectively, or learn it faster.

BILODEAU: I doubt for the length of training that he has reported today, that they would do anything particularly better than they were doing it to begin with.

ANDERSON: Okay, thank you.

LEON SMITH—UNIVERSITY OF IOWA: Have you done any retention studies following training to see how long they retain this skill? On control over motor units?

BASMAJIAN: Yes, some studies have been done on this, in Cleveland particularly. Again, they were interested in myoelectric devices. That was the reason and the carry-over is quite good. The man who probably consciously trained motor units first, Otto Mortenson at Wisconsin, so fully trained his first motor unit in tibialis anterior that with surface electrodes placed over it, he always got the same motor unit chattering, for months and even years afterward. He couldn't suppress that one. He didn't realize that we had ways of training motor units so that you could suppress one and recruit another. There was no one to train him; he just sat down and put the electrodes on himself, and it points up an interesting thing in science, too.

Dr. Mortenson, with a then graduate student, Virginia Harrison, was studying tibialis anterior. They were interested in kinesiology of tibialis anterior. They were using surface electrodes and they were on the defensive about surface electrodes. (I put a lot of people on the defensive about surface electrodes by talking about intramuscular ones.) So they were out to prove that you could record single motor units through the skin with surface electrodes. And while they were doing this, they began to fool around and discovered they could find one motor unit and then another motor unit. This is how this thing was born. Like all science, of course, when we began to look back we found that Olive Smith and Lindsley in the 30's and others had also been training motor units, but they didn't call it that. And the difficulty with Mortenson and Harrison's work is that they ran into a run of bad subjects, or didn't use right training techniques. When I heard of their work and got going, I ran into good subjects to start with. If you do a pilot study with all bad subjects, you can give up the whole research project, but if you are lucky enough to have all good subjects, then of course you're made, and well, I've been working on it for 10 years now.

That has more or less set the pattern of the research we do. Because the first few subjects I did turned out to be motor unit geniuses, we call them mugs. The opposite are the mums or motor unit morons. Oh, we've got all sorts of acronyms. Some of the gadgetry that we have devised and built have acronyms too, deliberately. The youngsters deliberately turn the letters around so they can make acronyms. We've got one machine call smut, single motor unit trainer, and we've got another one called smurd which is a response device (or reward device rather) a single motor unit reward device. I don't know how I got on to this, but it is interesting how research is not a straight line. I think Dr. Smith, probably like myself, is an universalist and would agree with this. Would you accept that designation?

LEON SMITH: I wouldn't call it a dirty word.

BASMAJIAN: Well, I think we are universalists who feel that the world is our oyster to open, and that we can move in different directions if it suits us as long as universities will pay us and keep us from having to go to the pawn broker, we are happy.

Aspects of Motor Learning, Vision and 'Natural' Linkage*

Joan C. Waterland
University of Wisconsin

Neurophysiologists concerned with movement patterning are currently turning their attention to the area of sensory-motor integration since normal willed movements are affected by sensory influences arising from all parts of the central nervous system. In addition, Paillard (1960) has stated that motor patterning is conversely affected by neuromuscular disorders which cause disruption or diminution in the stream of patterned sensory impulses which converge in the cerebral cortex. For example, a patient suffering from idiokinetic apraxia is aware of the objectives to be attained and movements to be carried out, but cannot control their correct execution even though motor commands are given. The movement which is impaired can, however, be *cortically directed* in perfect fashion when the subject is under the influence of an emotional experience since the neural connections apparently become mobilized and organized within the framework of *automatic reactions.* Emotional stress, augmented by a volley of *sensory stimuli,* finds release in motor expression.

The three "key" phrases used to describe Paillard's (1960) observations of a patient suffering from idiokinetic apraxia are: 1) sensory stimuli, 2) cortical direction, and 3) automatic reactions. An unpublished motion picture made by Hess (1943) and used by Jung and Hassler (1960) is a model for understanding successful and unsuccessful movement (Fig. 1). Hess uses three persons to represent the action and reaction inherent in any motor performance. The first person represents the cortical aspect of the volitional movement, the second the sensory stimuli involved in the movement process. The third person symbolizes the automatic reactions or the supportive framework within which intentional movement operates. The purposive act in Hess' model consists of one man jumping from the shoulders of another who is supported by the third person. For the jumper, who represents the willed component of the movement, to land upright on the floor, the supportive framework provided by the two men on the ground has to be utilized. When the involuntary aspects of the act are not utilized, the jumper falls forward

*Appreciation is expressed to Georgia M. Shambes, Susann G. Doody, and Marla J. Smith for their interest, and for their technical assistance.

for lack of proper reflex support and sensory modulation. Hess separates the three components of movement to emphasize diagrammatically the significance of each. However, within each individual the autonomous, sensory, and willed components should function at an optimal level of harmony for movement to be successful.

By identifying and studying the reflex or autonomous components of willed movement and ways of learning new movement patterns in the Motor Learn-

Fig. 1. The willed, sensory and autonomous components of movement are represented by figures 1, 2, and 3 respectively. *Left column:* successful movement; *right column:* unsuccessful movement. Reprinted with permission of W. R. Hess and the editors of the *Handbook of Physiology*.

ing Research Laboratory, it is hoped that "key" understandings can be translated into "key" cues which will then facilitate motor learning. This paper will include aspects of motor learning which relate to: (1) the influence of vision on the learning of motor patterns and (2) natural linkages which are considered part of the supportive framework of movement.

VISION AND MOTOR LEARNING

Charles E. Beevor, in a paper published by the American Medical Association in 1908, wrote: " . . . we have to take into account in performing a movement whether muscles forming the prime movers all contract together or whether there is any sequence, and whether the same sequence is preserved." This is a profound statement when it is remembered that Beevor's physiological approach to the study of muscle action consisted of inspection and palpation. In addition to specific temporal relationships found while working with the biceps brachii, brachioradialis and the supinator he also observed selected hip and knee muscles in order to gain further insight into his proposition. The action of the sartorius, rectus femoris and the vasti medialis and lateralis were studied in order to ascertain whether a particular prime mover contracts before another. The following quotation gives the movement Beevor (1908) studied and the results of his analysis which were obtained by inspection and palpation:

> . . . the person should stand erect on one leg and have the other resting on a chair, with the knee and thigh flexed. The person should incline slightly forward so as to bring the center of gravity in front of the foot on which he is standing. On then inclining backward, so as to shift the center of gravity behind the foot, the flexors of the hip of the leg resting on the chair will contract to prevent the trunk falling backward, and the only muscle which will be seen to contract is the sartorius. If then the person inclines still further back, the rectus femoris will be seen to act but without the vasti externus and internus. This by the way, illustrates the point that one part of an anatomic muscle can take part in a movement and not the rest of it. The important point is that we have no power to make the rectus contract before the sartorius.[1]

Beevor's study was repeated in the Motor Learning Research Laboratory with electromyography and photography (Hellebrandt, 1964). Center of gravity equipment was also used since it was known that if the vertical projection of the center of gravity was to "shift behind the foot" as directed

[1]Reprinted from Beevor (1908) with permission of the editor.

by Beevor that the integrity of body balance would be lost. Therefore, it was of interest to find out what happened to the center of gravity and also to the tibialis anterior and soleus muscles of the supporting leg (Hellebrandt, 1964). Beevor had only been interested in the lower extremity "resting on a chair with the knee and thigh flexed." Approximately fifty attempts to perform Beevor's experiment were failures. Every muscle sampled electromyographically sprang into action. It would have been easy to conclude that Beevor was wrong. However a systematic effort was made to achieve Beevor's theoretical objectives and it was not until the subject viewed her posture in a mirror that perception of the requirements of Beevor's study became apparent. Dr. Hellebrandt wrote in 1964, "Learning was instantaneous. In a flash of insight the supporting limb was fixed in a near vertical position, the pelvic girdle was stabilized, and the so-called forward and backward inclination of Beevor was restricted to trunk bending. The initial trial was a success, indeed a perfect experiment." Once the "key" cue was identified by the subject, who watched her own performance in a mirror, the experiment could be repeated at will.

Electromyography, photography and center of gravity equipment were again used to repeat Beevor's experiment with four uninformed subjects. The purpose of the investigations was to test the hypothesis that the "key" cue identified by the performer in Hellebrandt's study (1963) could be effectively used with other people. The subjects were entirely dependent on a verbal description of the desired task. They were asked to stabilize the supporting leg and the pelvic girdle. The forward and backward movement of the body was to be restricted to flexion and extension. Indeed, the first subject was immediately successful in reproducing the temporal relationships of the sartorius, rectus femoris and the vasti medialis and lateralis muscles as initially described by Beevor in 1908 (Figs. 2 and 3).

Three subjects elicited potentials from the sartorius muscle but were unsuccessful in bringing in the rectus femoris (Fig. 3). Photographs, with the frontal plane of the center of gravity drawn onto the pictures, showed that the subjects were compensating and not allowing the vertical projection of the center of gravity to shift backward during the extension phase of the act. The less strenuous movement did not require the participation of the rectus femoris.

Subsequently two subjects, one of whom was unsuccessful earlier, participated and greater emphasis was placed on the need for stabilization of the supporting leg and pelvis. The subjects were also directed to allow their weight to shift backward as far as possible during the extension phase of the movement. Assurance was given that an assistant would be behind them to prevent falling if balance was lost. Both of the participants were successful in confirming Beevor's findings (Fig. 3). The subject who performed the act for the second time said: "yes, but that's what I did the first time". The comment indicates that total perception of the movement was impaired by a lack of visual information. Decker and Smith (1961) also postulated that man is dependent upon vision for information about motor perception and performance, particularly during learning. In toto, however, motor behavior and learning are linked with a complex mass of incoming stimuli.

Fig. 2. Overt configurations recorded photographically of a subject who successfully repeated Beevor's experiment. The frontal plane of the center of gravity is shown on each picture. *Top row:* starting position, trunk flexion, and midposition of the sequential movement; *bottom row:* trunk extension with picture inserted in upper right corner which shows typical posture of unsuccessful subjects, final position.

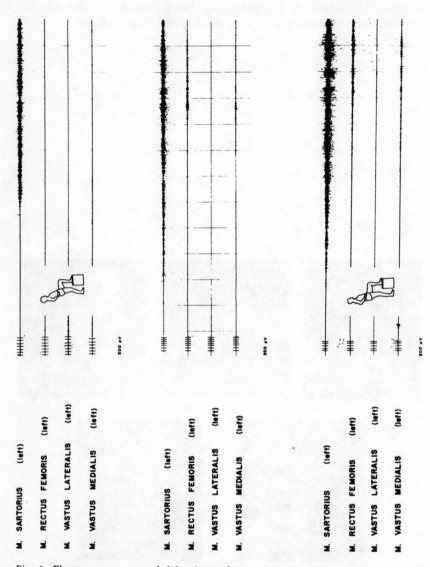

Fig. 3. Electromyograms recorded for three subjects while they were executing Beevor's experiment. *Upper record:* EMG for a performer who was unsuccessful in bringing in the rectus femoris with an insert of her posture showing the "back bend" position typical of the subjects who did not allow the vertical projection of the center of gravity to shift backward. *Middle and lower records:* EMG's for two subjects who were successful in repeating Beevor's experiment with insert on lower record showing the typical posture assumed when the rectus femoris became active so that action potentials were recorded.

Robison and co-workers (1965) studied the influence of vision and non-vision on the performance of abduction of the great toe. A statistically significant difference was found between the group who practiced with vision and the non-vision group. The results support the hypothesis that vision does indeed play a major role during the learning phase. Forward (1963) and McGraw (1963) also report that the initial learning stages of a motor act are facilitated by vision since it helps by selecting the proper motor response. However, when the new act becomes established, proprioceptive feedback is more important to motor performance.

NATURAL LINKAGES

The difference between stressful and nonstressful learning was investigated by Shaeffer (1954). Under stress, movement tends to lose its plasticity and instead assumes the characteristics of a stereotype. He hypothesized that there is a shift in dominance between cortical and subcortical centers. The primitive mechanisms known to be subcortically located become activated and dominate the cortically influenced movements.

Stress which is systematically imposed on a subject can magnify movement responses called upon when the machinery of the human body is forced to draw upon its reserve power to prevent breakdown. In 1964 Waterland and Hellebrandt designed a series of wrist ergographic exercises to stress a subject and bring him to the limits of his functional capacity. The importance of aspiring always for a truly maximal physiological performance, irrespective of the conditions imposed, was impressed on the subjects. The severity of the effort put forth by the subjects was evidenced by fatigue manifested in the agonist/antagonist complex and the irradiation of activity into the supportive or synergistic musculature.

Fatigue Factors Influencing Movement

Electromyograms of prime movers recorded in the Motor Learning Research Laboratory suggested a linear relationship between the amount of contraction and the magnitude of the weight lifted during wrist ergographic exercise. The first evidence of stress, as observed by a decrease in the range of joint motion, was associated with increased amplitude and density of the recorded electrical activity from the prime movers. Poudrier and Knowlton (1964) have also shown that when fatigue sets in with maximal isometric or isotonic contractions of the biceps brachii, there is a decrease in the muscular tension produced and thus a reduction in the contractibility of the muscles as recorded by strain gauges. However, excitation expressed by the action potential voltages did not decrease. The theory was therefore advanced by Poudrier and Knowlton (1964) that fatigue takes place within the muscle fibers themselves rather than at the neuromuscular junction, as assumed by most investigators.

In the gradation of muscular contractions, the recruitment of additional
motor units of higher threshold level is generally considered to be a very
potent factor. Increased frequency of firing and "synchronization of motor
units" are also known to affect muscle tension. The findings of Poudrier and
Knowlton (1964) concerning the decrease in contractibility and not excitation of the muscle relate to the onset of fatigue. Electromyograms recorded
in the Motor Learning Research Laboratory show that at the culmination of
an "all-out" effort, the amplitude of the agonist tends to fall off. The number
of acting units appears to diminish, as suggested by a less dense tracing of the
action potentials.

An increased activation of the central nervous system is reflected in the
synergistic muscles. The muscles linked with the agonist to form a total limb
synergy and the antagonist of the prime mover build to a crescendo while
the action potentials of the agonist diminish as fatigue makes itself manifest
(Fig. 4). The electromyographic pattern of the antagonist is usually less than
that of the prime mover, but occasionally it may supersede it during the ter-

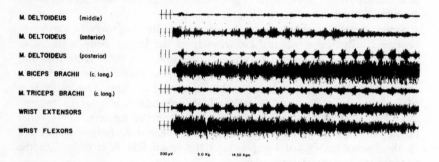

Fig. 4. Electromyogram recorded during wrist ergography for the twenty-repetition
maximum bout. The subject performed right wrist flexion from a radioulnar
position of supination.

minal phase of an "all-out" effort. It is conceivable that muscles acting as
antagonists serve to: (1) modulate the action produced by the prime mover,
and/or (2) produce or stabilize another joint action.

Limb Synergies[2]

Associated motor activity taking place in muscle groups removed from
actively contracting muscles is noted during reciprocal motions at the wrist
joint (Fig. 5). Alternate flexion and extension wrist movements have been

---

[2]The following sections of this paper are adapted from: Waterland, J. C. Proprioceptive Integration and Motor Learning. Proceedings International Symposium on Bio-
mechanics (Eindhoven, Holland) S. BARGER Basel-New York-London, in press.

M. BRACHIALIS

M. TRICEPS BRACHII (c. lat.)

200 μV

WRIST   FLEXION - EXTENSION

Fig. 5. Electrical activity recorded from synergistic musculature during wrist flexion and extension performed against gravity. The brachialis muscle is tied with wrist flexion and lateral head of triceps brachii is linked with extension.

found to elicit action potential activity in the ipsilateral brachialis muscle during volitional wrist flexion against gravity and excitation in the lateral head of the triceps muscle during active wrist extension. The irradiation of muscular activity observed in the synergistic musculature of the ipsilateral extremity may be attributed to proprioceptive influences from the initially contracting muscles. As early as 1927, Cooper and Creed demonstrated that contraction of the tibialis anterior muscle evoked flexor patterning in the entire ipsilateral limb. The total limb synergy thus elicited from the sensory inputs of actively contracting muscles may be regarded as the reflex or supportive background necessary for volitional movements.

In the radioulnar joints, nature provides an admirable device for varying sensory inputs, and Gellhorn (1953) was the first to study this in relation to proprioceptive inputs. He evoked what he called a "biceps and a triceps complex" by electrically stimulating appropriate cortical areas in rabbits, cats, and monkeys and subsequently demonstrated that muscle patterning could be changed by varying the radioulnar joint position. In 1947 he demonstrated the same patterning complexes in humans by using voluntary isometric contractions in the upper extremities. Wrist ergographic exercises designed to stress a subject systematically and bring him to the limits of his functional capacity were later used by Waterland and Hellebrandt (1964) to differentiate influences emanating from the prime movers activated volitionally from inputs elicited by modifying the position of the radioulnar joints. A total flexor limb synergy was called forth when wrist flexion was performed against resistance with the radioulnar joint in the anatomical or supinated position (Fig. 4). Wrist extension performed from the same radioulnar positioning augmented a limb synergy comprised of extensor muscles (Fig. 6). The action of supportive musculature was in harmony with that of the prime mover., However, the same wrist movements performed from a position of pronation evoked activity in associated muscles which was in conflict with the volitional act; wrist extension was linked with a flexor limb synergy and wrist flexion with an extensor synergy.

Head-Shoulder Linkages

The radioulnar joint has a profound influence on the upper appendage

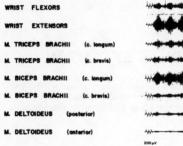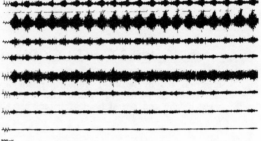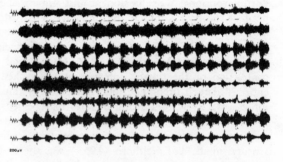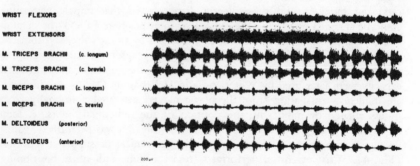

Fig. 6. Electromyograms recorded during wrist ergography. The subject performed right wrist extension from a radioulnar position of supination. *Upper record:* initial bout with 0.5 Kg., work output 1.93 Kg.m.; *middle record:* optimal bout with load of 3.0 Kg. with work output of 5.70 Kg.m.; *lower record:* twenty-repetition maximum with load of 4.0 Kg., work output of 3.40 Kg.m. It is interesting and perhaps of some importance to note that inhibition of the biceps brachii during the optimal bout occurred when the shoulder moved from a slightly protracted position to one of frank retraction.

during ergographic exercise and also affects the patterning of its contiguous parts, thus implicating the shoulder girdle, spine, and head. Covert and overt behavioral changes occurred in association with the maintenance of capacity in the face of mounting stress (Waterland and Hellebrandt, 1964). A head-shoulder girdle linkage was demonstrated by all subjects, and this appeared to be a physiological constant under the conditions imposed (Fig. 7). Some of the stereotypes that were identified are as follows: *First,* unilateral shoulder girdle retraction was always associated with the ipsilateral head turning while protraction of the shoulder girdle was always linked wih contralateral head turning. *Second,* certical spine ventral flexion was associated with shoulder girdle protraction and cervical spine dorsi-flexion was related to shoulder girdle retraction.

The head-shoulder girdle linkage was in no way affected by the way a subject performed the exercise task even though some substituted stronger proximal muscle groups for the wrist joint agonist. The invariability of the head-shoulder linkage was so impressive that a study of "nonstressful" vo-

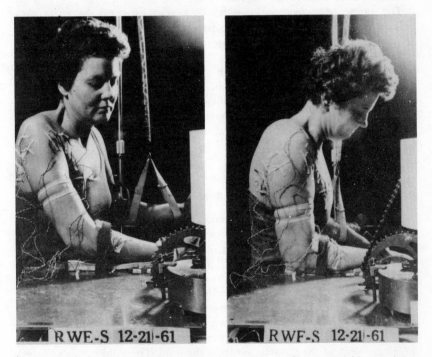

Fig. 7. Overt patterning evoked by exercise stress during a first ergographic experience. The patterning recorded for the same subject during the failing bout of wrist extension contrasts sharply with that photographed for wrist flexion. *Left:* profile picture of right wrist extension from a radioulnar position of supination; *right:* profile picture of right wrist flexion performed with the forearm in supination.

litional upper extremity, shoulder girdle, and head movements was undertaken (Waterland and Munson, 1964). This investigation showed that the head, shoulder girdle, and glenohumeral joints are mutually dependent; activity in one affected the behavior of the others, and the linkages observed were then classified as two-way stereotypes.

The movements of a child with central nervous system deficits who ex- hibited marked tonic neck reflex activity were investigated (Waterland, 1969). It was found that when an experimenter blocked shoulder girdle movement unilaterally, steretotyped tonic neck reactions were disrupted during the time of stabilization. Even though the youngster could with difficulty turn her head away from the side of shoulder stabilization in response to her name being called, the head rotation did not elicit flexion of the upper ex- tremity on the skull side where the shoulder was fixed. Photographs taken during unrestricted head rotation movements definitely revealed shoulder girdle involvement which is in keeping with head-shoulder linkages. His- torically, only one researcher has alluded to more proximal body parts in the "classical" tonic neck reflex literature (Hoff and Schilder, 1927).

The primitive stereotyped movements characteristic of the tonic neck reflexes in infants never become completely submerged in the motor repertory of an adult. Vestiges of the reflex are later expressed as the head-shoulder linkages. Twitchell has stated (1965), " . . . wholly new and distinct re- actions are not added at successively higher levels of the nervous system, but more primitive reactions become modified and elaborated as the stimulus of their response becomes more discriminating." The mechanism responsible for integration of the head-shoulder linkage observed in adults might be attributed to reflexes arising as a result of stimulation of the cervical joint receptors (C 1, 2, 3) and/or the muscle spindles and golgi tendon organs in the neck and shoulder area.

Head-Shoulder Linkages and Skill Achievement

Head-shoulder linkages may influence motor learning since some move- ments seem to rely on suppression of the innate pattern associates while others depend upon the preservation of the natural linkages. Fundamental motor activities taught to young children or to beginners of any age are probably characterized by the retention of natural and strong head-shoulder two-way linkages, while complex activities may be more dependent on partial or total volitional suppression of these natural pattern associates.

Cinematographic recordings of a two and a half year old child's throwing a ball suggest that the young do not have the capacity to disturb volitionally the natural yoke of the shoulder girdle to the head. The child stands with feet in a side-stride position, with the shoulders and head facing the direction of the intended throw. The activity is mostly restricted to movement in the glenohumeral joints. Perhaps this is the natural developmental pattern which must be later modified to attain a more forceful throw.

One of the most common teaching cues for a beginning tennis player is "side to the net." A novice has a natural tendency to face the net and attempts to hit the ball from this position without interfering with innate head-shoulder linkages. However, the golf swing demands that one separate head mobility from shoulder girdle movement. A skillful golfer learns to rotate the hips, trunk and shoulders between two stationary pivots, the feet and the head. A skilled bowler has developed by cortical control the ability to let the arm swing against a relatively stabilized shoulder girdle. The latter enhances the accuracy of the throwing arm, and the associated head movements are negligible.

Spontaneous overt pattern configurations of the head, shoulder girdle and the upper limbs are evident in skilled and unskilled performers, jumping for maximal distance. However, the unskilled jumpers fail to realize the full potential of an activated and integrated neuromuscular mechanism. The autonomous components of the movement are diminished but adequate for the distance jumped (Waterland, 1967).

Violin playing requires an unnatural head-shoulder positioning. Barlow (1954) reported that it is not uncommon for violinists to complain of shoulder and arm muscle spasms. A violinist, a patient of Barlow's, " . . . after playing for a while begins to pull his head over to the right . . . [and] he cannot prevent it when he becomes engrossed in his playing . . . even after his position has been corrected." He assumes a natural head-shoulder stereotype instead of the one dictated.

Hess (1954) has explained that "the course of a movement is nothing else but a projection to the outside of a pattern of excitation taking place in a corresponding setting in the central nervous system." Integration of sensory-motor elements is therefore essential for coordinated performances since movement is affected by both proprioceptive and exteroceptive influences. After a movement has been learned, motor control is partially "dethroned" from the cortex and relegated to lower areas of the central nervous system. Sensory stimuli and automatic responses then provide the supportive framework within which cortically directed movement operates.

REFERENCES

Barlow, W. Posture and the resting state. *Ann. Phys. Med.*, 1954, 2, 113-122.

Beevor, C. E. The coordination of single muscular movements in the central nervous system. *J. Am. Med. Assoc.*, 1908, LI, 89-97.

Cooper, S. and Creed, R. S. Reflex effects of active muscular contraction. *J. Physiol.*, 1927, 62, 273-279.

Decker, R. and Smith, L. *Motor Integration.* Springfield, Illinois: Charles C. Thomas, 1961.

Forward, E. Implications of research in motor learning for physical therapy. *J. Am. Phys. Ther. Assoc.*, 1963, 43, 339-344.

Gellhorn, E. Patterns of Muscular Activity in Man. *Arch. Phys. Med.*, 1947, 28, 568-574.

Gellhorn, E. *Physiological Foundations of Neurology and Psychiatry.* Minneapolis: The Univ. of Minnesota Press, 1953.

Hellebrandt, F. A. Living anatomy, *Wis. Med. J.*, 1964, 63, 525-535.

Hess, W. R. *Diencephalon-Automatic and Extrapyramidal Functions.* New York: Grune & Stratton, 1954.

Hess, W. R. Unpublished motion picture, 1943.

Hoff, H., and Schilder, P. Die Lagereflexe des Menschen. Klinische Untersuchungen uber Haltungs—und Stellreflex und verwandte Phanomene. Vienna: Julius Springer, 1927.

Jung, R. and Hassler, R. The extrapyramidal motor system. Vol. II of *Handbook of Physiology* (Chap. 35 of Section 1, Neurophysiology). Edited by J. Field, H. W. Magoun, and V. E. Hall. Washington, D. C.: American Physiological Society, 1960.

McGraw, M. B. *The Neuromuscular Maturation of the Human Infant.* New York: Hafner Publishing Company, 1963.

Paillard, J. The patterning of skilled movements. Vol. III of *Handbook of Physiology* (Chap. 67 of Section 1, Neurophysiology). Edited by J. Field, H. W. Magoun, and V. E. Hall. Washington, D. C.: American Physiological Society, 1960.

Poudrier, C. and Knowlton, G. C. Command-force relations during voluntary muscle contraction. *Am. J. Phys. Med.,* 1964, 43, 109-116.

Robison, M. E., Doudlah, A. M. and Waterland, J. C. The influence of vision on the performance of a motor act. *Am. J. Occ. Ther.,* 1965, 19, 202-204.

Schaffer, H. Behavior under stress; a neurophysiological hypothesis. *Phychol. Rev.,* 1954, 61, 323-333.

Twitchell, T. E. Attitudinal reflexes. In: *The Child with Central Nervous System Deficit.* Washington, D. C.: U. S. Government Printing Office, 1965.

Waterland, J. C. and Hellebrandt, F. A. Involuntary patterning associated with willed movement performed against progressively increasing resistance. *Am. J. Phys. Med.,* 1964, 43, 13-30.

Waterland, J. C. and Munson, N. Reflex association of head and shoulder girdle in nonstressful movements of man. *Am. J. Phys. Med.,* 1964, 43, 98-108.

Waterland, J. C. The effect of force gradation on motor patterning: standing broad jump. *Quest,* 1967, VIII, 15-25.

Waterland, J. C. Unpublished motion picture, 1969.

CRITIQUE OF WATERLAND'S PAPER
by J. B. Basmajian

In the area of Dr. Waterland's presentation, no laboratory in America (and probably in the entire world) has had a longer and richer experience than the Motor Learning Research Laboratory at the University of Wisconsin. The very real weight of authority that has characterized the work of Dr. Hellebrandt and her colleagues has left very little to be said by others who would venture into the same field. I have not escaped this feeling of trepidation. Yet the organizers of this conference asked me to offer a critique of Dr. Waterland's paper, not the eulogy which comes more naturally. Thus, my comments are hypercritical so as to generate fresh thoughts.

First, let me say that the general theses put forward are quite acceptable. On the other hand, most neurologists would consider Paillard's statements, quoted by Dr. Waterland, to be so obvious as to be trite. The same probably can be said of the model proposed by Hess and apparently illustrated by the motion picture of Jung and Hassler. Apt though the analogy of little men jumping off shoulders may be, it is simplistic to the point of being misleading. Having learned the lessons offered, one must wipe it clear out of one's mind to be able to deal with real patients with real disturbances in neuromuscular control mechanisms. More specifically, the role played by vision on the learning of motor patterns has much more subtle an influence. Happily, Dr. Waterland and her colleagues have recognized this and emphasized it.

Beevor's experiment on the muscles of the thigh is an excellent illustration of a number of phenomena in science besides the valid one he was then illustrating—the specificity of muscle action in patterned form. As you have learned, Dr. Hellebrandt then showed the real significance of the visual feedback mechanisms in obtaining the expected reactions. But in addition, the cited experiments emphasize the importance of controlling as many of the factors as possible in experiments with human subjects. One change in the setup and a totally opposite effect may be obtained!

This inescapable difficulty can be greatly reduced, but I sometimes fear that it can never be eliminated. This leads to the next requirement pointed up by the cited examples: one must employ as many subjects as will give valid statistical results before making generalized conclusions. Beevor, a brilliant observer, had a spotty record in this regard simply because his era came before medical scientists recognized the danger of generalizing from short series. His greatness lay in the insights he often obtained about muscular function with techniques we would consider primitive today. None of us who published papers on muscle function in the early days of the bioelectronic age is free of guilt in this regard. Nowadays, about the only error of scientific judgement that I freely admit about the past is the use of short series in some of my early electromyographic research. To make amends in recent years I have repeated—or more accurately, my students have repeated—almost everything. I derive cold comfort from the fact that practically all my generalizations have withstood the second testing.

"Limb Synergies"

The truly important contribution of the Wisconsin group represented by Dr. Waterland is their categorizing of the "limb synergies." Admittedly, the idea of a widespread overflow of activity in muscles that are not performing the prime movement is part of the ancient medical dogma. Indeed, the medieval physicians made a fetish of observing such activity for the purpose of diagnosis. The unique contribution Dr. Waterland and her colleagues have derived from Dr. Hellebrandt's leadership and their own experiments is the repeatable patterns of irradiation obtained under stress. My main criticism here concerns their terminology and perhaps this is a quibble. The use of "limb synergies" is misleading because it implies a useful function in the irradiation. I prefer the simpler and more accurate "natural linkages" now used by Dr. Waterland.

In a similar vein, Vladimir Janda and his colleagues (1963, 1965) demonstrated the natural linkages of muscular activity in the lower limb. They studied the role of the adductors in children and adults during flexion and extension of both the hip and the knee, with and without resistance. In almost every child the adductors were activated during flexion or extension of the knee and they were very active against resistance. Most adults showed activity during flexion of the knee, but only a minority were active during extension. With resistance almost all adult subjects showed great activity. During movements of the hip the role of the adductors was localized to their upper parts. During flexion against resistance, all the children and half the adults showed activity. During resisted extension, all were active.

Janda and Stará (1965) suggest that this labile response of the adductors is related to a postural response. They believe that these muscles are facilitated through reflexes of the gait pattern rather than being called upon as prime movers. With this view one can readily agree. Spruit's (1965) theoretical analysis of the adductors adds conviction to the opinion.

Linked muscular activity under stress in muscles far removed and apparently unrelated is in a class by itself. Along the same line, experiments were done by Sills and Olsen (1958) in the hope of demonstrating activity in the unexercised arm while the opposite arm was exercised by normal subjects. There was in these normal persons, little if any such "spread" to the opposite limb musculature unless extremely powerful movements were made. Their findings and conclusions effectively demolish the basis for certain contralateral exercises that have been advocated for developing muscles, especially for an injured limb too painful or too immobilized to be moved itself.

In very young normal children, especially premature babies, Fényes, Gergely and Tith (1960) reported "flexion reflexes" observed electromyographically. Both agonists and antagonists contract in what they term a "co-reflex phenomenon." The same is true in spastic children with cerebral palsy during locomotion (Kenney and Heaberlin, 1962). There is an abrupt onset of the agonists and a rapid response of the antagonists with sufficient power to be obstructive. Under considerable resistance, normal children give the same response of exuberant (but wasteful or useless) overactivity of antagonists.

In a study of reflex reactivity of biceps and triceps in children at different developmental stages, Missiuro (1963) found a spread of electrical activity to other muscles of the same extremity. With increasing age this decreases so that in adult life it is minimal.

Finally, let me hazard a suggestion that for fine performance the overflow of activity is both primitive and "undesirable" rather than useful. It is a reversion pattern and one which must be suppressed for improved performance. Indeed, I have suggested elsewhere (1967) that motor learning is a progressive suppression of the overflow patterns. Superior performers seem to be superior because the neural controls rapidly acquire the necessary inhibition of exuberant overactivity in the un-needed muscles. Thus, the coaching plea of "relax" seems to have a scientific rationale.

REFERENCES

Basmajian, J. V., *Muscles Alive: Their Functions Revealed by Electromyography.* 2nd edition, 1967, Baltimore, Maryland: Williams & Wilkins.

Fenyes, I., Gergely, Ch. & Tith, Sz. Clinical and electromyographic studies of "Spinal Reflexes" in premature and full-term infants. *J. Neurol., Neurosurg. & Psychiat.* (1960) *23:* 63-68.

Janda, V. & Stará, V. The role of thigh adductors in movement patterns of the hip and knee joint. *Courrier (Centre Internat. de L'Enfance)* (1965) *15:* 1-3.

Janda, V. & Véle, F. A polyelectromyographic study of muscle testing with special reference to fatigue. *Proc. of IX World Rehabilitation Congress,* Copenhagen 1963, 80-84.

Kenney, W. E. & Heaberlin, P. C., Jr. An Electromyographic study of the locomotor pattern of spastic children. *Clin. Orthop.,* 1962, *24:* 139-151.

Missiuro, W. Studies on developmental stages of children's reflex activity. Child Development, 1963, *34:* 33-41.

Sills, F. D. & Olsen, A. L. (1958) Action potentials in unexercised arm when opposite arm exercised. Res. Quart. 1958, *29:* 213-221.

Spruit, R. Een Analyse van Vorm en Ligging van de M.M. Glutaei en de Adductoren (An Analysis of Form and Location of Gluteal and Adductor Muscles) (Dutch text with English summary), Drukkerij, Albani-Den. Haag, Leiden, 1965.

WATERLAND'S REPLY TO
Basmajian's Critique, and Discussion

BILODEAU: The title of Dr. Waterland's presentation is "Aspects of Motor Learning: Vision and 'Natural' Linkages."

DR. WATERLAND: Thank you, the only thing I would like to add to the introduction is that my field is physical education.

OPEN DISCUSSION: BILODEAU: Thank you, Dr. Basmajian. Dr. Waterland do you want to agree, disagree or refuse to comment?

WATERLAND: I would like to respond to Dr. Basmajian's reactions. As far as Dr. Basmajian's comments concerning Dr. Paillard and Dr. Hess I feel that one should recognize and give credit to those people who have greatly influenced the work of the Motor Learning Research Laboratory. For example, Dr. Hess is responsible for the diagram I showed at the beginning of my talk. The illustration is basic to understanding the philosophy of the Motor Learning Research Laboratory. In addition, Dr. Hess and I have gotten to know each other quite well through correspondence. He writes to me in German and I have someone translate the letter and then write back to him in English. Knowing Dr. Hess and being able to discuss our research work with him has added dimensions to our work which would otherwise not exist. Dr. Hess is world famous and was once the recipient of a Nobel Prize. I believe that it is my privilege to be able to use his work and his basic diagram in introducing the work of the Motor Learning Research Laboratory.

Dr. Beevor is likewise one of my favorite scholars. I do not know if his work was done on one or more people. However, I must disagree with Dr. Basmajian since I do *not* believe that Dr. Beevor used crude methods but rather highly developed techniques. His eyes apparently were developed like our finest microscope. We as physical educators, I believe, should watch our subjects more carefully. We are apt to direct our attention to the electronic equipment which can be so fascinating.

I must give Dr. Basmajian part credit for using the term linkages. We both spoke at a conference in Chicago in 1962 and Dr. Basmajian capitalized on the word linkages and I had, at that time, used it quite inadvertently. After a bit of reflective thinking I allowed as how the term linkages was much better than synergies and have used it ever since.

I knew full well when I prepared my paper that Dr. Basmajian would mention his friend from Czeckoslovakia and I must be honest with him and tell you that he has mentioned him before. Not only that, but Dr. Basmajian was gracious enough to send me reprints of Dr. Janda's work and I was not thoughtful enough to include them in my presentation. I knew at the time that I would probably get called on it, but I just chuckled to myself and went on. Funny what you do.

Yes, I do agree with Dr. Basmajian that in some of your sport activities the linkages talked about are probably suppressed.

I believe there is time for one question. Dr. Lockhart from California has the privilege of asking a question.

LOCKHART: I am wondering in the light of the crucial role vision played in the subject's being able to watch her movement in a mirror, in the earlier part of your paper, if you would care to comment on the almost studied way of doing away with the use of demonstration by thinking you should put greater emphasis on the kinesthetic aspects during the early learning of a motor skill.

WATERLAND: I will give you my views, they do not necessarily represent other people's. I myself am not opposed to demonstration since you can get your message across to some people in this way and you may have to use other avenues for other people. This particular experiment was set up with the thought in mind that if we understood the movement we would be able to communicate verbally with our subjects and *not* use demonstration. This was the purpose of the study. Had we demonstrated I think we would have gotten the results, or the anticipated results as outlined by Dr. Beevor, much faster than we did.

LOCKHART: But in the end it took vision and the mirror to be able to produce this. Is that correct?

WATERLAND: On the original study done with Dr. Hellebrandt in 1963, yes. The initial study, however, was set up with a different purpose in mind. When we repeated the study in 1969, however, we did not use the mirrors. We studied the "failures" in order to clarify our understanding of the movement and thus the verbal description of the task. We were then able to communicate with the subjects.

Motor Abilities In Studies of Motor Learning

Harold P. Bechtoldt
University of Iowa

INTRODUCTION

In recent years rather serious consideration has been given to investigating hypotheses about the relationship of abilities and of individual differences to performance in learning situations (Bilodeau, 1966; Gagné, 1967; Glaser, 1962). In these several discussions, two so-called psychological trends might be noted. The first of these, a commitment phenomenon, is evidenced by a tendency for an author to repeat and expand on his previously stated position with respect to some debated issue. I intend to do this myself today. In this connection I am reminded of one of the laws collected by Don Lewis; this law states "if you say something often enough, you will even begin to believe it yourself" (Lewis, personal communication). The second trend is for the writers to support generally one of two positions reminiscent of Cronbach's two disciplines of psychology, one experimentally oriented and one psychometrically oriented (Cronbach, 1957). I will straddle the usual gulf here but not for the usual reasons. My suggestion is that the second trend arises in part from confusion about the notions of abilities and individual differences and in part from differences in the problems of interest to investigators.

My first objective is to consider briefly how confusion involving the notions of individual differences and of abilities is related to the evaluation of the usefulness of these concepts. The effect of differences in goals or purposes or problems characteristic of different investigators will not be considered. My second objective is then to consider critically but necessarily incompletely some recent statements by E. A. Fleishman and his associates about motor abilities and learning; the statements are based in part on the results of factor analytic studies and in part on experimental investigations. Although similar statements were criticized rather severely a number of years ago by Bechtoldt (1962) and by Jones (1962), these statements have influenced at least one writer of an elementary textbook (Anastasi, 1968). More recently, two writers have noted that Fleishman has failed to answer directly these criticisms (Adams, 1964, p. 191; Noble, 1968, p. 245); Fleishman, however, apparently considers that he has answered these earlier criticisms since he repeats his earlier statements and indicates that the same basic findings have been obtained with a variety of factor analytic designs and experimental methods (Fleishman and Bartlett, 1969, p. 358; Fleishman, 1966, p. 159; Fleishman, 1967b, p. 355).

The relationships under consideration are summarized by four statements repeated by Fleishman and his associates in at least three publications since the earlier criticisms. The statements are: (1) the particular combination of abilities contributing to performance (on a perceptual-motor task) changes as practice continues; (2) these changes are progressive and systematic and eventually become stabilized; (3) the contribution of "nonmotor" abilities relative to that of motor abilities decreases systematically with practice; and (4) there is also an increase in a factor specific to the task itself. Since such summary statements clearly have considerable appeal to psychologists (Irion, 1966), an analysis of these statements will be made in terms of the criticisms previously indicated and in terms both of the experimental data reported by Fleishman and of the results obtained by reanalyzing three factor analytic studies using more appropriate statistical procedures. The results are consistent with the conclusion that, while the four summary statements may be reasonable and appealing working hypotheses, our reanalyses of the data obtained by Fleishman offer little or no support for these hypotheses. Suggestions regarding procedures for the investigation of these working hypotheses will be made.

INDIVIDUAL DIFFERENCES AND ABILITIES

The confusion associated with the notion of individual differences is too vast to be recounted here. In addition, only that part of the discussion that deals with motor abilities in studies of motor learning is relevant. The relevant part can be presented in terms of three questions: First, what are individual differences? Second, what are abilities? Third, how do abilities and individual differences enter into studies of motor learning?

An answer to the first question requires only the definition of the term "individual differences." In the several collections of papers noted above, no definition of this term was found. Yet confusion or misunderstanding about this concept does seem to be common. In addition, such treatments as that by Cronbach (1957) of two disciplines of psychology indicate that different evaluative judgments of the usefulness of this notion of individual differences have long been with us.

According to the English and English dictionary of psychological terms, an "individual difference" is "any psychological character, quality, or trait, or difference in the amount of a character, by which an individual may be distinguished from others" (1958, p. 152). That definition is rejected as inadequate since the emphasis is on one of the functions that might be served by a classification procedure rather than on the concept itself. It is suggested that the term "individual difference" can be usefully and objectively defined by the considerations used by Ferguson in his treatment of test discrimination (1949). The proposed definition implies that any distribution of observations with a variance greater than zero contains one or more individual differences; the term "individual differences variable" might be applied to any defined variable with two or more categories, each of which has at least one member. The term "individual difference" refers to the binary relation of different, i.e., not the same; the relation is defined for each pairwise comparison of the results of applying a classification, assessment, or measurement rule for any attribute or property of the subjects of a psychological investigation. The definition of the relation *different* is that the two members of the pairwise comparison are not in the same class, category or level as appropriate for the procedure used. This definition indicates that every series of observations on any one defined property of each member of a sample of two or more subjects will lead to the judgment of one or more individual differences provided that two or more non-null categories of observations are obtained.

The second question also formally calls only for a definition of the term "abilities;" the term, however, is regularly used in two distinctly different ways. The first of these ways is indicated by English and English (1958, p. 1-2) when they define ability as the "actual power to perform an act, physical or mental, whether or not attained by training and education." Since power to perform an act refers to a property of behavior, an ability is often named by the term "behavioral variable." If the performance of the act is clearly specified by a set of standard observational conditions as in a testing situation, the observed test score constitutes an operational definition of the value of the ability or behavioral variable. It is important for our discussion here to recall also that Thurstone in his treatment of multiple factor analysis (1947) specified that an ability is defined by a specific test procedure and the method of scoring. Every conceivable test will define a separate ability; tests dealing with the same content but with different methods of presentation of stimuli or with different response systems will define different abilities (Bechtoldt, 1959).

The concept of individual differences is more general than that of ability; individual differences are not restricted to levels of a behavioral variable. If the distribution of the results of applying a definition to a sample of two or more cases leads to the observation of one or more pairwise "different" judgments, then the ability (behavioral) variable turns out to be also an individual differences variable for the data under consideration. Individual differences are also found in physiological states or treatment conditions which lead to such categories as male, seven feet tall, twenty years old, drugged, lesioned, hungry, hypnotized, informed, highly practiced, and so forth. Such individual differences are defined by the manipulative and selective activities of an investigator.

The second way in which the term "ability" is commonly used in psychology is also indicated by English and English (1958, p. 1-2) with the introduction of two adjectives to form the combination "primary mental abilities." This combination of words is said to refer to hypothetical units, various combinations of which constitute all distinguishable (defined) abilities. These hypothetical units appear in empirical studies as the constructed or artificial (not observable) statistical values implied by the set of factor analysis equations. An equally frequent and related use of the term "ability" appears in discussions of true scores in test theory (Lord, 1952), of latent structure of variables (Torgerson, 1958), and of postulated abilities (Ferguson, 1949) when the investigator *infers* or *assumes* (not defines) that subjects with higher test scores have as much or more ability than subjects with lower test scores.

The distinction between defined and hypothetical abilities must be kept in mind when evaluating a hypothesized relationship of motor abilities to motor learning as stated by Fleishman. For a number of years, Fleishman and his associates (Fleishman, 1966, 1967; Fleishman and Bartlett, 1969; Parker, 1967) have discussed the term "abilities" as referring to general traits which represent classes of mediating processes postulated to account for observed consistencies and for specific kinds of changes in performance. These consistencies represent instances of transsituational, empirical generalization of responses over some degree of variation in the stimulus and response conditions present in a set of tasks chosen for a factor analysis. Individual differences in skilled performances, i.e., in level of proficiency attained on a specific task, are considered by Fleishman as functions of these general traits which the individual brings with him as he attempts to learn a new task. The *skill* notion, as used by Fleishman, corresponds to the operationally defined *ability* notion of English and English while his *ability* notion is that of the *primary mental ability* class as presented by English and English. For Fleishman, an ability is not explicitly defined; any of a series of alternative testing situations apparently can be used interchangeably. The abilities are unobservable, inferred internal states or conditions of the subject which are said by Fleishman and his associates to resemble in some unspecified way mechanisms or capacities characteristic of an information processing or cognitive type of model of behavior. These mechanisms are then considered as influencing verbal and nonverbal response systems by modifying in some way the sensory input.

Statements about how a variable or a mechanism influences behavior as practice continues or modifies the stimulus input are statements about relationships involving behavioral variables. The question under consideration is how individual differences variables and abilities enter into testable statements of relationships involving behavioral variables of the type utilized in studies of learning.

There are two clearly distinguishable ways in which such variables appear in psychological investigations; these two ways correspond to the independent and dependent variables of an experiment or of a prediction situation. Since every behavioral variable with a variance greater than zero is both a defined ability variable and an individual differences variable and since the dependent or criterion variable in a learning situation is a behavioral variable with variance greater than zero, the first and most important use of individual differences and ability variables in studies of learning is as the dependent variable. No investigator would object to using behavioral variables with nonzero variance as criterion measures.

Concern expressed in the usual discussions of abilities about their usefulness is regularly associated with the second way in which these variables are used; this second way is as one of the independent variables of an investigation. Investigators are properly concerned with the variables they use as the independent variables. Such variables constitute the logical and empirical bases for explaining the systematic observed individual differences in the criterion variable; such an explanation expresses the results of the criterion measure as a function of the individual differences derived from the manipulative and selective activities of an experimenter which, in turn, represent the defining operations of each independent variable. From the viewpoint expressed here, there is no reason for rejecting individual differences variables as independent variables. If there were no individual differences in the independent or predictor variables, there would be no variables and no variation to be related to the variation observed in the criterion variable. Individual differences in both the dependent and independent variables must be present in any empirical behavioral study involving two or more subjects.

It is suggested here that actually the use of ability variables as independent variables is the only point at issue in recent discussions of individual differences and learning (Gagné, 1967). Both of the two classes of ability variables, the defined variables and the hypothetical variables, create special interpretative problems for an investigator when they are used as independent variables. However, the problems are entirely different in these two cases.

Since the operational definition of an ability or behavioral variable can be shown to have the formal features of a test score, the use of defined abilities as independent variables introduces the problems of using test scores as such variables. From an explanatory point of view, one problem encountered in using test scores as independent variables in an experiment is that the given behavior represented in a test score can arise from many different combinations of prior experience and experimental conditions. These different sequences of experience and sets of conditions would have different theoretical implications and would probably lead, if the differences were known, to different predictions. This explanatory problem in the sense of theory evaluation is less serious when, as is the case with most studies of adult human behavior, the question is one of prediction rather than explanation of performance. Test scores, representing abilities, singly and in combination have been shown to be useful in the prediction situation, although there are statistical issues to be considered, for example, in a regression problem.

Although a defined ability may be used either as an independent or a dependent variable, how is an experimenter to use a hypothetical ability either as an independent or as a dependent variable to investigate specific hypotheses about behavior? No definition of the hypothetical ability is available to indicate the class, category, or level to which each individual is to be assigned in order to evaluate the accuracy of statements about the hypothetical ability. This problem is a special case of the more general one of evaluating the undefined or postulated constructs of construct validity (Bechtoldt, 1959). More recently, Turner (1961) has emphasized some additional points involved in this hypothetical variable issue.

Since we are not dealing with ghosts, when empirical investigations of conjectures or speculations about factors and other such hypothetical abilities are conducted, temporary explicit definitions of the hypothetical ability must be introduced. Such definitions usually are expressed as a composite of one or more test scores. Specific instances of the use of this test score definitional procedure are found in studies of motor learning by Fleishman and Rich (1963) and by Fleishman and Hempel (1955). In these studies, performance on a single perceptual-motor task, as one of several possible factor measures, was used to section the original sample; the results were then said to show the relation of hypothetical motor and non motor abilities to motor learning. However, since no definition of the hypothetical ability was given, the statement of the relationship is an accurate one only in the sense of an ability as defined and not as a general trait or factor.

Unfortunately, the results obtained from using one definition of a factor are not necessarily comparable to those found with another definition. Alternative choices as to "ability measuring procedures" do not necessarily lead even to similar relationships with other variables. Certainly, variations in the method of presentation, in the type of stimuli involved, in the specific response systems required, as well as in the opportunities for differential amounts of prior experience with the defining tasks, can be expected to lead to variations in the relationships both with other behavioral variables and with treatment variables. This point has been recently demonstrated by Carver who reported on the danger involved in the use of tests which measure factors (1968). Carver used the two tests, shuttle run and softball throw, recommended by Fleishman, Thomas, and Munroe (1961) as defining measures for the factor named "explosive strength" in an experimental study of the effects of high altitude on selected physical fitness measures. Carver reported a treatment effect on shuttle run performance but not on softball throw performance. The selection of these two tests as dependent variables in a study of the effects of specified treatments on a factor, therefore, leads to different conclusions; what then, can one say about relationships involving the factor of explosive strength? Unless a specific operational definition has been proposed as the referent of a factor name, an experimenter using any treatment condition may report either no effect, a marked effect, or even that both statements are true, depending on the measure selected.

The selection of a single test to be used to define factors appearing as independent variables is also fraught with danger. Fleishman and Hempel (1955, p. 310) noted that the results of stratifying the sample on any one variables, as in a levels type of design, may not accurately represent the relations of the factor to the practiced performance. These authors demonstrated for four of their reference tests differential changes in mean Discrimination Reaction Time performance at upper and lower quartiles of the four test score distributions. Since statistical tests in these exploratory post hoc data searching procedures are not available, the statements by Fleishman and Hempel about systematic changes in abilities with practice are *hypotheses* about interaction effects to be investigated with *new* samples of cases rather than conclusions about relationships. However, no replication or follow up study of these statements has been located.

Fleishman and Hempel carefully indicated the name of the specific test used to stratify their subjects in the 1955 study although, as can be seen by inspection of the correlations in their Table 1 (Fleishman & Hempel, 1955, p. 305), other sets of reference tests could be used to demonstrate trends similar to those noted by the authors. This descriptive naming approach was not evident in the subsequent study by Fleishman and Rich (1963); in that study a hypothetical ability or factor approach was approximated with reference being made to spatial and kinesthetic measures. A rapid inspection of any of their published tables of correlations of reference tests with practiced performance will indicate those tests for which changing or unchanging trends in performance for extreme quartiles will be found; a crucial question is whether the predicted interaction (or no interaction) or level by trials effect will be found for new groups of cases.

This discussion of the three questions involving individual differences and abilities in motor learning can be briefly summarized. Individual differences must exist in both the dependent and independent variables. Defined abilities or behavioral variables are used in motor learning as the dependent variables and, in some instances also as one or more of the independent variables, either in a levels type of experimental design or in a regression problem. There is nothing empirically problematical about the use of defined abilities as independent variables although interpretative questions can be expected. The problematic situation is associated with the notion of hypothetical abilities. While explicit definitions of these abilities are required for each empirical investigation, if the defining operations are not invariant from one investigation to the next, the result is confusion if not chaos.

Since statements by Fleishman and his associates about hypothetical abilities constitute the major part of the literature dealing with the relation of abilities to perceptual-motor learning, their statements will now be considered and because their summary statements are based in large part on data obtained from the correlational techniques of factor analysis, the acceptability of these techniques for the hypotheses under consideration is a relevant issue.

CORRELATIONAL ANALYSES

In earlier critiques, Bechtoldt (1962) and Jones (1962, 1966) noted several issues in the discussions of the relationship of abilities to motor learning. The criticism by Jones was responded to by Fleishman with a restatement of his earlier views (1966). Jones had emphasized the view of Guttman

(1957) that the patterns of correlations of scores on successive practiced trials, which Jones names the superdiagonal pattern, is not appropriately represented by the simple linear model of factor analysis. Using the idea of increased specificity with practice, Jones indicates how this idea might be used to generate the superdiagonal form. However, since Corballis (1965) shows that alternative sets of assumptions about practice also can generate the same superdiagonal form, the important point in the papers by Jones and Corballis is that the application of factor analysis to practice data is *not* recommended.

None of these writers seem to have noticed that a study by Lewis *et al* (1953) is relevant to this discussion. Using a series of task reversed-task alternations on the Complex Coordination device, Lewis et al reported increases in the magnitude of the correlations from the last trial of one task to the initial trial of the other task as the alternation sequence continued, even though mean decrements in performance at the point of shift were evident until the end. The superdiagonal pattern, which was so evident on each one of the two tasks in the early stages of training, tended to be less evident in the later stages of training when performance levels were high. The application of factor analytic methods to these data is not open to some of the criticisms noted here, since the analysis was confined to observations on successive trials of a given stimulus situation; however, the evaluation of the resulting hypotheses by nonfactorial methods has not as yet been accomplished.

A serious criticism by Bechtoldt (1962) of the early studies by Fleishman (1960) and by Fleishman and Hempel (1954, 1955, 1956) was that the conventional orthogonal rotated factor analytic methods used by them were inappropriate techniques for the analyses of the data in terms of the hypotheses under consideration. The point was that the usual factor analysis model is not applicable to the analysis of data with respect to empirical questions or hypotheses involving the distinction between independent and dependent variables. Fleishman and his associates are concerned with possibly interesting hypotheses about how a combination of abilities contributes to performance as practice continues; such hypotheses imply a dependent ability variable of practiced performance and one or more independent ability variables. Factor analysis of such data *eliminate* the status differential associated with the dependent-independent variable feature of these hypotheses. The result of using inappropriate methods is that the data simply are not relevant to the hypotheses as stated; in such cases no one can determine from the reported results whether conclusions about practice effects are consistent or inconsistent with the data. However, when the design of the study is sound, relevant results may be obtained by reanalyzing the data using appropriate techniques. Such a reanalysis by Bechtoldt (1960) of a well designed factor analytic study by Coombs has been published by Fruchter (1966).

Since strong methodological criticism of statistical techniques is properly suspect, most readers would expect a clear cut refutation of this fundamental methodological point at once if the position stated were incorrect. However, no counter argument has been offered. Instead, in a recent review of human abilities by Fleishman and Bartlett (1969, p. 358), the critique by Bechtoldt (1962) was noted in passing as a *preference* for a multiple regression model applied to the reference and practice test data in the early Fleishman series. These two reviewers also state that the same basic findings (as in the criticized factor analytic studies) have been obtained with a variety of alternative factor analytic designs and experimental methods. This statement repeats earlier summaries of this work by Fleishman (1962, 1966) which emphasized the still earlier conclusions of the factor analytic studies of Fleishman and Hempel (1954, 1955) and of Fleishman (1960).

More recently a further discussion of the inappropriate use of factor analysis with repeated trial data has been published by the mathematical statistician, T. W. Anderson (1963). Anderson presents some of the theoretical reasons why conventional factor analysis methods are inappropriate methods of analysis of practice data; he is primarily concerned with the more general problem of the analysis of multiple time-series data; however, studies of practice effects over a set of trials constitute examples of a time-series problem. Anderson indicated that both the relevant status differences and the crucial time relationships are disregarded in the usual applications of factor methods (p. 9-11).

The resolution suggested by Bechtoldt (1962) for this problem of the status differences requires the separation of the data into two parts, one part consisting of the observations on one or more dependent variables and the other part the observations on one or more independent variables. This separation of the data is maintained in such statistical techniques as analysis of variance and regression analysis. Anderson (1963) also recommends separating the variables on the basis of such status differences. Both Bechtoldt and Anderson recommended the use of regression techniques as preferable to factor analytic methods in an investigation of relationships of abilities to dependent variables. For certain other hypotheses, different statistical methods would be more appropriate than the regression techniques.

The similarity of the factor analysis model to the regression model, noted by Bechtoldt (1961, 1962) and by Anderson (1963), has long been known (Holzinger & Harmon, 1941). The several reasons for the recommendation of the regression model over the factor analysis model apparently are not clear to Fleishman and Bartlett (1969, p. 358) since they indicate the choice to be simply a preference of the investigator. However, the reasons include appropriateness and applicability as well as efficiency; the application of factor analytic methods to combinations of reference and practice data is simply incorrect.

MULTIPLE REGRESSION REANALYSES

Since Fleishman has made repeated reference since 1962 in his statements about the relation of abilities to the results of three factor analyses, (Fleishman & Hempel, 1954, 1955; Fleishman, 1960), regression analyses have been made of these three sets of published data to secure some information from these studies relevant to the hypotheses about abilities in motor learning. The first problem encountered in making these reanalyses, however, is the definition of the hypothetical ability variables which are supposedly contributing as independent variables to performance in varying degrees as practice continues. This issue was also one of those raised earlier by Bechtoldt (1962); some aspects of this problem have been noted under the previous discussion of hypothetical abilities. The resolution suggested earlier was to define each hypothetical variable by a specified composite of one of more behavioral variables; such a definitional step changes the hypothetical ability to a defined ability. The procedure has been demonstrated (Bechtoldt, 1960, 1961, 1962). Similar procedures have been used also by Fleishman and Fruchter (1960) and by Parker and Fleishman (1960); such procedures also have been referred to by Fleishman and Bartlett (1969, p. 358) as relevant for the investigation of hypotheses about abilities.

The problem of developing operational definitions of behavioral concepts is indeed a difficult creative or judgmental act with serious scientific implications. Experts in the field, such as Fleishman and his associates, are the logical persons to provide suggested initial trial definitions. Although Fleishman (1953) has discussed cogently the difficulties of comparing factor analysis results, he provides only a verbal description of his factors and states that the factors are "best measured" by performance on one or more of a set of tasks; for example, he recently suggested five tests, including the Two Hand Coordination and Complex Coordination tests as measures of the *Multilimb Coordination* factor (1966, p. 152). In an earlier report (1962), Fleishman considered the *Control Precision* factor as best measured by such tests as Rotary Pursuit, Complex Coordination (of the Multilimb Coordination factor set), and Rudder Control. In his work on physical education fitness tests, Fleishman et al (1961) have been more specific in specifying given tests as the best of the series for measuring a set of factors. The list of suggested "best measures" apparently changes from time to time as new data are obtained; the changes, however, are not accompanied by any indication of the effect of these changes in measuring operations on the relationships of abilities to practiced performance.

A judgment as to the definition of such behavioral concepts as abilities or traits would surely be based on the results of nonfactorial studies as well as on the outcomes of factor analytic computations. The amount of confusion arising from alternative "best measures" of the hypothetical state or postulated construct in place of single explicit operational definitions can be expected to increase in the future if experimenters take at all seriously the suggestion of Ferguson that abilities can be studied in terms of transfer functions (1956) or the suggestion of Melton (1967) that we frame hypotheses about individual differences variables in terms of process constructs.

It has been pointed out that two desirable outcomes can be expected when concepts as factors, abilities, or traits are defined by explicit operational definitions (Bechtoldt, 1959, 1961, 1962). The first outcome is the elimination of confusion as to the referent of the term; invariance of ability scores with changes in the set of reference tasks and in the sample is assured when the ability is defined. The second outcome is the possibility of evaluating the tenability of hypotheses about such defined concepts in nonfactorial investigations. Of course, a defining function involving a composite of two or more behavioral variables is also a single definition in one sense of the word; such composite functions are convenient and useful definitions of independent variables which are used in an experimental design or as predictor variables, but these composites would create serious interpretive problems if they were to be used as dependent or criterion variables.

For the purpose of multiple-regression reanalyses of the three factor analytic studies under consideration, ten test variables were selected for use as predictor variables; these ten variables provided the largest possible number of test-defined factor variables common to at least two of the three studies. As noted earlier, the multiple regression model in the single group situation can be matched term by term to the linear factor analysis model when the separation of the variables into dependent and independent sets is maintained in the analysis and when the factors are explicitly defined by the predictor variables. The selected test variables to be used as predictors in the three analyses are shown in Table 1.

While the nine or ten variables of each of the three studies are experimentally independent, they are not statistically independent. The hypothesis of independence of these variables is rejected by the statistical test using the determinant of the correlation matrix for all three sets of predictor variables. Another indication of the degree of "overlap" or lack of independence of these predictor variables is provided by the multiple-correlation coefficients, computed for each variable used, in turn, as a criterion variable while all other test scores of each set appear as predictor variables. As shown in Table 1, these statistically significant multiple correlations range from a value of .40 to a value of .71.

Since the factor analytic results presented by Fleishman and his associates have emphasized the "variance contribution" of the factors to practiced performance, a linear regression analog of this very questionable notion will be employed. The factor analytic indices as the squares of projections on orthogonal axes are as subjective as the location of the axes and, in addition, include, inappropriately, part-whole components. The problem of evaluating "the contribution of each predictor" to the prediction of any single criterion variable in the regression model also is a matter of some dispute and complexity. Two indices of predictor contribution or usefulness will be employed; these are the partial correlation coefficients computed for a criterion measure paired with each predictor, in turn, and the index of predictive usefulness proposed by Darlington for this situation (Bechtoldt,

1962; Bottenberg & Ward, 1963; Cohen, 1968; Darlington, 1968; Hoffman, 1962). Table 1 also presents the partial correlation coefficients of each dependent or criterion variable, denoted CV in the table, with each available predictor; the criterion variables are the first trial or block of each practiced task. These correlations represent the pairwise relationships independent of

TABLE 1

Multiple and Partial Correlation Coefficients[1]

Computed Using Data For Ten Selected Variables From

Three Factor-Analytic Studies.[2]

Name of Variable	Multiple Correlations[3]			Partial Correlations[4]		
	1954	1955	1960	1954	1955	1960
Visual Jump Reaction Time	40	41	45	-15	02	09
General Mechanics	43	40	39	21	15	07
Visual Pursuit	52	47	48	18	-03	14
Rate of Movement	43	34	34	07	04	07
Speed of Identification	68	54	58	12	18	-04
Speed of Marking	61	--	49	19	--	11
Santa Ana Dexterity	--	53	55	--	12	12
Complex Coordination	71	61	63	(CV)	24	20
Discrimination Reaction Time	63	53	63	19	(CV)	-06
Rotary Pursuit	57	50	46	35	07	(CV)

1. All multiple correlations and those partial correlations exceeding $\pm$ .10 are significant at .05 level. Values rounded and multiplied by ·100 to remove decimals.

2. The three factor analytic studies are Fleishman and Hempel, 1954, Fleishman and Hempel, 1955, and Fleishman, 1960.

3. Multiple correlations computed from set shown with variable named as criterion.

4. Partial correlations computed between variable named and criterion variable designated (CV) holding remaining variables of set "constant".

(i.e., orthogonal to) the remaining predictor variables. These correlations indicate that both motor and nonmotor abilities are related to psychomotor performance over and above the contribution made by the other variables of the system. The changing pattern of significant partial correlations also is consistent with the suggestion that the several abilities are differentially related to performances on different psychomotor tasks.

Darlington (1968, p. 165) proposed defining the predictive usefulness index of a variable as the amount of reduction in the square of the multiple correlation which would be shown if that variable had been omitted from the set of predictor variables. These values are proportional to the squares of the corresponding partial correlation coefficients. While tests of significance of this index are available in terms of differences between squares of multiple-correlation coefficients, the sampling distributions for a repeated-trials situation have not been developed. For the purpose of showing the relationship of each predictor to the several practiced trials, these predictive usefulness indices will be shown in Tables 2, 3, and 4 only for the variables having significant partial regression coefficients in the regression equation. The square of the multiple correlation coefficient for each practiced trial also will be shown in Tables 2, 3, and 4; these values represent the ratio of predicted to total variance for each criterion trial. All of the multiple-correlation coefficients are significant by the usual tests.

The results of two reanalyses of the 1954 factor analysis study by Fleishman and Hempel are shown in Table 2; practice had been given on the Complex Coordination task. The upper half of Table 2 presents the usefulness coefficients for each of the eight blocks of practiced trials when all variables except a block of trials on the criterion task are used as predictors. The lower half shows the usefulness coefficients for the last seven blocks of trials when the first block of trials was added to the set of predictors. These results indicate that at each of the eight blocks of practice, three or more predictors of the set were making appreciable contributions to the R^2 values; in addition, the trend of the R^2 coefficients for the initial set of predictors indicates a general decrease in the accuracy of prediction as practice is continued. Two variables, Visual Pursuit and Rotary Pursuit, have significant partial-regression coefficients with each of the 8 criterion blocks of trials. However, no systematic changes in relationship to the criteria are shown for these two variables either by the usefulness coefficients of Table 2 or by the basic data which consists of the zero order correlation coefficients with blocks of trials as provided by Fleishman and Hempel (1954, p. 243). Slight evidence for a differential relationship between test abilities and early and late stages of practice might be provided by the small changes in the usefulness coefficients early in practice for the General Mechanics task and the Discrimination Reaction Time task and by the small coefficients for the Rate of Movement and, possibly, for the Reaction Time task later in practice. Since no specific hypotheses were being investigated when these studies were designed, statistical tests of the differences between regression coefficients

TABLE 2

Selected Predictive Usefulness Coefficients[1] for

Set of Predictors and Squares of Multiple Correlation Coefficients[2]

for Successive Trial Blocks of Complex Coordination Performance[3]

Predictor Variables Names and Code Numbers	Reaction Time	General Mechanics	Visual Pursuit	Rate of Movement	Speed of Identification	Speed of Marking	Rotary Pursuit	Discrimination Reaction Time	Complex Coordination (CC)	
	(25)	(12)	(15)	(26)	(13)	(19)	(21)	(23)	(1)	
(First Analysis[4]) CC Trial Block	Predictive Usefulness Coefficients									R^2
1-5	01	02	02	..	..	02	07	02	..	51
12-16	..	01	04	..	..	..	06	..	..	46
17-21	..	..	03	..	..	01	11	01	..	52
28-32	02	..	03	..	..	01	07	..	..	43
33-37	01	..	03	01	..	..	07	..	..	40
44-48	..	..	02	03	..	..	06	..	..	35
49-53	03	..	02	..	..	03	07	..	..	40
60-64	..	..	03	01	..	..	07	..	..	37
(Second Analysis[4]) CC Trial Blocks	Predictive Usefulness Coefficients									R^2
12-16	01	..	02	..	..	..	01	..	17	79
17-21	01	..	01	..	..	..	04	..	12	64
28-32	03	..	01	..	..	..	02	..	11	54
33-37	03	..	..	..	..	..	02	..	11	51
44-48	02	..	..	02	..	..	02	..	09	43
49-53	05	..	..	..	..	..	02	..	12	52
60-64	02	..	01	..	..	..	02	..	09	45

1. Predictive usefulness coefficients (Darlington, 1968) shown only for predictors with significant partial regression coefficients.

2. All multiple correlations (R^2) and all pairwise increments in (R^2) from the first to the second analysis are significant. All values rounded and multiplied by 100 to remove decimals.

3. Data from Fleishman and Hempel, 1954.

4. The second analysis uses the set of predictors of the first analysis augmented by the first trial block of Complex Coordination performance.

at these different stages of practice were not computed. At best, the results of this as well as those of the next two studies can provide specific hypotheses to be tested on new samples of cases in carefully designed studies.

The results of the second regression analysis of the 1954 data shown on the lower half of Table 2 indicate a change, as expected, in the pattern of predictive usefulness coefficients when the first block of practiced trials of the Complex Coordination (CC) task was used as a predictor variable. A crucial interpretative feature of a regression analysis is that the relationship of a given predictor variable to a criterion measure changes with changes in the set of predictor variables when the set is not a statistically independent one. In this second analysis, the Rotary Pursuit task and the Reaction Time task appeared with significant regression coefficients at each block of CC trials while these coefficients for the Visual Pursuit task were not as consistently significant as was the case in the first analysis. In this analysis as well as in the other regression analyses to be presented, the inclusion of the first stage or block of practice in the set of predictor variables increased significantly the multiple-correlation coefficient at all stages of practice.

The usefulness coefficients for block one as a predictor of the subsequent CC trials exhibit a slight trend toward a decrease in value from block 2 to block 8. Stronger decreasing trends in these coefficients appeared in each of the other two sets of reanalyses. This trend would be expected since the pattern of correlations between practiced trials, both before and after partialing out the sets of predictors, is the superdiagonal pattern emphasized by Jones (1962, 1966) and by Gutman (1957). In this analysis and in the others to be presented, the only clear evidence of changes in abilities with practice is provided by the data from the block one performances; there is little or no evidence supporting the hypothesis of differential changes in relationship of the set of defined abilities to performance on the Complex Coordination task as practice continued. Since some behavioral variables are better predictors than are others, the regression coefficients do vary between predictors.

The results of the 1955 factor analysis study of Fleishman and Hempel have been cited by Fleishman and his associates as providing strong evidence for the hypothesis that the relationship between ability and practiced performance changes as practice is continued. The results of the two multiple regression analyses of the data of the 1955 study are shown in Table 3.

In this study, practice was given on the Discrimination Reaction Time (DRT) task. Performances on the Speed of Identification and Complex Coordination tasks had significant regression coefficients in the equation for each of the eight DRT trials. By contrast, the regression coefficients for the Reaction Time task were significant only for the last five selected trials of DRT while the coefficients for the General Mechanics task and for the Santa Ana Dexterity task tended to be significant ones in the early stages of practiced performance. As noted earlier, the design of the study did not warrant evaluating the hypothesis of constant regression coefficients over the series of trials (Bechtoldt, 1962). However, neither the correlation co-

TABLE 3

Selected Predictive Usefulness Coefficients[1] for Set of Predictors and

Squares of Multiple Correlation Coefficients[2] for Odd-Numbered

Trials of Discrimination Reaction Time Performance[3]

Predictor Variables Names and Code Numbers	Reaction Time	General Mechanics	Visual Pursuit	Rate of Movement	Speed of Identification	Santa Ana Dexterity	Complex Coordination	Rotary Pursuit	Discrimination Reaction Time	R^2
	(24)	(12)	(17)	(20)	(14)	(19)	(26)	(27)	(1)	
(First Analysis[4]) DRT Trials				Predictive Usefulness Coefficients						R^2
1	..	02	..	..	02	..	04	..	..	29
3	..	..	..	..	03	05	05	..	..	38
5	..	01	..	..	04	02	03	..	..	34
7	02	..	..	01	02	01	04	..	..	32
9	03	..	..	02	02	..	02	..	..	32
11	02	..	..	..	04	..	02	..	..	27
13	01	..	..	..	04	03	03	..	..	34
15	04	01	..	..	03	..	01	..	..	31
(Second Analyses[4]) DRT Trials				Predictive Usefulness Coefficients						R^2
3	..	..	..	..	01	02	01	..	25	63
5	..	..	..	..	01	01	..	..	23	57
7	01	..	..	01	..	..	..	..	23	55
9	02	..	..	01	..	..	..	..	14	48
11	02	..	..	..	02	..	..	..	15	42
13	01	..	..	..	02	01	01	..	10	44
15	04	..	..	..	01	..	..	..	12	43

1. Predictive usefulness coefficients (Darlington, 1968) shown only for
    predictors with significant partial regression coefficients.

2. All multiple correlations (R^2) and all pairwise increments in (R^2) from the
    first to the second analysis are significant. All values rounded and
    multiplied by 100 to remove decimals.

3. Data from Fleishman and Hempel, 1955.

4. The second analysis uses the set of predictors of the first augmented
    by the first trial of Discrimination Reaction Time performance.

efficients reported by Fleishman and Hempel (1955, p. 305) nor the usefulness coefficients of Table 3 indicated any appreciable change in relationship
of defined abilities and practiced DRT performance as practice continued.
The most noticeable feature of the original correlational data was the differences in average (over trials) correlations of DRT performance for the
series of test performances.

The results of adding Trial 1 of the Discrimination Reaction Time task
to the set of predictors are shown in the lower half of Table 3; these data
indicate that only the relationship of Reaction Time performance from the
initial set of abilities with DRT performance remains invariant with the
addition of Trial 1. The decreasing usefulness of Trial 1 as a predictor
is clearly evident in the coefficients shown in the table; the pattern of zero-
order correlation coefficients shows the same changes as practice continues.

One of the problems of attempting to study changes in practiced performance with a single group of subjects using test-defined abilities can be presented in terms of the differences in the results shown in Tables 2 and 3.
In Table 2, DRT performance appeared as a poor predictor of CC criterion
performance while in Table 3 CC performance was a useful predictor of
DRT criterion performance. However, the two sets of zero-order correlation
coefficients directly involved in these comparisons are nearly identical; the
differences in the regression results are largely in the magnitude of the other
correlation coefficients of the study. Similar changes over samples are evident
in the statistics of Table 1. Since the sampling variation of sets of correlation
coefficients is at least as great as that for sets of arithmetic means, systematic
replication of every important study, correlational or not, is needed to establish the stability of the descriptive statistics and to permit the testing of
specific hypotheses on new samples of cases. In addition, the introduction
of explanatory concepts as contrasted to predictive ones will be easier when
the manipulative and selective activities of an experimenter are a part of the
defining operations of the independent variables of a study.

The results of the final pair of regression reanalyses are shown in Table
4; ten test variables are utilized as predictors of performance in eight stages
of practice of Rotary Pursuit (RP) performance. The multiple-correlation
coefficients shown in the upper half of Table 4 are the lowest of those found
in the three sets of computations. Although the usefulness coefficients corresponding to the significant partial-regression coefficients indicate some predictive value for the Speed of Marking and Santa Ana Dexterity tasks, when
Rotary Pursuit performance is the criterion in both analyses represented in
Table 4, the corresponding factor analytic factors of Aiming and Finger
Dexterity, according to Fleishman, were not involved in RP performance
(1960, p. 168). However, the zero-order correlations published by Fleishman (1960, p. 165) are consistent with the regression analysis results; the
correlations with Rotary Pursuit were highest for the Complex Coordination,
Speed of Marking, and Santa Ana Dexterity tasks. The change in usefulness
coefficients for RP performance as a predictor of CC criterion performance

TABLE 4

Selected Predictive Usefulness Coefficients[1] for Set of Predictors and

Squares of Multiple Correlation Coefficients[2] for

Odd-Numbered Trials of Rotary Pursuit Performance[3]

Predictor Variables Names and Code Numbers	Reaction Time	General Mechanics	Visual Pursuit	Rate of Movement	Speed of Identification	Speed of Marking	Santa Ana Dexterity	Complex Coordination	Discrimination Reaction Time	Rotary Pursuit	
	(22)	(9)	(13)	(20)	(11)	(15)	(17)	(24)	(25)	(1)	
(First Analysis[4]) RP Trials			Predictive Usefulness Coefficients								R^2
1	..	..	02	..	..	..	..	03	..	..	22
3	..	..	02	..	..	02	03	..	..	..	27
5	..	..	..	..	..	02	03	..	..	..	26
7	..	..	..	..	..	02	03	01	..	..	24
9	..	..	..	..	..	..	03	..	..	..	22
11	..	..	..	..	..	04	03	..	..	..	23
13	..	..	..	..	..	05	03	02	..	..	26
15	..	..	..	02	..	03	..	03	..	..	26
(Second Analysis[4]) RP Trials			Predictive Usefulness Coefficients								R^2
3	..	..	..	..	..	01	01	..	..	59	71
5	..	..	..	..	..	01	01	..	..	33	59
7	..	..	..	..	..	..	01	..	..	33	57
9	..	..	..	..	..	01	..	..	..	26	48
11	..	..	..	..	..	02	01	..	..	26	49
13	..	..	..	..	..	03	01	..	..	18	44
15	..	..	..	..	..	02	..	..	..	14	40

1. Predictive usefulness coefficients (Darlington, 1968) shown only for predictors with significant partial regression coefficients.

2. All multiple correlations (R^2) and all pairwise increments in (R^2) from the first to the second analysis are significant. All values are rounded and multiplied by 100 to remove decimals.

3. Data from Fleishman, 1960.

4. The second analysis uses the set of predictors of the first analysis augmented by the first trial of Rotary Pursuit performance.

in the 1954 data of Table 2 to the values for CC performance as a predictor of RP criterion performance in the 1960 data of Table 4 represents mainly a change over samples in the zero-order correlations directly involved; the 1954 correlations between these two variables ranged over trials of CC from .49 to .59, while the 1960 correlations ranged over trials of RP from .31 to .39.

The results of the present regression analysis using ten predictors can hardly be compared to those of an earlier reanalysis (Bechtoldt, 1962) since only three of the predictor variables are common to the two analyses. Nevertheless, both analyses indicated the predictive usefulness of performance on the paper-pencil task of Speed of Marking for performance on the criterion apparatus task of Rotary Pursuit. In addition, neither analysis offered any support for the notion of differential changes in abilities as practice progressed except for the performance on Trial 1 of RP when this trial is used as a predictor.

The selection of seven independent variables to define the factors in the previous reanalysis was made in terms of that study alone; in the present reanalysis, as large a common set of predictors as possible was desired since statements about differential changes in relationship of abilities to practiced performance on different tasks were of interest. Of course, none of the desired statistical procedures could be used in between-group comparisons since different practiced tasks were used with different groups observed at different times and with different sets of reference abilities presented in different orders. When the studies are designed to investigate the hypotheses of interest, the several statistical procedures of multivariate analysis appropriate to repeated measurements and time-series data will be applicable; significant interaction effects of various specific kinds will be observed if the suggested differential relationships involving specific abilities and practiced performance on given classes of tasks are to be accepted even as working hypotheses.

The results of the several regression analyses of the three sets of data under consideration can be briefly summarized by six statements. It must be emphasized that these statements apply to the results of the regression analyses as modeled on the factor analytic studies; they may not apply to results from all possible sets of two or more predictors. (1) Significant levels of prediction of CC, DRT, and RP performance from a set of eight or nine ability scores were found. (2) The inclusion of the first trial or block of trials of the practiced task as a predictor variable significantly improved the level of prediction in each study. (3) The predictive usefulness of the initial trial of the practiced task tends to decrease as practice continues. (4) The predictive usefulness of performances on such non apparatus (or nonmotor) tasks as Speed of Marking, Speed of Identification, and Visual Pursuit tends to be only slightly less than that for performances on apparatus tasks; in terms of the regression analyses, the more useful apparatus tasks were Santa Ana Dexterity, Complex Coordination, Visual Jump Reaction Time, and Rotary Pursuit tests. (5) There is at best only slight evidence (involving scores on General Mechanics) of any decrease with practice in the usefulness of nonmotor abilities as compared to that of motor abilities as claimed by Fleishman; (6) There is some slight evidence in each of the three sets of data for nonsystematic changes as practice continues in the predictive usefulness of given abilities (excluding the initial practiced trial), but the clearest trend is for one or more of these abilities to maintain a constant level of predictive usefulness as practice continues.

In general, the results do not support the claims made by Fleishman on the basis of the early inappropriate factor analyses of the three sets of data. The six summary statements are offered only as working hypotheses rather than conclusions since the studies were not designed for multiple-regression analysis tests of these hypotheses. Until such studies are designed for, and analyzed by, appropriate statistical procedures, discussion of the relationships of abilities to motor learning will remain the confusing series of conjectures, speculations, and differences of opinion characteristic of the field today.

REFERENCES

Adams, J. A. Motor skills. *Annual Review of Psychology, 15,* 181-202, Palo Alto: Annual Reviews Inc., 1964.

Anastasi, A. *Psychological Testing,* 3rd edition, New York: Macmillan, 1968.

Anderson, T. W. The use of factor analysis in the statistical analysis of multiple time series. *Psychometrika,* 1963, *28,* 1-25.

Bechtoldt, H. P. Construct validity: a critique. *American Psychologist,* 1959, *14,* 619-629.

Bechtoldt, H. P. Statistical tests of predictions generated from factor hypotheses. Paper presented at *Midwestern Psychological Association:* St. Louis, Mo., April, 1960.

Bechtoldt, H. P. An empirical study of the factor analysis stability hypothesis. *Psychometrika,* 1961, *26,* 405-432.

Bechtoldt, H. P. Factor analysis and the investigation of hypotheses. *Perceptual and Motor Skills,* 1962, *14,* 319-342.

Bilodeau, E. A. (Ed.) *Acquisition of Skill.* New York: Academic Press. 1966.

Bottenberg, R. A., & Ward, J. N. *Applied multiple linear regression* (PRL-TDR-63-6) Lackland AF Base, Texas, 1963.

Carver, R. P. Brief report: on the danger involved in the use of tests which measure factors. *Multivariate Behavioral Research,* 1968, *3,* 509-512.

Cohen, J. Multiple regression as a general data-analytic system. *Psychological Bulletin,* 1968, *70,* 426-443.

Corballis, M. C. Practice and the simplex. *Psychological Review,* 1965, *72,* 399-406.

Cronbach, L. J. The two disciplines of scientific psychology. *American Psychologist,* 1957, *12,* 671-684.

Darlington, R. B. Multiple regression in psychological research and practice. *Psychological Bulletin,* 1968, *69,* 161-182.

English, H. B., & English, A. C. *A Comprehensive Dictionary of Psychological and Psychoanalytic Terms.* New York: David McKay, 1958.

Ferguson, G. A. On the theory of test discrimination. *Psychometrika,* 1949, *14,* 61-68.

Ferguson, G. A. On transfer and the abilities of man. *Canadian Journal of Psychology,* 1956, *10,* 121-131.

Fleishman, E. A. Testing for psychomotor abilities by means of apparatus tests. *Psychological Bulletin,* 1953, *50,* 241-262.

Fleishman, E. A. Abilities at different stages of practice in rotary pursuit performances. *Journal of Experimental Psychology,* 1960, *60,* 162-171.

Fleishman, E. A. The description and prediction of perceptual-motor skill learning. In

Training Research and Education, 137-176. (Glaser, R., Ed., N.Y.: Wiley, 596 pp., 1962).

Fleishman, E. A. Human abilities and the acquisition of skill. In *Acquisition of Skill,* 147-167. (Bilodeau, E. A., Ed., New York: Academic Press, 539 pp., 1966).

Fleishman, E. A. Individual differences and motor learning. In *Learning and Individual Differences,* 165-192 (Gagné, R. M., Ed., Columbus: Merrill, 265 pp., 1967) (a)

Fleishman, E. A. Performance assessment based on an empirically derived task taxonomy. *Human Factors,* 1967, *9,* 349-366. (b)

Fleishman, E. A., & Bartlett, C. J. Human abilities. *Annual Review of Psychology, 20,* 349-380, Palo Alto: Annual Reviews, Inc., 1969.

Fleishman, E. A., & Fruchter, B. Factor structure and predictability of successive stages of learning Morse Code. *Journal of Applied Psychology,* 1960, *44,* 96-101.

Fleishman, E. A., & Hempel, W. E. Changes in factor structure of a complex psychomotor test as a function of practice. *Psychometrika,* 1954, *19,* 239-252.

Fleishman, E. A., & Hempel, W. E. The relation between abilities and improvement with practice in a visual discrimination reaction task. *Journal of Experimental Psychology,* 1955, *49,* 301-310.

Fleishman, E. A. & Hempel, W. E. Factorial analysis of complex psychomotor performance and related skills. *Journal of Applied Psychology,* 1956, *40,* 96-104.

Fleishman, E. A. & Rich, S. Role of kinesthetic and spatial-visual abilities in perceptual-motor learning. *Journal of Experimental Psychology,* 1963, *66,* 6-11.

Fleishman, E. A., Thomas P., & Munroe, P. *The Dimensions of Physical Fitness—A Factor Analysis of Speed, Flexibility, Balance, and Coordination Tests.* ONR Technical Report 3, New Haven: Yale University, 1961.

Fruchter, B. Manipulative and hypothesis-testing factor-analytic experimental designs. 330-354. In *Handbook of Multivariate Experimental Psychology,* (Cattell, R. B., Ed., Chicago, Ill.: Rand McNally, 959 pp. 1966).

Gagné, R. M. Ed. *Learning and Individual Differences* Columbus: (Merrill, 1967).

Glaser, R. (Ed.) *Training Research and Education,* New York: Wiley, 1962.

Guttman, L. Empirical verification of the radex structure of mental abilities and personality traits. *Educational and Psychological Measurement,* 1957, *17,* 391-407.

Hoffman, P. J. Assessment of the independent contributions of predictors. *Psychological Bulletin,* 1962, *59,* 77-80.

Holzinger, K. J., & Harman, H. *Factor Analysis.* Chicago: Univ. Chicago Press, 1941.

Irion, A. L. A brief history of research on the acquisition of skill. In *Acquisition of Skill,* 1-46 (Bilodeau, E. A., Ed., New York: Academic Press, 1966).

Jones, M. B. Practice as a process of simplification. *Psychological Review,* 1962, *69,* 274-294.

Jones, M. Individual differences. In *Acquisition of Skill,* 109-146 (Bilodeau, E. A., Ed., New York: Academic Press, 539 pp., 1966).

Lewis, D., Department of Psychology, University of Iowa, Personal Communication.

Lewis, D., McAllister, D. E., & Bechtoldt, H. P. Correlational study of performance during successive phases of practice on the standard and reversed tasks on the SAM Complex Coordinator. *Journal of Psychology,* 1953, *36,* 111-126.

Lord, F. A. Theory of test scores. *Psychometric Monograph,* 1952, No. 7.

Melton, A. W. Individual differences and theoretical process variables: general comments on the conference. In *Learning and Individual Differences,* 238-252. (Gagné, R. M., Ed., Columbus: Charles E. Merrill, 265 pp., 1967).

Noble, C. E. The learning of psychomotor skills. *Annual Review of Psychology, 19,* 203-205. Palo Alto: Annual Reviews, Inc., 1968.

Parker, J. F. The identification of performance dimensions through factor analysis. *Human Factors,* 1967, *9,* 367-373.

Parker, J. F., & Fleishman, E. A. Ability factors and component performance measures as predictors of complex tracking behavior. *Psychological Monographs,* 1960, *74,* No. 16 (Whole No. 503).

Thurstone, L. L. Multiple-factor Analysis. Chicago: Univer. of Chicago Press, 1947.

Torgerson, W. S. *Theory and Methods of Scaling.* New York: John Wiley & Sons, 1958.

Turner, W. S. A reexamination of the two kinds of scientific conjecture. *Psychological Record,* 1961, *11,* 279-298.

CRITIQUE OF BECHTOLDT'S PAPER
by D. H. Holding

Many of us may still fall into a category which Fleishman (1966) implied was obsolete. He wrote then that 'it was not too long ago when learning psychologists viewed individual differences as troublesome error variance, obscuring rather than clarifying the principles of skill learning.' The difficulty, of course, is that attempts to unscramble the 'troublesome error variance' are fraught with problems of methodology and interpretation of a kind not met with in normal experimentation, so that many psychologists do not feel that the issues raised satisfactorily resolved until the hypotheses which emerge are removed from correlational to inferential, laboratory study.

In my own case, an attempt to find order in a correlational study, relating reaction time (RT) to measures of pursuit tracking ability, brought swift disillusion. Against root-mean-square error scores early and late in training, we (Loveless and Holding, 1959) correlated measures of simple, two-choice and discriminative RT. One might make a prima facie case for the importance of choice or discriminative RT in tracking, although only choice RT gave a significant correlation; on the other hand, simple RT appears almost irrelevant to the task presented to the operator but showed the highest correlation with practised tracking performance. At the same time, the measure of simple RT correlated best and significantly only with the discriminative RT measure, a finding which fails to assist interpretation. In the face of this kind of complication, one tends to cast about for further evidence of a directly experimental kind.

However, this natural tendency does not exonerate us from the task of attempting a conceptual resolution of the correlational issues. Dr. Bechtoldt has compelled us to a reappraisal of the factor-analytic findings which have tended to dominate the investigation of individual differences in skills. He has shown that Fleishman, in combining reference data with practice data, in the context of repeated trials, has used methods which are strictly inappropriate. This kind of problem occurs frequently in the analysis of psychological data, since learning and performance data tend to mesh awkwardly with the underlying assumptions of the statistical techniques which are otherwise appropriate. What we have to decide in each case is whether the infringements committed are merely technical, or whether they lead to substantial errors of interpretation.

Fleishman's (1966) admittedly cursory reply to Bechtoldt's (1962) earlier statement of his criticisms was that a variety of different approaches have been used, all confirming these basic findings.' The examples adduced were of cross-sectional analyses of skilled and unskilled performance, regression techniques, analyses of component-total task relations, and straight experimental procedures. It does appear true that support for many of the factor-analytic findings can be derived from other sources, although a confirmation in detail must clearly wait upon the establishment of a far broader basis of research.

The outlines of the individual difference picture seem tolerably clear. New factors will inevitably accumulate, while others will be assigned modified roles. Nevertheless, many of the factors identified by Fleishman correspond with the categories used by earlier workers in the analysis of skills, while some valuable confirmation can be drawn from research outside the context of apparatus tests. It is of interest, for instance, that an analysis of practical driving skill by Herbert (1963) revealed major loadings on five factors which could be identified as corresponding to those of Fleishman. Test scores obtained for maneuvering a truck in an artificial parking lot, parallel parking, hill starting, trailer backing and similar exercises yielded as factors (I) multilimb coordination (II) spatial orientation (III) proprioceptive (IV) response orientation, and (V) reaction time.

What is less clear, of course, is the status of changes brought about by repeated practice in the contribution of differing ability variables to task performance. Factor analysis, in the circumstances of learning trial application, appears to show systematic trends in the weighting of 'construct' abilities; while multiple regression analysis shows relatively stable prediction, by abilities defined as test scores, of successive performance levels at the criterion tasks. Although the factor analysis and multiple regression techniques involve differing rationale and intent, Bechtoldt has justified his preference for the second technique in this application. There are therefore good grounds for viewing the conclusions concerning changes in ability distribution with extreme reserve, particularly where the abilities are defined as hypothetical units.

We cannot, nevertheless, conclude that changes in ability distribution never occur as a result of practice. In at least one important instance, the changes in relative weighting of spatial-visual and kinestheitc ability, there is no real doubt that the findings of Fleishman and Rich (1963) are essentially correct. As Bechtoldt points out, this is in any case more in conformity with his criteria as a study in which abilities are effectively test-defined, but its basic credibility is rooted in the skills literature. It is clear that in many skilled activities the initial importance of visual information tends to give way to the feedback of kinesthetic data, so that the operator who is skilled in a sensorimotor task eventually becomes able to 'do it blindfold'. Since the relative importance of the two information channels changes as practice progresses, it is reasonable to expect differences in the demands on the corresponding abilities. It is also true (Welford, 1958) that the deterioration of skill with age tends to bring a return to dependence upon visual cues, so that we may predict a reversal of the differential ability trend with aging.

There seems therefore to be at least some truth in the statement that 'the particular combination of abilities contributing to performance changes as practice continues,' although the generality of the statement must be curtailed. A detailed resolution of the problem will depend in part upon further careful checks within the correlational literature. At the same time, the eventual residue of generally accepted findings must emerge from a continuing dialog between the psychometric and the exprimental sub-cultures.

REFERENCES

Bechtoldt, H. P. Factor analysis and the investigation of hypotheses. *Perceptual & Motor Skills,* 1962, 14, 319-342.

Fleishman, E. A. Human abilities and the acquisition of skill. In Bilodeau, E. A. (Ed.), *Acquisition of Skill.* New York: Academic Press. 1966.

Fleishman, E. A., & Rich, S. Role of kinesthetic and spatial-visual abilities in perceptual-motor learning. *Journal of Experimental Psychology,* 1963, 66, 6-11.

Herbert, M. J. Analysis of a complex skill: vehicle driving. *Human Factors,* 1963, 5, 363-372.

Loveless, N. E., & Holding, D. H. Reaction time and tracking ability. *Perceptual & Motor Skills,* 1959, 9, 134.

Welford, A. T. *Ageing and Human Skill.* London: Oxford University Press. 1958.

BECHTOLDT'S REPLY TO
Holding's Critique

HOLDING: I had better give Dr. Bechtoldt the chance to reply if he wishes.

BECHTOLDT: I would love to, even though the hour is late. There are some things that Thurstone said and very few people have understood; he said that factor analysis has its greatest usefulness at the borderline of science and that you take the results for checking into the laboratory. How are you going to take hypothetical underlying casual variables into the laboratory?

HOLDING: Well, I had better not try to reply to that. I know Dr. Henry wishes to get a word in and we shall see whether his remarks follow on directly from that or not.

HENRY: As a matter of fact, while I may not be quite precise in this, I have a feeling that a dissertation study by Robert Morford, at Berkeley, a few years ago, studying kinesthetic learning (using that thing I had labeled some years ago, kinesthetic dynamic process gismo) found a modification of this gadget that required strictly kinesthetic cues. Learning was impossible when he introduced large amounts of visual information to help the subject; it then became entirely a visual task. But if he used the proper gradation of supplementary visual information, kinesthetic cues could be used, and in subsequent trials the task was performed kinesthetically. It seems to me this does furnish rather direct information and later in practice —and in this instance as well—in a much simpler situation kinesthetic cues can be used effectively late in the task. I would hesitate to generalize very far from that. The real purpose, however, Mr. Chairman, for my wishing to have a chance at this microphone is that I've been entirely too placid and peaceful here. While I fully support the thesis that Dr. Bechtoldt has adopted this afternoon, I felt at first that I must be losing the ability to hear the entire range of tones at my age. I checked with K. U. Smith who should

still have his abilities available; we agreed together that he did indeed say
that if the variance in a set of scores is greater than zero, there is at least
one individual difference. Now, I may be paraphrasing slightly in that sense;
well, Sir, choose your weapons and let's have at it.

BECHTOLDT: You are right!

HENRY: And only one of us can emerge from this whole, because I do
not, I cannot, believe that a set of random scores has individual differences.
While I have never encountered a pair of honest dice, I understand that there
are such things as honest dice. If there were and one threw them many
times they would turn up scores, and I don't think that if they are honest
dice they can have individual differences. Now had you substituted—or
rather put in—one little word "true" in your statement—that is, if the
variance of a set of "true" scores is greater than zero—then you would have
individual differences. Then you see, you are dealing with true scores, and
the variance is greater than zero; you are not dealing with random numbers,
and I don't think there can be two positions on this issue. Either you, Sir,
are wrong, or I am wrong (and I might be; I was once).

BECHTOLDT: I have been wrong many times, but *this* is a definitional
problem that is right at the heart of this issue. There is no operational
definition for a true score or an error score. These ideas are based on a
conceptual formulation that is mathematically beautiful and elegant, that
leads to test theory, which in the Lord and Novick formulation leads to all
sorts of reliability notions, and on and on. Just realize that when you go
into a laboratory, you are looking at observed values; now you can use
various kinds of manipulations, including the statistical operations related
to a linear hypothesis and have those observed scores separated in an experiment into the grand mean, the row effects, the column effects, the interaction effects, and so on. What you have left at every stage is what you call
error. Error means that you either don't give a hoot about it or there isn't
anything that you can do about it. Now, these are pretty good operational
formulations of systematic and error effects in terms of statistical hypothesis.
Perfectly good! But notice that there was nothing in the term individual
difference—as I defined it (and that I can use in every situation)—that says
that individual differences have to be stable or systematic. The assumption
commonly made as a result of some of the surplus meanings in the term is
there is something magical or at least stable about individual differences.
You need two to tango; you need two observations to define a difference.
Assume there are two observations from two subjects. I have to have one
from each subject. This is where the individual comes in. You can count
the hairs on the head, measure the length of the nose, measure how well one
can wiggle his ears, or anything else. You've got two observations, one from
this particular case and one from that case. Do they fall in the same class
or not? If they fall in the same class, you have no individual difference in
that pair. If they fall in different classes you have one difference because the
two cases are now in different classes. You now have two non-null categories

with at least one case in each one. You can have a thousand in one category and one in another and you have a thousand individual differences, because the one in the one category is different from each of the thousand in the other category. All of the thousand are alike.

HOLDING: I don't know whether we are going to resolve the differences between Drs. Bechtoldt and Henry; would you like another half minute?

BECHTOLDT: No reply. We have a difference in our use of words. You may recall I started off by saying that words and the definition of words are important. When we have differences in definition of terms there is no use in talking more until we find out what the differences in the definitions are.

Theories and Research on Aggression In Relation to Motor Learning and Sports Performance

Emma McCloy Layman
Iowa Wesleyan College

The ubiquity of wars, the increase in crimes of violence, the ease with which riots flare up on college campuses and city streets in any part of the world, and the quickness of some police to wield the billy-club or pull the trigger—all these have pointed to the control of aggression as one of the major necessities of our time. They have heightened the interest in understanding the nature of aggression and in finding means for its inhibition, redirection, or harmless discharge. An understanding of aggression demands (a) that we be able to define it, (b) that we delineate its origin or antecedents, (c) that we recognize the forms which it may take, and (d) that we have knowledge concerning its relationship to other behavioral variables. Motor learning is one such variable.

The definition of aggression used by most laymen is more comprehensive but also more ambiguous than that usually accepted by the behavioral scientist. For the lay person, aggression may refer to fighting behavior, or it may refer to the act of pursuing *any* goal with initiative and vigor. These two types of behavior, of course, may not be mutually exclusive, but the existence of one does not necessarily imply the concomitance of the other. In contrast to this dual meaning of aggression in the layman's vocabulary, most psychologists and other behavioral scientists regard aggression as the initiation of an *attack,* and it is in this sense that we shall use the term in this paper.

THEORIES AND NATURE OF AGGRESSION

Following World War I, Freud voiced the theory that human aggression is instinctive—that in every individual there is a life instinct and a death instinct, with aggression being interpreted as a turning outward of the death instinct. Many of Freud's followers repudiated the idea of a death instinct, but most of the psychoanalytic group has clung to a belief in the instinctive nature of aggression, although they have accepted the evidence that aggressive *behavior* can be modified by learning. More recently the eminent ethologist, Konrad Lorenz (1966), drawing principally on observations of lower animals, reaffirmed the idea of an instinctive basis for aggression in man, insisted on the "spontaneity" of aggressive impulses, and even contended that love develops out of aggression.

In 1939 a group of Yale psychologists including Dollard and others went back to an idea found in some of Freud's early writings, and published their now classic monograph, *Frustration and Aggression,* in which they stated that aggression is the consequence of frustration and that frustration always leads to aggression. If their contention were supported by facts, it would explain the alleged universality of aggression, since there is no one who has not experienced frustration in some form.

The theories of the Yale group were not accepted uncritically by psychologists, but the frustration-aggression hypothesis did serve as the stimulus for hundreds of clinical and experimental studies of aggression which have resulted in modifications of the older theories and considerable illumination with reference to the nature and causes of aggressive behavior. Much of this research has been summarized and discussed in books by Scott (1958), Buss (1961), Berkowitz (1962), and Yates (1962), as well as in other books dealing with the psychology of war and peace. As a result of this research, most behavioral scientists have taken the point of view that, although there is a biological rudiment of animal aggression in man, the forms which human aggression takes are socially and culturally determined, with human aggressive behavior being principally learned behavior acquired by conditioning (Scott, 1968; Meerloo, 1968).

When we speak of aggression as "fighting" behavior or the act of initiating an attack, we can perhaps delineate two major types of aggression in human beings—*reactive* aggression and *instrumental* aggression.

Reactive aggression involves a goal-response which is the injury of the person or group of persons against whom the attack is directed. The person or group is perceived as the "enemy," who has been the agent of frustration, the source of some noxious stimulus, or the originator of a threat of frustration or unpleasantness of some kind. Both the perception of an enemy and the emotion of anger are involved in reactive aggression.

Instrumental aggression is attack in which the primary goal is not injury to the enemy, but the attainment of a reward. Instrumental aggression does not involve anger, and it is not a response to frustration or noxious stimuli. It should be noted that both frustration and noxious stimuli may lead to emotions other than anger and to behavior other than aggression. For example, they *could* lead to fear or anxiety, and to flight or withdrawal.

Several generalizations about aggression appear justified, whether we accept the instinct theory, learning memory, or some combined theory of the source of aggression, and whether we are speaking of reactive aggression or instrumental aggression.

(a) The tendency to engage in aggressive behavior is very nearly universal in the animal kingdom, including man. Although in lower animals it may have as its chief function the preservation of the species (Lorenz, 1966), modern technology has made it a force which threatens extinction of the human race.

(b) Whether reactive or instrumental, aggressive behavior has the same goal—the inflicting of injury on others.

(c) Aggression may be expressed actively or passively, and it may be expressed directly or indirectly, i.e., toward the perceived "enemy" or toward a substitute for the enemy. The expression of aggression toward a substitute for the enemy is referred to by behavioral psychologists as "displacement."

(d) Aggression may be destructive in its results but if appropriately directed and controlled it may contribute to constructive ends.

Aggression and Sports

Because learning is an intervening variable we cannot measure it directly but must assume that it has taken place on the basis of some measure of *performance*. Thus, if we were going to study the effects of aggression on motor learning or the effects of motor learning on aggression, our criterion of motor learning accomplished would have to be some measure of motor skill or motor performance.

The linkage between expression and performance in competitive sports has been of interest to behavioral scientists for some time. In recent years the recognition of this linkage has provided the basis for many theoretical discussions dealing with the psychodynamics of aggression and has produced a few empirical studies dealing with aggression and sports. Most of the empirical studies and theoretical formulations are only marginally or indirectly related to the psychology of motor learning. However, from research and discussions in which motor learning is not a central concern it is frequently possible to derive hypotheses concerning aggression in relation to motor performance. Hence, it seems worth while to sketch in some of the background of thinking about aggression in relation to sports and to review some of the research in this area before discussing specifically its implications from the standpoint of aggression in relation to motor learning.

Lorenz (1966) defines sport as "a specifically human form of nonhostile combat, governed by the strictest of culturally developed rules" (p. 280), and suggests that it was probably in highly ritualized but still seriously hostile fighting that sport had its origin. He indicates the chief values of sport as being two-fold—to provide a harmless outlet for the aggressive urge and to educate man to a conscious and responsible control of his own fighting behavior. Scott (1968) sees games and sports as providing important training in the control of aggression. He states that perhaps the most important kind of training involves passive inhibition—forming habits of being peaceful by bringing people together in enjoyable activities in a setting where they cannot commit destructive acts while engaged in these activities. He comments further that many games and sports have the effect of inducing situations which can easily lead to aggression but provide training which develops habits of restraint from violence in these situations, since one of the first principles in competitive sports is that the person who loses his temper is likely to lose the game, either because he loses his judgment or through violation of the rules.

Both Lorenz and Scott emphasize competitive sport as *non-hostile* aggression. This would imply that, for most participants, competitive sports involve principally instrumental aggression. That is, the player attempts to defeat his rival because of the satisfaction he will experience from proving his own competence, and because of the praise and approval he will receive, but he is not really angry at his opponent. However, we would contend that, for some athletes, sports participation involves reactive aggression. Because winning in a sports contest always involves doing some injury to another, either physically or psychologically; and because in our society people are frequently made to feel that it is wrong to hurt others except possibly in retaliation for injury received, there are some athletes who cannot force themselves to win unless they can perceive the opponent as the enemy and can become angry with him. Otherwise, their expression of aggression would generate intolerable feelings of guilt. Sometimes coaches try to cause the team members to become angry with the opponents so that they will make a greater effort to win.

Studies of the physiology of the emotions indicate that intense emotion serves to energize the organism for primitive emergency response. Thus, the angry individual may display greater endurance, strength, and speed than when he is not angry. However, anger is difficult to control and easily develops into disorganized rage, with the result that the quality of performance suffers. Strong emotion of any kind results in impairment of finer and more complex coordinations as well as in impairment of judgment, so the extremely angry tennis player, baseball pitcher, or boxer frequently displays an inferior performance. The situation for the player who is only mildly angry appears to be different, with mild anger serving as a motivator for more intense effort and apparently not serving as a hindrance to effective performance. All of this would imply that, when aggression in sports is instrumental aggression and the player is not uncomfortable with aggressive impulses when expressed in a ritualized form, there should be enhancement of motor performance, but when it is reactive aggression involving extreme anger, the quality of performance should suffer.

In discussing aggression in relation to sports and motor performance, there are three topics I would like to touch on. These are sports competition as frustration, the catharsis hypothesis, and the role of anxiety, feelings of guilt, and self-concept as intervening variables.

Competition as Frustration

Let us first look at competition in relation to frustration and aggression.

What is competition? According to Berkowitz (1962, p. 307), competition consists of "(a) two or more units . . . engaged in pursuing the same rewards, with (b) these rewards so defined that if they are attained by any one unit, there are fewer rewards for the other units in the situation." Although, as we have said, to a great extent the aggression expressed in competitive sports is instrumental aggression, in a sense competition must also be regarded as a frustration. It is obviously a frustration for the loser, who may be angry at having lost, but still further frustrated by the fact that he is supposed to be a good sport and conceal his anger. But it is a frustration also for the one who wins in the end, for the opponent is constantly trying to block him in attaining his goal, and this serves as an instigation to further aggression. We might assume that aggression would be at a maximum when two opposing individuals or teams are quite evenly matched, because the amount of frustration would be at a maximum, and the prospect of rewards for fighting well and winning are also present. When two opponents are very unevenly matched there may not be much aggression, for the stronger opponent will experience little frustration and the weaker opponent has little prospect of a reward at the end of the match.

Many athletes will go into a competitive situation with anger and resentment engendered by frustrations external to the competitive situation itself. For example, team members may be frustrated by the necessity of keeping training rules, or by the fact that the time which they must spend in practice is so extensive that they cannot do other things they would like to do. In such instances, some of the anger generated by these frustrations conceivably may be displaced to the opponent in the sports situation.

Two social factors should be mentioned in connection with expression of aggression in competitive team sports. One is the tendency for persons to be more aggressive toward the "out group" than toward members of the "in group." The other team is perceived as the out group, and even when it is not a real threat there may be hostile feelings that are readily expressed in aggression.

The second social factor we should note is the tendency for members of a group to imitate what other group members are doing. This means that aggressive behavior on the part of some group members, particularly if they are leaders, serves as an instigation to aggression for other group members, who copy the aggressive behavior of their team-mates.

One would expect that aggression would be strong in team competition in which there is a strong sense of group identity, in which there is a good relation among team members and a keen interest in the team by its supporters, who gives gratifying praise and commendation when the team is successful. In addition, if the first few games of the season are relatively easy wins, but later ones very close wins, the combination of instrumental aggression, group-induced aggression and reactive aggression would seem to result in the greatest total aggression within the limits of the rules and the bounds of sportsmanship.

With a team characterized by low cohesiveness, and in a situation where there is little spectator interest, both the social instigation to aggressive behavior against the opponent and the reward for winning are very slight. If, in addition, the team is weak and never wins, there can be no reward at all for winning. But wouldn't there be aggression generated by frustration? Actually, if a team never wins, and really doesn't expect to win, it is doubtful if winning is a real goal, and therefore there actually is little frustration, so both instrumental and reactive aggression should be low.

These points, of course, are all relevant for the coach who wants to have a successful team, for a fighting spirit expressed in action is synonymous with putting forth optimal effort in sports competition. However, there is not always a positive relation between effort and performance in a competitive situation. Several studies have shown that, regardless of the kind of activity involved, competition is a very powerful incentive to learning, with both children and adults working harder and more effectively when competing than when learning in a non-competitive setting, providing that each competitor has a reasonable chance of winning (Layman, 1960). Some studies show, however, that increased competition may increase output but decrease quality (Layman, 1960). Also, although competition is a strong incentive for learning all through the school years, there are wide individual differences in the responsiveness of students to competition. Some put forth great effort to excel, some remain fairly indifferent to competition, and others are so frustrated or threatened by it that learning is blocked entirely. These individual differences are undoubtedly related to differences in ability, but they may relate also to the ease with which anger is mobilized, and to stress tolerance.

Although not involving competition, a study by Waterhouse and Child (1953) on frustration and the quality of performance may be relevant to the variations in reactions to competitive frustration. These authors hypothesized that frustration will produce a decrease in the equality of ongoing performance to the extent that the frustration evokes other responses which interfere with ongoing performance. They found that students with a low frustration tolerance did relatively poorly in intellectual and motor tests when frustrated in their desire to perceive themselves as doing well, and those with high frustration tolerance did better under conditions of frustration than when not frustrated. The implications of this study for aggression are not entirely clear, however, since the criterion for low frustration tolerance was the tendency to engage in disruptive behavior when frustration and aggression was not always involved.

Catharsis Hypothesis

Prominent in psychoanalytic writings on aggression and suggested also by Dollard and his four co-authors (1939) is the catharsis hypothesis in relation to aggression. According to this hypothesis, the performance of an aggressive act releases pent-up aggressive energy, reduces tension, decreases the remaining instigation to aggression, and makes the individual feel better. Presumably it would therefore contribute to emotional health.

Along with the catharsis hypothesis Dollard and co-workers recognized the principle of displacement—the fact that, when direct expression of aggression toward the frustrating agent is inhibited by fear of punishment or feelings of guilt, both the *object* of the aggression and the *form* of the aggression may change. Combining the principle of displacement with the catharis hypothesis, the Yale psychologists postulated that there is an inverse relationship between the tendency of different forms of aggression to occur. As one form is inhibited, others are strengthened; when one form occurs, others are weakened.

Controlled studies indicate that when aggression occurs in the presence of anger there *is* a decrease in the level of anger and a decrease in the tendency to aggress for a short period. Also, unless the individual has feelings of guilt because of the aggressive act, there will be a reduction of tension and improved feeling of well-being. However, when aggression occurs in the absence of anger, there is an *increase* in the tendency to aggress, unless the tendency to aggress is weakened by guilt or anxiety. Thus, reactive aggression in general supports the catharsis hypothesis but instrumental aggression does not.

What is the relevance of this for sports? Lemkau (1952) expresses doubt that athletics are really an outlet for aggressive impulses because the controls involved in game rules make it possible for the participant to really express himself freely. Also, we might note that the unwritten rules of sportsmanship call on the individual to shake hands with his opponent and to congratulate the winner. Yet at the same time athletes are told by the coach to "get out there and fight" and the cheering fans shout, "Kill him," "Murder them," "Tear into them," "Fight, fight, fight." Probably in the beginning of an athletic competition most of the players are not angry, so any aggression they might express would be instrumental aggression. If they play vigorously there will be a discharge of energy through activity and at the end of the game the players should be fatigued and therefore not eager to repeat the performance immediately. But if the aggression has brought the reward of winning the game and the desired social approval for fighting hard, after a short rest the players will be ready for a more aggressive attack the next time. If the result of the aggressive behavior has been one of failure to win and failure to receive approval, there will be no reinforcement of the aggression and the team members will perhaps not fight as hard the next time, unless they become angry.

But it is not as simple as this. Some athletes try to make themselves aggressive by deliberately looking on the opponent as the enemy, so that they can be angry at him. Probably others respond to the suggestions of the coach and fans and work up at least mildly angry feelings. Some will be angry because of a tongue-lashing by the coach or for some other reason, and can readily displace this anger onto the opponent. Still others will become angry when fouled against, hit by an opponent, or outplayed in the game. In the average athletic contest there are many frustrations, and the most usual reactions to frustration are anger and aggression. Thus, for many players there will be opportunities for discharge of angry aggression even with the restrictions imposed by the rules, although this would probably be more possible in some sports than in others.

Despite Lemkau's reservations about the applicability of the catharsis theory in the field of sports, and the apparent complexity of the situation, some psychoanalytically-oriented psychiatrists contend that competitive sports do provide a satisfactory social outlet for the aggressive drive.

Several studies have attempted to test the catharsis hypothesis in an athletic situation.

Stone (1950) administered the TAT to college varsity football players before and after scrimmage and after the football season, and their responses were compared with the stories told by matched controls. There was no difference between the two groups in fantasy aggression before or after scrimmage, and no significant change in aggression resulting from scrimmage, but the football players showed less aggression at the end of the season. The fantasy aggression that the football players did display tended to be of a "projective" nature. That is, the hostility was attributed to an impersonal source. Stone argued that this projection was due to the football players' anxiety and guilt about aggresssion. Thus there is some question as to whether the reduction in aggression at the end of the season was due to the cathartic discharge of aggressive impulses or to feelings of guilt when positive reinforcement no longer occurred.

Johnson and Hutton (1955) reported a study in which the House-Tree-Person test was administered to eight varsity wrestlers before the wrestling season had begun, four to five hours before the first intercollegiate match of the season, and the morning after the competition. Among other findings it was reported that there were increased aggressive feelings before the match, and considerably less aggression after the match. Of interest was the fact that the heightened aggression before the match tended to be of the intrapunitive sort, suggesting possible feelings of guilt in connection with the anticipated aggressive activity. The decline in aggression following the match, however, did not seem to support the catharsis hypothesis.

In a subsequent study by Husman (1955) the Rosenzweig P-F study, several TAT cards, and a sequence completion test were administered at intervals in the competitive season to four groups: 9 boxers, 8 wrestlers, 9 cross country runners (non-combative controls), and 7 control subjects. The TAT showed the boxers to have significantly less fantasy aggression than the other groups, and the P-F study showed that the boxers' aggression tended to be more intrapunitive than was true for the other groups, with the cross country runners being extrapunitive, suggesting guilt and anxiety associated with the more aggressive sport of boxing. This difference was especially pronounced in tests given less than two days after a boxing match. Trends in the data which were not significant indicated that a season of participation tended to increase the aggression of the participants, as measured by the

TAT, while a season of participation tended to lower the Rosenzweig P-F scoring factors of extrapunitiveness, intrapunitiveness, and super-ego. Husman interpreted the findings as supporting both the catharsis and circular theories of aggression.

Any research performed in "real-life" situations is likely to be difficult to interpret because of the impossibility of avoiding contamination. In these studies there is the likelihood that both instrumental and reactive aggression entered into the picture and that some of the reduction in aggression was related to guilt and anxiety rather than representing a "draining off" of pent-up energy. There seems to be little support, then, for the idea that sports provide a catharsis, and so reduce the instigation to aggression. We tend to agree with Berkowitz, who says, "Most nondisturbed persons do *not* seem to have either (a) weaker aggressive inclinations or (b) less concern about their hostile tendencies after engaging in socially sanctioned aggressive sports. If hostile behaviors are less apparent following such competitive activities . . . these actions may have been inhibited by game-induced guilt or anxiety" (1962, p. 207).

The question concerning the catharsis hypothesis in relation to sports participation would seem to have more relevance to the role of sports participation in contributing to emotional health than to aggression in relation to motor learning, except insofar as the expression of aggression may result in a decreased instigation to aggression because of the inhibiting effect of anxiety and feelings of guilt mobilized by the aggressive act.

Feelings of Guilt, Anxiety, and Self-Concept as Intervening Variables

Numerous studies have demonstrated an inverse relationship between anxiety and quality of motor performance, including performance in both athletic and non-athletic types of activities (see Nelson and Langer, 1963; Nelson and Langer, 1965; Cofer and Appley, 1965; Langer, 1966; Deese, 1958). One common source of anxiety is a feeling of guilt about hostility and aggressive acts or impulses. We have considerable evidence that such feelings are related to impairment of motor learning and performance.

A number of years ago Bruno Bettelheim, Director of the Sonia Shankman Orthogenic School for emotionally disturbed children at the University of Chicago, wrote a book called *Love is not Enough*. In this book he makes the statement that he has never seen a child with a severe emotional disturbance who did not also have problems in the area of motor incoordination. He quotes case material to show how one child is unable to learn to throw a ball because he is afraid that if he learns, his aggressions will get the better of him and he will throw the ball at someone whom he wishes to hurt. Another child is afraid to develop competencies of any kind because he fears that if he becomes skillful he will be held responsible and will be punished for an aggressive act committed years ago by accident.

Arnold Beisser (1967), a psychiatrist and former ranking tennis player, has specialized in the psychiatric treatment of champion athletes, and is especially interested in tennis players with emotional problems. He notes that many athletes are unable to be sufficiently aggressive to let themselves win unless they can cast the opponent in the role of the villain. That is, they can tolerate reactive aggression in themselves, but cannot force themselves to be aggressive when the opponents are perceived as good fellows who have done them no harm. Under the latter circumstances they play poorly and manage to lose in competitive play, although the reasons for this are not usually consciously grasped.

The problem of guilt and aggression in sports has been discussed by Johnson (1965), who utilized hypnosis for exploring the feelings, conflicts, and experiences of athletes with problems in sports performance relating to feelings of guilt about aggression. Their problems with aggression manifested themselves in the sports situation in various ways—inability to *feel* aggressive, dislike for aggressive sports, having to whip up feelings of rage before and during games, and losing contests which could have been won had the opponents not been perceived as friendly. In each instance feelings of guilt about aggression were found to be associated with repressed experience in which aggression had resulted in harm to someone.

Anxiety and feelings of guilt have been mentioned as possible intervening variables involved in the relationship between aggression and motor performance. Another such variable may be the self-concept. Conceivably, a person with poor *motor* control might picture himself as having poor *emotional* control, with consequent problems in control of aggression. Conversely, a person with poor emotional control might perceive himself as uncontrolled in general, with consequent poor motor control. Relevant to this are observations of brain-damaged children and Warren Johnson's work in the Physical Developmental Clinic at the University of Maryland, in progress since 1957.

Psychiatrists and clinical psychologists working with brain-damaged children have listed among the most common symptoms observed the existence of motor incoordination and difficulties with impulse control—especially control of aggressive impulses (Doll, 1951; Strauss and Lehtinen, 1947; Strauss and Kephart, 1955). They have noted also that brain-damaged children and adolescents are frequently quite anxious about their problems with control of aggressive impulses. It has sometimes been suggested that the problems with motor control may have contributed to the development of a self-concept in which the individual sees himself as an individual without self-control, and that the problems with impulse control may be in part an expression in action of the self-concept stemming from perceptual-motor difficulties. If this were the case, we would anticipate that when a program of physical activities has resulted in improved motor coordination, it would result also in a changed self-concept and a lessening of problems relating to the control of aggressive impulses. The work of Johnson and others, to be described later, has shown that, in fact, this is what happens when children with a variety of problems are treated with an individualized program designed to improve motor coordination.

Aggression and Motor Learning

In considering the problem of relations between aggression and motor learning, we are faced with the question of how we are going to assess aggression, and what criteria of motor performance we are going to use as evidence that motor learning has taken place. When we review the literature relevant to the relationships between these two variables, we find that there are very few studies in which a clear-cut relationship can be demonstrated, because so frequently we have to *infer* that one variable not *called* aggression actually is a measure of aggression, or that another variable not called motor performance or motor skill actually does measure this variable. In fairness to the investigators, we should say that, in most studies the understanding of aggression in relation to learning is not one of the purposes of the research, but whenever we are just beginning the exploration of a topic we seek for hypotheses in studies of only marginal significance as well as seeking for hypotheses and conclusions to be derived from studies dealing directly with the issues involved.

In the literature on personality in relation to exercise and sports we find aggression as a personality trait revealed by several projective techniques, including the Rorschach test, Thematic Apperception Test, Sentence Completion Test, House-Tree-Person Test, and the Rosenzweig Picture-Frustration Study, as well as by the Aggression Scale of the Edwards Personal Preference Inventory. With the exception of the Edwards test, these all lend themselves to analysis in terms of the strength of the instigation to aggression, ease of arousal, the direction of expression (extrapunitive versus intrapunitive), and the objects toward which aggression is expressed. But they do not always differentiate between indications of hostile feelings and aggressive actions. In other studies we find personality assessed by instruments such as the MMPI, the Cattell 16 PF Questionnaire, the California Personality Inventory, and the California F-Scale. None of these list aggression as a specific dimension being tested, but in some instances the results have been interpreted as having certain implications about aggression in relation to motor performance.

In assessing motor performance, some studies have used objective measures of achievement, such as the tests involved in a Physical Efficiency Profile, or records of speed in a competitive swimming meet. Others have used achievement indices based on an Extra-curricular Information Form, or ratings by coaches. Some have based assessment of achievement on selection for an Olympic or varsity team versus non-selection, or attainment of championship status versus non-attainment. In other studies participants have been compared with non-participants and in these studies it is sometimes assumed that a participant in a sport is likely to have a higher skill level in that sport than is a non-participant. Participants in different sports, also, have been compared on different personality dimensions.

Johnson and Fretz (1966) report the results of preclinic and postclinic evaluations of 79 children enrolled in a summer program at the Children's Physical Developmental Clinic at the University of Maryland. These children had a variety of disorders ranging from brain injury, mental retardation, and emotional-social disturbances to speech, vision, and orthopedic disorders. The program of the clinic included individualized, systematic, enjoyable neuromotor-perceptual training in a gymnasium and swimming pool setting. The testing program included tests of many aspects of performance and different personality variables. Of particular interest to our present concern were the results with reference to motor performance, frustration tolerance, and aggression. Motor skills were measured with a mirror-drawing technique in which the child was asked to trace a diamond and a star reflected in a mirror. Frustration tolerance was measured by placing the child in a "high-card-wins-an M & M" game in which the dealer palmed and used high cards, and the dealer could conspicuously eat and enjoy his winnings whereas the child was told that as soon as he ate one M & M the game would stop. The child's score equaled the number of seconds he endured up to 5 minutes. Direction of expression of aggression was derived from the Rosenzweig Picture-Frustration Test, on which scoring was in terms of extrapunitive (aggression directed outward), intropunitive (aggression directed upon self), and impunitive (no aggression shown). Scores were computed also for obstacle-dominance (emphasis on the barrier causing the frustration), ego-defense, and need-persistence (emphasis on the solution of the problem). The results showed improved motor performance, and an improvement in frustration tolerance for most of those retested (those who had endured the entire five minutes in pretesting were not retested for frustration-tolerance). Changes in aggression were from extrapunitiveness to intropunitiveness to impunitiveness, and from need-persistence to obstacle-dominated. The implications here from the standpoint of motor learning suggest that a motor learning experience results in less need to express aggression because of greater frustration tolerance, and to the use of aggressive energy for problem solving rather than engaging in non-productive whining.

Dowell, Badgett, and Chevrette (1968) report on a study relating motor skills achievement to authoritarian dimensions as measured by the F-Scale. Several of these dimensions are related to aggression. The subjects were 574 male university freshmen. All were given the Texas A. & M. Physical Fitness Test and were assigned athletic achievement indices and non-athletic achievement indices based on information obtained on the Extra-curricular Information Form. All were given the California "Fascism" Scale. Correlations computed between F-scale scores and other variables showed no significant relations between F-scale scores and physical fitness nor any significant relation between authoritarianism and non-athletic achievement. A significant relation was found between athletic achievement and the following authoritarian dimensions: authoritarian aggression (.11), authoritarian submission (.12), anti-intraception (.12), conventionalism (.10), power and "toughness" (.11), projectivity (.12), and superstition and stereotypy (.14). Although these correlation coefficients are positive and are statistically significant, they are quite low, and no very impressive relationship between aggression and athletic achievement is suggested.

We have already mentioned Langer's study (1966) in which he explored football performance in relation to anxiety. In this study he also studied football performance in relation to personality as measured by the Cattell 16 PF test, with football performance being based on coaches' ratings after each game. The subjects included 55 varsity football players at a state university. Although the Cattell 16 PF does not include a factor identified as "aggressiveness," the author identified a variable which he called "hardnosed"—a term often used by coaches to describe the player characterized by high aggressiveness, self-assurance, and ability to respond to stress in a controlled manner, without disruption of performance by the effects of anxiety. The results of this study, then, suggest that high aggressiveness is associated with successful performance in football in players whose anxiety is at a low level.

Kroll (1967) studied 94 amateur and collegiate wrestlers, using the Cattell 16 PF test. Personality profiles were studied across different levels of achievement in wrestling, with members of the United States Olympic team being rated "superior," varsity wrestlers who had won at least 60 percent of their matches during the season being rated "excellent," and less successful wrestlers on the college teams being designated as "average." The personality profiles showed no significant differences between groups at different athletic achievement levels, but the group as a whole differed from the norms on a factor indicating tough-mindedness, self-reliance, and masculinity. Aggression is quite prominent in this factor. Although this study does not demonstrate differences in aggression related to differences in quality of performance, this may be due to the fact that even those rated as "average" were good enough to make the varsity team, and there is some suggestion that these wrestlers as a group are individuals who are fairly comfortable with the expression of aggression, despite Husman's (1955) finding that intrapunitive aggression in wrestlers was relatively high.

Brown (1958) compared 79 wrestlers from three high school teams with a representative sample of 25 non-athletics from one of these schools. Based upon coaches' ratings, wrestlers were divided into high or low competitive-aggressiveness. When compared on the Edwards' Personal Preference Schedule, the high rated wrestlers were found to be significantly higher than the low-rated wrestlers on the aggression variable of the test.

Merriman (1960) evaluated the motor ability of 808 high school boys, using the JCR test, and classified the subjects into upper and lower motor-ability groups, athletes and non-athletes, and participants in team sports, individual sports, and team-individual sports. The various groups were compared on the different scales of the California Personality Inventory. The upper motor-ability group scored significantly higher than the lower motor-ability group on measures of ascendancy, poise, self-assurance, and on measures of interest modes. Few significant differences were found when athletes and non-athletes were matched on motor ability, and few significant differences were found between those competing in team and individual sports. In this study, no mention is made of aggression, but the trait of "ascendance" (sometimes called "dominance") may be related to aggressiveness.

Booth (1958) studied 145 non-athletes and 141 athletes in a single college, comparing them on the MMPI. Among other findings, he reported varsity athletes to have significantly lower scores in anxiety than did freshman athletes, upperclass non-athletes, and freshman non-athletes. He also found that varsity athletes and upperclass non-athletes scored higher in "dominance" than did the freshmen, and that varsity athletes participating in team sports had lower scores on "depression" (intrapunitive aggression) than those participating in individual sports.

Johnson, Hutton, and Johnson (1954) reported a study of twelve assorted contact and non-contact sports athletes of All-American or national champion caliber, with the athletes being evaluated on the Rorschach and House-Tree-Person Projective tests. They concluded that champion college athletes showed relatively extreme aggressiveness, a freedom from great emotional inhibition, high generalized anxiety, high level of intellectual aspiration, and feelings of exceptional self-assurance.

In another study LaPlace (1954) made a comparison between major league and minor league baseball players by means of the MMPI. Again the exceptional performers were characterized by high "drive" (expressed as ambitiousness and aggressiveness), self-discipline, initiative, and a tendency to worry.

There is some discrepancy between the fact that motor performance and anxiety usually have a negative relationship and the relatively high anxiety level of champion athletes. With the level of aggression in the champions being relatively high, it is possible that in these groups the anxiety relates to factors other than aggression.

Summary and Conclusions

A review of theories of aggression and consideration of the research on aggression in relation to sports and other types of motor activity makes it clear that there are many more questions than answers available about aggression in relation to motor learning. However, we can offer a few tentative conclusions or hypotheses that seem supported by everyday observations, clinical evidence, or systematic research.

(1) Human aggression is learned behavior, but is easily mobilized either by frustration or by positive reinforcement. Both frustration and positive

reinforcement are involved in competitive sports.

(2) In competitive sports, controlled expression of aggression is usually associated with effective performance.

(3) Learning experiences involving positive reinforcement of sportsmanlike behavior and fair play are basic to the learning of controlled expression of aggression in competitive sports.

(4) Uncontrolled aggression makes for lack of control and inefficiency in motor performance.

(5) For individuals with no serious conflicts relating to aggression, instrumental aggression is associated with superior motor performance, as is reactive aggression involving only a mild or moderate degree of anger; reactive aggression involving rage or extreme anger is more likely to result in poor motor coordination or uncontrolled behavior.

(6) There is a wide range of individual differences in frustration tolerance and in ability to maintain motor control when under stress involving anger. For some persons a given degree of frustration and/or anger would enhance performance whereas for others it would impair the quality of performance.

(7) For some athletes, being rewarded for attacking others arouses such intense feelings of guilt that motor performance suffers under conditions of instrumental aggression.

(8) Whether instrumental aggression or reactive aggression is more effective in enhancing motor performance in competitive sports depends upon whether or not the individual has easily mobilized anxiety and feelings of guilt centering on aggression. For the person who is uncomfortable with aggression, effective performance is possible only if the individual can perceive the opponent as a "villain" and work up feelings of anger toward him.

(9) Poor motor control may contribute to the development of a self-concept in which the individual sees himself as one who cannot control his impulses, and this may find expression in uncontrolled aggression. With improvement in motor control there may be a change in self-concept, with consequent improvement in control of aggressive impulses.

(10) Improvement of motor coordination results in greater frustration tolerance and decreased reactive aggression expressed in extrapunitive behavior.

Need for Research

In closing, I would like to say a few words about needed research. As has frequently been pointed out, research on aggression in real-life situations involving sports is hard to carry out, because of the difficulty in maintaining adequate controls and the difficulty in differentiating between hostile feelings and the tendency to express these feelings in action, as well as the fact that coaches and players are reluctant to have anything done that would interfere with the game. Nevertheless, it would be possible to plan research more directly relevant to aggression in relation to motor learning than most of the studies reported in the literature. In studies where aggression as a personality characteristic is to be considered as the independent variable and motor performance resulting from learning as the dependent variable, it is suggested that the kind of aggression being studied be carefully defined and an instrument such as the Rosenzweig P-F study, the TAT, or the Rorschach test be used for assessing aggression rather than a personality questionnaire such as the MMPI or 16 PF test; and that objective measures of achievement be used to assess the results of motor learning.

In attempting to answer questions about the relationship between aggression and motor learning, it is necessary to check the influence of many variables, such as the nature and direction of aggression, the nature and complexity of the motor skills, the age, sex, stress tolerance, and emotional health of the subjects, and the nature of the frustrating or reinforcing agent. A great deal of research will have to be completed before we can offer any conclusions about aggression and motor learning that are more than hunches or educated guesses. But there are many challenging and fascinating problems to be explored by the psychologist as well as by the physical educator interested in this area, which cuts across the legitimate concerns of both disciplines.

REFERENCES

Beisser, A. *The madness of sport.* New York: Appleton-Century-Croft, 1967.

Berkowitz, L. *Aggression: A Social-Psychological analysis.* New York: McGraw-Hill, 1962.

Bettelheim, B. *Love is not enough.* Glencoe, Ill.: Free Press, 1950.

Booth, E. G., Jr. Personality traits of athletes as measured by the MMPI. *Research Quarterly,* 1958, *29,* 127-138.

Brown, E. A. *Personality characteristics of wrestlers.* Unpublished master's thesis, University of Minnesota, 1958.

Buss, A. H. *The psychology of aggression.* New York: Wiley, 1961.

Cofer, C. N., & Appley, M. H. *Motivation: theory and research.* New York: Wiley, 1965.

Deese, J. *The psychology of learning.* New York: McGraw-Hill, 1958.

Doll, E. A. Neurophrenia. *American Journal of Psychiatry.* 1951, *108,* 5-53.

Dollard, J. and Others. *Frustration and aggression.* New Haven: Yale University Press, 1939.

Dowell, L., Badgett, J., & Chrevrette, J. Motor skills achievement and authoritarian dimensions. *Perceptual and Motor Skills,* 1968, *27.* 469-470.

Husman, B. F. Aggression in boxers and wrestlers as measured by projective techniques. *Research Quarterly,* 1955, *26,* 421-425.

Johnson, W. R. The problem of aggression and guilt in sports. Paper presented before the 1st International Congress of Sport Psychology, Rome, Italy, April, 1965 (mimeographed).

Johnson, W. R., & Fretz, B. R. Changes in measures of neuromotor perceptual organization and psychosocial adjustment after a children's physical development program. College Park: University of Maryland, 1966 (mimeographed).

Johnson, W. R., & Hutton, D. C. Effects of a combative sport upon personality dynamics as measured by a projective test. Research Quarterly, 1955, *26,* 49-53.

Johnson, W. R., Hutton, D. C., & Johnson, G. B., Jr. Personality traits of some champion athletes as measured by two projective tests: Rorschach and H-T-P. *Research Quarterly,* 1954, *25,* 484-485.

Kroll, W. Sixteen Personality Factor profiles of collegiate wrestlers. *Research Quarterly.* 1967. *38,* 49-57.

Langer, P. Varsity football performance. *Perceptual and Motor Skills* 1966, *23,* 1191-1199.

LaPlace, J. P. Personality and its relationship to success in professional baseball. *Research Quarterly,* 1954, *25,* 313-319.

Layman, E. M. Contributions of exercise and sports to mental health and social adjustment. In W. R. Johnson (Ed.). *Science and medicine of exercise and sport.* New York: Harper, 1960, Chap. 29.

Lemkau, P. V., quotation in *Desirable athletic competition for children.* Washington, D. C.: American Association for Health, Physical Education and Recreation, 1952.

Lorenz, K. *On aggression.* New York: Harcourt, Brace & World, 1966.

Meerloo, J. A. Human violence versus animal aggression. *Psychoanalytic Review,* 1968, *55,* 37-56.

Merriman, J. B. Relationship of personality traits to motor ability. *Research Quarterly,* 1960, *31,* 163-173.

Nelson, D. O., & Langer, P. Getting to really know your players. *Athletic Journal.* 1963, *39,* 88-93.

Nelson, D. O. & Langer, P. Comments on the athlete's playing performance and his anxiety. *Coaching Athletics,* 1965, *28,* 12-23.

Newman, E. N. Personality traits of faster and slower competitive swimmers. *Research Quarterly,* 1968, *39,* 1049-1053.

Scott, J. P. *Aggression.* Chicago: University of Chicago Press, 1958.

Scott, J. P. Sport and aggression. Paper presented before the 2nd International Congress of Sport Psychology, Washington, D. C. October, 1968.

Stone, A. The catharsis theory of aggression. *Laboratory Bulletin.* Laboratory of Social Relations, 1950, *2* 9-13.

Strauss, A. A., & Kephart, N. C. *Psychopathology and education of the brain-injured child.* New York: Grune & Stratton, 1955.

Strauss, A. A. & Lehtinen, L. E. *Psychopathology and education of the brain-injured child.* New York: Grune & Stratton, 1947.

Waterhouse, I. K., & Child, I. L. Frustration and quality of performance. Journal of Personality, 1953, *21,* 298-311.

Yates, A. J. *Frustration and conflict.* New York: Wiley, 1962.

CRITIQUE OF LAYMAN'S PAPER
by Walter Kroll

Any reaction to Mrs. Layman's paper must be conditioned by a very important consideration: the reaction must not reveal undesirable aggressive intentions even if such behavior serves cathartic purposes. Reactive aggression on the part of Mrs. Layman could be disastrous since she is scheduled to review my paper later this afternoon. Mrs. Layman has stated, however, that "there are many more questions than answers available about aggression in motor learning" and it seems a safe strategy to raise a few more questions and question a few answers in the area of aggression and motor performance.

First of all, I want to call attention to a point I will later treat in my own paper. The research available represents a theme which emphasizes psychiatric insight and confirmation of general theories of aggression rather than a research strategy which searches for illumination of positive forces in athletic personality and motor learning fields. Thus, the Johnson and Hutton (1955) study "did not seem to support the catharsis hypothesis" in regard to an observed decline in aggression. Husman (1955) "interpreted the findings as supporting both the catharsis and circular theories of aggression." I do not disavow the need to do research which seeks to show the congruency of general theories of aggression with problems in motor learning and sports performance. The amount and quality of such research in athletics is such to cause us all enough embarrassment and frustration to generate high instrumental aggression. But such efforts merely transfer theory and serve chiefly to cross-validate or refute the validity of general theory using athletics as another sample set. Such studies do not directly broaden the prospects of a satisfactory knowledge structure for athletics per se.

Let me illustrate my point by asking a few questions which might elicit answers more pertinent to athletic work rather than general theory. Instead of attempts to enhance general theory concerning aggression, a more specific attack would involve the issue of which kind of aggression athletes display and whether one kind or another is better than the other for achievement of objectives. What kind of aggressive intent is found in different sports, at different age levels, and at different quality levels of competitive talent? And lastly, a question which I believe is of extreme importance, do athletes perceive aggression in the manner in which it is usually defined and studied? Answers to these kinds of questions would then need to be considered in the light of sportsmanship ideals and the achievement of educational goals.

An interesting paradox arises if competitive sports really do provide a release or "harmless outlet for aggressive urges" as forwarded by the catharsis hypothesis for aggression. Using competitive sport as a vehicle for venting pent-up aggression may be appropriate in a therapeutic setting, but would it be acceptable in an educational environment? Reactive aggression with its constructs of attacking a person, perception of an enemy, and emotion of anger is antagonistic to sportsmanship ideals and educational objectives. Even if "reactive aggression involving only a mild or moderate degree of anger" could be "associated with superior motor performance," it might still be debated whether encouragement of reactive aggression was sound in an educational sense. Compounding the dilemma is the possibility that the catharsis hypothesis is wrong while Berkowitz (1969) is right in his contention that aggressive behavior is learned and can be reinforced. If so, then the encouragement of aggression in competitive sport would seem contraindicated in any setting, therapeutic, recreational, or educational.

Now such questions, I contend, are more legitimate and more important questions to be asked concerning aggression and motor performance because they contribute to knowledge in the athletic domain first and to general theory second. Such a research strategy, moreover, might even contribute more to general theory than presumable direct research efforts at verifying general theory in athletics. Aggression in competitive sport situations might just reveal data of importance to general theory which are not attainable in contrived laboratory experiments.

There would seem to be several situations in athletics, for example, in which reactive aggression and extreme anger may be beneficial to performance. In competitive sports where control is important—say golf or bowling —anger may be detrimental to performance, but in other sports the coach welcomes the display of anger. Defensive lineman, for instance, seem to charge the quarterback with more gusto if their own quarterback was "unnecessarily" injured in the previous series of downs. One or two poor calls by an official can infuriate a whole team and result in improved performance. One could argue that such examples of reactive aggression were really accompanied by only mild anger. Real life experiences in such situations would seem to indicate that such anger was extreme but controlled and directed effectively.

Although not mentioned in Mrs. Layman's paper, the perceived aggressive intent of the opponent is also a factor in the initiation of aggression. As Epstein and Taylor (1967) have shown, "perception of the intent of the aggressor is a more potent instigator to aggression than frustration per se." The subjects used in this study, of course, were male undergraduates enrolled in an introductory psychology class and one cannot be sure athletes would exhibit similar aggressive reactions. Interestingly enough, opponents who assumed the role of unmitigating aggressors (always delivered the strongest electrical shock to the opponent) were viewed by subjects in a negative manner as far as intelligence, sociability, and adjustment. The unmitigating aggressors who won, however, were also considered strong, dominant, a leader, competitive, and independent by their defeated opponents. Once again we can see the likelihood of a difficult paradox. If the development of dominance, leadership, competitiveness, and independence is desirable in an educational sense, how does one cope with the concomitant influence of perceived maladjustment, lesser intelligence, and lack of sociability?

This reaction to Mrs. Layman's paper, unfortunately, represents little more than speculation by extrapolation with a good dose of subjective opinion. Until more evidence is available concerning aggression and sport we must agree with Mrs. Layman's observation that "there are many more questions than answers available." When such evidence is supplied, furthermore, I predict there will be even more confusion. The general theory developed in some degree through careful observation of the Greylag Goose (Lorenz), the lemurs of Madagascar, herring gull colonies, and gibbons (Ardrey), or the hairy ape (Morris) will not fit the above normal human behavioral situation represented by competitive athletics.

REFERENCES

Berkowitz, L. *Aggression: A Social-Psychological Analysis.* New York: McGraw-Hill, 1962.

Epstein, Seymour and Taylor. Stuart P. Instigation to aggression as a function of degree of defeat and perceived aggressive intent of the opponent. *Journal of Personality* 1967, *35*, 265-289.

Husman, B. F. Aggression in boxers and wrestlers as measured by projective techniques. *Research Quarterly*, 1955, *26*, 421-425.

Johnson, W. R. & Hutton, D. C. Effects of a combative sport upon personality dynamics as measured by a projective test. *Research Quarterly*, 1955, *26*, 49-53.

LAYMAN'S REPLY TO
Kroll's Critique

SIMON: Thank you Professor Kroll. I would like to ask Professor Layman if she would care to respond to anything Professor Kroll has said and also if she would like to entertain questions from the floor.

LAYMAN: Well, I agree with what Professor Kroll has said and I appreciate his calling my attention to the Epstein and Taylor study which I will certainly look into. But what he said is right, that whether or not one is giving a paper on this subject or is criticizing a paper on this subject because there is really so very little in the way of specific concrete evidence and so much of the research has been done on lower animals rather than on human beings that we are always in a highly speculative realm. This is one area in which it is extremely difficult to do very well controlled research because of the difficulty of maintaining adequate controls. And the difficulty of differentiating between hostile feelings and aggressive behavior, and so far our measures don't really distinguish between those two very well. I think that in a decent approach to this problem of aggression in relating to motor learning, probably what we have to do is to first of all decide on what our criterion of learning is going to be and to give individuals a learning experience in which we do our assessment of learning on a before and after basis and then experimentally produce a situation in which there is instigation to aggression. In which we deliberately make people angry or in the case of instrumental aggression in which we supply a situation in which we reward them for aggressive behavior. So far we have no studies of this type and they would be very tricky to carry out. I think we have a need for real experimental work in this area. Are there any questions?

DISCUSSION

UNKNOWN PERSON: I would like to thank you for a very earthy presentation and the other thing is that I would like to ask you a question as a coach. Assuming that the team does perceive the opponent as the enemy, and also assuming that their winning is their goal and assuming that this goal is not accomplished; how do we as a coach structure the situation immediately after the game? To channel this kind, I think, of frustration that fills the team with aggression and hostility. How can we then allow them to act this out socially within the social contacts of the situation. Because I think you alluded to what will happen in the next athletic contest. But a more nitty gritty situation is what will happen immediately after this kind of experience.

LAYMAN: Do you have ideas about that Dr. Kroll?

KROLL: Well, you suffer a lot. Laughter.

VOICE FROM AUDIENCE: That's very true.

LAYMAN: This is a very practical question and I think it is an important one. I think that it is a very knotty question, because I think we have the question of the balance between fighting as hard as you can and playing the game or regarding this as something real and earnest. That is, I think that after the contest, the game aspect of it can again be brought in, that this can be put in perspective and the feelings that have been generated in the course of the contest which has become something frequently which is over and beyond the game situation can then be dispelled. Of course it is a platitude I suppose to emphasize things like, "Oh, you tried as hard as you could, you worked hard and better luck next time", that, "this is only a game", to put the whole thing into perspective as it weren't a matter of life or death. Unfortunately, I think that varsity competition has reached the point now where we forget sometimes that it is a game, and the opponents are not really enemies.

UNKNOWN: It seems to be in our standard of conduct almost written in and it seems that in light of so many things that have come to light in the field of psychology that it seems to be somewhat unrealistic that we should not encourage, I don't think we should, that kids are to go together and smile and say you played a wonderful game—it is just so unrealistic—

LAYMAN: It is unrealistic in terms of what is expected by their peers, by the crowd. It isn't enough that they played a good game. And I think this is matter of education of the public as much as it is coping with players themselves.

BASMAJIAN: I have a comment which may or may not be relevant. I think it is. I am thinking in terms of the learning experience and aggressiveness and so on as exhibited by one's children as you are teaching them competitive games. Now, those of us who have raised children and tried to teach them games are quite aware of the interplay that goes on between elements of aggressiveness in the teacher and, the parent, and the naked aggressiveness of the child who is trying to bait Daddy or Mother. I don't know if there has been anything written on this sort of love-hate relationship except by the Freudian psychologists. Does Professor Layman have any comment to make on it?

LAYMAN: Yes, there has been some work done by Sears and his co-workers that deals with the methods that parents use in coping with children's aggressive impulses, particularly aggression toward them, in relation to whether this serves to increase it or to decrease it. In general they have found that when the reaction of the parent is either a punitive reaction or is a reaction in which the aggression is permitted to be expressed uncontrolled, that either of these results in an increase in the instigation to aggression; that the kind of behavior which results in a decrease of aggression is behavior in which children are not permitted to express aggression to their parents in such ways as to actually harm their parents. In which the parent's attitude is one of firmness in dealing with it rather than an attitude of permissiveness or an attitude or punishment, but aside from clinically oriented case study approaches. I think that is about the only one I recall. Now, material in play therapy shows that actually when children in play therapy are encouraged to express their feelings of hostility toward their parents through play activities, that this does not result in a decrease of the instigation to aggression, it results in an increase of it. It is a permissive attitude toward the expression of aggressive impulses toward the parents, even symbolically.

SIMON: Thank you Professor Layman.

Current Strategies and Problems
In Personality Assessment
of Athletes

Walter Kroll
University of Massachusetts

The profession of physical education has long been aware of the importance of personality variables in its conduct of educational physical activity programs. Ever since the beginning of the twentieth century when the New Physical Education was espoused by leaders like Thomas D. Wood and Clark Hetherington, aims of the profession have universally included at least one specific objective dealing with desirable personality development. Whether called emotional-impulsive (Nash), development of instinct mechanisms (Hetherington), or personal-social attitudes (Cowell and Schwenn), physical education has continuously held itself obligated to the structuring of satisfactory learning experiences in an educational environment for inculcation of suitable personality traits and attitudes. In no small way, social and moral aspects of personality dynamics have often tended to overshadow the importance and emphasis given to physical or neuromuscular objectives in physical education. Even when the nation was in an uproar over the physical unfitness of American youths, for example, a well-received article in the Association's journal appeared with the revealing title, "Is Physical Fitness Our Most Important Objective?" (Weiss, 1964).

Belief in the principle of mind-body unity extends beyond the domain of professional physical education in an educational setting. The role of physical activity has been explored concerning its therapeutic potential in social adjustment, mental health, juvenile delinquency, and as an aid in the diagnosis and treatment of maladjustment (Layman, 1960a). As a result of such inquiries, physical activity is accepted in many quarters as an adjunctive therapy in socio-medical seettings (Layman, 1960b; Davis, 1952). Release of aggressive feelings, reduction of anxiety, social mobility, and enhanced sociometric status have also been linked to physical activity. Currently, preliminary reports on perceptual-motor relationships are capturing the profession's imagination as evidence suggesting that physical activity may actually contribute to cognitive development in a direct and casual manner rather than via some indirect route.

Although physical activity and personality are recognized as interacting components of some consequence to professional physical education in an educational setting and to adjunctive therapies in a socio-medical environ-ment, it is in athletics where personality is accorded its most notable position as a factor of accentuated importance. Based upon considerably less ob-jective evidence than exists for the role of personality variables and physical activity in educational or therapeutic endeavors, personality is rather uni-versally proclaimed an important and essential prerequisite for successful athletic performance. Few coaches or athletes would deny that personality is a factor of crucial significance in achieving athletic success (winning). Some experienced observers even go so far as to suggest that certain per-sonality traits are the only real differentiators between success and failure in athletics. Support of such a position is based upon the thesis that concerted efforts to equalize physical athletic talent at any particular quality level of competitive sports have been highly successful.

This brief introduction could be greatly amplified but I believe it is sufficient to suggest that personality has been widely acknowledged as an important aspect of physical activity. Research concerning personality and physical activity has, of course, been conducted from each of the reference frames mentioned, i. e., educational physical education, therapeutics, and athletics. Although the primary emphasis in this paper is upon personality in athletics and current strategies (and problems) in assessment and research, such a focus does not exclude the domains of therapeutics and professional physical education from consideration. If personality factors are operative in physical activity then studying extreme or classical samples as typified by athletes has implications for all levels of physical activity. Such a posture implies acceptance of a dimensional rather than a categorical system for personality and is in accord with Eysenck's (1964) doctrine of continuity in which personality is assumed to be "due to a combination of quantitative variations along some designated continua." In Eysenck's model, of course, the major continua are represented by introversion-extraversion and stable-unstable.

By studying personality in athletics we accept the notion that elements of the same description are likely to apply at lower intensity levels of physical activity, i. e., in intramural sports, physical education classes, volun-tary participation, etc. Research findings at either end of a continuum may contribute to a knowledge structure applicable at the other end as well as at any points along the continuum. Studying non-athletes, for example, may contribute as much (or more) as studying champion athletes just as studying psychotics may produce knowledge about normals. This is not to say that descriptions or assessment techniques developed at either end of the con-tinuum would be completely—or even partially—satisfactory at the other end without some modification. Need for such moderation in extrapolation is reflected in Holtzman's (1965) contention that " . . . the MMPI is not a satisfactory instrument for determining personality dimensions since it was constructed for an entirely different purpose." Even though it was designed to provide "clinical scales for the diagnosis of psychiatric populations (Holtzman, 1965)" the MMPI has produced research data of interest to other levels of personality research.

My purpose is, then, to review with you some of the problems in athletic personality research. The comments made are bound to elicit debate since many are contrived to make implicit assumptions explicit. Anytime you try to tell someone—much less an entire field—what they are trying to say and accomplish, you are sure to get into trouble. Trouble in this case appears in the form of the reactor to the paper, Mrs. Layman, who is well-equipped for pointing out the nonsense in any paper. She ought to have a field day with this one.

GOALS AND OBJECTIVES OF PERSONALITY RESEARCH IN ATHLETICS

A basic premise of almost quasi-mystical potency for personality research in athletics is that athletes possess unique and definable personality attributes different from nonathletes. It is also commonly held, moreover, that in addition to differentiation from nonathletes, athletes in one sport can be distinguished from athletes in another sport. The basis for such sweeping assumptions is partly generated by widespread acceptance of classification schemes for athletic and physical activities. One of the most frequently cited classification systems, for example, dichotomizes athletic activities into team sports versus individual sports. Other categorical plans suggest combative versus noncombative, indoor versus outdoor, or use of a missile and/or implement versus nonuse of a missile and/or implement in the activity. A variety of classification plans exist including some with more categories such as that provided by the Committee on Curriculum Research of the National College Physical Education for Men (LaPorte, 1955): aquatics, dancing, team sports (court and diamond games plus field sports), gymnastics, and individual and dual sports.

Such classification schemes have been popularized chiefly by physical education curriculum experts in order to provide some framework for establishing an ideal educational program. Individual activities are typically evaluated for potential contribution to achievement of stated educational objectives. Thus, weight training is rated as contributing to a physical fitness objective but making a smaller contribution to a social objective. Golf, on the other hand, is typically rated as a good contributor to the social objective and a poor developer of physical fitness. With such assessments of activity potential for contribution to achievement of educational ends, a curriculum is designed which hopefully balances learning experiences for optimum results.

Implicit in the curriculum decision-making process is the belief that: (a) different physical activities make unequal contributions to individual objectives in a heterogeneous set; and (b) different physical activities make distinctive kinds of contributions to the same objective. Some activities are excellent for development of physical fitness while others make their major contribution to a social objective. But even when several activities are mutually linked to the same objective their contributions may be distinctively different. Thus, while both contact and non-contact sports may contribute to a social objective they do so in different ways: contact sports are assumed to be developers of aggressiveness and masculinity while a non-contact sport such as golf is judged good for development of social and cultural refinement. Although such curriculum decisions and judgments must be made, the factual basis for much of the accepted policy guiding classification systems and evaluative curriculum decision-making remains obscure.

If personality attributes of athletes could be found which are capable of differentiating athletes from nonathletes and athletes in one sport from another, certain advantages would result. First, there would be promise for development of personality techniques for screening of potential athletic talent eventually leading to a procedure by which aspiring candidates for athletics could be matched with a sport (or sports) for which they were best suited and in which they would be most likely to experience success. Coupled with the knowledge already available and quickly being accumulated on motor characteristics necessary for success, a practical system of athletic counseling could be realized. Secondly, if success prerequisites in terms of personality attributes were established for an athletic sport then the manner in which participants were trained could be modified so as to promote optimum cultivation of the personality success attributes. In a similar manner, knowledge of the effects and demands of particular athletic activities could permit therapeutic uses of physical activity and curriculum rather than subjective insight and an opinion consensus.

Research Strategy and Research Problems

The amount of research data concerning personality and athletics is not very extensive but it is admittedly confusing. The amount of research data concerning personality in general is, of course, both extensive and confusing. Thus, we are only behind in one phase of our work. Several excellent reviews of the literature have recently appeared (Layman, 1960a; Kane, 1964; and Husman, 1969) describing the present status of knowledge concerning personality factors in athletics. Universal acknowledgement was made of the problem of valid and reliable assessment techniques in these reviews and lack of suitable measurement instruments continues to plague definitive research undertakings. In addition to lack of acceptable measurement tools, a superabundance of theoretical models for personality structure, personality dynamics and development results in an entangling web of conflicting results.

Since the personality researcher in athletics makes use of the theories and research tools developed by personality research in general, he inherits both the good and the bad in his attempts at defining a personality model for athletics. At best, then, research dealing with personality in athletics will find iself beset with many irritating problems of considerable potency. Some of the general problems in personality are needlessly compounded in athletic personality work, however, because of inadequately conceived paradigms and less than adequate attention to matters of experimental design and statistical analysis. Other specific problems stem from nonrecognition of the fact that problems in general personality work carry over into athletic personality research. A few of the more important of these research problems will be considered as they relate to relatively specific issues in athletic personality work.

Measurement problems. In the opening sentence dealing with personality in the 1969 *Annual Review of Psychology,* Adelson said: "The field of personality these days is marked by abundance, diffusiveness, and diversity." Shortly thereafter Adelson cited Sanford's (1968) description of personality research as a "disconcerting sprawl" and suggested that personality research is characterized by a conglomerate of loosely related topics "each of which more or less goes its own way." Fiske's (1963) chapter on Problems in Measuring Personality likewise acknowledged the "critical weakness in the scientific study of personality" due in some part to the "relative lack of adequate measurement operations." He cited inadequacy of common personality definitions as leading to damaging specificity of personality measurement instruments. Thus, personality inventories purporting to measure the same or highly similar components seldom show intercorrelations above .50. When assessment of the same component is attempted by different methods —e.g., inventories versus projective techniques—the intercorrelations are even lower.

Such abundance, diffusiveness, and diversity is not peculiar to studies of personality structure alone for Adelson also points out that there is no general agreement as to the composition of anxiety even though hundreds of studies have been conducted. Cofer and Appley (1964) concur with such a description for motivation as they note: "It is clear that a comprehensive, definitive psychology of motivation does not yet exist." The goal of synthesis and integration for personality structure and personality dynamics, both singly and together, seems less achievable today than it was before in that "we appear to be in era of such extreme methodological and conceptual specialization that communication between investigators, never satisfactory to begin with, threatens to break down (Wiggins, 1968)."

Compounding such acknowledged dilemmas in personality structure and personality dynamics has been the relatively recent "Crisis in Methodology (Adelson, 1969)" generated by the disturbing findings concerning response sets. Studies delineating the effects of social desirability (SD) and acquiescence (Acq) have suggested that such response sets can have equivocal and pervasive effects upon the derived scores from many personality inventories. This issue, according to Christie and Lindauer (1963), entails more than internal psychometric argument involving preferences in methodological measurement strategy, and, instead, lays open the question of the validity of a good deal of completed and on going personality research. Thus, the question has been raised of whether response sets are more important in self-report inventories than the substantive content of items in such inventories themselves.

Several reports have shown, for example, that the effect of response sets is of considerable importance in an inventory such as the widely used MMPI. Edwards (1966) disregarded substantive content and constructed an artificial MMPI by matching his own personality statements with MMPI items simply on the basis of known endorsement frequency (EF) and social desirability scale values (SDSV). The first two factors on the EF and SDSV constructed MMPI correlated .98 and .67 respectively with actual MMPI factor loadings. Similarly, Jackson and Messick (1961; 1962) divided MMPI scales into true and false-keyed subscales. Factor analytic results showing a factor comprised of almost all the true subscales and another factor containing almost all the false subscales led to the conclusion that direction of item-keying was an important "determinant of the factorial structure of the MMPI." The amount of concern with such contamination of test validity by response sets is reflected in the fact that approximately 25 per cent of the articles between 1964 and 1967 reviewed by Wiggins (1968) dealt with this problem.

As overwhelming as these and other measurement problems are in personality research, they do not—in my opinion—constitute the greatest source of difficulty for the athletic personality researcher. Indeed, even if the measurement deficiencies currently being debated were to be cleared up to the satisfaction of personality experts I doubt the muddled picture seen in athletic personality research would be much affected. Such an attention getting and easily criticized position is based upon two major arguments each of which has some merit even if outweighed by deficiency.

Psychiatric versus normal. First of all, much of the theoretical frame-of-reference in personality research is heavily imbued with clinical identification of psychiatric or quasipsychiatric populations. As Garfield (1963) has pointed out, the clinician's view of personality emphasizes pathology and usual appraisals of normal personality are likely to be couched in terms of susceptibility to maladjustment or the presence of latent pathological features. Tests devised for compatibility with mental health or psychiatric goals, no matter how well constructed, rather than assessment of normal personality would seem to promise less help in athletic personality work than is needed.

As Crites (1964) has argued, dissatisfaction with the abnormal personality orientation has led counseling psychologists to the practice of adapting personality instruments for the assessment of normal personality. Outside of the California Psychological Inventory (CPI, Gough, 1957) and, to a lesser extent, the Cattell Sixteen Personality Factor Questionnaire (16 PF, Cattell, and Eber 1957), there hardly exists a satisfactory inventory capable of assessing normal personality with adequately established internal and external validity. An inventory such as the MMPI, for example, was developed for identification of psychiatric populations and its empirically constructed clinical scales are poorly suited to dimensional analysis of personality structure in normals (Holtzman, 1965). Studies employing the MMPI on athletes typically result in conclusions dealing with psychopathic deviation (Pd), paranoia (Pa), depression (D), hysteria (hy), or other psychiatric features rather than a discussion of normal or "successful" personality (see, for example, Slusher, 1964. Although identification of psychiatric obstacles is of acknowledged importance, athletic personality research would seem better suited to a different reference frame.

Major pre-occupation with psychiatric deficiencies and clinical-therapeutic approaches to athletic personality seems to fix attention at one end of the personality continuum. Although capable of making important contributions, it tends to emphasize weaknesses and neglects consideration of the personality strengths necessary for successful athletic performance. In many respects there seems to be some correspondence between clinical-therapeutic approaches in athletic personality work and the prevention and treatment of athletic injuries. As any team physician or coach can attest, the absence of physical injury does not insure the physical condition necessary for success. In the same way, then, the absence of psychiatric deficiency does not insure the presence of personality attributes necessary for success. It would seem that personality attributes necessary for success are of at least equal importance to personality attributes of a psychiatric nature preventing success. Research effort in athletic personality should be encouraged, therefore, in a manner paralleling work in athletic conditioning as opposed to athletic injury management.

There are currently two good examples of the kind of contributions made by a clinical-therapeutic approach to athletic personality work. One of these is a book by a practicing psychiatrist, *The Madness in Sports* (Beisser, 1967) in which an intriguing set of case studies is used to exemplify the psychodynamics of psychiatric disturbances in athletes. The other is a book by a pair of widely published clinical psychologists titled *Problem Athletes and How to Handle Them.* (Ogilvie and Tutko, 1966). In both of these books there is the usual absence of cited scientific references for support of clinical observations and conclusions other than Recommended Reading or Bibliography. Although one book noted that "psychological investigations must provide the reliable data that will enhance and complement coaching skill (p. 10), the authors did not choose to "present the more scholarly experimental documentation of our research findings in the area of athletic motivation (p. 12)."

Too often, as reflected in these examples, the bulk of clinical-therapeutic efforts is presented in a form resistant to affirmation or cross-validation by reasonably objective techniques. Since affirmation is made difficult, denial of findings is almost impossible except by judgment. Although definitive work is provided full of strong assertions and packed with practical suggestions for immediate application, such work demands complete reliance upon the author's capability to translate and apply general theory to the behavioral situation being examined. One must recognize the genuine contributions that insight and personal analysis of psychodynamics can make when applied to athletic personality work, but one must also weigh Meehl's (1954) study showing how poor clinical diagnoses are when compared to even weak objective tests. Thus, many choose to follow Cattell's recommendation (Cattell and Butcher, 1968) concerning clinically derived insights: " . . . it is necessary to distinguish insight from fantasy by rigorous empirical methods."

My point is that the psychiatric and mental health overtones which influence a good share of personality work are likely to hold center stage for quite some time. If one's goal is to define the personality deficiencies preventing successful athletic performance then the wealth of clinical-therapeutic research will be of inestimable value. If, however, one's goal is closer to the one described earlier for athletic personality then such clinical-therapeutic research will be of value in a narrower and quite limited dimension. Acceptance of a dimensional system for personality (Eysenck, 1964) does not automatically obligate the athletic personality researcher to complete reliance upon the methodology and set of operations pertinent to the study of personality deficiencies. Just as we recognize that health is more than the absence of disease, we must recognize that athletic personality is more than the absence of psychiatric deficiencies. Even further, we must recognize that the instruments and techniques suitable in one area may not be completely satisfactory in the other.

Normal versus super-normal. Even if we can hope that personality instruments will be developed which are adequate for the assessment of normal rather than deficient personality, the probability of achieving implicit research goals in athletic personality work will only be minimally increased. I base this contention partly on the results of studies dealing with the prediction of academic achievement, job placement and personnel classification, and guidance counseling in which personality instruments have been of minor value, far overshadowed by more specific ability tests. Involved also is the innocent idea that competitive sports are a special kind of a behavioral situation resembling the unique and exceptional more than they do the average and general; .i e., competitive sports represent a super-normal rather than a normal system.

The belief that personality attributes are important to academic achievement is probably as widespread as the belief that personality is important in athletics. Although various personality attributes have been linked to academic achievement, however, few studies have been able to show any dramatic rise in prediction over and above that produced by traditional ability measures. Certainly personality has not been shown to correlate with academic achievement to the extent that popular belief would predict. The point to be emphasized here is that personality measures must add to the predictive efficiency obtainable through standardized ability tests. Attempts to improve prediction by use of personality and other non-intellectual components have, in the words of Middleton and Guthrie (1959), "yielded quite discouraging results." Some individuals, on the other hand, would become excited over the finding reported by Cattell and Butcher (1968) that addition of the fourteen factors of the High School Personality Questionnaire improved prediction of the total score on the Stanford Achievement Test over and above the predictive capability of ability scores alone. Others would note that this significant increase was actually a rise from .72 to .79 and agree with Cattell and Butcher's observation that the "effects reported are not spectacular (p. 196.)"

Research done in conjunction with the National Merit Scholarship Corporation has shown that academic achievement in college can be predicted from several personality inventories. The California Psychological Inventory was reported to be the most successful instrument with several scales predicting college grades in the high .10's and .20's, hardly an overwhelming result (Astin, 1964). Astin also noted, moreover, that simple self-ratings on such traits as scholarship, persistence, or drive to achieve actually predicted grade point average better than the personality inventories. Astin concluded that it was economically unwise to use elaborate personality inventories in attempts to improve prediction of academic achievement when simple self-ratings were generally superior. Parallel evidence suggests that the CPI can hardly be called a valid predictor of college grade point average (Holland, 1959; Johnson and Pacine, 1961) nor does it predict college major very well (Hase and Goldberg, 1967). Indeed, in the study by Hase and Goldberg college major was simply a dichtomy between liberal arts versus non-liberal arts and 11 CPI empirical scales gave a cross validated multiple R of .30.

Such studies are representative of many which could be cited in defense of the argument that personality inventories alone have not been shown to be adequate instruments for prediction of academic success or for choice of college major. Similar evidence is available to show that personality inventories are not adequate for job placement or vocational guidance. In place of personality instruments we find employment of specifically designed assessment techniques. The inherent demand characteristics of the task, be it academic achievement or an occupation, are analyzed and specific, relevant assessment measures devised which emphasize empirical rather than rational validity.

A Model For Personality In Athletics

Throughout our previous discussion we have assumed that athletic personality research had a definite and universally accepted purpose. Let us turn our attention away from problems and strategies in measurement which supposedly prevent achievement of our expressed goals to an even more important issue, that of the conceptualized role of personality in athletics. Needless to say, the scientific goal of personality research in athletics calls for development of a comprehensive knowledge structure in the form of an accepted theory or predictive model. It is not unfair to say that studies done so far on athletes seem guided by the single objective of demonstrating personality differences between athletes and nonathletes (or between athletes in one sport from another) in order to identify personality traits characteristic of athletes in a specific sport. When significant differences are shown the inference is often made that such traits are desirable prerequisites for entry into a particular sport and that either by inherent possession or environmental development these traits should exist in high concentration for successful performance in the sport.

Personality attributes which have been demonstrated as significant differentiators between athletes and nonathletes or between athletes in different sports are certainly personality features somehow linked to athletics. Contending that such traits are essential characteristics for success in a sport, however, is quite a different matter. Not only must a personality attribute differentiate athletes from nonathletes but it must be shown to differ on logical dimensions between known levels of ability in the same sport and/or that participation enhances the magnitude of the trait before any confidence can be attached to the claim that it is related to successful performance. Even then the trait might still represent a necessary but not a sufficient personality characteristic for success in the sport. If another research uncovers successful athletes who do not possess the trait in established dimensions then the whole argument for the trait representing a personality success prerequisite fails.

Now achievement of such a personality model in athletics—i. e., one which identifies unique characteristics essential to success—may be highly desirable, but there is no guarantee that such a state of affairs actually exists and such a model is still only a hope rather than a fact. There are, in fact, other possibilities and a short time ago several hypothetical models were suggested for personality research in athletics (Kroll, 1967). These alternative reference frames appeared as part of an article dealing with experimental data and do not seem to have received much attention. At this early stage of development, it may be a good idea to keep as many plausible options open as possible for athletic personality research. Hence, these models will again be presented in modified form along with some brief arguments as to their suitability. Several of these models are less appealing than others to goal-oriented fields such as education and adjunctive therapy which understandably prefer more teleologically acceptable theories. Nature, however, often has ideas of its own in such matters and the well-intentioned researcher may have difficulty imposing his own will upon reality. My argument is not for acceptance of these models but rather that there is a need to acknowledge the options and not to pursue a pre-conceived and limited objective regardless of how wholesome and advantageous that goal may be in certain professional applications.

First, there may be a set of personality factors which prompt individuals to elect participation in a particular sport. Those individuals who possess the most fortunate combination of these features are then seen as continuing on and experiencing success in the sport. Any individual lacking these traits would fail to survive very long even if he elected to begin participation. In this hypothetical model both those individuals entering the sport as well as successful veterans in the sport would exhibit similar personality profiles possibly differing only in intensity. A second alternative is that no pattern exists which is associated with initial entry into a sport, but either by modification of existing and alterable personality characteristics or attrition of inappropriate patterns only those individuals possessing suitable or alterable patterns will persist and experience success. In this case, early participants may exhibit heterogeneous patterns but successful veterans would possess homogeneous personality patterns. Both of these two cases would hold promise for identification of personality features characteristic of an athlete which are essential for successful performance and allow practical applications in educational and therapeutic settings.

Most athletic personality researchers seem to express overwhelming preference for these two potential models but there are other alternatives. A third possibility is that both neophytes and successful veterans possess dissimilar and nondiscriminant patterns: i.e., unique personality factors appear to be non-existent and unrelated to athletic performance. Fourth, a similar pattern may exist at entry but participation and attrition results in a dissimilar and nondiscriminant pattern among successful veterans. These latter two models postulate the absence of identifying success characteristics for talented performers and seem professionally if not scientifically less attractive than the first two cases. Thus, whenever results compatible with options three or four occur there appears an expression of apologetic embarrassment and the researcher often reveals his disappointment by second guessing his study blaming lack of precision, poor subject cooperation, faulty measurement instruments, sample composition, and the like for non-significant findings.

A fifth model alternative can be added in which opposite discriminatory patterns may be demonstrated in untried novices and successful veterans. Under this scheme the presence of certain traits in novice participants could indicate that just the opposite traits were required for success and characeristic of veteran performers. Some support for such a model was presented in a study on amateur collegiate level wrestlers (Kroll, 1967) when it compared its results with a study done by Slusher (1964) involving high school athletes. Slusher concluded that wrestlers and football players displayed the most neurotic MMPI profile of the five athletic groups and norm sample studied. Results from the collegiate level sample, however, suggested just the opposite was true since the wrestlers demonstrated a low factor I score on the Cattell 16 PF Test. It was speculated that participation in the sport of wrestling might conceivably be responsible for amelioration of a "dominate neurotic profile" and development of a tough, masculine, and aggressive profile.

Although support for each of these five models is scarce, evidence from a parallel search for physical success prerequisites and distinguishing characteristics suggests that model possibilities other than the more attractive ones (models one and two) merit careful consideration. We know, for example, that successful dash men are seldom developed from a non-descript set of physical capabilities. The chances of developing middle and long distance runners, however, are much better. As far as physical characteristics, then, one might say dash men conform to model one and distance runners to model two. Disallowing extremes of ecto- and endomorphy in somatotypes, there is good evidence to assume that amateur wrestlers in the United States requires no specific somatotype prerequisite for success (Rasch, 1958; Kroll, 1954). Thus, beginning and successful wrestlers would each exhibit dissimilar and nondiscriminating somatotype profiles and generally conform to model three predictions.

Model four, meanwhile, calls for discriminating characteristics among beginners but not among successful veterans. Several studies have demonstrated support for the idea that strength is more important for beginning wrestlers than for advanced wrestlers (Gross, Griesel, and Stull, 1956; Kroll, 1954, 1958; and Rasch and Kroll, 1964). Among beginning wrestlers in college physical activity classes Gross, Griesel, and Stull reported a correlation of .498 between McCloy's General Strength Quotient and the ability to learn wrestling. The other studies showed that the importance of strength declined as the skill level of wrestling went up. To some degree, at least, these data suggest conformity to the postulates of model four. Thus, in the same sport we see need for model three to understand somatotypes and model four to incorporate strength findings. Work done by Fleishman (1963) and others (Jones, 1962) also support the idea that the importance of various component abilities is modified with changes in criterion skill performance.

Model five proposes that an opposite set of discriminating characteristics may be present in untried novices and successful veterans. Such a model would appear to be most attractive for use in educational and therapeutic environments since it infers acceptance of the premise that the demand characteristics of an activity can be achieved through the developmental effect of participation itself. Such an outlook also prescribes acceptance of a kind of deficiency-compensation principle whereby individuals seek to overcome some deficiency by participation in an activity which is perceived as necessitating just the opposite of the deficiency for success. Thune's (1949) finding of an inferiority complex among weight trainers, for example, has been widely interpreted as conforming to this deficiency-compensation principle. Individuals dissatisfied with their physique and muscular strength would thus elect partcipation in weight training while competitive weight lifters would be characterized by diametrically opposite characteristics.

Whether or not any of these models will ever be shown to be valid remains to be seen but they can at least be used to moderate our interpretation of unsettled personality research in athletics. Bland acceptance of *any* preconceived and poorly verified paradigm can be disruptive to productive research efforts. A noted researcher in this area (Husman, 1969), for example, reviewed the vast array of conflicting results and implied a sort of predilection to models one or two by his statement that "such conflicting evidence . . . is undoubtedly due to instrumentation and methodological inaccuracies." Reacting to Husman's paper at the same conference, Singer (1969) also generally implied acceptance of a model one or two reference frame as he expressed the hope for future "application of such information to the sports' scene." In common with Husman, Singer also saw promise that "with better measuring devices and techniques . . . there will occur greater agreement between experimental results." Contrasted against these two homogeneous positions is one forwarded by Rushall (1968) who, after a comprehensive study of athletic personality, concluded that "personality is not a significant factor in sport performance."

My point is this: we know from much more extensive evidence concerning exercise physiology that physical characteristics and physiological success prerequisites are related to athletic performance in a multiplicity of ways. Because of the amount of accumulated reliable knowledge, we are not surprised when a study shows dash men do not possess excellent levels of cardiovascular endurance or that weight training regimes fail to improve maximal oxygen uptake. We are not disturbed by such findings because we more fully understand the role of aerobic and anaerobic energy sources and recognize that sprints and weight lifting require anaerobic energy and should not be expected to develop or require aerobic fitness characteristics. Thus, even though we classify cardiovascular endurance as an important component of physical fitness we accept the fact that all competitive sports do not make equal demands upon fitness components.

We also know that some activities make very little demand for *any* physical fitness factors but instead require high levels of skill for success. Bowling is an example of such a low fitness and high skill activity. Other sports, such as distance running, necessitate superb levels of physical fitness for competitive success and make much smaller demands upon skill. Thus, we see a physical trait such as cardiovascular fitness varying from nil to high importance as far as an essential characteristic in successful athletic performance. In light of such evidence it would seem unwise to conclude that skill is unimportant in athletics because cardiovascular fitness rather than skill is the chief success prerequisite for distance running nor is it prudent to judge fitness unimportant because skill is the major differentiator between good and bad bowlers. Why, then, is it unreasonable to hold open the possibility that personality attributes may represent an important success factor in some sports but not in others, or at some quality levels but not at others? When viewed from model one alone, such personality data would indeed appear confusing. Viewed from other models—which are already accepted in the physical realm—the results would not seem conflicting at all.

Thus, when personality studies fail to show distinguishing characteristics between athletes and nonathletes we must be ready to consider the findings as evidence for a model three or four and not quickly and resolutely classify the results as conflicting or question the research procedures employed. To be sure, measurement in personality is far less than adequate. But we cannot proclaim its inadequacy for non-significant or conflicting results and implicitly accept its adequacy when findings more to our liking are realized. In a similar manner, we cannot allow a review of confusing data to prompt a conclusion that there is no order for personality factors in athletics. We have far too little acceptable research dealing with athletic personality to venture definitive conclusions at the present time.

We have also learned through physiological studies, by the way, that many (if not most) competitive sports do not supply sufficient development of demand characteristics by mere participation. Thus, physiological preparedness necessary for the mile run is not achieved by running one mile a day nor is the physical condition demanded by football developed by game like scrimmages alone. Complicated training programs are instead devised to attain the necessary physiological characteristics demanded by the activity. Whether called supplemental, off-season, or pre-season conditioning, such training programs are considered essential for successful athletic performance. The same is true for skill as exemplified by the numerous specific drills that are utilized in athletic training. If the physical analogy holds, there may be need to examine the potential models for athletic personality from the same reference frame. There may very well be need for personality training regimes as well as special physical conditioning programs in athletics.

Janus' Outlook

Any honest appraisal of the work in athletic personality must conclude that the picture is unsettled. Only clinical interpretations have been able to come up with anything approaching a definite conclusion while studies with objective measurements of personality continue to offer conflicting results. Part of the acknowledged confusion, however, is due to the fact that we have naively expected too much of personality inventories and other general assessment techniques. Because of an abundance of encapsulated personality philosophies and unrelated measurement instruments, structural personality factors cannot always be expected to discriminate in the kinds of operations and situations in which we have hoped for significant differences. Disregarding methodological measurement problems, personality inventories postulate a number of static traits each of which is poorly defined as to composition and thus poorly represented in the item pool. Such a catholic lens for personality may not have the proper focal length for identification of the elusive characteristics important in athletic personality research. We have, in effect, gone fishing for minnows with a nomological net designed for whales and have no right to complain about the poor catch.

A similar observation would seem to hold for efforts in the area of personality dynamics. We have little knowledge, for example, of the potency of various situations in athletics to elicit activity of personality features and allow prediction of behavior. Even if motivation for success were a general and consistent factor in individuals and even if the demand characteristics of athletic tasks were specified, the individual incentive for success in particular tasks could vary sufficiently to disallow predictable and discriminating behavior. One of the outstanding authorities in the field of motivation, moreover, cautions against acceptance of a generalized achievement motivation rather than a situation locked and specific multidimensional structure. In fact, Heckhausen (1967) suggests that an achievement motivation in "practically every situational relationship" is observed in "certain apparently neurotic cases." Anxiety, likewise, can be situation locked to particular conditions, is modified by experience, and lacks a common agreed upon definition.

In this connection Hunt (1965) discussed the problem of whether static personality traits constituted the major source of behavioral variance, or, as social psychology argues, that variations in particular situations mediate behavior. The conclusion reached was that interactions between the two determined behavior. The recommendation given by Hunt was to seek instruments capable of predicting behavior of individuals in various kinds of situations rather than clinging to the belief in "static dimensional traits." Thus, the depicting of stable and permanent personality traits (structure) or the description of behavior in specific, monetary situations (dynamics) alone is not sufficient.

It is embarrassing to suggest that Lewin's equation of $B = f (P, E)$ requires acknowledgement in athletic personality research. The bulk of research in athletic personality, however has been aimed at specific definition of personality structure through use of a variety of inventories. Much less has been done on the interaction of supposedly stable personality attributes and the demand characteristics of particular environmental situations. Almost nothing has been accomplished on developing specific and pertinent measurement tools for assessment of personality attributes in athletic situations.

This latter observation is, I believe, the major cause of discouraging results in athletic personality research, i. e., lack of effort in developing specific and unique assessment tools for athletics. Due to a traditional practice of borrowing knowledge constructs and research tools from related disciplines in an eclectic and parasitic manner, physical education research in the area of athletic personality can be typified as one continuous series of "piggy-back" rides. Progress in general personality research is awaited with the enthusiastic expectation that new strategies developed in the psychiatric ward or the college admissions office will provide the needed illumination in athletic personality work. *It may be time for athletic personality researchers to recognize that the unaccounted for variance characteristic in general personality research constitutes a more important challenge than the duplication of accounted for variance.* The methodological research strategies developed in other areas may be efficiently employed to identify discriminatory personality features in athletics. Once having netted our whale, however, we should seek to expand its meaning in both depth and breadth, and seek to refine its discriminating power in the specific and pertinent realm of athletics.

It seems very unlikely that the measurement instruments designed for the study of general personality structure and dynamics will ever offer more than guideposts for the kind of definitive work demanded by the goals of athletic personality research. What seems needed is concerted effort to develop specific assessment techniques capable of explaining behavior in situations pertinent (and perhaps unique) to athletics. Having established our own measurement operations we can back-track through to establish relationships with general personality assessment techniques. The major shift in strategy will be that low correlations between general tests and our empirically successful specific tests will be viewed as unaccounted for variance in the general standardized tests and not vice-versa.

I am not suggesting abandonment of general personality theory and measurement techniques. I am suggesting that contemporary research strategy almost totally emphasizes use of general personality theory in an attempt to reproduce or verify the presence of accounted for variance in athletic situations. Rather than being satisfied when a general instrument also accounts for some variance in our pertinent athletic situations, our attention should be directed toward the variance for which these instruments fail to account. The development of achievement tests in specific academic areas, for example, extends the accounted for variance beyond that attributable to a general intelligence measure. In the same measure, more intense effort is needed in the area of extending accounted for variance in athletic personality work beyond that provided by general personality assessment techniques. We need to transmute and not merely transfer personality theory to athletic personality research.

It would be expected of me to suggest research topics worthy of execution, and I can at least give you one good example of the kind of change in research strategy I am advocating. For several years now Kenyon at Wisconsin has been at work developing an instrument capable of assessing the multidimensional-structure of attitude toward physical activity. Based upon the idea that physical activity can be reduced to logical subsets by use of "perceived instrumentality" of various classes of physical activity, Kenyon (1968a) has defined six model dimensions of attitude toward physical activity which have survived cross validation rather well. These six dimensions are not reproducible by any metamorphosis of existing personality scales and constitute the unique and specific dimensions of attitude toward physical activity: (1) a social experience; (2) health and fitness; (3) pursuit of vertigo; (4) an aesthetic experience; (5) catharsis; and (6) an ascetic experience. Some consideration has also been given to a seventh, chance.

Kenyon (1968b) has justifiably claimed that adequate assessment of attitude(s) toward physical activity could "aid in the development of a sociopsychological theory of sport." If anything, Kenyon has been most unassuming in forwarding the importance of the implication and potential application of his work in this area. Over and above these potential applications and important returns, however, is the fact that his work represents the first major and concerted effort which has not depended upon use of "standardized" personality instruments for definition of the model domain. Instead, certain variables with established importance in explaining related social phenomena were compared against the instrument developed to assess attitude(s) toward physical activity. Thus, variance represented by the attitude toward physical activity domain has to be accounted for by other general assessment tools. Some may argue this change reflects only a transfer of confusion from one area to the other. If so, at least the amount of reliable knowledge which exists is in our special interest domain and not the other.

Before closing, I want to emphasize once again that I am not advocating abandonment of general personality theory and use of current assessment techniques. We will continue to need application of general personality theory in athletic situations in order to help identify the more promising areas for further work. At the same time, however, I have suggested that such confirmation of general theory should be coupled with equal efforts at new applications and development research. It seems doubtful to me that general personality theory will ever be successful in adequately defining the structure of the areas most pertinent to athletic psychology. The unaccounted for variance in competitive spirit, physical motivation, athletic anxiety, sportsmanship, and competitive stress warrants direct attack. Until such time as we stop the piggy-back rides and change the copy-cat strategy, the bright hope for advances in athletic personality will remain a dim prospect.

REFERENCES

Adelson, Joseph. Personality. *Annual Review of Psychology,* 1969, 20, 217-252.

Astin, Alexander W. The use of tests in research on students of high ability. *Journal of Counseling Psychology,* 1964, 11, 400-404.

Beisser, Arnold R. *The Madness in Sports.* New York: Appleton-Century-Crofts, 1967.

Cattell, Raymond B., and Butcher, H. John. *The Prediction of Achievement and Creativity.* New York: Bobbs-Merrill, 1968.

Cattell, Raymond B., and Eber, H. W. *Handbook for the Sixteen Personality Factor Questionnaire.* Champaign: Institute for Personality and Ability Testing, 1957.

Christie, Richard and Lindauer, Florence. Personality structure. *Annual Review of Psychology,* 1963, 14, 201-230.

Cofer, C. N., and Appley, M. H. *Motivation: Theory and Research.* New York: Wiley, 1964.

Crites, John O. The California Psychological Inventory, I. As a measure of the Normal personality. *Journal of Counseling Psychology,* 1964, 11, 197-202.

Davis, John Eisele. *Clinical Applications of Recreational Therapy.* Springfield: Charles C. Thomas, 1952.

Edwards, A. L. A comparison of 57 MMPI scales and 57 experimental scales matched with the MMPI scales in terms of item social desirability scale values and probabilities of endorsement. *Educational and Psychological Measurement,* 1966, 26, 15-27.

Eysenck, H. J. Principles and methods of personality description, classification and diagnosis. *British Journal of Psychology,* 1964, 55, 284-294.

Fiske, Donald W. Problems in measuring personality. In J. M. Wepman and R. W. Heine, (Eds.), *Concepts of Personality.* Chicago: Aldine Publishing Company, 1963. Pp. 449-473.

Fleishman, Edwin A., and Rich, Simon. Role of kinesthetic and spatial-visual abilities in perceptual-motor learning. *Journal of Experimental Psychology,* 1963, 66, 6-11.

Garfield, Sol L. The clinical method in personality assessment. In J. M. Wepman and R. W. Heine (Eds.), *Concepts of Personality.* Chicago: Aldine Publishing Co., 1963. Pp. 474-502.

Gough, H. G. *Manual for the California Psychological Inventory.* Palo Alto: Consulting Psychologists Press, 1957.

Gross, Elmer A.; Griesel, Donald C.; and Stull, Alan. Relationships between two motor educability tests, a strength test, and wrestling ability after eight weeks' instruction. *Research Quarterly,* 1956, 27, 395-402.

Hase, Harold D. and Goldberg, Lewis R. Comparative validity of different strategies of constructing personality inventory scales. *Psychological Bulletin,* 1967, 67, 231-248.

Heckhausen, Heinz. *The Anatomy of Achievement Motivation.* New York: Academic Press, 1967.

Holland, J. L. The prediction of college grades from the California Psychological Inventory and the Scholastic Aptitude Test. *Journal of Educational Psychology,* 1959, 50, 135-142.

Holtzman, Wayne H. Personality structure. *Annual Review of Psychology,* 1965, 16, 119-156.

Hunt, J. McV. Traditional personality theory in the light of recent evidence. *American Scientist.* 1965, 53, 80-96.

Husman, Burris F. Sport and personality dynamics. *NCPEAM Proceedings,* 1969, 72, 56-70.

Jackson, D. N. and Messick, S. Acquiescence and desirability as response determinants on the MMPI. *Educational and Psychological Measurement,* 1961, 21, 771-790.

Jackson, D. N. and Messick, S. Response styles on the MMPI: comparison of clinical and normal samples. *Journal of Abnormal and Social Psychology,* 1962, 65, 285-299.

Jackson, D. N. and Pacine, L. Response styles and academic achievement. *Educational and Psychological Measurement* 1961, 21, 1015-1028.

Jones, Marshall B. Practice as a process of simplification. *Psychological Review,* 1962, 4, 274-294.

Kane, John E. Personality and physical ability. *Proceedings of the International Congress of Sports Sciences.* Tokyo, 1964.

Kenyon, Gerald S. A conceptual model for characterizing physical activity. *Research Quarterly,* 1968a, 39, 96-105.

Kenyon, Gerald S. Six scales for assessing attitudes toward physical activity. *Research Quarterly,* 1968b, 39, 566-574.

Kroll, Walter. Sixteen personality factor profiles of collegiate wrestlers. *Research Quarterly,* 1967, 38, 49-57.

Kroll, Walter. Selected factors associated with wrestling success. *Research Quarterly,* 1958, 29, 396-406.

Kroll, Walter. An anthropometric study of some Big Ten varsity wrestlers. *Research Quarterly,* 1954, 25, 307-312.

LaPorte, Wm. Ralph. *The Physical Education Curriculum.* Los Angeles: College Book Store, 1955.

Layman, Emma M. Contributions of exercise and sports to mental health and social adjustment. In Warren R. Johnson (Ed.), *Science and Medicine of Exercise and Sports.* New York: Harper, 1960a. Pp. 560-599.

Layman, Emma M. Physical activity as a psychiatric adjunct. In Warren R. Johnson (Ed.), *Science and Medicine of Exercise and Sports.* New York: Harper, 1960b. Pp. 703-725.

Meehl, Paul E. *Clinical Versus Statistical Prediction: A Theoretical Analysis and Review of the Evidence.* Minneapolis: University of Minnesota Press, 1954.

Middleton, G., and Guthrie, G. M. Personality syndromes and academic achievement. *Journal of Educational Psychology,* 1959, 60, 66-69.

Ogilvie, Bruce C., and Tutko, Thomas A. *Problem Athletes and How to Handle Them.* London: Pelham Books, 1966.

Rasch, Philip J. Indices of body build of United States freestyle wrestlers. *Journal of the Association for Physical and Mental Rehabilitation,* 1958, 12, 91-94.

Rasch, Philip J. and Kroll, Walter. *What Research Tells the Coach About Wrestling.* Washington, D. C.: AAHPER, 1964.

Rushall, Brent S. An evaluation of the relationship between personality and physical performance categories. Proceedings of the 2nd International Congress of Sport Psychology, Washington, D. C., 1968.

Sanford, Nevitt. Personality-the field. In David L. Sills (Ed.), *International Encyclopedia of the Social Sciences.* New York: Crowell Collier and Macmillan, 1968. Vol. 11, 587-606.

Singer, R. N. Reaction to "Sport and personality dynamics." *NCPEAM Proceedings,* 1969, 72, 76-79.

Slusher, Howard S. Personality and intelligence characteristics of selected high school athletes and nonathletes. *Research Quarterly,* 1964, 35, 539-545.

Thune, John B. Personality of weightlifters. *Research Quarterly,* 1949, 20, 296-306.

Weiss, Raymond A. Is physical fitness our most important objective? *JOHPER,* 1964, 35, 17-18 and 61-62.

Wiggins, Jerry S. Personality structure. *Annual Review of Psychology,* 1968, 19, 293-350.

CRITIQUE OF KROLL'S PAPER
by Emma McCloy Layman

My overall reaction to Dr. Kroll's paper is that he has done an excellent job of reviewing the current strategies and problems in the personality assessment of athletes, as well as in his outlining of possible models for personality in relation to athletics and suggestions for future approaches in research. Consequently, my comments will be mostly in the nature of underscoring some of Dr. Kroll's points, amplifying others, and raising some questions rather than creating the kind of trouble which he seems to anticipate. However, the dynamics of personality are so complex that one nearly always has some reservations about any generalization based on personality research.

Investigators of relationships between personality and sports are constantly being frustrated by the fact that the same personality variables may have different relationships to performance in different persons. For example, assuming the validity of the bipolar personality variables suggested by Eysenck and others, it might be hypothesized that there is a positive relationship between strength of aggressive impulses and athletic success. Such an hypothesis, however, overlooks the possibility that athletic success might be a reaction formation against passivity or some other personality characteristic in some persons, as well as the possibility that aggressive impulses in an individual who feels guilty about them could contribute to lack of success in sports. The difficulty if not impossibility of controlling for these many intervening variables that do not always lend themselves to quantitative measurement doubtless obscures some of the real relationships which exist between personality trends and performance in physical activities.

I would agree with Dr. Kroll that those who study personality in relation to athletics do tend to accept the notion that elements of the same description are likely to apply at lower intensities of physical activity, but I am not sure that this assumption is justified. There may be different personality variables operating at different levels of physical activity or the same variables may differ in strength between one participant and another.

In his section on Goals and Objectives, Dr. Kroll lists three premises which are commonly accepted and are involved in personality research in athletics. He also states three advantages which would result if personality attributes could be found which are capable of differentiating athletes from non-athletes and athletes in one sport from athletes in another sport.

In commenting on the premises and the objectives which have grown out of them, I would like to make several remarks. To begin with, I think we need more precise and consistent ways for defining the "athlete" and the "non-athlete." When we speak about an athlete, do we mean one who enjoys sports, one who is skilled in sports, or both? Is a non-athlete one who does not like to participate, one who likes to participate but doesn't do so, or one who is unskilled? And what kinds of activities does he have to participate in if we are to call him an athlete? Is he an athlete if he is an expert bowler or is a good marksman with a rifle? Also, in the case of personality assessment we have to distinguish between external behavioral manifestations and the significance of these manifestations in terms of the functions which they serve as well as the findings with which they are associated.

I would certainly concur with the statement about the importance of basing therapeutic use of sports on empirical determinations of the personality variables associated with different sports. And I would agree that athletic counseling and inclusion of personality development techniques as a part of sports training should also be based on such empirical determinations. A recent study by Sappenfield (1969) shows that consensus with respect to perception of personality traits of acquaintances frequently conforms to accepted stereotypes and tends to be at variance with more objective measures of the traits in question. An example applicable to the field of athletics is the tendency of the naive stereotyper to perceive the male athlete as a "super-male" and to perceive team sports as more masculine than individual sports (Layman, 1968), with failure to recognize the possibility that often the apparently very masculine athlete is reacting against role identity confusion and that the competitive swimmer may be both physically and psychologically just as masculine as the bulkier helmeted and shoulder-padded football player. Another obvious example of the distortions associated with stereotyping is the tendency to perceive the woman athlete as masculine in her psychological orientation, with little in the way of empirical support for such a consensus (Layman, 1968).

Apropos of the inclusion in an athletic training program of methods to cultivate those personality characteristics associated with success in the sport, it would be superfluous to point out that this is easier said than done, even if we know what traits we are trying to develop. We can, of course, talk about the desired behavior and reinforce it if and when it occurs, but we are going to have to arrange situations so that it *can* occur. Also, we know from other fields that some behavior patterns we are not going to change unless our approach involves attention to the causes of the behavior, and that the likelihood of our changing those patterns that are manifestations of a person's basic life style is not very great unless we are prepared to involve ourselves in lengthy and intensive therapeutic programs.

In the section on research problems, Dr. Kroll has summarized very effectively the general problems of personality measurement and research, and then has discussed the special problems involved in athletic research. I shall comment about several points in both of these areas.

The criticism of personality tests made by Adelson (1969) is certainly justified, for very few of the personality tests on the market are based on an internally consistent conceptual system. With reference to the inadequacy of personality definitions, different test-makers and personality theorists not only disagree on the components of a given personality trait, but may use the same "label" for entirely different personality patterns.

The significance of response sets in affecting personality test results is widely recognized, but it is extremly difficult to build into a personality test a correction formula to take this into account. For instance, with reference to the social desirability factor the problem is not so much that SD affects responses, but, rather, why one person needs to present himself in the best possible light and another in the worst. Both could be for the same reason but the two persons may differ in the adequacy of their defenses. Jacobson, Berger, and Millham (1969) reported a study in which students with high self-esteem were more prone to cheat than those with low self-esteem. Presumably, one group would tend to give the socially desirable response on a personality test and the other would not.

Another question about response set is that of whether the response set is specific to the test, or represents a "trait." For example, McNair and Fisher (1967) reported drug research in which persons of high "acquiescence" gave glowing reports on both tranquilizers and placebos whereas those of low acquiescence reacted negatively to both.

With reference to special problems that weigh heavily for the athletic researcher, Dr. Kroll mentions two in particular—(1) the tendency of personality research to be oriented toward the clinical identification of abnormal populations and (2) the general inadequacy of personality evaluation instruments to predict the *super-normal* performance. I should like to address myself to some of the discussion in connection with each of these points.

First, with reference to the criticism about the orientation of personality tests toward detection of the abnormal, I would most certainly agree that we need tests to assess personality traits which are relevant to the most effective functioning of the normal person in different areas of endeavor and standardized on a normal population, and which conceivably could involve assessment of personality characteristics irrelevant to a psychiatric diagnosis. I would not go along with any implication that normal and abnormal operate according to two sets of "laws," and I do not believe that Dr. Kroll intends to imply this. I would agree also that the MMPI is not a test with a scoring system that readily lends itself to ease of application to athletic personality research, although some of the supplementary scoring scales that have been developed since the original standardization are more relevant to the normal personality than the original scales which were in terms of psychiatric diagnostic entities. However, if the researcher understood the dynamics of the different psychiatric disorders the results could be translated into personality traits more meaningful in a normal frame of reference than usually is the case in most reports of athletic personality research based on the MMPI.

Dr. Kroll has pointed out that the results of personality tests have usually added very little to prediction of academic achievement or vocational performance when prediction is based on measures of ability, and he has cited evidence in support of this view. My comments will relate only to the prediction of academic achievement. In this connection, it is common practice to use high school class rank, high school grade-point average, and standardized test scores as the independent variables and college grade-point average as the dependent variable. Of these, the test scores represent the only variable not subject to possible confounding by the effects of subjectivity—variations within the same instructor and between instructors, especially when instructor evaluations are based on essay type examinations. If there were complete objectivity in both independent and dependent variables, we don't know how accurately we would be able to predict performance, either with or without personality tests. Most studies currently published do indicate that adding personality test results to measures of ability does not add greatly to the effectiveness of attempts at predicting academic achievement. However, in a study of freshmen entering Iowa Wesleyan College in the fall of 1968 it was found that, when high school class rank, high school grade-point average, and scores on the ACT were the independent variables the multiple r with college grade-point average the freshman year was .46, and this was raised to .67 when personality variables measured by the OAIS were included.

The implication of all this, as far as athletic personality research is concerned, is that the researcher cannot assume that personality measures will be effective or ineffective in contributing to his ability to predict athletic success, but it *is* important that, in research to test the effectiveness of personality measures to improve prediction, all variables involved be as objective as possible.

Dr. Kroll's point that several different models may be necessary in order to express the relationship between personality and athletic performance is well taken, and each of the models he suggests would seem to have areas of applicability. Other models, of course, could be developed. For example, fruitful research might come from a model involving the "need" concept, "dissonance," or some other concept stressing in one way or another the congruity or incongruity between the perceived self and ideal self.

It was pointed out that physiological preparedness for effective participation in some sports requires complicated physical conditioning programs, and it was suggested that, if the physical analogy holds in the field of personality, there may well be also a need for personality training regimes in the preparation of the athlete. I think a great deal more research is going to be necessary before we can know whether the physical analogy holds or not, but right now I find it difficult to imagine what a personality conditioning program might be like outside of the context of sports participation.

Dr. Kroll's final point on the importance of developing measurement tools for the assessment of personality in *athletic situations* I think is one of the most important points he makes, and I would certainly concur in his statement that we need to transmute and not merely transfer personality theory to athletic personality research.

There are several types of study that have been largely neglected and should be pursued if we are to answer our questions about personality in relation to athletics. We need follow-up studies of former atheltes who have given up sports participation in adulthood, to determine whether or not personality differences between athletes and non-athletes persist after participation has been discontinued. We need more research on girls and women and on individuals of different ages to note sex and age differences. I think we may have overemphasized a trait approach to personality assessment and could perhaps learn something from a self-concept type of research, perhaps using a technique such as the Q-sort. We need also to develop more objective criteria of success in athletics and to make some decisions about what sort of validity we should rely on in constructing instruments for the assessment of personality in athletic situations. We could continue the list indefinitely.

In conclusion, Dr. Kroll's paper makes it apparent that there are enough problems and unanswered questions pertaining to research in personality assessment of athletes to challenge our ingenuity and occupy our time for years to come, but he has provided us with some useful guidelines for at least making a start toward straightening out the confusion which now exists.

REFERENCES

Adelson, Joseph. Personality. Annual review of Psychology, 1969, 20, 217-252.

Jacobson, L. I., Berger, S. E., & Millham, J. Self-esteem, sex differences, and the tendency to cheat. *Proceedings, 77th Annual Convention, American Psychological Association,* 1969. Pp. 353-354.

Layman, Emma M. Attitudes toward sports for girls and women in relation to masculinity-feminity stereotypes of women athletes. Paper read to the 135's meeting of the American Association for Advancement of Science, Dallas, Texas, December 27, 1968.

McNair, D., & Fisher, S. Personal communication, 1967.

Sappenfield, B. R. Stereotypical perception of a personality trait in personal acquaintances. *Proceedings, 77th Annual Convention, American Psychological Association.* 1969. P. 409-410.

DISCUSSION

KROLL: Well, Dr. Layman and I are even, I think it took more effort on her part because my paper did take a serious and too critical view of the clinical therapeutic approach for someone who uses the technique so well. At least one must admit it had an invigorating effect upon critical powers.

SIMON: Would you like to entertain questions?

WILLIAM STRAUB, ITHACA COLLEGE: I would like to also congratulate Dr. Kroll for the far reaching approach that he has given during his paper. I would like to disagree with him though on how bleak the picture of personality assessment of athletes looks at this point and cite the work that is being done in this area by Tutko and Ogilvie at San Jose State and it is interesting to note that these two researchers have developed their own personality assessment inventory; they have founded the institute for motivation in athletics and have also involved more than 45 teams and several professional teams in this work. Coaches, physical educators, are hungry for help in this area, all of us realize that mental preparation in athletics is the unanswered question in this area. We have talked about weight training and physiological ways in which we can increase performances but one person has decided that the real way we can improve the performances of the athlete is to understand the whole man—his emotional, physical and personality assessment, so we can do a better job working with individuals. I would also like to cite the vibrant work, having studied it somewhat, I feel that this is quite a bit of sensationalism in and of itself in reporting athletic personality and although we might laugh at Sports Illustrated and some of the other professional magazines in terms of their approach, I feel that this criticism might also be levied at other people, and it seems to me that we have identified rather conclusively the traits of the outstanding athlete in a variety of sports; we know that they are highly servient and slightly group dependent and that most of them are rather tough minded. It seems to me now that one question we haven't brought up here this afternoon is how do we help the practitioner utilize this information? How do we help him do a better job in preparing his athletes for better performances? I think once we uncover that along with doing some of the things that Professor Kroll pointed out in our research, we are going to make some significant contributions in this area. Thank you.

SIMON: Did you have anything you wanted to say?

KROLL: I would just like to make the comment that Ogilvie and Tutko are very close friends of Dr. Leon Smith and most of us here; they are the ones that this quote comes from—they did "not choose to present the more scholarly experimental documentation of our research findings in the area of athletic motivation." Where is it? I can read the conclusions, I can read the insight and the interpretations, but where are the data? I acknowledge that clinical interpretations can give you strong assertions and strong assumptions, definitive suggestions for what to do and what not to do. Whether or not they are in fact accurate or not remains to be seen. I am not aware, by the way, of any personality study which has employed the relatively simple technique of cross validation with the hold out sample to make sure that the significant differences found in that study were not just artifacts or accidents.

FRANKLIN HENRY: I might very well have given the talk that Walter Kroll gave, my title would have been just slightly different, I would have said, personality and athletics thirty years later. But aside from that, I think it would be substantially the same thing. I wonder why psychology in this area as well as in certain others has gained so little in such a long time. I would make just a little further comment on a point in which I do agree. (I don't agree with every word, Walter, and I hope someday you will take a positive approach to life and start more research that will take us forward with respect to the unsolved problems, but these things are beside the issue to be considered now). I would suggest the following: that first I respect and have great sympathy for those who see the great need for practical help with practical problems. First, I say, don't be so damn impatient, you have got to do more than just complain about paying your income tax. Typically, in physical education research meetings, what do you get? A bunch of school teachers and coaches are in there. They say: you research people live with your heads in the clouds and you don't give us anything that we can make use of, namely, research that will help us with our problems, or how to use it. This is ridiculous, of course. In professions that are truly professions, the professional people get a professional education and are prepared to read and interpret their own and other professional literature. I think there are still some M.D.'s that are so damned oriented to the practical that they give antibiotics for viruses, although they could have obtained correct scientific information at conventions, but by and large professional people are or should be educated professionally. So I say, there is no hope for us if we have to orient ourselves towards the practical needs of the moment, and it is not fair of the potential customers to expect us to concentrate on these issues—they don't know what their real needs are. When we do our job and tell them the right way to do things, they pay little attention to us. In fact, in a footnote, you once said something nice about me, about the use of best scores. This example has a long history, but who among the customers ever pays a damn bit of attention to it. A minor thing, perhaps, but then I don't think they (the customers) are receptive unless we give them the magic thrill, and guarantee success from minor or biased results. So I think our approach should not be what are the practical needs for the football players (or whoever). Furthermore, why should research be oriented towards picking out the successful people; why not just say here are our athletes—let's see how much they have personality differences among themselves and as compared with other people. And I fully agree with you people that it is rather ridiculous to try to find out whether some of the athletes should or should not be in the California State Hospital. So, I think that we should be oriented in a different direction from the abnormal. I don't think athletes are abnormal. Thirty years ago (this may be off a year or two) I gave a paper on personality and weight lifting at a meeting of the American Psychological Association, which happened to be at the west coast that year. The wire services picked up the story—I had lots of long distance telephone calls that evening, and then the letters began coming in. They really were stereotyped, because they all started out this way,—first, "who is this S B Henry", and point two, "why doesn't he keep his so and so mouth shut", which I thought was beautiful, perhaps not conclusive, but at least beautifully valid. Actually, I felt that for most people going into weight lifting at that time, it was wonderful psychotherapy for them. Although I wouldn't call them abnormal, many were people with certain personality needs, and this was a wonderful way to help them out. So let's find out why and to what extent athletes are different, rather than woryying too much about how we can either make them better athletes or pick out those who are destined to be great athletes. Our only hope to do this is to approach the problem correctly. I never did much publishing of these results, but I directed a study on weight lifters by John Thune. A later study was done by Harlow of Harvard, using a couple of projective or so called depth techniques, coming out with essentially the same results. This is the only positive thing that came out. Thune's work was really eclectic—we found that the available personality tools were designed for other purposes. If one would approach the research more empirically, and perhaps use more imagination, there would be ways of getting at the problem. Now, it is true that I have changed a lot and the world has changed a lot, but I think in this respect it hasn't changed substantially in thirty years. I see this study within normality as the only possible way to approach the problem. Now, I was heartened a little bit by the comments of the psychologists among us, who seem to feel that we in physical education might develop our own personality tests. I think we need some help; also there is a lot to learn about psychology, indeed there is. It requires some very extensive study on our part, if we are to do this work. Psychologists are not going to solve our problems for us, they are not truly interested in our problems, they are interested in using us to solve their own problems, as Harlow was. Now, I don't know how to evaluate Dr. Ogilvie, but let's not be too harsh, Walter, there might be a lot of good there. I agree with you that one must withstand the rigors of publication, but we should be more sympathetic. I just point this out as a possibility, so let's get this show on the road; I will be looking forward to some of the papers along this line from Walter Kroll a little later on.

KROLL: The only point I can make, Dr. Henry, is that if you can't criticise your friends, you can't criticise anyone, so we could pick on Ogilvie and Tutko.

SYMPOSIUM ON THE PSYCHOLOGY OF MOTOR LEARNING

UNIVERSITY OF IOWA

OCTOBER 10-12, 1969

SPEAKERS

CAROL H. AMMONS
ROBERT B. AMMONS
University of Montana

J. V. BASMAJIAN
Emory University

HAROLD BECHTOLDT
University of Iowa

INA McD. BILODEAU
Tulane University

FRANKLIN M. HENRY
University of California

D. H. HOLDING
Tulane University

WALTER KROLL
University of Massachusetts

EMMA McCLOY LAYMAN
Iowa Wesleyan

RICHARD A. SCHMIDT
University of Maryland

J. RICHARD SIMON
University of Iowa

KARL U. SMITH
University of Wisconsin

JOAN WATERLAND
University of Wisconsin

PARTICIPANTS

PEARL BERLIN
University of Massachusetts

JULIA BROWN
University of Wisconsin

LES BRUWITZ
University of Illinois

LINDA BUNKER
University of Illinois

SUSAN BURROUGHS
University of Illinois

ALYCE CHESKA
University of Illinois

M. J. ELLIS
University of Illinois

LOLAS E. HALVERSON
University of Wisconsin

ROBERT JONES
Ithaca College

GLENN KIRCHNER
Simon Fraser University

BILL KOZAR
Texas Tech. University

LAWRENCE LOCKE
University of New Mexico

CLAIRE MARCIL
University of Illinois

LORETTA STALLINGS
The George Washington University

MARY OST
University of Minnesota

WILLIAM STRAUB
Ithaca College

KAY PETERSEN
University of Wisconsin

MARGARET THOMPSON
University of Missouri

JERALYN PLACK
University of Minnesota

GEORGE VANIS
University of Michigan

JOANNE SAFRIT
University of Wisconsin

MARILYN VINCENT
University of Georgia

JACQUES SAMSON
University of Illinois

HARRIET WILLIAMS
University of Toledo

ROBERT SINGER
Florida State University

IAN WILLIAMS
University of Illinois

A. T. SLATER-HAMMEL
Indiana University

MARJORIE WILSON
University of Minnesota

JUDITH SMITH
UCLA

WANEEN WYRICK
University of Texas

FRANK SMOLL
University of Wisconsin

MARY YOUNG
University of Minnesota

MARJORIE SOUDER
University of Illinois

OLIVE YOUNG
University of Illinois